FRANKLIN: *THE AUTOBIOGRAPHY* AND OTHER WRITINGS ON POLITICS, ECONOMICS, AND VIRTUE

Benjamin Franklin (1706–1790) is one of the best-known and least-understood figures in the history of eighteenth-century political thought. Though a man of extraordinary intellectual accomplishment, he was an occasional writer who left no major treatise. Though the author of essays and pamphlets on a wide range of topics, he is often known only through his two most famous productions, the *Autobiography* and *Poor Richard's Almanack.* Though a pivotal actor in and keen observer of colonial and revolutionary American politics, Franklin has resisted classification using the terms of contemporary historical analysis; he is neither classical republican nor Lockean liberal.

The present volume provides the textal foundation for a comprehensive reassessment of Franklin's political thought. Alan Houston makes available, for the first time, a full and representative selection of Franklin's most important political writings. He pairs a new edition of the *Autobiography* with letters, essays, pamphlets, and manuscript notes on topics ranging from political economy, moral psychology, religious belief and practice, voluntary association, and the public sphere of news and communication, to the dynamics of international migration and the design of political institutions. Through these texts Franklin emerges as an active participant in debates over the modern commercial republic.

ALAN HOUSTON is Associate Professor of Political Science at the University of California, San Diego.

CAMBRIDGE TEXTS IN THE
HISTORY OF POLITICAL THOUGHT

Franklin: *The Autobiography* and Other Writings on Politics, Economics, and Virtue

CAMBRIDGE TEXTS IN THE HISTORY OF POLITICAL THOUGHT

Cambridge Texts in the History of Political Thought is now firmly established as the major student textbook series in political theory. It aims to make available to students all the most important texts in the history of western political thought, from ancient Greece to the early twentieth century. All the familiar classic texts will be included, but the series seeks at the same time to enlarge the conventional canon by incorporating an extensive range of less well-known works, many of them never before available in a modern English edition. Wherever possible, texts are published in complete and unabridged form, and translations are specially commissioned for the series. Each volume contains a critical introduction together with chronologies, biographical sketches, a guide to further reading and any necessary glossaries and textual apparatus. When completed the series will aim to offer an outline of the entire evolution of western political thought.

For a list of titles published in the series, please see end of book

FRANKLIN

The Autobiography
and Other Writings on Politics, Economics, and Virtue

EDITED BY

ALAN HOUSTON

University of California, San Diego

PUBLISHED BY THE PRESS SYNDICATE OF THE UNIVERSITY OF CAMBRIDGE
The Pitt Building, Trumpington Street, Cambridge, United Kingdom

CAMBRIDGE UNIVERSITY PRESS
The Edinburgh Building, Cambridge, CB2 2RU, UK
40 West 20th Street, New York, NY 10011–4211, USA
477 Williamstown Road, Port Melbourne, VIC 3207, Australia
Ruiz de Alarcón 13, 28014 Madrid, Spain
Dock House, The Waterfront, Cape Town 8001, South Africa

http://www.cambridge.org

First published 2004

Printed in the United Kingdom at the University Press, Cambridge

Typeface Ehrhardt 9.5/12 pt. *System* LaTeX 2ε [TB]

A catalogue record for this book is available from the British Library

Library of Congress Cataloguing in Publication data
Franklin, Benjamin, 1706–1790.
[Selections. 2004]
Franklin: the autobiography and other writings on politics, economics, and virtue / edited by Alan Houston.
p. cm. – (Cambridge texts in the history of political thought)
Includes bibliographical references and index.
ISBN 0 521 83496 1 – ISBN 0 521 54265 0 (pb.)
1. Franklin, Benjamin, 1706–1790. 2. Statesmen – United States – Biography. 3. United States – Economic conditions – To 1865. 4. United States – Politics and government – To 1775. 5. United States – Politics and government – 1775 – 1783. 6. Political culture – United States – History – 18th century. 7. Political science – Early works to 1800. 8. Political science – United States – History – 18th century. 9. Virtue. 10. Social values. I. Houston, Alan Craig, 1957 – II. Title. III. Series.
E302.6.F7A2 2004
973.3′092 – dc22
[B] 2004045103

ISBN 0 521 83496 1 hardback
ISBN 0 521 54265 0 paperback

Contents

Acknowledgements

The holograph manuscript of Franklin's *Autobiography*, HM 9999, is reproduced by permission of the Huntington Library, San Marino, California. Selections from *The Papers of Benjamin Franklin* are reproduced by permission of Yale University Press. Two poems by Franklin's uncle Benjamin are reproduced by permission of the American Antiquarian Society; Franklin's final speech at the Constitutional Convention is reproduced courtesy of the Division of Rare and Manuscript Collections, Cornell University Library.

Quentin Skinner first suggested this edition. He subsequently provided detailed and insightful comments on the Introduction, as did Douglas Anderson, Don Herzog, Steve Pincus, Nancy Rosenblum, Shannon Stimson, and an anonymous reviewer. Richard Fisher of Cambridge University Press was unfailingly supportive as this project matured. David Selby assisted with the final stages of research. Kelsey and Jamie helped me appreciate Franklin's complex role in American popular culture. To all of these friends, colleagues, and relations, I offer my heartfelt thanks.

Introduction

Benjamin Franklin's life-story is legendary. The youngest son and fifteenth child of a Boston tallow chandler and soap boiler, he received only two years' formal education before being apprenticed to his brother, a local printer. But by the time of his death he was world-famous for his accomplishments. A writer of wit, grace and intelligence, he crafted a series of complex and distinct literary voices. An experimental scientist, he conducted original research on electricity, was elected to the Royal Society, and founded the first scientific society in North America. A practical engineer, he invented the lightning rod, bifocal glasses, and the first truly efficient wood-burning stove. A born improver, he fathered the first subscription library, the first volunteer fire department, and the first charity hospital. A political leader in colonial Pennsylvania and revolutionary America, he helped draft the Declaration of Independence, represented the United States in negotiations with France and Great Britain, and participated in the Constitutional Convention.

Franklin's political writings reflect his engagement with this wider world. He was not an abstract or systematic thinker. At no point did he articulate a developed conception of justice, or defend a theory of human nature. And yet *The Papers of Benjamin Franklin* – now in its thirty-seventh volume, with nearly a decade of his life still to be covered – reveals a mind of extraordinary critical intelligence. By trade a printer, Franklin actively participated in the public sphere of news and communication. He wrote to influence opinions and shape events, to entertain friends and demolish enemies, to share ideas and attain commercial success. He addressed topics ranging from monetary policy to sexual mores, and from the conduct of business to the sins of slavery. He employed a wide array of literary forms, including journalistic essays, popular broadsides, public letters, political pamphlets, scientific treatises and bagatelles. Well schooled in the use of irony, satire and invective – he taught himself to write by miming Addison's *Spectator* – he understood the value of a good hoax, and delighted in the construction of dramatic *personae*. Some of Franklin's most famous productions were "authored" by fictional characters like Silence Dogood and Richard Saunders.

Faced with these riches, scholars have found it difficult to agree on Franklin's contribution to the history of ideas. In scores of monographs he has been variously cast as Puritan, Deist and atheist; as Newtonian empiricist and Enlightenment rationalist; as democratic populist and liberal individualist; as petit bourgeois and proto-capitalist; as principled pragmatist and opportunistic scoundrel. American popular culture has had an easier time of it. Franklin is best known as prophet of the American dream: if you work hard and play by the rules, then you will succeed. Power and privilege are the fruit of industry and effort, not birth and ascriptive social roles. The American dream is closely associated with some of Poor Richard's most famous phrases: "A penny saved is a penny earned," "There are no gains without pains," and "Early to bed and early to rise/Make a man healthy wealthy and wise." Proof of these maxims is provided by Franklin's own life, which affirms the power of individuals to shape their own destiny.

Franklin's appeal has not been limited to adults. Children's literature – with titles like *Ben and Me: A New and Astonishing Life of Benjamin Franklin as Written by His Good Mouse Amos* (in which Amos assumes responsibility for Franklin's discoveries and inventions), *The Hatmaker's Sign* (based on a parable Franklin told Jefferson when the latter balked at congressional attempts to edit the Declaration of Independence) and *Fart Proudly: The Writings of Benjamin Franklin You Never Read in School* (whose title derives from Franklin's satiric proposal for the scientific study of flatulence, *Letter to the Royal Academy*) – testifies to the complex emotional appeal of Franklin's life and writings. With the possible exception of George Washington, none of Franklin's contemporaries has played as important a role in the moral and political imaginations of Americans; and Washington, distant as Cato, lacks Franklin's immediacy and intimacy.

Ironically, Franklin's importance to American culture has made it more difficult to understand him. Consider, for example, D. H. Lawrence's well-known attack on Franklin's moral and political ideals. In the *Autobiography* Franklin described his "bold and arduous project of arriving at moral perfection," complete with a table of virtues and a method for rendering them habitual. Lawrence railed against the "barbed wire moral enclosure" that Franklin "rigged up": "The soul of man is a vast forest, and all Benjamin intended was a neat back yard." Why did Franklin do this? "Out of sheer cussedness." Franklin "hated England, he hated Europe . . . he wanted to be an American," and his whole life was dedicated to "destroying the European past." Lawrence was a brilliant writer, but his argument rested on dubious interpretative protocols. Like many before and after, he reduced Franklin's writings to the *Autobiography* and the *Almanack*; and like many before and after, he naively (or perhaps mischievously) assumed that the man born in Boston was identical to the characters he created.[1]

Lawrence identified Franklin with the desire to be an "American," and this, too, is a stumbling block. During most of Franklin's life the term "American" referred to an inhabitant of a geographic region, whether Native American or British colonist. Only in the wake of the imperial crises of the 1760s and the revolutionary struggles of the 1770s did it begin to assume unique social, political, and cultural meanings. Franklin certainly played a role in the construction of the type "American" – not least when, as minister to France, he played to European visions of natural genius by wearing a beaver cap and simple wool coat. However, the identification of Franklin with America confuses four potentially distinct things: the biographical origins of the author, the social and political problems that dominated his thoughts, the audience he addressed, and the intellectual resources he brought to bear on them. Franklin spent his first two decades in Boston and the following three in Philadelphia. Throughout his life his attention was riveted on the dilemmas of civic life in North America. But during long missions to England (1757–62, 1764–75) and France (1776–85) he wrote at length and with great sophistication for European audiences. And there was nothing parochial about his reading habits. As a child, he eagerly read Bunyan's *Pilgrim's Progress*, Plutarch's *Lives*, Mather's *Bonifacius*, and Defoe's *Essay on Projects*; as a lad of 18, in a journal kept at sea, he debated Machiavellian dicta; as a budding political economist of 23, he exploited the arguments of William Petty and Marchamont Nedham. Other early papers indicate familiarity with the poetry of Thomson, Waller, Cowley, Swift, and Pope. At his death he left a library of 4,276 volumes in English, French, Italian, Latin, Spanish, and German.

[1] D. H. Lawrence, "Benjamin Franklin," in *Studies in Classic American Literature* (New York, 1923), 13–31.

There is one final dimension to the problems posed by Franklin's "American" identity, this time having to do with historiographical conventions and commitments. Beginning in the 1960s, widely shared principles governing the study of political thought came under fire. Rejecting approaches that drew their bearings from canonical texts and teleological narratives, scholars sought to recover the meaning of texts by focusing on the linguistic contexts within which they were written. The significance of a claim or utterance could be grasped only in relationship to the range of idioms available at a given point in time. Shop-worn distinctions between philosophy and history, or between reason and rhetoric, were called into question. Complex works of literature were placed alongside analytic nonfiction. In England these arguments led to vital new interpretations of familiar figures like Machiavelli, Hobbes, and Locke, and to the recovery of less well-known writers like James Harrington. In the United States the new histories of political thought coincided with – and were largely absorbed by – the "republican" interpretation of the American Revolution. As late as 1955 Louis Hartz could argue that the key to American political thought was to be found in the writings of John Locke. But by the early 1960s scholars had discovered, in the pamphlet literature of the mid-eighteenth century, a language of virtue and corruption that appeared to be distinct from and in tension with the liberal logic of rights and interests. Within a few short years, the concept of republicanism dominated the landscape. Taking cues from the path-breaking work of Bernard Bailyn, Gordon Wood, and J.G.A. Pocock, historians and political theorists recast the Revolution as a struggle to preserve republican liberty against the hazards of moral and political corruption.

Benjamin Franklin is a strikingly marginal figure in the pages of republican revisionists, and plays no greater role in the work of critics seeking to reassert a liberal paradigm. There is a simple reason for this: he was neither a "classical republican" nor a "Lockean liberal." Though concerned with virtue and corruption, he did not assume – as republican theory seemed to require – that a stable and successful polity rested on moral purity and selfless devotion to the commonwealth. Though dedicated to self-reliance and economic growth, he did not assume – as Lockean theory seemed to require – that property rights were natural, or that the language of natural jurisprudence fully captured the meaning of modern citizenship.

The present volume provides the textual foundation for a comprehensive reassessment of Franklin's political thought. Freed from the confines of the liberalism/republicanism debate, it uses the tools of historical research to open new questions and frame new arguments. At the center of this collection is Franklin's *Autobiography* [1],[2] the clearest statement of his lifelong commitment to personal and civic improvement. The language of improvement – of gain and profit, progress and perfection, increase and expansion, benefit and amelioration – runs throughout Franklin's writings. Its meaning was not simply – or even primarily – economic. In an influential essay on the emergence of "the peculiar modern Western form of capitalism," Max Weber argued that Franklin exhibited, with "almost classic purity," the ethos of rational acquisition. Franklin's ideal was the "credit-worthy honest man"; all of life was subordinated to the task of earning "more and more money" while scrupulously avoiding "all spontaneous enjoyment of life." This duty to a calling, once sanctified by Puritanism, had lost its religious basis by Franklin's day. But, according to Weber, it continued to mobilize men around the rational pursuit of profit.[3] There is much in Franklin to support this view, from *Advice to a Young Tradesman* ("Remember that Time is Money" [12]) to the wildly popular preface to the 1758 edition of *Poor Richard Improved* [22]. But the production of wealth was only part of the ethos Franklin sought to cultivate. He praised industry and frugality, but he also commended the pursuit of knowledge, the cultivation of friendship, and the satisfaction of need. "Improvement," in Franklin's lexicon, was nothing less than shorthand for the civilizing process. It captured his deepest values and commitments, and tied him to some of the most important debates of the eighteenth century.

The *Autobiography* is a rich and complex work. Franklin intended to review his entire life, but the narrative we possess is incomplete and ends in his sixth decade. At the outset, he admitted to mixed motives: he wanted to provide a family history for his son, to vindicate his reputation from aspersions cast by his enemies, and to indulge his vanity by recounting his success in the world. But the *Autobiography* is also a deliberate work of moral and political education. Franklin thought his life "fit to be imitated." As he explained to a friend, he hoped "to benefit the young reader, by showing him from my example, and my success in emerging from poverty, and acquiring some degree of wealth, power, and reputation,

[2] Numbers in brackets refer to documents listed in the table of contents.

[3] Max Weber, *The Protestant Ethic and the Spirit of Capitalism*, 1920, trans. Talcott Parsons (London, 2001), 47–78.

the advantages of certain modes of conduct which I observed, and of avoiding the errors which were prejudicial to me."[4] Countless readers have debated the merits of Franklin's example. Rushed into print immediately after Franklin's death, the *Autobiography* has been published in over a dozen major and literally hundreds of minor editions. Translated into French, Dutch, and German in the 1790s, it has also been rendered in Spanish, Italian, Danish, Portuguese, Swedish, Hebrew, Russian, and Chinese. It is the most important work of its kind in American letters, and one of the most influential works of world literature.

Part Two of the *Autobiography* describes Franklin's "bold and arduous project of arriving at moral perfection," and provides the clearest statement of a moral theory in all his writings. But it is by far the briefest of the three major sections of the memoir. The biographical material surrounding it is equally important: it is intended to demonstrate the practical validity of Franklin's insights and arguments. As a youth of 18 Franklin traveled to London. There, under the influence of dissolute friends and freethinking ideas, he committed a number of painful indiscretions. During the long voyage home he resolved upon a "Plan of Conduct" that he might "live in all respects like a rational creature" [2]. He settled on four goals: frugality, industry, honesty, and sincerity. To his chagrin he found the task exceedingly difficult. His challenge was not cognitive, but psychological. The content of virtue was easily distilled from the many and varied lists he encountered in his reading. (In the end, he settled on thirteen.) But the practice of virtue was an altogether different matter. Custom, habit, and inclination repeatedly triumphed over reason and conviction. Legislating moral reform – even self-legislating moral reform – was generally ineffective.

The intellectual foundation for this "discovery" lay in John Locke's *An Essay concerning Human Understanding*, which Franklin read with care. According to Locke, moral freedom rests on the capacity to "*suspend* the prosecution of this or that desire, as every one daily may Experiment in himself." Each man has the capacity to "be determined in *willing* by his own Thought and Judgment"; but "'tis not easie for the Mind to put off those confused Notions and Prejudices it has imbibed from Custom, Inadvertency, and common Conversation." Locke argued that the solution to this problem lay in a keen awareness of man's utter dependence on God. Only the threat of punishment in the afterlife could lead men to resist

[4] To Benjamin Vaughan, 4 October 1788, in Writings 9:675–6.

the temptations of pleasure in the present.[5] Here Franklin and Locke parted company. Locke was concerned with the stability and justification of moral claims, Franklin with the psychological bases of moral action. Though some might need religious reasons to be moral, not all did [23]. Virtue was a matter of habit, and what Franklin needed was an art or method for securing the virtues he possessed and acquiring the ones he lacked. To this end he devised a novel system of moral bookkeeping. In a small book he drew a table with a row for every virtue and a column for each day of the week. Each time he committed a fault, he made a black mark in the appropriate square. Each week he focused his attention on one of the virtues. Over time, through repetition, he hoped to experience the pleasure of "viewing a clean Book." Franklin readily admitted that this did not happen. But he saw improvement, and attributed his long and happy life to the effects of his method. Later in life he commended this system and its correlates to friends who were faced with difficult decisions and errant passions [24, 35].

The rhetorical framework of the *Autobiography* would have been familiar to Franklin's audience from seventeenth- and eighteenth-century moral and religious writings. A man of promise and ability leads a life of dissipation; awakening to this fact, he is disgusted with himself and resolves to change; through reflection and self-observation, he struggles to purge himself of vice; over time, with the helping hand of God, he moves ever closer to a life of purity and perfection. This narrative, concerned with the fate of a single soul, was deeply personal. But it was told for public purposes, and not simply that we might learn from the struggles and mistakes of others. The self created through self-discipline was an exemplary self. It represented the qualities and characteristics of a life infused with God's grace, and it expressed God's grace through benevolent action in the world. Good works were an outward manifestation of inner piety. As Cotton Mather put it in *An Essay upon the Good* – another work that Franklin read with care – "a workless faith is a worthless faith."[6]

Franklin often expressed his moral ideals in precisely these terms: "What is Serving God? 'Tis doing good to man".[7] Yet he profoundly transformed their meaning. Franklin's table of virtues included temperance,

[5] John Locke, *An Essay concerning Human Understanding*, ed. Peter Nidditch (Oxford, 1975), 2.21.47, 2.21.48, 2.13.27.

[6] Cotton Mather, *Bonifacius: An Essay upon the Good*, 1710, ed. David Levin (Cambridge, MA, 1966), 29.

[7] Poor Richard, 1747, in Papers 3:105; see also [7].

silence, order, resolution, frugality, industry, sincerity, justice, moderation, cleanliness, tranquility, chastity, and humility. He constructed no comparable table of vices, but we can infer them from his characterizations of men and events. The list would be short: argumentativeness (young Ben), idleness (James Ralph), indecision (Lord Loudon). These habits made men unhappy and prevented them from working in concert with others. They were known by their consequences, not by their coherence with divine revelation. "Vicious Actions are not hurtful because they are forbidden, but forbidden because they are hurtful, the Nature of Man alone considered."

Morality was a matter of actions and effects, not motives and intentions. In 1749 Poor Richard opined that "*Words* may shew a man's Wit, but *Actions* his Meaning." Seven years later he made the point with flourish:

> At the Day of Judgment, we shall not be asked, what Proficiency we have made in Languages or Philosophy; but whether we have liv'd virtuously and piously, as Men endued with Reason, guided by the Dictates of Religion. In that Hour it will more avail us, that we have thrown a Handful of Flour or Chaff in Charity to a Nest of contemptible Pismires, than that we could muster all the Hosts of Heaven, and call every Star by its proper Name. For then the Constellations themselves shall disappear, the Sun and Moon shall give no more Light, and all the Frame of Nature shall vanish. But our good or bad Works shall remain for ever, recorded in the Archives of Eternity.[8]

We sometimes say that actions speak louder than words, particularly when we seek to expose the hypocrisy of others. Franklin had something different in mind: moral identity is established by, and known through, action. Properly speaking, it is not a matter of will, at least not as the will was understood by Puritan moralists. The self was a constellation of passions and interests, integrated into a productive whole through good habits. Purity of heart was not possible, nor was it necessary to moral improvement. Franklin's contemporary, Jonathan Edwards, vehemently rejected this idea. According to Edwards, virtuous actions were the fruit of virtuous motives. A theory based on habit could not explain an original commitment to virtue ("How came he by that virtue from which he acted when he first began to reform?"[9]). Nor could it protect men against the sins

[8] Papers 3:331, 7:89.

[9] Jonathan Edwards, Miscellany 73, quoted in Norman S. Fiering, "Benjamin Franklin and the Way to Virtue," *American Quarterly* 30 (1978): 221.

of hypocrisy and self-deception. But Franklin did not participate in the Puritan inner drama of guilt, self-doubt, and self-accusation. Nor did he linger, with fear and trembling, over backsliding and the recrudescence of sin. He tallied his mistakes – his "errata" – and sought to change himself by changing his habits. In this effort he did not insist that his motives be pure. As he quipped in the *Autobiography*, vanity and pride made him a better man.

Franklin cast his beliefs in latitudinarian terms. This rejection of doctrinal precision enabled him to address a difficult practical problem. Pennsylvania was the most heterodox colony in British North America. Founded in the late seventeenth century by William Penn, it was originally intended as a "holy experiment," an asylum for Quakers and other persecuted people. In Franklin's day Quakers were in the minority but dominated Philadelphia civic life and controlled the colonial Assembly. In the city they were joined by "new" and "old" Presbyterians; in the backcountry lived large numbers of Mennonites, Dunkers, and Moravians. The Penns, no longer Quaker, were the single largest landholders in Pennsylvania, and retained the powers and privileges of the Proprietors. Colonial prosperity and security required cooperation among these groups, but doctrinal differences and sectarian conflicts often precluded it. Franklin thought it possible to agree on actions without delving too deeply into their justification. Civic improvements – paving roads, providing hospitals for the poor, protecting against the menace of fire – were goals all could agree to. Cooperation emerged from the attempt to solve specific and local problems. Instrumental reasoning was a bond of union among men divided by custom, habit, and inclination.

On one occasion Franklin's practical Christianity landed him in the lap of doctrinal controversy. In late 1734 the Rev. Mr. Samuel Hemphill, a Presbyterian clergyman ordained in Ireland, was invited to assist Jedediah Andrews, the ageing minister of Philadelphia. Franklin was a member of Andrews' congregation, but did not attend his sermons because he found them "dry, uninteresting and unedifying, since not a single moral Principle was inculcated or enforc'd, their Aim seeming to be rather to make us Presbyterians than good Citizens." Hemphill's sermons were altogether different. According to Franklin, they were not "dogmatical . . . but inculcated strongly the Practice of virtue or what in the religious Stile are called Good Works." Here was a man after Franklin's own heart. But in 1727 the Synod of Philadelphia, in an attempt to unite warring factions, had voted that all ministers subscribe to the Westminster Confession of

Faith. Hemphill's sermons did not meet this requirement, and orthodox Presbyterians, led by Andrews, brought charges before the Synod in April 1735. Hemphill was "a *New-Light Man*, a *Deist*, one who preach'd nothing but *Morality*."

Franklin sprang to Hemphill's defense in four long and impassioned essays.[10] He instructed his fellow congregants on the meaning of Christianity. The Sermon on the Mount was an "excellent moral Discourse." Jesus preached that "Morality or Virtue is the End, Faith only a Means to obtain that End: And if the End be obtained, it is no matter by what Means." Indeed, "a virtuous Heretick will be saved before a wicked Christian." Improvement came through a gradual transformation of habits, not an abrupt conversion or turning of the soul. Original sin was "absurd," a "Bugbear set up by Priests . . . to fright and scare an unthinking Populace out of its Senses." Brandishing anti-clerical weapons forged by English Dissenters a century before, Franklin went on the offensive. The judgment of man is fallible, and disagreement over doctrine is inevitable. Reformation is gradual, as partial truths displace partial errors. The free exchange of ideas is essential to this process. Every man must be permitted to speak and be heard. (Franklin used the same logic to defend the right and duty of printers to print unorthodox ideas [4].) In their persecuting zeal the Presbyterian clergy emulated "that hellish Tribunal the *Inquisition*." They must be humbled, and their repressive power destroyed, through the assertion of "natural rights and liberties" by "the brethren of the laity."

Franklin's defense failed and Hemphill was forced to leave Philadelphia. The loss was bitterly personal. Hemphill sought to incite lives of virtuous action, and Franklin had long embraced that goal. But in the course of defending Hemphill Franklin discovered just how unorthodox his ideas were. Even fellow supporters of Hemphill were troubled by Franklin's antinomian appeal to the laity. Within a few years he formed a fast friendship with the charismatic evangelist George Whitefield, and in so doing helped to bring the Great Awakening to Philadelphia. But Franklin repeatedly resisted Whitefield's invitation to live by faith and grace. A life dedicated to doing good was sanctified; from a religious point of view, that was sufficient. But what held together the habits of personal

[10] In addition to *A Dialogue* (April 1735), reprinted here [6]: *Some Observations on the Proceedings against The Rev. Mr. Hemphill* (July 1735); *A Letter to a Friend in the Country* (September 1735); *A Defence Of the Rev. Mr. Hemphill's Observations* (October 1735), in Papers 2:37–125. All quotations in this paragraph are from these tracts.

improvement? What social forms and political institutions were appropriate to civic improvement? And how were these goals held together?

From an early age Franklin had a "projecting public Spirit." He saw enormous benefits in organized and enlightened collective action. As he put it in his proposal for a charity hospital, "The Good particular Men may do separately . . . is small, compared with what they may do collectively, or by a joint Endeavour and Interest."[11] Franklin's description of the first subscription library is paradigmatic. The members of Franklin's Junto were avid readers, but as humble tradesmen they could not afford many books. Franklin suggested that they pool their resources in a "common Library." They did so, but quickly discovered that their combined collection was much smaller than expected. Worse yet, over time the few books they had were mistreated and mislaid. After one year, the experiment was ended. It was in response to this crisis of the commons that Franklin "set on foot" his "first Project of a public Nature, that for a Subscription Library." Fifty subscribers agreed to fund the library for fifty years; lists were drawn and books were ordered; hours were set, and subscribers were permitted to borrow books only if they promised to pay a fine for volumes unreturned. Franklin proudly reported that "the institution soon manifested its utility" and was imitated in other towns and provinces. "These Libraries have improv'd the general Conversation of the Americans, made the common Tradesmen and Farmers as intelligent as most Gentlemen from other Countries." And "perhaps," Franklin added, they "have contributed in some degree to the Stand so generally made throughout the Colonies in Defence of their Privileges."

Franklin was equally successful in getting the streets of Philadelphia paved and swept. In wet weather unpaved streets became quagmires; in dry weather they were a dirty nuisance. Finding a "poor industrious man" who was willing to undertake the labor, Franklin "wrote and printed a Paper setting forth the Advantages" of hiring him at the rate of sixpence per house per month. The agreement was unanimously subscribed to, and "all the Inhabitants of the City were delighted with the Cleanliness of the Pavement that surrounded the market." This "raised a general Desire to have all the Streets paved, and made the People more willing to submit to a Tax for that purpose."

[11] "Appeal for the Hospital," 8 August 1751, in Papers 4:150.

> Some may think these trifling Matters not worth minding or relating, but when they consider that tho' Dust blown into the Eyes of a single Person or into a single Shop on a windy Day, is but of small Importance, yet the great Number of the Instances in a populous City and its frequent Repetitions give it Weight and Consequence, perhaps they will not censure very severely those who bestow some Attention to Affairs of this seemingly low Nature. Human Felicity is produced not so much by great Pieces of good Fortune that seldom happen as by little Advantages that occur every Day.

Happiness, like character itself, was built slowly and piecemeal. It required self-discipline and the ability to identify with proper objects of desire and ambition [34].

Not all Franklin's projects were confined to the "little Advantages" of everyday life. In 1747 he led the formation of the Association, a private militia that enrolled 10,000 Pennsylvanians to defend the colony against French and Spanish privateers [10, 11]. As a middle colony removed from the coast, Pennsylvania had been relatively insulated from the imperial conflicts of the 1730s and 1740s. Then in the fall of 1747 rumors of an attack up the Delaware River began circulating. Colonists grew anxious, but the Assembly – dominated by Quakers – refused defensive preparations. Working with associates, Franklin campaigned to create a broad base of support for direct action. Though "the whole Province" was "one Body, united by living under the same Laws, and enjoying the same Privileges," Pennsylvanians were divided by regional, religious, and class loyalties. Some of these differences could not be easily transcended. The "religious Scruples" of the Quakers prevented them from taking defensive measures. Rich merchants, consumed by spite, refused to take a lead because in so doing they might help the Quakers. "Most unhappily circumstanced indeed are we, the middle People, the Tradesmen, Shopkeepers, and Farmers of this Province and City!" Franklin reminded his audience that "*Protection* is as truly due from the Government to the People, as *Obedience* from the People to the Government." If the Assembly was unwilling to defend Pennsylvania, then it ought not to object if the people took matters into their own hands. "All we want is Order, Discipline, and a few Cannon."

The Association was an extraordinary experiment. Soldiers – each of whom signed the *Form of Association* – were divided into companies whose social composition was intentionally mixed: "'Tis designed to mix the Great and Small together, for the sake of Union and Encouragement.

Where danger and Duty are equal to All, there should be no Distinction from Circumstances, but All be on the Level." (Fifty years later Franklin used the same argument to support proportional representation in the United States Congress [43] and oppose the representation of property in Pennsylvania's upper house [44]. "The Combinations of Civil Society are not like those of a Set of Merchants.") In their companies, soldiers directly elected their officers. Franklin hoped that this arrangement, when combined with rotation in office, would ensure the selection of good men and foster incentives to perform well.

Order and discipline required planning, but cannons were an altogether different matter. Soldiers were responsible for their own guns, but cannons were expensive and exceeded the capacity of most individuals. Franklin addressed this problem by selling tickets to a lottery. Pennsylvanians were familiar with the device: lotteries had been used in England since the days of Queen Elizabeth; and though opposed by Quakers on moral grounds, they were used throughout the eighteenth century to fund large-scale public and private ventures. Indeed, prior to the development of a stable bond market, lotteries were an essential mechanism for raising capital in colonial America. But Franklin's use of a lottery is particularly striking because it called on the vice of cupidity channeled through a game of chance to fund the efforts of citizen-soldiers.

The Association was successful in all but one regard: it was an expression of "the people out of doors," and as such – as an extra-legal and extra-political organization – it drew the ire of Pennsylvania's Proprietors. Thomas Penn thought the Association little less than "a Military Common Wealth," and worried that Franklin had become "a Sort of Tribune of the People." He was "licentious." He was a "leveller." He was, in short, a "republican."[12]

Franklin's ability to think of civic needs in political-economic terms points to a final context for his thought. At precisely the moment when Franklin framed his "Plan of Conduct," in precisely the place where he had committed his indiscretions and made his self-discoveries, men of letters were engaged in a heated debate over the relationship between moral philosophy and political economy. In *The Fable of the Bees* – printed in a third and revised edition in 1724, just as Franklin landed in London – Bernard Mandeville argued that society was an aggregation of self-interested individuals, bound together not by civic devotion or moral rectitude but by the

[12] Thomas Penn, quoted in Papers 3:186.

tenuous bonds of envy, competition, and exploitation. During his first trip to London Franklin met Mandeville – whom he found a "most facetious, entertaining companion" – and participated in the intellectual life of clubs and coffee-houses. In these settings he encountered men steeped in the books and essays he had absorbed as a boy: Addison's *Spectator*, Trenchard and Gordon's *Cato's Letters*, Shaftesbury's *Characteristics*, Steele's *Tatler*, Defoe's *Essay on Projects*.

The controversy surrounding Mandeville's *Fable* was part of a broad debate over the language of sociability and the logic of commercial society. All parties accepted that humans were capable of improvement, and that the weaknesses of individuals were to be overcome through combination with others. But what enabled humans to cooperate? What ties held them together in collective endeavors? It was here that the argument was joined. Christian moralists invoked love and the bonds of an inclusive church. Shared values and practices were the cement of social order. Machiavellians appealed to the power of necessity, imposed by the institutional constraints of a well-ordered polity. Sumptuary laws, military service, and a strong civil religion overcame the divisive effects of private interests. A third group, concerned with the emergence of commercial society, found these options politically implausible and morally unpalatable, and sought instead to explain the emergence of cooperative social relations through the power of needs and interests. Humans joined together because they were useful to each other. Through the reciprocal exchange of goods and services men acquired the skills needed to sustain and navigate the complex relations of a commercial society.

Franklin embraced the claim that the bonds of cooperation were forged on the anvil of utility. But his practical context was North America, not Great Britain, and the colonies of his youth lacked the institutional density of the mother country. There were few clubs and coffee-houses for enlightened conversation, no societies to foster natural philosophy. Commercial relations were unstable and unevenly distributed. Regional differences hindered common undertakings. Faced with these deficits, Franklin was forced to improvise. The debate over commercial society provided new tools for thinking about growth and change. Returning to North America in 1726, Franklin discovered that underdevelopment presented novel opportunities for enlightened action. As was so often the case, Franklin's interventions in complex debates took the form of incidental tracts and practical proposals.

Franklin's first political pamphlet concerned the monetary policy of Pennsylvania [3]. Seventeenth-century colonial economies were plagued by a shortage of circulating media of exchange. Gold and silver were extremely scarce: mercantilist policies led Parliament to prohibit the export of coin to the colonies in 1695, and English creditors generally required balance-of-trade payments to be made in the few coins that could be found. At times the colonies came close to operating on a barter basis. This was massively inefficient, and posed substantial obstacles to development. Beginning in 1690, colonial governments sought to resolve this liquidity crisis by issuing paper money in the form of bills of credit. Pennsylvania first did so in 1723, and the success of that venture led to a renewal in 1726. These experiments pleased many, especially merchants and debtors; but because the expansion of the money supply was accompanied by inflation, it dismayed landowners and creditors. *A Modest Enquiry* was Franklin's attempt to influence the outcome of this debate.

According to Franklin, "Commerce, or the Exchange of one Commodity or Manufacture for another, is highly convenient and beneficial to Mankind" because it eliminates the inefficiencies and instabilities of barter exchange. Money is simply a socially agreed-upon medium of exchange, and a plentiful money supply enables efficient market institutions to develop. In so doing it spurs immigration, which serves as a stimulus to continued growth. Scarce money, by contrast, frustrates commercial exchange and encourages recourse to barter. Prices increase, the value of commodities varies, labor is discouraged, and population is depressed. Many of these ideas were derived from William Petty's *Treatise of Taxes*. Franklin's contribution lay in his explicit attention to the political determinants of economic development. Property rights were conventional, not natural [38]. In colonial Pennsylvania there were classes of men who did not favor commercial development. "Men will always be powerfully influenced in their Opinions and Actions by what appears to be their particular Interest," and it was the interest of those who profited from inefficiency – the very wealthy, money lenders, and lawyers who built their business on failed contracts – to keep money scarce. These men and their interests were represented in the Assembly. The dynamics of electoral politics led to fluctuating monetary policies; this, in turn, exacerbated Pennsylvania's economic woes. The key to commercial growth was political integration.

The fluid and underdeveloped nature of colonial economies provides one context for understanding some of Poor Richard's maxims. The population of British North America was growing rapidly but was still highly dispersed. Commercial exchange primarily occurred in local settings where the stability of transactions rested on personal character, not impersonal market institutions. In the *Autobiography* Franklin observed that "in order to secure my Credit and Character as a Tradesman" in Philadelphia, "I took care not only to be in *Reality* Industrious and frugal, but to avoid all *Appearances* to the Contrary." This was not a confession – Franklin was unembarrassed by his success at performing a role – but a statement of necessity. Commercial success rested on personal reputation, and reputation was a matter of appearance, of living up to the expectations of an audience. Doing so was not "natural"; it was hard work, and required extraordinary self-discipline [17, 42]. Franklin's harsh criticisms of the English poor law stem from his belief that public assistance undermined the very qualities of character he thought essential to the development of a stable market [25]. In this context, Weber's analysis is illuminating. Franklin called on colonists to subordinate their desires to an economic "calling." Poor Richard's ethos of industry and frugality was a strategic response to the challenges of an economically backward society.

During the late 1760s, industry and frugality were also weapons in the growing imperial conflict. As the British Empire was increasingly conceived in commercial terms, so restraint of trade was thought to be an effective bargaining tool. The non-importation agreements of the late 1760s were designed to influence British policy by creating a crisis among English merchants. In so doing they made the consumption patterns of ordinary Americans a matter of strategic concern.

Prosperity and economic development were important goals, but they were not Franklin's only goals. Consider the Junto, the "club for mutual improvement" that Franklin and his Philadelphia friends – printers, scriveners, shoemakers, and joiners – formed in 1727. Meeting on Friday evenings, members of the Junto provided mutual support, exchanged information and discussed moral, political, economic and scientific topics. Among the topics they handled were:

> Whether Men ought to be denominated Good or ill Men from their Actions or their Inclinations?
>
> If the Sovereign Power attempts to deprive a Subject of his Right, (or which is the same Thing, of what he thinks his Right) is it justifiable in him to resist if he is able?
>
> Does the Importation of Servants increase or advance the Wealth of our Country?

> Whence comes the Dew that stands on the Outside of a Tankard that has cold Water in it in the Summer Time?[13]

Franklin bragged that the Junto's debates were "conducted in the sincere spirit of inquiry after Truth, without Fondness for Dispute or Desire of Victory." This aspiration may not always have been achieved; to encourage good manners, small fines were imposed for uncivil conduct.

The Junto met for nearly forty years, and was, in Franklin's own opinion, "the best School of Philosophy, Morals, and Politics that then existed in the Province." It was also a hard-headed practical institution, combining moral uplift and self-help in roughly equal proportions. At each meeting members asked themselves questions like:

> Hath any citizen in your knowledge failed in his business lately, and what have you heard of the cause?
>
> Have you lately heard any member's character attacked, and how have you defended it? [5]

The education provided by the Junto was fine-tuned to the needs and interests of tradesmen confronting the complex and changing world of colonial British North America. Lacking patrons and disparaging masters, Franklin and his associates turned to each other for help. Improvement was a collective process, resting on the character of the participants and the quality of their interactions.

The Junto was the first of many educational institutions Franklin founded. In 1743, in order to address the imbalance of economic development and cultural opportunity in North America, he proposed what later became the American Philosophical Society [8]. "The first Drudgery of Settling new Colonies, which confines the Attention of People to mere Necessaries, is now pretty well over," wrote Franklin. "There are many in every Province in Circumstances that set them at Ease, and afford Leisure to cultivate the finer Arts, and improve the common Stock of Knowledge." But owing to "the extent of the Country such Persons are widely separated, and seldom can see and converse or be acquainted with each other, so that many useful Particulars remain uncommunicated, die with the Discoverers, and are lost to Mankind." The Society was to provide an institutional bond between individual scholars, holding regular meetings and distributing copies of communications. Its subject was anything and everything "new": "all new-discovered Plants," "New Methods of Curing

[13] "Proposals and Queries to be Asked the Junto, 1732," in Papers 1:259–64.

or Preventing Diseases," "all philosophical Experiments that let Light into the Nature of Things, tend to increase the Power of Man over Matter, and multiply the Conveniences or Pleasures of Life." As electrician and natural philosopher, of course, Franklin was one of the most important sources of new knowledge in the eighteenth century. But curiosity and flexibility were not restricted to science. In 1749 Franklin helped found the Philadelphia Academy (the future University of Pennsylvania) [13]. His hope, he explained two years later, was that youth might "come out of this School fitted for any Business, Calling or Profession." But from the start he was engaged in a fevered battle over the curriculum. Some favored a classical education, but Franklin thought this anachronistic. "There is in mankind an unaccountable Prejudice in favour of ancient Customs and Habitudes, which inclines to a Continuance of them after the Circumstances, which formerly made them useful, cease to exist." Such was the habit of teaching Greek and Latin, in preference to English; having outlived their utility, these languages – "the quackery of literature" – survived as little more than a mark of wealth and breeding.[14]

Finally, consider Franklin's most influential work of social analysis, his 1751 *Observations concerning the Increase of Mankind* [14]. In this brief treatise he made two predictions that proved remarkably accurate: that the population of the United States would double every twenty-five years, and that the population of North America would outstrip that of Great Britain within a hundred years. The significance of these predications lay in a widely shared assumption of late seventeenth- and early eighteenth-century political economy, that the key to public prosperity and national independence lay in a growing population.

If populousness was the key to prosperity, then the eighteenth-century Anglo-American world suffered an embarrassment of riches. The combined population of the British Isles and mainland North America grew from roughly 8.4 million in 1700 to 13.3 million in 1770. This growth was unevenly distributed in space and time, and its impact was often devastating. In Scotland and Ireland land shortages drove thousands into poverty, and spurred waves of emigration in the decades prior to the Revolution. From Germany came many more, pushed by war and pulled by the promise of a better life. These changes were unexpected and only

[14] "Idea of the English School," 1749, in Papers 4:108; "Observations Relative to the Intentions of the Original Founders of the Academy at Philadelphia," 1789, in Writings 10:29–31; "Excerpts from the Papers of Dr. Benjamin Rush," *Pennsylvania Magazine of History and Biography* 29 (1905): 27.

dimly understood, and challenged the capacities of basic social and political institutions. Parliament, fearing depopulation and economic devastation – a labor shortage would drive up the price of wages, rendering British manufactures uncompetitive on the world market – sought to stop emigration from Britain and impose strict limits on American economic development.

Franklin skewered moral objections to population growth in one of his most famous hoaxes, *The Speech of Miss Polly Baker* [9]. In the *Observations* he turned to demography. The primary limit to population growth was the availability of free land. There was "no Bound to the prolific Nature of Plants or Animals, but what is made by their crowding and interfering with each others' Means of Subsistence." This meant that theories and policies devised for "full settled old Countries, as Europe," were unsuited to "new Countries, as America." It also meant that population varied with stages of economic development. When first discovered, America was fully settled – but by hunters, not husbandmen. The introduction of agriculture by Europeans created ecological space for a population explosion. Moreover, the distinct stages of development in England and America enabled them to cooperate rather than compete. Manufacturing relied on an oversupply of labor. The sheer size of the North American land mass ensured that it would remain agricultural for many generations; the abundance of uncultivated land made manufacturing unprofitable. And while land in North America provided refuge for many a poor Irish or Scotch farmer, it produced no net drain on the population of the British Isles. "What an Accession of Power to the *British* Empire by Sea as well as Land! What Increase of Trade and Navigation!"

Franklin's analysis of the relationship between land and population gave him confidence that the continent would be occupied. But by whom? In "Rattle-Snakes for Felons" [16] he mocked the British practice of transporting criminals to the colonies. Slaves represented a much larger addition to the population of North America; but according to the *Observations*, slavery consumed, rather than produced, lives. Franklin's sharpest comments were directed at German immigrants: "Why should the Palatine Boors be suffered to swarm into our Settlements . . . Why should Pennsylvania, founded by the English, become a Colony of *Aliens*, who will shortly be so numerous as to Germanize us instead of our Anglifying them?" Pennsylvania Germans possessed a strong work ethic, but they refused to be culturally assimilated: they supported German printing houses, patronized German stores, and taught their children in German.

Even more threatening, they outnumbered the English in many counties and carried all but a few elections. They possessed a potent combination of cultural distinctness and political clout [17]. Franklin was not alone in these worries; manuscript copies of the *Observations* were eagerly read by friends and politicians on both sides of the Atlantic. Franklin embraced proposals to establish free English schools in German communities, and to require that all legal documents be written in English, and that all officeholders be competent to speak English. But he rejected draconian suggestions that German printing houses be suppressed: "Their fondness for their own Language and Manners is natural: it is not a Crime" [18].

The political divisiveness of Franklin's language and political programs was evident to his contemporaries. When he published the *Observations* in 1760, he left out the sections treating German immigrants. Copies of the original manuscript survived, however, and were reprinted during the Assembly election of 1764 in an attempt to turn German voters against him. Franklin professed not to understand the fuss, but he felt the sting of electoral defeat nonetheless.

By 1754 Franklin had shifted his attention to the continent as a whole and to the unique threat posed by the French. Successful expansion of the British Empire required political cooperation; but intercolonial conflict was endemic, leaving the colonies vulnerable to French predation [15]. Franklin's "Albany Plan" of 1754 sought to resolve this colonial security dilemma by creating a federal union in North America [20]. A General Council, explicitly modeled on the House of Commons, represented the people; a President General provided a link to the crown. The primary purpose of the union would have been to manage the western frontier of the Empire by regulating the Indian trade and supervising the formation of new colonies. Through frequent meetings, Franklin hoped that the colonists would learn to consider themselves "not as so many independent states, but as members of the same body."

Franklin's projects brought him into diplomatic contact with Native Americans. At times he cast Indians as primitive peoples, exhibiting noble simplicity; at other times he cast them as savages, mired in vice. To modern eyes these views are repugnant. But eighteenth-century prose was highly inflected – recall the sharp satire of Swift, or the bleak irony of Mandeville – and it is not always clear that Franklin's rhetoric should be taken at face value. Hostile to bigotry, he also argued that Native Americans possessed their own cultures, distinct from those of Europeans, that could be understood with empathy and imagination [39]. He acknowledged that frontier violence was often the fruit of white provocation, and that brutality was not the monopoly of any one race or nation. He was appalled by the Paxton Boys – a band of backcountry Pennsylvanians who slaughtered defenseless Indians in late 1763 – and wrote an impassioned defense of their victims.[15] Unlike many of his contemporaries – including Thomas Jefferson – he neither proposed nor embraced a policy of extermination. Franklin's faith in the benevolent effects of a commercial economy was so strong that he did not confront – or perhaps even contemplate – the human consequence of an expanding frontier population.

The Albany Plan was rejected by both the colonies and the crown. Franklin recapitulated many of his basic ideas twenty years later, in a draft "Articles of Confederation" [32]. But in the interim he continued to reflect on the relationship between demography and politics. In 1757 he was sent to London by the Pennsylvania Assembly to persuade the British to change the terms of the colonial charter. Franklin painfully misjudged the situation and failed in his mission. But, with the exception of a trip home in 1762–64, he remained in London until 1775 as official representative of up to four colonies. During this time he emerged as a leading spokesman for the American people. In this capacity he wrote well over a hundred pamphlets and letters to the press concerning the nature and basis of the British Empire.

By the second quarter of the eighteenth century the term "British Empire" had come to be identified with a distinct ideology: it was Protestant, maritime, commercial, and free. But the terms of integration between the mother country and the colonies of North America remained a bone of contention [26]. Were they partners and co-nationals, or were the colonies a politically dependent economic resource for the metropolis? Franklin saw this issue, first and foremost, in demographic and economic terms. He sought to reassure the Britons that the open expanse of land in North America guaranteed that it would remain agricultural for at least a century. He warmly embraced David Hume's 1760 essay "Of the Jealousy of Trade" in the optimistic faith that it might "abate" English anxieties about American development. But Franklin's enthusiasm masked a threatening possibility: that the wealth of North America was not subject to gross political manipulation. The British Empire rested on its domination of international markets. But markets have their own laws, imposing limits

[15] *A Narrative of the Late Massacres, in Lancaster County, of a Number of Indians, Friends of this Province, by Persons Unknown*, 1764, in Papers 11:42–69.

on those who live by them. As Hume commented in another of his essays, trade had become "an affair of state," and no nation could either afford to ignore it or hope to completely control it.[16] Franklin's insistence on the economic limits to imperial policy laid the foundation for thoughts of independence in 1767. As he explained to the Scottish jurist and philosopher Lord Kames, the advantages of Union are "not so apparent": "America, an immense Territory, favor'd by Nature with all Advantages of Climate, Soil, great navigable Rivers and Lakes, &c. must become a great Country, populous and mighty; and will in a less time than is generally conceiv'd, be able to shake off any Shackles that may be impos'd on her, and perhaps place them on her Imposers" [26].

Demography and political economy also played a critical role in Franklin's reflections on the rights of the colonists. By 1767 he embraced the radical claim that the colonies had been discovered and settled by individuals, at their own expense, and owed nothing to the British state. The king was sovereign, but "talk of the *Sovereignty of Parliament* and of the *Sovereignty of this Nation* over the Colonies" was nonsensical.[17] Seven years later John Adams invoked this claim to undermine the legitimacy of the British Empire. Franklin, writing to persuade a British audience, did not publicly permit himself this conclusion. Instead, he repeatedly attempted to explain that government policies were destined to fracture the Empire. Two of his most famous satires – "Rules by Which a Great Empire May be Reduced to a Small One" [29] and "An Edict by the King of Prussia" [30] – date from this period.

Franklin's return to America in 1775 brought him into direct contact with a new generation of American statesmen. His complaisance – his sedulous avoidance of direct conflict – was well marked. Thomas Jefferson considered Franklin "the greatest man & ornament of the age and country in which he lived," and urged his grandson to imitate Franklin, "the most amiable of men in society," because he made it a rule "'never to contradict any body.' If he was urged to announce an opinion, he did it rather by asking questions, as if for information or by suggesting doubts." John Adams, by contrast, thought Franklin's "whole life . . . one continued Insult to good Manners and to Decency." He was particularly troubled

[16] *The Interest of Great Britain Considered, With Regard to her Colonies*, 1760, in Papers 9:59–100; To David Hume, 27 September 1760, in Papers 9:227; David Hume, "Of Civil Liberty," in *Essays, Moral, Political, and Literary*, ed. E. F. Miller (Indianapolis, 1985), 88.

[17] This argument is especially clear in the marginalia of Franklin's copies of English pamphlets from this period; see Papers 13:207–32, 16:276–372, 17:317–400.

by Franklin's amiable demeanor: "He loves his ease, hates to offend, and seldom gives any opinion till obliged to do it . . . Although he has as determined a soul as any man, yet it is his constant policy never to say yes or no decidedly but when he cannot avoid it."[18] Jefferson and Adams each recognized that Franklin's complaisance was a conscious choice – a "rule" or "policy" – and not (simply) an affect or instinct. Adams thought it self-serving and nationally humiliating, especially when Franklin blandly endured the precise and complex rituals dictated by the court of Louis XVI. Jefferson, by contrast, was convinced that Franklin's mode of conduct expressed a valuable political ideal. "I never yet saw an instance of one of two disputants convincing the other by argument. I have [on the other hand] seen many on their getting warm, becoming rude, and shooting one another." We do not need to choose between these two interpretations; on more than one occasion, good manners were Franklin's weapon of choice.

Adams and Jefferson knew Franklin as a man in his seventies, coping with the challenges of war-making and state-building. The personal style they observed had been honed during five decades of public life. As was so often the case, Franklin's defense of complaisance linked method and purpose with personal narrative. In a letter to Samuel Mather, he recalled a hard lesson learned at the hands of Samuel's father Cotton:

> The last time I saw your father was in the beginning of 1724, when I visited him after my first trip to Pennsylvania. He received me in his library, and on my taking leave showed me a shorter way out of the house through a narrow passage, which was crossed by a beam over head. We were still talking as I withdrew, he accompanying me behind, and I turning partly towards him, when he said hastily, "*Stoop, stoop!*" I did not understand him, till I felt my head hit against the beam. He was a man that never missed any occasion of giving instruction, and upon this he said to me, "*You are young, and have the world before you;* STOOP *as you go through it, and you will miss many hard thumps.*" This advice, thus beat into my head, has frequently been of use to me; and I often think of it, when I see pride mortified, and misfortunes brought upon people by their carrying their heads too high.[19]

[18] Thomas Jefferson to Samuel Smith, 22 August 1798, and Thomas Jefferson to Thomas Jefferson Randolph, 24 November 1808, in *The Writings of Thomas Jefferson*, ed. Paul Leicester Ford (New York, 1892–99), 7:275–6, 9:232–3; John Adams to James Warren, 13 April 1783, in *Warren–Adams Letters* (Boston, 1917–25), 2:209, 74; John Adams, *Diary and Autobiography*, 27 May 1778, ed. L. H. Butterfield (Cambridge, MA, 1961), 4:118.

[19] Franklin told the story twice, in letters of 7 July 1773 (Papers 20:286) and 12 May 1784 (Writings 9:209).

Franklin was too proud to be humble, but he relished the comedy of the scene and the utility of Mather's advice. As a young man he mastered the Socratic method and took delight in his ability to draw people "into Concessions, the Consequences of which they did not foresee, entangling them in Difficulties out of which they could not extricate themselves." But he found that his victims – like Socrates' – were angered by his stratagems and ended his enemies rather than his friends. As a consequence he gradually set aside his "positive dogmatical Manner," and retained only the habit of expressing himself "in terms of modest Diffidence . . . This Habit I believe has been of great Advantage to me, when I have had occasion to inculcate my Opinions and persuade Men into Measures that I have been from time to time engag'd in promoting." Modesty, not frankness, was the hallmark of political speech. Improvement was a collective endeavor; Franklin's projects and ideas were futile unless embraced by others. But even well-intentioned men disagreed over the content of the public good and the means needed to attain it. Democratic politics was inseparable from negotiation, persuasion and compromise. And so Franklin met privately with associates and like-minded men, printed newspapers and almanacs containing news and information reinforcing his views, circulated petitions and organized public meetings to broaden support, and wrote pamphlets and essays by the hundred. In a widely read bagatelle Franklin argued that playing chess taught "valuable qualities of the Mind," like foresight, patience, and courtesy, that were "useful in the course of human Life" [33]. But as he explained to a French friend late in life, politics was not like chess, capable of being played "by a skilful hand, without a fault."[20]

In 1785 Franklin was replaced as Minister Plenipotentiary to France by Thomas Jefferson. Returning to the United States, he was elected President of the State of Pennsylvania; soon thereafter he was nominated to the Constitutional Convention. An elder statesman, he brokered peace by proposing compromise and praising moderation. At one particularly delicate moment he sought to buy time and cool tempers by calling for prayers. His final speech, read for him on 17 September, brilliantly expressed his style: "I confess that I do not entirely approve of this Constitution at present, but, Sir, I am not sure I shall never approve it: For having lived long, I have experienced many Instances of being obliged by

[20] To Dupont de Nemours, 9 June 1788, in Writings 9:659.

better Information or fuller Consideration, to change Opinions even on important Subjects, which I once thought right, but found to be otherwise" [43].

Franklin's final public gestures addressed slavery and the slave trade. As a young printer he had published slave notices in the *Gazette*; as colonial leader, he kept slaves in Philadelphia and London; as a middle-aged pamphleteer he voiced the shibboleths of white racism. In the *Observations* of 1751 he observed in passing that "almost every Slave" is "*by Nature* a Thief." But during the 1760s Franklin's attitudes began to change. After visiting "the Negro School" in Philadelphia in 1763 he "conceiv'd a higher Opinion of the natural Capacities of the black Race, than I had ever before entertained." In all respects the black students were "equal to that of white Children." As to his old attitudes, Franklin was characteristically unapologetic: "You will wonder perhaps that I should ever doubt it, and I will not undertake to justify all my Prejudices, nor to account them."[21] By 1769 the *Observations'* "*by Nature* a Thief" had become "from the nature of slavery a thief." Between 1770 and 1772 Franklin's descriptions of slavery and the slave trade shifted from defensive to critical. Mocking British hypocrisy [28], he began cooperating with anti-slavery advocates in England (Granville Sharp) and America (Anthony Benezet). With increasing clarity he recognized the colonists' inconsistency in calling for liberty while buying and selling human chattels. In early 1790, as president of the Pennsylvania Society for Promoting the Abolition of Slavery, Franklin signed a memorandum to Congress calling for an end to slavery. Senator James Jackson of Georgia responded with outrage; Franklin countered with a hoax, a bitter parody defending the custom of enslaving Christians by Barbary pirates [45].

We have no way of knowing how Franklin would have responded to the persistence of slavery, the neglect of the North, and the intransigence of the South, during the nineteenth century. Nor can we know how he would have responded to the brutal treatment of Native Americans as the descendants of Europeans spread across the continent. We can, however, plausibly imagine how he would have begun these tasks. In 1787 Franklin presided over the creation of one final philosophical association, the Society for Political Enquiries. "The arduous and complicated science of government" had been too long "left to the care of practical politicians, or

[21] To John Waring, 17 December 1763, in Papers 10:395.

the speculations of individual theorists." Meetings were held in Franklin's house. In early May, Tench Coxe – soon to assist Hamilton at the Treasury – read a paper on the future commercial system of the United States.[22] The problems and prospects of the modern republic were inseparable from individual effort, voluntary association, and the logic of commercial society. The strengths and weaknesses of Franklin's political thought are inseparable from these ideals and institutions.

[22] *Rules and Regulations of the Society for Political Enquiries* (Philadelphia, 1787), 2; [Tench Coxe], *An Enquiry Into The Principles On Which a Commercial System For The United States Should Be Founded* (Philadelphia, 1787).

Chronology

1706	Born 17 January (6 January 1705, Old Style) in Boston.
1718	Apprenticed to brother James, a printer.
1722	"Silence Dogood" essays published in *New England Courant*.
1723	Runs away to Philadelphia, arriving 6 October.
1724	Sails for London.
1725	Works as printer; meets Mandeville; publishes *A Dissertation on Liberty and Necessity*.
1726	Returns to Philadelphia.
1727	Nearly dies of pleurisy; rejoins Keimer's print shop; forms Junto.
1728	Opens own print shop with Hugh Meredith.
1729	Buys *Pennsylvania Gazette* from Samuel Keimer; birth of son, William.
1730	Common-law marriage to Deborah Read, 1 September.
1731	Joins Freemasons; founds Library Company of Philadelphia.
1732	First volume of *Poor Richard's Almanack* (continued annually until 1757).
1733	Conceives "bold and arduous Project of arriving at moral Perfection."
1735	Hemphill controversy.
1736	Appointed clerk of Pennsylvania Assembly; son Francis, age 4, dies of smallpox; establishes Union Fire Company.
1737	Appointed postmaster of Pennsylvania.
1739	George Whitefield visits Philadelphia for first time.

1741	Designs Pennsylvania Fireplace ("Franklin stove").
1743	Founds American Philosophical Society; birth of daughter Sarah.
1745	Begins electrical experiments.
1747	Sends letters on theory of electricity to Peter Collinson; organizes Pennsylvania militia.
1748	Forms partnership with David Hall, retires from business.
1748–50	Experiments with lightning.
1749	Proposes Philadelphia Academy (future University of Pennsylvania).
1751	*Experiments and Observations on Electricity*, Part 1, published in London; elected to Pennsylvania Assembly (re-elected annually until 1764).
1752	Performs kite experiment.
1753	Appointed joint deputy postmaster general of North America; Carlisle conference.
1754	Attends Albany Congress and proposes intercolonial union.
1755	Supplies Gen. Braddock; struggles with Proprietors.
1756	Commands defense of Northampton County; elected Fellow of the Royal Society.
1757	Appointed agent of Pennsylvania Assembly to negotiate dispute with Proprietors; sails for London.
1761	Coronation of George III.
1762	Returns to Philadelphia.
1763	Seven Years War ends with Peace of Paris; Paxton Boys massacre.
1764	Defeated in Assembly election but sent to London as its agent.
1765	Stamp Act passed.
1766	Testifies against Stamp Act in Parliament.
1768	Appointed agent of Georgia Assembly.
1769	Joins Ohio Company; appointed agent by New Jersey House of Representatives.
1770	Appointed agent by Massachusetts House of Representatives.
1771	Writes Part One of *Autobiography*.
1772	Sends Hutchinson-Oliver letters to Massachusetts.
1773	Boston Tea Party.

1774	Denounced in Parliament; dismissed from post office; Deborah Franklin dies in Philadelphia, 19 December.
1775	Returns to Philadelphia; battles of Lexington and Concord; elected to Second Continental Congress; George III declares colonies in open rebellion.
1776	Helps draft Declaration of Independence; elected commissioner to France.
1777	Settles in Paris suburb of Passy.
1778	Treaties of amity and commerce with France; John Adams arrives in Paris as commissioner; Congress appoints Franklin Minister Plenipotentiary to France.
1779	First edition of Franklin's *Political, Miscellaneous, and Philosophical Pieces.*
1781	Cornwallis surrenders at Yorktown.
1782	Negotiates, with John Adams and John Jay, peace treaty with Britian.
1783	Treaty of Paris, marking end of American Revolution.
1784	Writes Part Two of *Autobiography.*
1785	Replaced by Jefferson as Minister to France; returns to Philadelphia.
1787	Elected to Constitutional Convention; named president of Pennsylvania Society for the Abolition of Slavery.
1788	Begins Part Three of *Autobiography.*
1790	Petitions Congress against slavery; dies of pleurisy, 17 April.

Bibliographical note

The authoritative edition of Franklin's writings is *The Papers of Benjamin Franklin*, ed. Leonard W. Labaree *et al.* (New Haven, 1959–). Currently in its thirty-seventh volume, and covering Franklin's life through 1782, the *Papers* is comprehensive, scrupulously edited, and packed with annotations. The most reliable source for Franklin's writings after 1782 is *The Writings of Benjamin Franklin*, ed. Albert H. Smyth, 10 vols. (New York, 1905–7). The best single-volume collection is *Writings*, ed. J. A. Leo Lemay (New York, 1987). A scholarly edition of Franklin's memoirs is *The Autobiography of Benjamin Franklin: A Genetic Text*, ed. J. A. Leo Lemay and P. M. Zall (Knoxville, 1981).

Modern biographies begin with Carl Van Doren's still-vital *Benjamin Franklin* (New York, 1939), which argues that Franklin's mind was "a federation of purposes," his soul "a harmonious human multitude." Recent retellings include H. W. Brands, *The First American* (New York, 2000) and Walter Isaacson, *Benjamin Franklin* (New York, 2003). Edmund Morgan's *Benjamin Franklin* (New Haven, 2002) is an excellent short biography. Robert Middlekauf seeks to balance Van Doren by focusing on Franklin's "organizing animosities" in *Benjamin Franklin and His Enemies* (Berkeley, 1996). *Benjamin Franklin: An Extraordinary Life, an Electric Mind* (PBS, 2002) is an award-winning documentary.

Franklin's Philadelphia is the subject of Carl and Jessica Bridenbaugh, *Rebels and Gentlemen* (Oxford, 1942). James Hutson, *Pennsylvania Politics 1746–1770* (Princeton, 1972) focuses on the movement for royal government. Gary Nash, *The Urban Crucible* (Cambridge, MA, 1979) stresses social and economic cleavages. Fred Anderson, *The Crucible of War* (New York, 2000) definitively treats the Seven Years War. For the

Albany Congress, see Robert Newbold, *The Albany Congress and the Plan of Union* (New York, 1955) and Timothy Shannon, *Indians and Colonists at the Crossroads of Empire* (Ithaca, 2000). The Stamp Act crisis is the focal point of Edmund and Helen Morgan, *The Stamp Act Crisis* (Chapel Hill, 1953) and P. D. G. Thomas, *British Politics and the Stamp Act Crisis* (Oxford, 1975). Lawrence Gipson, *The Coming of the Revolution, 1763–1775* (New York, 1954) illuminates the imperial context. R. R. Palmer's *The Age of the Democratic Revolution*, 2 vols. (Princeton, 1959–64) places the American Revolution in a comparative Atlantic perspective. For the Continental Congress, see Jack Rakove, *The Beginnings of National Politics* (New York, 1979). Robert Middlekauf's *The Glorious Cause* (Oxford, 1982) is a concise account of the Revolution. For diplomacy, see Jonathan Dull, *The Diplomatic History of the American Revolution* (New Haven, 1985). The best account of the Constitutional Convention is still Max Farrand, *The Framing of the Constitution of the United States* (New Haven, 1913).

For nearly forty years scholars have disputed the "liberal" or "republican" character of the American Revolution. The literature is voluminous; leading contributions include the following. Louis Hartz identified a liberal Lockean consensus in *The Liberal Tradition in America* (New York, 1955). Caroline Robbins, *The Eighteenth-Century Commonwealthmen* (Cambridge, MA, 1959) called attention to radical Whig theorists. Bernard Bailyn acknowledged Locke's influence but emphasized radical rhetoric in explaining *The Ideological Origins of the American Revolution* (Cambridge, MA, 1967). Gordon Wood, *The Creation of the American Republic, 1776–1787* (New York, 1969) cast the Revolution as a struggle to preserve republican liberty and virtue. J. G. A. Pocock, *The Machiavellian Moment* (Princeton, 1975) identified a distinctively republican language. Challenges include Isaac Kramnick, "Republican Revisionism Revisited," *American Historical Review* 87 (1982): 629–64 and Joyce Appleby, *Liberalism and Republicanism in the Historical Imagination* (Cambridge, MA, 1992).

An essential starting-point for the intersection of political economy and moral psychology in the eighteenth century is Istvan Hont and Michael Ignatieff, eds., *Wealth and Virtue* (Cambridge, 1983). See also Albert Hirschman, *The Passions and the Interests* (Princeton, 1977). Ideas of empire are the subject of Anthony Pagden, *Lords of All the World* (New Haven, 1995) and David Armitage, *The Ideological Origins of the British Empire* (Cambridge, 2000).

Useful collections of essays on Franklin include: Esmond Wright, ed., *Benjamin Franklin* (New York, 1970); Brian M. Barbour, ed., *Benjamin Franklin* (Englewood Cliffs, 1979); J. A. Leo Lemay, ed., *Reappraising Benjamin Franklin* (Newark, 1993).

Franklin's political ideas are often identified as "pragmatic"; representative is Clinton Rossiter, "The Political Theory of Benjamin Franklin," *Pennsylvania Magazine of History and Biography* 76 (1952): 259–93. Gerald Stourzh, *Benjamin Franklin and American Foreign Policy*, 2nd edn (Chicago, 1969) admires Franklin's "liberal realism." Paul Conner counters, in *Poor Richard's Politics* (Oxford, 1965), that Franklin was a creature of "the Enlightenment," captivated by order, efficiency, stability, and structure. Drew McCoy brings Franklin into the republican fold in "Benjamin Franklin's Vision of a Republican Political Economy for America," *William and Mary Quarterly*, 3rd ser., 35 (1978): 605–28; John Patrick Diggins argues the contrary in *The Lost Soul of American Politics* (Chicago, 1984).

Franklin's moral psychology is the subject of fierce debate. Mark Twain's "The Late Benjamin Franklin" (1870) is a tragicomic defense of "boys" against Franklin's ethos of work and labor. D. H. Lawrence's "Benjamin Franklin," *Studies in Classic American Literature* (New York, 1923), 13–31, accuses Franklin of being a shallow, guileful materialist. Less acidic, but still within the Lawrence tradition, are Mitchell Robert Breitweiser, *Cotton Mather and Benjamin Franklin* (Cambridge, 1984) and Ormond Seavey, *Becoming Benjamin Franklin* (University Park, PA, 1988). Max Weber, *The Protestant Ethic and the Spirit of Capitalism*, 1920, trans. Talcott Parsons (London, 2001), argues that Franklin exhibited with "almost classic purity" the ethos of rational acquisition that gave rise to Western capitalism. David Levin, "The *Autobiography* of Benjamin Franklin: The Puritan Experimenter in Life and Art," *Yale Review* 53 (1963): 258–75, asserts that Franklin's religiosity was tempered by skeptical experimentalism. Norman Fiering holds that Franklin's emphasis on habit was "essentially neo-pagan" in "Benjamin Franklin and the Way to Virtue," *American Quarterly* 30 (1978): 199–223. Douglas Anderson, *The Radical Enlightenments of Benjamin Franklin* (Baltimore, 1997) deftly locates Franklin in the context of Mandeville, Hutcheson, and Shaftesbury.

Alfred Owen Aldridge argues in *Benjamin Franklin and Nature's God* (Durham, NC, 1967) that Franklin was a polytheist; Kerry Walters counters that Franklin espoused "theistic perspectivism" in *Benjamin Franklin and His Gods* (Urbana, 1998). There are several revealing essays in Barbara Oberg and Harry Stout, eds., *Benjamin Franklin, Jonathan Edwards, and the Representation of American Culture* (Oxford, 1993).

Franklin's economic ideas are explored in McCoy, Connor, and Anderson, *supra*. Lewis Carey's *Franklin's Economic Views* (New York, 1928) is dated but still useful. Essential background is provided by John J. McCusker and Russell R. Menard, *The Economy of British America, 1607–1789* (Chapel Hill, 1985).

Population and migration are the subject of Bernard Bailyn's landmark *The Peopling of British North America* (New York, 1986) and *Voyagers to the West* (New York, 1986). Franklin's contributions to pre-Malthusian population doctrines are discussed in Alfred Owen Aldridge, "Franklin as Demographer," *Journal of Economic History* 9 (1949): 25–44. See also James Cassedy, *Demography in Early America* (Cambridge, MA, 1969) and James C. Riley, *Population Thought in the Age of the Demographic Revolution* (Durham, NC, 1985). Franklin's reflections on German immigration are treated by Philip Gleason in "A Scurrilous Colonial Election and Franklin's Reputation," *William and Mary Quarterly*, 3rd ser., 18 (1961): 68–84, and "Trouble in the Colonial Melting Pot," *Journal of American Ethnic History* 20 (2000): 3–17.

Franklin's early involvement in the slave trade is discussed in Gary Nash, "Slaves and Slaveowners in Colonial Philadelphia," *William and Mary Quarterly*, 3rd ser., 30 (1973): 225–56. Franklin's opposition to slavery in the 1780s is captured by Joseph Ellis in *Founding Brothers* (New York, 2001), 81–119. There are no adequate studies of Franklin and Native Americans.

Colonial and revolutionary militias are the subject of heated debate in the United States; unfortunately, there are no satisfactory studies of the Association. For the mid-1750s, see Leonard Labaree, "Benjamin Franklin and the Defense of Pennsylvania 1754–1757," *Pennsylvania History* 29 (1962): 7–23. Fred Anderson, *A People's Army: Massachusetts Soldiers and Society in the Seven Years' War* (Chapel Hill, 1984) provides valuable comparative material. The use of lotteries to fund public ventures is described in John Samuel Ezell, *Fortune's Merry Wheel: The Lottery in America* (Cambridge, MA, 1960). Eric Hinderaker and Peter Mancall, *At the Edge of Empire* (Baltimore, 2003) sets the Paxton Boys in frontier context.

Franklin's life as a colonial printer is the subject of C. William Miller, *Franklin's Philadelphia Printing, 1728–1766* (Philadelphia, 1974). See also:

Stephen Botein, "'Meer Mechanics' and an Open Press: The Business and Political Strategies of Colonial American Printers," *Perspectives in American History* 9 (1975): 127–228; Charles Clark, *The Public Prints* (Oxford, 1994). In *The Letters of the Republic* (Cambridge, MA, 1990), Michael Warner argues that Franklin's embrace of "print culture" permitted him to embody a new kind of representativeness.

Franklin's educational ideas are highlighted in Bernard Bailyn's *Education in the Forming of American Society* (Chapel Hill, 1960). See also Lawrence Cremin, *American Education: The Colonial Experience, 1607–1873* (New York, 1979). The dean of Franklin science studies is I. Bernard Cohen; *Science and the Founding Fathers* (New York, 1995) traces the relationship between Franklin's science and his political ideas.

Franklin was astutely aware of the power and importance of his popular image. Charles Coleman Sellers, *Benjamin Franklin in Portraiture* (New Haven, 1962) provides a rich trove of data. Bernard Bailyn, "Realism and Idealism in American Diplomacy: Franklin in Paris, *Couronné par la Liberté*," in *To Begin the World Anew* (New York, 2003), 60–115, shows how Franklin used his image to diplomatic advantage. Nian-Sheng Huang, *Benjamin Franklin in American Thought and Culture* (Philadelphia, 1994) meticulously catalogs references to Franklin from 1790 to 1990.

Scholarly studies of Franklin's life and writings appear with regularity. An increasing number are available electronically. For an updated bibliography, including links to the Internet, see: http://www.cambridge.org/0521542650.

Biographical guide

ADAMS, JOHN (1735–1826). Lawyer, leading statesman and political philosopher from Massachusetts. Served in Continental Congress; helped negotiate with France and England during Revolution. Second president of the United States.

ALLEN, WILLIAM (1704–80). Philadelphia merchant and chief justice of Pennsylvania. Early ally of Franklin; broke during fight over proprietary privileges. Loyalist in the Revolution.

BACHE, SARAH ("SALLY") FRANKLIN (1743–1808). Franklin's daughter.

BRADDOCK, EDWARD (1695–1755). Commander of British forces in North America in 1755; fatally wounded in battle with French and Indians.

BRADFORD, ANDREW (1686–1742). Philadelphia printer and competitor of Franklin's.

BRILLON DE JOUY, ANNE-LOUISE BOIVIN D'HARDANCOURT (1744?–1824?). Franklin's neighbor and close friend at Passy.

BUFFON, GEORGES-LOUIS LECLERC, COMTE DE (1707–88). French naturalist and experimental scientist.

COLDEN, CADWALLADER (1688–1776). Scottish-born American politician and naturalist. Loyalist; made lieutenant-governor of New York in 1761.

COLLINSON, PETER (1694–1768). Quaker merchant in London. Patron and agent for Library Company. Naturalist and antiquary; corresponded with Franklin about science.

FOTHERGILL, JOHN (1712–80). Quaker physician and scientist in London.

FRANKLIN, BENJAMIN (1650–1727). Franklin's favorite uncle. Emigrated to Philadelphia in 1715.

FRANKLIN, DEBORAH READ (*c.* 1704–74). Franklin's wife; entered common-law union in 1730.

FRANKLIN, JAMES (1697–1735). Franklin's brother and first printing master.

FRANKLIN, JOSIAH (1657–1745). Franklin's father.

FRANKLIN, WILLIAM (1729?–1813). Franklin's son by an unknown mother. Raised in Franklin household. Last royal governor of New Jersey. Loyalist; imprisoned in 1776; released and fled to England in 1780.

FRANKLIN, WILLIAM TEMPLE (*c.* 1760–1823). Illegitimate son of William, raised largely by Franklin. Printed collection of Franklin's writings.

GALLOWAY, JOSEPH (1731–1803). Philadelphia lawyer and statesman. Franklin's ally in colonial Pennsylvania Assembly. Loyalist; fled to England in 1778.

HALL, DAVID (1714–72). Scottish printer. Emigrated to Philadelphia at Franklin's invitation in 1744; became managing partner in 1748.

HEMPHILL, SAMUEL (dates unknown). Irish Presbyterian minister, installed in Philadelphia in 1734. Unorthodox views banned by Synod in 1735; defended in print by Franklin.

HILLSBOROUGH, WILLS HILL, LORD (1718–93). English president of Board of Trade, 1763–65, 1766–68; secretary of state for colonies, 1768–72. Opposed concessions to colonies.

HOWE, LORD RICHARD (1726–99). British admiral; commander-in-chief in North America, 1776–78. Attempted negotiation with Franklin in 1775.

HUME, DAVID (1711–76). Scottish philosopher and historian.

HUTCHINSON, THOMAS (1711–80). Boston-born royal governor of Massachusetts, 1771–74.

INGENHOUS, JAN (1730–99). Dutch physician and physicist; corresponded with Franklin about electricity.

JAMES, ABEL (1724–90). Quaker official in Pennsylvania. Worked on Indian affairs with Franklin in 1750s. Recovered Part One of *Autobiography*.

KAMES, HENRY HOME, LORD (1696–1782). Scottish judge and moral philosopher.

KEIMER, SAMUEL (*c.* 1688–1742). London-born Philadelphia printer. Franklin's first employer, and subsequent competitor.

KEITH, WILLIAM (1680–1749). Scottish-born governor of Pennsylvania, 1716–26.

LOGAN, JAMES (1674–1751). Irish-born American scholar, scientist, and book collector. Member of Governor's Council; leader of Quaker party in Pennsylvania Assembly.

MATHER, COTTON (1663–1728). Prominent Puritan clergyman in Boston.

MECOM, JANE FRANKLIN (1712–94). Franklin's sister and favored correspondent.

MORRIS, ROBERT (1734–1806). English-born American banker. Signed Declaration of Independence. Superintendent of finance for Congress, 1781–84. Member of Constitutional Convention.

PENN, THOMAS (1702–75). Son of William Penn. After 1746, became primary Proprietor of Pennsylvania; resided in London.

PITT, WILLIAM, EARL OF CHATHAM (1708–78). English statesman. Prime minister during Seven Years War, 1756–63. Worked with Franklin in 1774–76 to avoid war.

PRICE, RICHARD (1723–91). English Unitarian minister, economist, and political philosopher. Publicly opposed war with America.

PRIESTLEY, JOSEPH (1733–1804). English scientist, educator and Unitarian theologian.

RALPH, JAMES (1695–1762). English writer. Traveled with Franklin to London in 1724.

SHIPLEY, JONATHAN, BISHOP OF ST. ASAPH (1714–88). Outspoken supporter of American cause. Part One of *Autobiography* written at his home in Twyford.

STRAHAN, WILLIAM (1714–85). London printer; published Hume, Smith, Gibbon, and others.

VAUGHAN, BENJAMIN (1751–1835). English diplomat and political economist. Edited first edition of Franklin's writings, 1779. Helped negotiate Anglo-American peace in 1782.

WHITEFIELD, GEORGE (1714–70). English evangelist. Missions to America helped spark the Great Awakening.

A note on the texts

Franklin began writing his memoirs in the summer of 1771, while visiting Jonathan Shipley, bishop of St. Asaph, at his country estate near Twyford, Hampshire, England. He completed the first draft of Part One within six weeks, but did not write Part Two until 1784, during his residence in France. Parts Three and Four were written in Philadelphia between 1788 and 1790. At this time Franklin also made numerous revisions to Parts One and Two. During the last decade of his life Franklin corresponded with friends in England and America about the nature, purpose, and publication of his memoirs. Ill health prevented him from completing the manuscript, however, and the narrative breaks off abruptly in 1757. Franklin's outline of 1771 indicates that he conceived his memoirs as a single work covering the whole of his life.

The holograph manuscript of the *Autobiography* is held by the Huntington Library, HM 9999. The present edition provides a clear text, based on this manuscript, and is intended for general readers. In preparing the text, I have adopted the following guidelines:

- The conventional division of the text into four parts has been preserved, though there are no headings in the original manuscript.
- Franklin's insertions and cancellations have been silently incorporated into the text. Supplementary texts have been included where Franklin indicated.
- Eighteenth-century spelling and punctuation have been preserved. However, Franklin's spelling has been made consistent, and obvious misspellings have been corrected.

- Superscripts have been lowered, and symbols and abbreviations have been expanded. Dashes that appear throughout the manuscript have been retained.

Many of Franklin's writings were published in his life. Whenever possible the texts reproduced here are the original manuscript or the first printed edition. Most are drawn from the following sources, abbreviated thus:

Gazette	*The Pennsylvania Gazette.*
LC	Benjamin Franklin Papers, Manuscript Division, Library of Congress.
Papers	*The Papers of Benjamin Franklin*, ed. Leonard W. Labaree *et al.*, 37 vols. to date (New Haven: Yale University Press, 1957–).
Temple	William Temple Franklin, ed., *Memoirs of the Life and Writings of Benjamin Franklin*, 3 vols. (London: Henry Colburn, 1817–18).
Vaughan	Benjamin Franklin, *Political, Miscellaneous, and Philosophical Pieces*, ed. Benjamin Vaughan (London: J. Johnson, 1779).
Writings	*The Writings of Benjamin Franklin*, ed. Albert H. Smyth, 10 vols. (New York: Macmillan, 1905–7).

Franklin's correspondence often dealt with subjects other than politics, and in a handful of cases has been edited. Missing portions are clearly indicated by ellipses. With the exception of *Proposals Relating to the Education of Youth* – whose lengthy footnotes have been abbreviated – all other texts are reprinted in their entirety.

Franklin frequently did not title his pieces. The ones given here are customary, having been assigned by his first editors. Explanatory footnotes are placed within square brackets; all others are Franklin's. As with the *Autobiography*, eighteenth-century spelling and punctuation has been preserved. And – in keeping with Franklin's wishes – Substantives are capitalized.[1]

[1] To Noah Webster, 26 December 1789, in Writings 10:79–80.

CHAPTER I
The Autobiography

Part One

Twyford, at the Bishop of St. Asaph's 1771.

Dear Son,

I have ever had a Pleasure in obtaining any little Anecdotes of my Ancestors. You may remember the Enquiries I made among the Remains of my Relations when you were with me in England; and the Journey I took for that purpose. Now imagining it may be equally agreable to you to know the Circumstances of *my* Life, many of which you are yet unacquainted with; and expecting a Weeks uninterrupted Leisure in my present Country Retirement, I sit down to write them for you. To which I have besides some other Inducements. Having emerg'd from the Poverty and Obscurity in which I was born and bred, to a State of Affluence and some Degree of Reputation in the World, and having gone so far thro' Life with a considerable Share of Felicity, the conducing Means I made use of, which, with the Blessing of God, so well succeeded, my Posterity may like to know, as they may find some of them suitable to their own Situations, and therefore fit to be imitated.——That Felicity, when I reflected on it, has induc'd me sometimes to say, that were it offer'd to my Choice, I should have no Objection to a Repetition of the same Life from its Beginning, only asking the Advantage Authors have in a second Edition to correct some Faults of the first. So would I if I might, besides correcting the Faults, change some sinister Accidents and Events of it for others more favourable, but tho' this were deny'd, I should still accept the Offer. However, since such a Repetition is not to be expected, the next Thing most like living one's Life over again, seems to be a *Recollection* of that Life; and to make that Recollection as durable as possible, the putting it down in Writing. Hereby, too, I shall indulge the Inclination so natural in old Men, to be talking of themselves and their own past Actions, and I shall indulge it, without being troublesome to others who thro' respect to

Age might think themselves oblig'd to give me a Hearing, since this may be read or not as any one pleases. And lastly, (I may as well confess it, since my Denial of it will be believ'd by no body) perhaps I shall a good deal gratify my own *Vanity*. Indeed I scarce ever heard or saw the introductory Words, *Without Vanity I may say*, &c. but some vain thing immediately follow'd. Most People dislike Vanity in others whatever Share they have of it themselves, but I give it fair Quarter wherever I meet with it, being persuaded that it is often productive of Good to the Possessor and to others that are within his Sphere of Action: And therefore in many Cases it would not be quite absurd if a Man were to thank God for his Vanity among the other Comforts of Life.——

And now I speak of thanking God, I desire with all Humility to acknowledge, that I owe the mention'd Happiness of my past Life to his kind Providence, which led me to the Means I us'd and gave them Success.——My Belief of This, induces me to *hope*, tho' I must not *presume*, that the same Goodness will still be exercis'd towards me in continuing that Happiness, or in enabling me to bear a fatal Reverso, which I may experience as others have done, the Complexion of my future Fortune being known to him only: and in whose Power it is to bless to us even our Afflictions.

The Notes one of my Uncles (who had the same kind of Curiosity in collecting Family Anecdotes) once put into my Hands, furnish'd me with several Particulars relating to our Ancestors. From these Notes I learnt that the Family had liv'd in the same Village, Ecton in Northamptonshire, for 300 Years, and how much longer he knew not, (perhaps from the Time when the Name *Franklin* that before was the Name of an Order of People, was assum'd by them for a Surname, when others took Surnames all over the Kingdom.[1]) on a Freehold of about 30 Acres, aided by the Smith's

[1] As a proof that FRANKLIN was anciently the common name of an order or rank in England, see Judge Fortescue, *De laudibus Legum Angliae*, written about the year 1412, in which is the following passage, to show that good juries might easily be formed in any part of England.

"Regio etiam illa, ita respersa refertaque est *possessoribus terrarum* et agrorum, quod in ea, villula tam parva reperiri non poterit, in qua non est *miles*, *armiger*, vel pater-familias, quails ibidem *Franklin* vulgariter nuncupatur, magnis ditatus possessionibus, nec non libere tenentes et alii *valecti* plurimi, suis patrimoniis sufficientes ad faciendum juratam, in forma praenotata."

"Moreover, the same country is so filled and replenished with landed menne, that therein so small a Thorpe cannot be found wherein dweleth not a knight, an esquire, or such a householder, as is there commonly called a *Franklin*, enriched with great possessions; and also other freeholders and many yeomen able for their livelihoods to make a jury in form aforementioned."——(*Old Translation.*)

Business which had continued in the Family till his Time, the eldest Son being always bred to that Business. A Custom which he and my Father both followed as to their eldest Son.——When I search'd the Register at Ecton, I found an Account of their Births, Marriages and Burials, from the Year 1555 only, there being no Register kept in that Parish at any time preceding.——By that Register I perceiv'd that I was the youngest Son of the youngest Son for 5 Generations back. My Grandfather Thomas, who was born in 1598, lived at Ecton till he grew too old to follow Business longer, when he went to live with his Son John, a Dyer at Banbury in Oxfordshire, with whom my Father serv'd an Apprenticeship. There my Grandfather died and lies buried. We saw his Gravestone in 1758. His eldest Son Thomas liv'd in the House at Ecton, and left it with the Land to his only Child, a Daughter, who with her Husband, one Fisher of Wellingborough sold it to Mr. Isted, now Lord of the Manor there. My Grandfather had 4 Sons that grew up, viz. Thomas, John, Benjamin and Josiah. I will give you what Account I can of them at this distance from my Papers, and if those are not lost in my Absence, you will among them find many more Particulars. Thomas was bred a Smith under his Father, but being ingenious, and encourag'd in Learning (as all his Brothers like wise were) by an Esquire Palmer then the principal Gentleman in that Parish, he qualify'd himself for the Business of Scrivener, became a considerable Man in the County Affairs, was a chief Mover of all publick Spirited Undertakings, for the County or Town of Northampton and his own Village, of which many Instances were told us at Ecton and he was much taken Notice of and patroniz'd by the then Lord Halifax. He died in 1702 Jan. 6. old Stile, just 4 Years to a Day before I was born. The Account we receiv'd of his Life and Character from some old People at Ecton, I remember struck you as something extraordinary from its Similarity to what you knew of mine. Had he died on the same Day, you said one might have suppos'd a Transmigration.——John was bred a Dyer, I believe of Woollens. Benjamin, was bred a Silk Dyer, serving an Apprenticeship at London. He was an ingenious Man, I remember him

Chaucer too calls his Country Gentleman, a *Franklin*, and after describing his good housekeeping thus characterizes him:

> "This worthy Franklin bore a purse of silk,
> Fix'd to his girdle, white as morning milk.
> Knight of the Shire, first Justice at th' Assize,
> To help the poor, the doubtful to advise.
> In all employments, generous, just, he proved;
> Renown'd for courtesy, by all beloved." [Temple 1:3]

well, for when I was a Boy he came over to my Father in Boston, and lived in the House with us some Years. He lived to a great Age. His Grandson Samuel Franklin now lives in Boston. He left behind him two Quarto Volumes, M.S. of his own Poetry, consisting of little occasional Pieces address'd to his Friends and Relations, of which the following sent to me, is a Specimen.[2]

Sent to My Name upon a Report
of his Inclination to Martial affaires
7 July 1710

Beleeve me Ben. It is a Dangerous Trade
The Sword has Many Marr'd as well as Made
By it doe many fall Not Many Rise
Makes Many poor few Rich and fewer Wise
Fills Towns with Ruin, fields with blood beside
Tis Sloths Maintainer, And the Shield of pride
Fair Citties Rich to Day, in plenty flow
War fills with want, Tomorrow, & with woe
Ruin'd Estates, The Nurse of Vice, broke limbs & scarss
Are the Effects of Desolating Warrs

Sent to B.F. in N.E. 15 July 1710

B e to thy parents an Obedient Son
E ach Day let Duty constantly be Done
N ever give Way to sloth or lust or pride
I f free you'd be from Thousand Ills beside
A bove all Ills be sure Avoide the shelfe
M ans Danger lyes in Satan sin and selfe
I n vertue Learning Wisdome progress Make
N ere Shrink at Suffering for thy saviours sake
F raud and all Falshood in thy Dealings Flee
R eligious Always in thy station be
A dore the Maker of thy Inward part
N ow's the Accepted time, Give him thy Heart
K eep a Good Conscience 'tis a constant Frind
L ike Judge and Witness This Thy Acts Attend
I n Heart with bended knee Alone Adore
N one but the Three in One Forevermore.

[2] [Benjamin Franklin (1650–1727), Notebooks 1666–1725, *c.* 1783, vol. 1, page 145, American Antiquarian Society, Worcester, MA.]

He had form'd a Shorthand of his own, which he taught me, but never practicing it I have now forgot it. I was nam'd after this Uncle, there being a particular Affection between him and my Father. He was very pious, a great Attender of Sermons of the best Preachers, which he took down in his Shorthand and had with him many Volumes of them.——He was also much of a Politician, too much perhaps for his Station. There fell lately into my Hands in London a Collection he had made of all the principal Pamphlets relating to Publick Affairs from 1641 to 1717. Many of the Volumes are wanting, as appears by the Numbering, but there still remains 8 Vols. Folio, and 24 in 4to and 8vo.——A Dealer in old Books met with them, and knowing me by my some times buying of him, he brought them to me. It seems my Uncle must have left them here when he went to America, which was above 50 Years since. There are many of his Notes in the Margins.——

This obscure Family of ours was early in the Reformation, and continu'd Protestants thro' the Reign of Queen Mary, when they were sometimes in Danger of Trouble on Account of their Zeal against Popery. They had got an English Bible, and to conceal and secure it, it was fastned open with Tapes under and within the Frame of a Joint Stool. When my Great Great Grandfather read in it to his Family, he turn'd up the Joint Stool upon his Knees, turning over the Leaves then under the Tapes. One of the Children stood at the Door to give Notice if he saw the Apparitor coming, who was an Officer of the Spiritual Court. In that Case the Stool was turn'd down again upon its feet, when the Bible remain'd conceal'd under it as before. This Anecdote I had from my Uncle Benjamin.——The Family continu'd all of the Church of England till about the End of Charles the 2ds Reign, when some of the Ministers that had been outed for Nonconformity, holding Conventicles in Northamptonshire, Benjamin and Josiah adher'd to them, and so continu'd all their Lives. The rest of the Family remain'd with the Episcopal Church.

Josiah, my Father, married young, and carried his Wife with three Children unto New England, about 1682. The Conventicles having been forbidden by Law, and frequently disturbed, induced some considerable Men of his Acquaintance to remove to that Country, and he was prevail'd with to accompany them thither, where they expected to enjoy their Mode of Religion with Freedom.——By the same Wife he had 4 Children more born there, and by a second Wife ten more, in all 17, of which I remember 13 sitting at one time at his Table, who all grew up to be Men and Women, and married;——I was the youngest Son and the youngest Child but two, and was born in Boston, N. England.

My Mother the 2d Wife was Abiah Folger, a Daughter of Peter Folger, one of the first Settlers of New England, of whom honourable mention is made by Cotton Mather, in his Church History of that Country, (entitled Magnalia Christi Americana) as a *godly learned Englishman*, if I remember the words rightly. I have heard that he wrote sundry small occasional Pieces, but only one of them was printed which I saw now many Years since. It was written in 1675, in the homespun Verse of that Time and People, and address'd to those then concern'd in the Government there. It was in favour of Liberty of Conscience, and in behalf of the Baptists, Quakers, and other Sectaries, that had been under Persecution; ascribing the Indian Wars and other Distresses, that had befallen the Country to that Persecution, as so many judgments of God, to punish so heinous an Offence; and exhorting a Repeal of those uncharitable Laws. The whole appear'd to me as written with a good deal of Decent Plainness and manly Freedom. The six last concluding Lines I remember, tho' I have forgotten the two first of the Stanza, but the Purport of them was that his Censures proceeded from *Goodwill*, and therefore he would be known as the Author,

> because to be a Libeller, (says he)
> I hate it with my Heart.
> From[3] Sherburne Town where now I dwell,
> My Name I do put here,
> Without Offence, your real Friend,
> It is Peter Folgier.

My elder Brothers were all put Apprentices to different Trades. I was put to the Grammar School at Eight Years of Age, my Father intending to devote me as the Tithe of his Sons to the Service of the Church. My early Readiness in learning to read (which must have been very early, as I do not remember when I could not read) and the Opinion of all his Friends that I should certainly make a good Scholar, encourag'd him in this Purpose of his. My Uncle Benjamin too approv'd of it, and propos'd to give me all his Shorthand Volumes of Sermons I suppose as a Stock to set up with, if I would learn his Character. I continu'd however at the Grammar School not quite one Year, tho' in that time I had risen gradually from the Middle of the Class of that Year to be the Head of it, and farther was remov'd into the next Class above it, in order to go with that into the third at the End

[3] In the Island of Nantucket.

of the Year. But my Father in the mean time, from a View of the Expence of a College Education which, having so large a Family, he could not well afford, and the mean Living many so educated were afterwards able to obtain, Reasons that he gave to his Friends in my Hearing, altered his first Intention, took me from the Grammar School, and sent me to a School for Writing and Arithmetic kept by a then famous Man, Mr. Geo. Brownell, very successful in his Profession generally, and that by mild encouraging Methods. Under him I acquired fair Writing pretty soon, but I fail'd in the Arithmetic, and made no Progress in it.——At Ten Years old, I was taken home to assist my Father in his Business, which was that of a Tallow Chandler and Sope-Boiler. A Business he was not bred to, but had assumed on his Arrival in New England and on finding his Dying Trade would not maintain his Family, being in little Request. Accordingly I was employed in cutting Wick for the Candles, filling the Dipping Mold, and the Molds for cast Candles, attending the Shop, going of Errands, &c.——I dislik'd the Trade and had a strong Inclination for the Sea; but my Father declar'd against it; however, living near the Water, I was much in and about it, learnt early to swim well, and to manage Boats, and when in a Boat or Canoe with other Boys I was commonly allow'd to govern, especially in any case of Difficulty; and upon other Occasions I was generally a Leader among the Boys, and sometimes led them into Scrapes, of which I will mention one Instance, as it shows an early projecting public Spirit, tho' not then justly conducted. There was a Salt Marsh that bounded part of the Mill Pond, on the Edge of which at Highwater, we us'd to stand to fish for Minews. By much Trampling, we had made it a mere Quagmire. My Proposal was to build a Wharf there fit for us to stand upon, and I show'd my Comrades a large Heap of Stones which were intended for a new House near the Marsh, and which would very well suit our Purpose. Accordingly in the Evening when the Workmen were gone, I assembled a Number of my Playfellows, and working with them diligently like so many Emmets, sometimes two or three to a Stone, we brought them all away and built our little Wharff.——The next Morning the Workmen were surpriz'd at Missing the Stones; which were found in our Wharff; Enquiry was made after the Removers; we were discovered and complain'd of; several of us were corrected by our Fathers; and tho' I pleaded the Usefulness of the Work, mine convinc'd me that nothing was useful which was not honest.——

I think you may like to know Something of his Person and Character. He had an excellent Constitution of Body, was of middle Stature, but well set and very strong. He was ingenious, could draw prettily, was skill'd a little in Music and had a clear pleasing Voice, so that when he play'd Psalm Tunes on his Violin and sung withal as he sometimes did in an Evening after the Business of the Day was over, it was extreamly agreable to hear. He had a mechanical Genius too, and on occasion was very handy in the Use of other Tradesmen's Tools. But his great Excellence lay in a sound Understanding, and solid judgment in prudential Matters, both in private and publick Affairs. In the latter indeed he was never employed, the numerous Family he had to educate and the straitness of his Circumstances, keeping him close to his Trade, but I remember well his being frequently visited by leading People, who consulted him for his Opinion in Affairs of the Town or of the Church he belong'd to and show'd a good deal of Respect for his Judgment and Advice. He was also much consulted by private Persons about their Affairs when any Difficulty occur'd, and frequently chosen an Arbitrator between contending Parties.——At his Table he lik'd to have as often as he could, some sensible Friend or Neighbour, to converse with, and always took care to start some ingenious or useful Topic for Discourse, which might tend to improve the Minds of his Children. By this means he turn'd our Attention to what was good, just, and prudent in the Conduct of Life; and little or no Notice was ever taken of what related to the Victuals on the Table, whether it was well or ill drest, in or out of season, of good or bad flavour, preferable or inferior to this or that other thing of the kind; so that I was bro't up in such a perfect Inattention to those Matters as to be quite Indifferent what kind of Food was set before me; and so unobservant of it, that to this Day, if I am ask'd I can scarce tell, a few Hours after Dinner, what I din'd upon.——This has been a Convenience to me in travelling, where my Companions have been sometimes very unhappy for want of a suitable Gratification of their more delicate because better instructed Tastes and Appetites.——

My Mother had likewise an excellent Constitution. She suckled all her 10 Children. I never knew either my Father or Mother to have any Sickness but that of which they dy'd, he at 89 and she at 85 Years of age. They lie buried together at Boston, where I some Years since plac'd a Marble stone over their Grave with this Inscription

Josiah Franklin
And Abiah his Wife
Lie here interred.
They lived lovingly together in Wedlock

Fifty-five Years.
Without an Estate or any gainful Employment,
By constant Labour and Industry,
With God's Blessing,
They maintained a large Family
Comfortably;
And brought up thirteen Children,
And seven Grand Children
Reputably.
From this Instance, Reader,
Be encouraged to Diligence in thy Calling,
And distrust not Providence.
He was a pious & prudent Man,
She a discreet and virtuous Woman.
Their youngest Son,
In filial Regard to their Memory,
Places this Stone.
J.F. born 1655 — Died 1744. Ætat 89
A.F. born 1667 — died 1752 — 85

By my rambling Digressions I perceive my self to be grown old. I us'd to write more methodically.——But one does not dress for private Company as for a publick Ball. 'Tis perhaps only Negligence.——

To return. I continu'd thus employ'd in my Father's Business for two Years, that is till I was 12 Years old; and my Brother John, who was bred to that Business having left my Father, married and set up for himself at Rhode Island, there was all Appearance that I was destin'd to supply his Place and be a Tallow Chandler. But my Dislike to the Trade continuing, my Father was under Apprehensions that if he did not find one for me more agreable, I should break away and get to Sea, as his Son Josiah had done to his great Vexation. He therefore sometimes took me to walk with him, and see Joiners, Bricklayers, Turners, Braziers, &c. at their Work, that he might observe my Inclination, and endeavour to fix it on some Trade or other on Land. It has ever since been a Pleasure to me to see good Workmen handle their Tools; and it has been useful to me, having learnt so much by it, as to be able to do little Jobs my self in my House, when a Workman could not readily be got; and to construct little Machines for my Experiments while the Intention of making the Experiment was fresh and warm in my Mind. My Father at last fix'd upon the Cutler's Trade, and my Uncle Benjamin's Son Samuel who was bred to that Business in London being about that time establish'd in Boston, I was sent to be with him some time on liking. But his Expectations of a Fee with me displeasing my Father, I was taken home again.——

From a Child I was fond of Reading, and all the little Money that came into my Hands was ever laid out in Books. Pleas'd with the Pilgrim's Progress, my first Collection was of John Bunyan's Works, in separate little Volumes. I afterwards sold them to enable me to buy R. Burton's Historical Collections; they were small Chapmen's Books and cheap, 40 or 50 in all.——My Father's little Library consisted chiefly of Books in polemic Divinity, most of which I read, and have since often regretted, that at a time when I had such a Thirst for Knowledge, more proper Books had not fallen in my Way, since it was now resolv'd I should not be a Clergyman. Plutarch's Lives there was, in which I read abundantly, and I still think that time spent to great Advantage. There was also a Book of Defoe's called an Essay on Projects, and another of Dr. Mather's, call'd Essays to do Good which perhaps gave me a Turn of Thinking that had an Influence on some of the principal future Events of my Life.[4]

This Bookish Inclination at length determin'd my Father to make me a Printer, tho' he had already one Son, (James) of that Profession. In 1717 my Brother James return'd from England with a Press and Letters to set up his Business in Boston. I lik'd it much better than that of my Father, but still had a Hankering for the Sea.——To prevent the apprehended Effect of such an Inclination, my Father was impatient to have me bound to my Brother. I stood out some time, but at last was persuaded and signed the Indentures, when I was yet but 12 Years old.——I was to serve as an Apprentice till I was 21 Years of Age, only I was to be allow'd Journeyman's Wages during the last Year. In a little time I made great Proficiency in the Business, and became a useful Hand to my Brother. I now had Access to better Books. An Acquaintance with the Apprentices of Booksellers, enabled me sometimes to borrow a small one, which I was careful to return soon and clean. Often I sat up in my Room reading the greatest Part of the Night, when the Book was borrow'd in the Evening and to be return'd early in the Morning lest it should be miss'd or wanted. And after some time an ingenious Tradesman Mr. Matthew Adams who had a pretty Collection of Books, and who frequented our Printing House, took Notice of me, invited me to his Library, and very kindly lent me such

[4] [John Bunyan, *A Pilgrim's Progress* (1678); Nathaniel Crouch wrote popular histories under the name "R. Burton"; Daniel Defoe, *An Essay upon Projects* (1697); Cotton Mather, *Bonifacius. An Essay Upon the Good* (1710).]

Books as I chose to read. I now took a Fancy to Poetry, and made some little Pieces. My Brother, thinking it might turn to account encourag'd me, and put me on composing two occasional Ballads. One was called the *Light House Tragedy*, and contain'd an Account of the drowning of Capt. Worthilake with his Two Daughters; the other was a Sailor Song on the Taking of *Teach* or Blackbeard the Pirate. They were wretched Stuff, in the Grubstreet Ballad Stile, and when they were printed he sent me about the Town to sell them. The first sold wonderfully, the Event being recent, having made a great Noise. This flatter'd my Vanity. But my Father discourag'd me, by ridiculing my Performances, and telling me Verse-makers were generally Beggars; so I escap'd being a Poet, most probably a very bad one. But as Prose Writing has been of great Use to me in the Course of my Life, and was a principal Means of my Advancement, I shall tell you how in such a Situation I acquir'd what little Ability I have in that Way.

There was another Bookish Lad in the Town, John Collins by Name, with whom I was intimately acquainted. We sometimes disputed, and very fond we were of Argument, and very desirous of confuting one another. Which disputacious Turn, by the way, is apt to become a very bad Habit, making People often extreamly disagreable in Company, by the Contradiction that is necessary to bring it into Practice, and thence, besides souring and spoiling the Conversation, is productive of Disgusts and perhaps Enmities where you may have occasion for Friendship. I had caught it by reading my Father's Books of Dispute about Religion. Persons of good Sense, I have since observ'd, seldom fall into it, except Lawyers, University Men, and Men of all Sorts that have been bred at Edinborough. A Question was once some how or other started between Collins and me, of the Propriety of educating the Female Sex in Learning, and their Abilities for Study. He was of Opinion that it was improper; and that they were naturally unequal to it. I took the contrary Side, perhaps a little for Dispute sake. He was naturally more eloquent, had a ready Plenty of Words, and sometimes as I thought bore me down more by his Fluency than by the Strength of his Reasons. As we parted without settling the Point, and were not to see one another again for some time, I sat down to put my Arguments in Writing, which I copied fair and sent to him. He answer'd and I reply'd. Three or four Letters of a Side had pass'd, when my Father happen'd to find my Papers, and read them. Without entring into the Discussion, he took occasion to talk to me about the Manner of my Writing, observ'd that tho' I had the Advantage of my Antagonist in correct Spelling and pointing[5] (which I ow'd to the Printing House) I fell far short in elegance of Expression, in Method and in Perspicuity, of which he convinc'd me by several Instances. I saw the Justice of his Remarks, and thence grew more attentive to the *Manner* in Writing, and determin'd to endeavour at Improvement.——

About this time I met with an odd Volume of the Spectator.[6] It was the third. I had never before seen any of them. I bought it, read it over and over, and was much delighted with it. I thought the Writing excellent, and wish'd if possible to imitate it. With that View, I took some of the Papers, and making short Hints of the Sentiment in each Sentence, laid them by a few Days, and then without looking at the Book, try'd to compleat the Papers again, by expressing each hinted Sentiment at length and as fully as it had been express'd before, in any suitable Words, that should come to hand.

Then I compar'd my Spectator with the Original, discover'd some of my Faults and corrected them. But I found I wanted a Stock of Words or a Readiness in recollecting and using them, which I thought I should have acquir'd before that time, if I had gone on making Verses, since the continual occasion for Words of the same Import but of different Length, to suit the Measure, or of different Sound for the Rhyme, would have laid me under a constant Necessity of searching for Variety, and also have tended to fix that Variety in my Mind, and make me Master of it. Therefore I took some of the Tales and turn'd them into Verse: And after a time, when I had pretty well forgotten the Prose, turn'd them back again. I also sometimes jumbled my Collections of Hints into Confusion, and after some Weeks, endeavour'd to reduce them into the best Order, before I began to form the full Sentences, and compleat the Paper. This was to teach me Method in the Arrangement of Thoughts. By comparing my work afterwards with the original, I discover'd many faults and amended them; but I sometimes had the Pleasure of Fancying that in certain Particulars of small Import, I had been lucky enough to improve the Method or the Language and this encourag'd me to think I might possibly in time come to be a tolerable English Writer, of which I was extreamly ambitious.

My Time for these Exercises and for Reading, was at Night after Work, or before Work began in the Morning; or on Sundays, when I contrived to

[5] [Pointing: punctuation.]
[6] [Joseph Addison and Richard Steele, *The Spectator* (1711–12).]

be in the Printing House alone, evading as much as I could the common Attendance on publick Worship, which my Father used to exact of me when I was under his Care: And which indeed I still thought a Duty; tho' I could not, as it seemed to me, afford the Time to practise it.

When about 16 Years of Age, I happen'd to meet with a Book written by one Tryon, recommending a Vegetable Diet. I determined to go into it. My Brother being yet unmarried, did not keep House, but boarded himself and his Apprentices in another Family. My refusing to eat Flesh occasioned an Inconveniency, and I was frequently chid for my singularity. I made my self acquainted with Tryon's Manner of preparing some of his Dishes, such as Boiling Potatoes or Rice, making Hasty Pudding, and a few others, and then propos'd to my Brother, that if he would give me Weekly half the Money he paid for my Board I would board my self. He instantly agreed to it, and I presently found that I could save half what he paid me. This was an additional Fund for buying Books: But I had another Advantage in it. My Brother and the rest going from the Printing House to their Meals, I remain'd there alone, and dispatching presently my light Repast, (which often was no more than a Bisket or a Slice of Bread, a Handful of Raisins or a Tart from the Pastry Cook's, and a Glass of Water) had the rest of the Time till their Return, for Study, in which I made the greater Progress from that greater Clearness of Head and quicker Apprehension which usually attend Temperance in Eating and Drinking. And now it was that being on some Occasion made asham'd of my Ignorance in Figures, which I had twice failed in learning when at School, I took Cocker's Book of Arithmetick, and went thro' the whole by my self with great Ease.—— I also read Seller's and Sturmy's Books of Navigation, and became acquainted with the little Geometry they contain, but never proceeded far in that Science.——And I read about this Time Locke on Human Understanding, and the Art of Thinking by Messrs du Port Royal.[7]

While I was intent on improving my Language, I met with an English Grammar (I think it was Greenwood's) at the End of which there were two little Sketches of the Arts of Rhetoric and Logic, the latter finishing with a Specimen of a Dispute in the Socratic Method. And soon after I procur'd Xenophon's Memorable Things of Socrates, wherein there are many Instances of the same Method. I was charm'd with it, adopted it,

[7] [Thomas Tryon, possibly *Wisdom's Dictates* (1691), or *The Way to Save Wealth* (1695); Edward Cocker, *Arithmetic* (1677); John Seller, *Practical Navigation* (1681); Samuel Sturmy, *The Mariner's Magazine* (1669); John Locke, *Essay concerning Human Understanding* (1690); Antoine Arnauld and Pierre Nicole, *Logic: or the Art of Thinking* (1687).]

dropt my abrupt Contradiction, and positive Argumentation, and put on the humble Enquirer and Doubter. And being then, from reading Shaftsbury and Collins, become a real Doubter in many Points of our Religious Doctrine, I found this Method safest for my self and very embarassing to those against whom I used it, therefore I took a Delight in it, practis'd it continually and grew very artful and expert in drawing People even of superior Knowledge into Concessions the Consequences of which they did not foresee, entangling them in Difficulties out of which they could not extricate themselves, and so obtaining Victories that neither my self, nor my Cause always deserved.[8]——I continu'd this Method some few Years, but gradually left it, retaining only the Habit of expressing my self in Terms of modest Diffidence, never using when I advance any thing that may possibly be disputed, the Words, *Certainly, undoubtedly*, or any others that give the Air of Positiveness to an Opinion; but rather say, *I conceive*, or *I apprehend a Thing to be so or so, It appears to me*, or *I should think it so or so for such and such Reasons*, or *I imagine it to be so*, or *it is so if I am not mistaken.*——This Habit I believe has been of great Advantage to me, when I have had occasion to inculcate my Opinions and persuade Men into Measures that I have been from time to time engag'd in promoting.——And as the chief Ends of Conversation are to *inform*, or to be *informed*, to *please* or to *persuade*, I wish wellmeaning sensible Men would not lessen their Power of doing Good by a Positive assuming Manner that seldom fails to disgust, tends to create Opposition, and to defeat every one of those Purposes for which Speech was given us, to wit, giving or receiving Information, or Pleasure: For if you would *inform*, a positive dogmatical Manner in advancing your Sentiments, may provoke Contradiction and prevent a candid Attention. If you wish Information and Improvement from the Knowledge of others and yet at the same time express your self as firmly fix'd in your present Opinions, modest sensible Men, who do not love Disputation, will probably leave you undisturb'd in the Possession of your Error; and by such a Manner you can seldom hope to recommend your self in *pleasing* your Hearers, or to persuade those whose Concurrence you desire.——Pope says, judiciously,

Men should be taught as if you taught them not,
And things unknown propos'd as things forgot,——

[8] [James Greenwood, *An Essay towards a Practical English Grammar* (1711); Anthony Ashley Cooper, third Earl of Shaftesbury, *Characteristic of Men, Manners, Opinions, Times* (1711); Anthony Collins, *A Discourse of Free Thinking* (1713).]

farther recommending it to us,

> *To speak tho' sure, with seeming Diffidence.*[9]

And he might have coupled with this Line that which he has coupled with another, I think less properly,

> *For Want of Modesty is Want of Sense.*

If you ask why, *less properly*, I must repeat the Lines;

> Immodest Words admit of *no Defence*;
> *For* Want of Modesty is Want of Sense.[10]

Now is not *Want of Sense* (where a Man is so unfortunate as to want it) some Apology for his *Want of Modesty?* and would not the Lines stand more justly thus?

> Immodest Words admit *but this* Defence,
> That Want of Modesty is Want of Sense.

This however I should submit to better Judgments.——

My Brother had in 1720 or 21, begun to print a Newspaper. It was the second that appear'd in America, and was called *The New England Courant*. The only one before it, was *the Boston News Letter*. I remember his being dissuaded by some of his Friends from the Undertaking, as not likely to succeed, one Newspaper being in their Judgment enough for America.——At this time 1771 there are not less than five & twenty.——He went on however with the Undertaking, and after having work'd in composing the Types and printing off the Sheets I was employ'd to carry the Papers thro' the Streets to the Customers.——He had some ingenious Men among his Friends who amus'd themselves by writing little Pieces for this Paper, which gain'd it Credit, and made it more in Demand; and these Gentlemen often visited us.——Hearing their Conversations, and their Accounts of the Approbation their Papers were receiv'd with, I was excited to try my Hand among them. But being still a Boy, and suspecting that my Brother would object to printing any Thing of mine in his Paper if he knew it to be mine, I contriv'd to disguise my Hand, and writing an anonymous Paper I put it in at Night under the Door of the Printing House. It was found in the Morning and communicated to his Writing Friends when they call'd in as Usual. They read it, commented

[9] [Alexander Pope, *Essay on Criticism* (1711), lines 574–5, 567.]
[10] [Wentworth Dillon, earl of Roscommon, *Essay on Translated Verse* (1684), lines 113–14.]

on it in my Hearing, and I had the exquisite Pleasure, of finding it met with their Approbation, and that in their different Guesses at the Author none were named but Men of some Character among us for Learning and Ingenuity.——I suppose now that I was rather lucky in my Judges: And that perhaps they were not really so very good ones as I then esteem'd them. Encourag'd however by this, I wrote and convey'd in the same Way to the Press several more Papers, which were equally approv'd, and I kept my Secret till my small Fund of Sense for such Performances was pretty well exhausted, and then I discovered it; when I began to be considered a little more by my Brother's Acquaintance, and in a manner that did not quite please him, as he thought, probably with reason, that it tended to make me too vain. And perhaps this might be one Occasion of the Differences that we began to have about this Time. Tho' a Brother, he considered himself as my Master, and me as his Apprentice; and accordingly expected the same Services from me as he would from another; while I thought he demean'd me too much in some he requir'd of me, who from a Brother expected more Indulgence. Our Disputes were often brought before our Father, and I fancy I was either generally in the right, or else a better Pleader, because the Judgment was generally in my favour: But my Brother was passionate and had often beaten me, which I took extreamly amiss;[11] and thinking my Apprenticeship very tedious, I was continually wishing for some Opportunity of shortening it, which at length offered in a manner unexpected.

One of the Pieces in our News-Paper, on some political Point which I have now forgotten, gave Offence to the Assembly. He was taken up, censur'd and imprison'd for a Month by the Speaker's Warrant, I suppose because he would not discover his Author. I too was taken up and examin'd before the Council; but tho' I did not give them any Satisfaction, they contented themselves with admonishing me, and dismiss'd me; considering me perhaps as an Apprentice who was bound to keep his Master's Secrets. During my Brother's Confinement, which I resented a good deal, notwithstanding our private Differences, I had the Management of the Paper, and I made bold to give our Rulers some Rubs in it, which my Brother took very kindly, while others began to consider me in an unfavourable Light, as a young Genius that had a Turn for Libelling and Satyr. My Brother's Discharge was accompany'd with an Order of

[11] I fancy his harsh and tyrannical Treatment of me, might be a means of impressing me with that Aversion to arbitrary Power that has stuck to me thro' my whole Life.

the House, (a very odd one) *that James Franklin should no longer print the Paper called the New England Courant.* There was a Consultation held in our Printing House among his Friends what he should do in this Case. Some propos'd to evade the Order by changing the Name of the Paper; but my Brother seeing Inconveniences in that, it was finally concluded on as a better Way, to let it be printed for the future under the Name of *Benjamin Franklin.* And to avoid the Censure of the Assembly that might fall on him, as still printing it by his Apprentice, the Contrivance was, that my old Indenture should be return'd to me with a full Discharge on the Back of it, to be shown on Occasion; but to secure to him the Benefit of my Service I was to sign new Indentures for the Remainder of the Term, which were to be kept private. A very flimsy Scheme it was, but however it was immediately executed, and the Paper went on accordingly under my Name for several Months. At length a fresh Difference arising between my Brother and me, I took upon me to assert my Freedom, presuming that he would not venture to produce the new Indentures. It was not fair in me to take this Advantage, and this I therefore reckon one of the first Errata of my Life: But the Unfairness of it weigh'd little with me, when under the Impressions of Resentment, for the Blows his Passion too often urg'd him to bestow upon me. Tho' he was otherwise not an ill-natur'd Man: Perhaps I was too saucy and provoking.——

When he found I would leave him, he took care to prevent my getting Employment in any other Printing-House of the Town, by going round and speaking to every Master, who accordingly refus'd to give me Work. I then thought of going to New York as the nearest Place where there was a Printer: and I was the rather inclin'd to leave Boston, when I reflected that I had already made myself a little obnoxious to the governing Party; and from the arbitrary Proceedings of the Assembly in my Brother's Case it was likely I might if I stay'd soon bring myself into Scrapes; and farther that my indiscrete Disputations about Religion began to make me pointed at with Horror by good People, as an Infidel or Atheist. I determin'd on the Point: but my Father now siding with my Brother, I was sensible that if I attempted to go openly, Means would be used to prevent me. My Friend Collins therefore undertook to manage a little for me. He agreed with the Captain of a New York Sloop for my Passage, under the Notion of my being a young Acquaintance of his that had got a naughty Girl with Child, whose Friends would compel me to marry her, and therefore I could not appear or come away publickly. So I sold some of my Books to raise a little Money, Was taken on board privately, and as we had a fair Wind, in three

Days I found my self in New York near 300 Miles from home, a Boy of but 17, without the least Recommendation to or Knowledge of any Person in the Place, and with very little Money in my Pocket.

My Inclinations for the Sea, were by this time worne out, or I might now have gratify'd them. But having a Trade, and supposing my self a pretty good Workman, I offer'd my Service to the Printer of the Place, old Mr. Wm. Bradford, (who had been the first Printer in Pennsylvania, but remov'd from thence upon the Quarrel of Geo. Keith).——He could give me no Employment, having little to do, and Help enough already: But, says he, my Son at Philadelphia has lately lost his principal Hand, Aquila Rose, by Death. If you go thither I believe he may employ you.——Philadelphia was 100 Miles farther. I set out, however, in a Boat for Amboy, leaving my Chest and Things to follow me round by Sea. In crossing the Bay we met with a Squall that tore our rotten Sails to pieces, prevented our getting into the Kill, and drove us upon Long Island. In our Way a drunken Dutchman, who was a Passenger too, fell over board; when he was sinking I reach'd thro' the Water to his shock Pate and drew him up so that we got him in again.——His Ducking sober'd him a little, and he went to sleep, taking first out of his Pocket a Book which he desir'd I would dry for him. It prov'd to be my old favourite Author Bunyan's Pilgrim's Progress in Dutch, finely printed on good Paper with copper Cuts, a Dress better than I had ever seen it wear in its own Language. I have since found that it has been translated into most of the Languages of Europe, and suppose it has been more generally read than any other Book except perhaps the Bible. Honest John was the first that I know of who mix'd Narration and Dialogue, a Method of Writing very engaging to the Reader, who in the most interesting Parts finds himself as it were brought into the Company, and present at the Discourse. Defoe in his Cruso, his Moll Flanders, Religious Courtship, Family Instructor, and other Pieces, has imitated it with Success. And Richardson has done the same in his Pamela, &c.——

When we drew near the Island we found it was at a Place where there could be no Landing, there being a great Surff on the stony Beach. So we dropt Anchor and swung round towards the Shore. Some People came down to the Water Edge and hallow'd to us, as we did to them. But the Wind was so high and the Surff so loud, that we could not hear so as to understand each other. There were Canoes on the Shore, and we made Signs and hallow'd that they should fetch us, but they either did not understand us, or thought it impracticable. So they went away, and Night coming on, we had no Remedy but to wait till the Wind should abate, and in the mean time the Boatman and I concluded to sleep if we could, and so crouded into the Scuttle with the Dutchman who was still wet, and the Spray beating over the Head of our Boat, leak'd thro' to us, so that we were soon almost as wet as he. In this Manner we lay all Night with very little Rest. But the Wind abating the next Day, we made a Shift to reach Amboy before Night, having been 30 Hours on the Water without Victuals, or any Drink but a Bottle of filthy Rum: The Water we sail'd on being salt.——

In the Evening I found my self very feverish, and went ill to Bed. But having read somewhere that cold Water drank plentifully was good for a Fever, I follow'd the Prescription, sweat plentifully most of the Night, my Fever left me, and in the Morning crossing the Ferry, I proceeded on my Journey, on foot, having 50 Miles to Burlington, where I was told I should find Boats that would carry me the rest of the Way to Philadelphia.

It rain'd very hard all the Day, I was thoroughly soak'd, and by Noon a good deal tir'd, so I stopt at a poor Inn, where I staid all Night, beginning now to wish I had never left home. I cut so miserable a Figure too, that I found by the Questions ask'd me I was suspected to be some runaway Servant, and in danger of being taken up on that Suspicion. However I proceeded the next Day, and got in the Evening to an Inn within 8 or 10 Miles of Burlington, kept by one Dr. Brown.——

He entred into Conversation with me while I took some Refreshment, and finding I had read a little, became very sociable and friendly. Our Acquaintance continu'd as long as he liv'd. He had been, I imagine, an itinerant Doctor, for there was no Town in England, or Country in Europe, of which he could not give a very particular Account. He had some Letters, and was ingenious, but much of an Unbeliever, and wickedly undertook some Years after to travesty the Bible in doggrel Verse as Cotton had done Virgil. By this means he set many of the Facts in a very ridiculous Light, and might have hurt weak minds if his Work had been publish'd:——but it never was.——At his House I lay that Night, and the next Morning reach'd Burlington. But had the Mortification to find that the regular Boats were gone, a little before my coming, and no other expected to go till Tuesday, this being Saturday. Wherefore I return'd to an old Woman in the Town of whom I had bought Gingerbread to eat on the Water, and ask'd her Advice; she invited me to lodge at her House till a Passage by Water should offer and being tired with my foot Travelling, I accepted the Invitation. She understanding I was a Printer, would have had me stay at that Town and follow my Business, being ignorant of the Stock necessary to begin with. She was very hospitable, gave me a Dinner of Ox Cheek with great Goodwill, accepting only of a Pot of Ale in return. And I tho't my self fix'd till Tuesday should come. However walking in the Evening by the Side of the River a Boat came by, which I found was going towards Philadelphia, with several People in her. They took me in, and as there was no Wind, we row'd all the Way; and about Midnight not having yet seen the City, some of the Company were confident we must have pass'd it, and would row no farther, the others knew not where we were, so we put towards the Shore, got into a Creek, landed near an old Fence with the Rails of which we made a Fire, the Night being cold, in October, and there we remain'd till Daylight. Then one of the Company knew the Place to be Cooper's Creek a little above Philadelphia, which we saw as soon as we got out of the Creek, and arriv'd there about 8 or 9 a Clock, on the Sunday morning, and landed at the Market street Wharff.——

I have been the more particular in this Description of my Journey, and shall be so of my first Entry into that City, that you may in your Mind compare such unlikely Beginning with the Figure I have since made there. I was in my Working Dress, my best Cloaths being to come round by Sea. I was dirty from my Journey; my Pockets were stuff'd out with Shirts and Stockings; I knew no Soul, nor where to look for Lodging. I was fatigu'd with Travelling, Rowing and Want of Rest. I was very hungry, and my whole Stock of Cash consisted of a Dutch Dollar and about a Shilling in Copper. The latter I gave the People of the Boat for my Passage, who at first refus'd it on Account of my Rowing; but I insisted on their taking it, a Man being sometimes more generous when he has but a little Money than when he has plenty, perhaps thro' Fear of being thought to have but little. Then I walk'd up the Street, gazing about, till near the Market House I met a Boy with Bread. I had made many a Meal on Bread, and inquiring where he got it, I went immediately to the Baker's he directed me to in second Street; and ask'd for Bisket, intending such as we had in Boston, but they it seems were not made in Philadelphia, then I ask'd for a threepenny Loaf, and was told they had none such: so not considering or knowing the Difference of Money and the greater Cheapness nor the Names of his Bread, I bad him give me three pennyworth of any sort. He gave me accordingly three great Puffy Rolls. I was surpriz'd at the Quantity, but took it, and having no room in my Pockets, walk'd off, with a Roll under each Arm, and eating the other. Thus I went up Market Street as far as fourth Street, passing by the Door of Mr. Read, my future Wife's Father, when she standing at the Door saw me, and thought I made as I certainly did a most awkward ridiculous Appearance. Then I turn'd and went down Chestnut Street and part of Walnut Street, eating my Roll all the Way, and coming round found my self again at Market Street Wharff, near the Boat I came in, to which I went for a Draught of the River Water, and being fill'd with one of my Rolls, gave the other two to a Woman and her Child that came down the River in the Boat with us and were waiting to go farther. Thus refresh'd I walk'd again up the Street, which by this time had many clean dress'd People in it who were all walking the same Way; I join'd them, and thereby was led into the great Meeting House of the Quakers near the Market. I sat down among them, and after looking round a while and hearing nothing said, being very drowzy thro' Labour and want of Rest the preceding Night, I fell fast asleep, and continu'd so till the Meeting broke up, when one was kind enough to rouse me. This was therefore the first House I was in or slept in, in Philadelphia.——

Walking again down towards the River, and looking in the Faces of People, I met a young Quaker Man whose Countenance I lik'd, and accosting him requested he would tell me where a Stranger could get Lodging. We were then near the Sign of the Three Mariners. Here, says he, is one Place that entertains Strangers, but it is not a reputable House; if thee wilt walk with me, I'll show thee a better. He brought me to the Crooked Billet in Water-Street. Here I got a Dinner. And while I was eating it, several sly Questions were ask'd me, as it seem'd to be suspected from my youth and Appearance, that I might be some Runaway. After Dinner my Sleepiness return'd: and being shown to a Bed, I lay down without undressing, and slept till Six in the Evening; was call'd to Supper; went to Bed again very early and slept soundly till the next Morning. Then I made my self as tidy as I could, and went to Andrew Bradford the Printer's. I found in the Shop the old Man his Father, whom I had seen at New York, and who travelling on horse back had got to Philadelphia before me. He introduc'd me to his Son, who receiv'd me civilly, gave me a Breakfast, but told me he did not at present want a Hand, being lately supply'd with one. But there was another Printer in town lately set up, one Keimer, who perhaps might employ me; if not, I should be welcome to lodge at his House, and he would give me a little Work to do now and then till fuller Business should offer.

The old Gentleman said, he would go with me to the new Printer: And when we found him, Neighbour, says Bradford, I have brought to see you a young Man of your Business, perhaps you may want such a One. He ask'd me a few Questions, put a Composing Stick in my Hand to see how I work'd, and then said he would employ me soon, tho' he had just then nothing for me to do. And taking old Bradford whom he had never seen before, to be one of the Towns People that had a Good Will for him, enter'd into a Conversation on his present Undertaking and Prospects; while Bradford not discovering that he was the other Printer's Father, on Keimer's saying he expected soon to get the greatest Part of the Business into his own Hands, drew him on by artful Questions and starting little Doubts, to explain all his Views, what Interest he rely'd on, and in what manner he intended to proceed.——I who stood by and heard all, saw immediately that one of them was a crafty old Sophister, and the other a mere Novice. Bradford left me with Keimer, who was greatly surpriz'd when I told him who the old Man was.

Keimer's Printing House I found, consisted of an old shatter'd Press, and one small worn-out Fount of English, which he was then using himself, composing in it an Elegy on Aquila Rose before-mentioned, an ingenious young Man of excellent Character much respected in the Town, Clerk of the Assembly, and a pretty Poet. Keimer made Verses, too, but very indifferently. He could not be said to write them, for his Manner was to compose them in the Types directly out of his Head; so there being no Copy, but one Pair of Cases, and the Elegy likely to require all the Letter, no one could help him.——I endeavour'd to put his Press (which he had not yet us'd, and of which he understood nothing) into Order fit to be work'd with; and promising to come and print off his Elegy as soon as he should have got it ready, I return'd to Bradford's who gave me a little Job to do for the present, and there I lodged and dieted. A few Days after Keimer sent for me to print off the Elegy. And now he had got another Pair of Cases, and a Pamphlet to reprint, on which he set me to work.——

These two Printers I found poorly qualified for their Business. Bradford had not been bred to it, and was very illiterate; and Keimer tho' something of a Scholar, was a mere Compositor, knowing nothing of Presswork. He had been one of the French Prophets and could act their enthusiastic Agitations. At this time he did not profess any particular Religion, but something of all on occasion; was very ignorant of the World, and had, as I afterwards found, a good deal of the Knave in his Composition. He did not like my Lodging at Bradford's while I work'd with him. He had a House indeed, but without Furniture, so he could not lodge me: But he got me a Lodging at Mr. Read's before-mentioned, who was the Owner of his House. And my Chest and Clothes being come by this time, I made rather a more respectable Appearance in the Eyes of Miss Read, than I had done when she first happen'd to see me eating my Roll in the Street.——

I began now to have some Acquaintance among the young People of the Town, that were Lovers of Reading with whom I spent my Evenings very pleasantly and gaining Money by my Industry and Frugality, I lived very agreably, forgetting Boston as much as I could, and not desiring that any there should know where I resided, except my Friend Collins who was in my Secret, and kept it when I wrote to him. At length an Incident happened that sent me back again much sooner than I had intended.——

I had a Brother-in-law, Robert Homes, Master of a Sloop, that traded between Boston and Delaware. He being at New Castle 40 Miles below Philadelphia, heard there of me, and wrote me a Letter, mentioning the Concern of my Friends in Boston at my abrupt Departure, assuring me of their Goodwill to me, and that every thing would be accommodated to my Mind if I would return, to which he exhorted me very earnestly. I wrote an Answer to his Letter, thank'd him for his Advice, but stated my Reasons for quitting Boston fully, and in such a Light as to convince him I was not so wrong as he had apprehended. Sir William Keith Governor of the Province, was then at New Castle, and Capt. Homes happening to be in Company with him when my Letter came to hand, spoke to him of me, and show'd him the Letter. The Governor read it, and seem'd surpriz'd when he was told my Age. He said I appear'd a young Man of promising Parts, and therefore should be encouraged: The Printers at Philadelphia were wretched ones, and if I would set up there, he made no doubt I should succeed; for his Part, he would procure me the publick Business, and do me every other Service in his Power. This my Brother-in-Law afterwards told me in Boston. But I knew as yet nothing of it; when one Day Keimer and I being at Work together near the Window, we saw the Governor and another Gentleman (which prov'd to be Col. French, of New Castle) finely dress'd, come directly across the Street to our House, and heard them at the Door. Keimer ran down immediately, thinking it a Visit to him. But the Governor enquir'd for me, came up, and with a Condescension and Politeness I had been quite unus'd to, made me many Compliments, desired to be acquainted with me, blam'd me kindly for not having made my self known to him when I first came to the Place, and would have me away with him to the Tavern where he was going with Col. French to taste as he said some excellent Madeira. I was not a little surpriz'd, and Keimer star'd like a Pig poison'd. I went however with the Governor and Col. French, to a Tavern the Corner of Third Street, and over the Madeira he propos'd my Setting up my Business, laid before me the Probabilities of Success, and both he and Col. French assur'd me I should have their Interest and Influence in procuring the Publick Business of both Governments. On my doubting whether my Father would assist me in it, Sir William said he would give me a Letter to him, in which he would state the Advantages, and he did not doubt of prevailing with him. So it was concluded I should return to Boston in the first Vessel with the Governor's Letter recommending me to my Father. In the mean time the Intention was to be kept secret, and I went on working with Keimer as usual, the Governor sending for me now and then to dine with him, a very great Honour I thought it, and conversing with me in the most affable, familiar, and friendly manner imaginable. About the End of April 1724. a little Vessel offer'd for Boston. I took Leave of Keimer as going to see my Friends. The Governor gave me an ample Letter, saying many flattering things of me to my Father, and strongly recommending the Project of my setting up at Philadelphia, as a Thing that must make my Fortune. We struck on a Shoal in going down the Bay and sprung a Leak, we had a blustring time at Sea, and were oblig'd to pump almost continually, at which I took my Turn. We arriv'd safe however at Boston in about a Fortnight.——I had been absent Seven Months and my Friends had heard nothing of me; for my Br. Homes was not yet return'd; and had not written about me. My unexpected Appearance surpriz'd the Family; all were however very glad to see me and made me Welcome, except my Brother. I went to see him at his Printing-House: I was better dress'd than ever while in his Service, having a genteel new Suit from Head to foot, a Watch, and my Pockets lin'd with near Five Pounds Sterling in Silver. He receiv'd me not very frankly, look'd me all over, and turn'd to his Work again. The Journey-Men were inquisitive where I had been, what sort of a Country it was, and how I lik'd it? I prais'd it much, and the happy Life I led in it; expressing strongly my Intention of returning to it; and one of them asking what kind of Money we had there, I produc'd a handful of Silver and spread it before them, which was a kind of Raree-Show they had not been us'd to, Paper being the Money of Boston. Then I took an Opportunity of letting them see my Watch: and lastly, (my Brother still grum and sullen) I gave them a Piece of Eight to drink and took my Leave.——This Visit of mine offended him extreamly. For when my Mother some time after spoke to him of a Reconciliation, and of her Wishes to see us on good Terms together, and that we might live for the future as Brothers, he said, I had insulted him in such a Manner before his People that he could never forget or forgive it. In this however he was mistaken.——

My Father receiv'd the Governor's Letter with some apparent Surprize; but said little of it to me for some Days; when Capt. Homes returning, he show'd it to him, ask'd if he knew Keith, and what kind of a Man he was: Adding his Opinion that he must be of small Discretion, to think of setting a Boy up in Business who wanted yet 3 Years of being at Man's Estate. Homes said what he could in favour of the Project; but my Father was clear in the Impropriety of it; and at last gave a flat Denial to it. Then he wrote a civil Letter to Sir William thanking him for the Patronage he had so kindly offered me, but declining to assist me as yet in Setting up, I being in his Opinion too young to be trusted with the Management of a Business so important, and for which the Preparation must be so expensive.——

My Friend and Companion Collins, who was a Clerk at the Post-Office, pleas'd with the Account I gave him of my new Country, determin'd to go thither also:——And while I waited for my Father's Determination, he set out before me by Land to Rhode Island, leaving his Books which were a pretty Collection of Mathematicks and Natural Philosophy, to come with mine and me to New York where he propos'd to wait for me. My Father, tho' he did not approve Sir William's Proposition was yet pleas'd that I had been able to obtain so advantageous a Character from a Person of such Note where I had resided, and that I had been so industrious and careful as to equip my self so handsomely in so short a time: therefore seeing no Prospect of an Accommodation between my Brother and me, he gave his Consent to my Returning again to Philadelphia, advis'd me to behave respectfully to the People there, endeavour to obtain the general Esteem, and avoid lampooning and libelling to which he thought I had too much Inclination; telling me, that by steady Industry and a prudent Parsimony, I might save enough by the time I was One and Twenty to set me up, and that if I came near the Matter he would help me out with the rest.——This was all I could obtain, except some small Gifts as Tokens of his and my Mother's Love, when I embark'd again for New York, now with their Approbation and their Blessing.——

The Sloop putting in at Newport, Rhode Island, I visited my Brother John, who had been married and settled there some Years. He received me very affectionately, for he always lov'd me. A Friend of his, one Vernon, having some Money due to him in Pennsylvania, about 35 Pounds Currency, desired I would receive it for him, and keep it till I had his Directions what to remit it in. Accordingly he gave me an Order.——This afterwards occasion'd me a good deal of Uneasiness.——At Newport we took in a Number of Passengers for New York: Among which were two young Women, Companions, and a grave, sensible Matron-like Quaker-Woman with her Attendants.——I had shown an obliging readiness to do her some little Services which impress'd her I suppose with a degree of Good-will towards me.——Therefore when she saw a daily growing Familiarity between me and the two Young Women, which they appear'd to encourage, she took me aside and said, Young Man, I am concern'd for thee, as thou has no Friend with thee, and seems not to know much of the World, or of the Snares Youth is expos'd to; depend upon it those are very bad Women, I can see it in all their Actions, and if thee art not upon thy Guard, they will draw thee into some Danger: they are Strangers to thee, and I advise thee in a friendly Concern for thy Welfare, to have no Acquaintance with them.——As I seem'd at first not to think so ill of them as she did, she mention'd some Things she had observ'd and heard that had escap'd my Notice; but now convinc'd me she was right. I thank'd her for her kind Advice, and promis'd to follow it.——When we arriv'd at New York, they told me where they liv'd, and invited me to come and see them: but I avoided it. And it was well I did: For the next Day, the Captain miss'd a Silver Spoon and some other Things that had been taken out of his Cabbin, and knowing that these were a Couple of Strumpets, he got a Warrant to search their Lodgings, found the stolen Goods, and had the Thieves punish'd.——So tho' we had escap'd a sunken Rock which we scrap'd upon in the Passage, I thought this Escape of rather more Importance to me.

At New York I found my Friend Collins, who had arriv'd there some Time before me. We had been intimate from Children, and had read the same Books together. But he had the Advantage of more time for reading, and Studying and a wonderful Genius for Mathematical Learning in which he far outstript me. While I liv'd in Boston most of my Hours of Leisure for Conversation were spent with him, and he continu'd a sober as well as an industrious Lad; was much respected for his Learning by several of the Clergy and other Gentlemen, and seem'd to promise making a good Figure in Life: but during my Absence he had acquir'd a Habit of Sotting with Brandy; and I found by his own Account and what I heard from others, that he had been drunk every day since his Arrival at New York, and behav'd very oddly. He had gam'd too and lost his Money, so that I was oblig'd to discharge his Lodgings, and defray his Expences to and at Philadelphia:——Which prov'd extreamly inconvenient to me.——The then Governor of New York, Burnet, Son of Bishop

Burnet hearing from the Captain that a young Man, one of his Passengers, had a great many Books, desired he would bring me to see him. I waited upon him accordingly, and should have taken Collins with me but that he was not sober. The Governor treated me with great Civility, show'd me his Library, which was a very large one, and we had a good deal of Conversation about Books and Authors. This was the second Governor who had done me the Honour to take Notice of me, which to a poor Boy like me was very pleasing.——We proceeded to Philadelphia. I received on the Way Vernon's Money, without which we could hardly have finish'd our Journey.——Collins wish'd to be employ'd in some Counting House; but whether they discover'd his Dramming by his Breath, or by his Behaviour, tho' he had some Recommendations, he met with no Success in any Application, and continu'd Lodging and Boarding at the same House with me and at my Expence. Knowing I had that Money of Vernon's he was continually borrowing of me, still promising Repayment as soon as he should be in Business. At length he had got so much of it, that I was distress'd to think what I should do, in case of being call'd on to remit it.——His Drinking continu'd, about which we sometimes quarrel'd, for when a little intoxicated he was very fractious. Once in a Boat on the Delaware with some other young Men, he refused to row in his Turn: I will be row'd home, says he. We will not row you, says I. You must or stay all Night on the Water, says he, just as you please. The others said, Let us row; what signifies it? But my Mind being soured with his other Conduct, I continu'd to refuse. So he swore he would make me row, or throw me overboard; and coming along stepping on the Thwarts towards me, when he came up and struck at me I clapt my Hand under his Crutch, and rising pitch'd him head-foremost into the River. I knew he was a good Swimmer, and so was under little Concern about him; but before he could get round to lay hold of the Boat, we had with a few Strokes pull'd her out of his Reach.——And ever when he drew near the Boat, we ask'd if he would row, striking a few Strokes to slide her away from him.——He was ready to die with Vexation, and obstinately would not promise to row; however seeing him at last beginning to tire, we lifted him in; and brought him home dripping wet in the Evening. We hardly exchang'd a civil Word afterwards; and a West India Captain who had a Commission to procure a Tutor for the Sons of a Gentleman at Barbadoes, happening to meet with him, agreed to carry him thither. He left me then, promising to remit me the first Money he should receive in order to discharge the Debt. But I never heard of him after. The Breaking into this Money of Vernon's was one of the first great Errata of my Life. And this Affair show'd that my Father was not much out in his Judgment when he suppos'd me too young to manage Business of Importance. But Sir William, on reading his Letter, said he was too prudent. There was great Difference in Persons, and Discretion did not always accompany Years, nor was Youth always without it. And since he will not set you up, says he, I will do it my self. Give me an Inventory of the Things necessary to be had from England, and I will send for them. You shall repay me when you are able; I am resolv'd to have a good Printer here, and I am sure you must succeed. This was spoken with such an Appearance of Cordiality, that I had not the least doubt of his meaning what he said.——I had hitherto kept the Proposition of my Setting up a Secret in Philadelphia, and I still kept it. Had it been known that I depended on the Governor, probably some Friend that knew him better would have advis'd me not to rely on him, as I afterwards heard it as his known Character to be liberal of Promises which he never meant to keep.——Yet unsolicited as he was by me, how could I think his generous Offers insincere? I believ'd him one of the best Men in the World.——

I presented him an Inventory of a little Printing House, amounting by my Computation to about 100£ Sterling. He lik'd it, but ask'd me if my being on the Spot in England to chuse the Types and see that every thing was good of the kind, might not be of some Advantage. Then, says he, when there, you may make Acquaintances and establish Correspondencies in the Bookselling and Stationary Way. I agreed that this might be advantageous. Then says he, get yourself ready to go with Annis; which was the annual Ship, and the only one at that Time usually passing between London and Philadelphia. But it would be some Months before Annis sail'd, so I continu'd working with Keimer, fretting about the Money Collins had got from me, and in daily Apprehensions of being call'd upon by Vernon, which however did not happen for some Years after.——

I believe I have omitted mentioning that in my first Voyage from Boston, being becalm'd off Block Island, our People set about catching Cod and hawl'd up a great many. Hitherto I had stuck to my Resolution of not eating animal Food; and on this Occasion, I consider'd with my Master Tryon, the taking every Fish as a kind of unprovok'd Murder, since none of them had or ever could do us any Injury that might justify the Slaughter.——All this seem'd very reasonable.——But I had formerly been a great Lover of Fish, and when this came hot out of the Frying Pan, it smelt admirably well. I balanc'd some time between Principle and Inclination: till I recollected, that when the Fish were opened, I saw smaller Fish taken out of their Stomachs: Then thought I, if you eat one another, I don't see why we mayn't eat you. So I din'd upon Cod very heartily and continu'd to eat with other People, returning only now and than occasionally to a vegetable Diet. So convenient a thing it is to be a *reasonable Creature*, since it enables one to find or make a Reason for every thing one has a mind to do.——

Keimer and I liv'd on a pretty good familiar Footing and agreed tolerably well: for he suspected nothing of my Setting up. He retain'd a great deal of his old Enthusiasms, and lov'd Argumentation. We therefore had many Disputations. I us'd to work him so with my Socratic Method, and had trapann'd him so often by Questions apparently so distant from any Point we had in hand, and yet by degrees led to the Point, and brought him into Difficulties and Contradictions that at last he grew ridiculously cautious, and would hardly answer me the most common Question, without asking first, *What do you intend to infer from that?* However it gave him so high an Opinion of my Abilities in the Confuting Way, that he seriously propos'd my being his Colleague in a Project he had of setting up a new Sect. He was to preach the Doctrines, and I was to confound all Opponents. When he came to explain with me upon the Doctrines, I found several Conundrums which I objected to, unless I might have my Way a little too, and introduce some of mine. Keimer wore his Beard at full Length, because somewhere in the Mosaic Law it is said, *thou shalt not mar the Corners of thy Beard.* He likewise kept the seventh day Sabbath; and these two Points were Essentials with him.——I dislik'd both, but agreed to admit them upon Condition of his adopting the Doctrine of using no animal Food. I doubt, says he, my Constitution will not bear that. I assur'd him it would, and that he would be the better for it. He was usually a great Glutton, and I promis'd my self some Diversion in half-starving him. He agreed to try the Practice if I would keep him Company. I did so and we held it for three Months. We had our Victuals dress'd and brought to us regularly by a Woman in the Neighbourhood, who had from me a List of 40 Dishes to be prepar'd for us at different times, in all which there was neither Fish Flesh nor Fowl, and the whim suited me the better at this time from the Cheapness of it, not costing us above 18d. Sterling each, per Week.——I have since kept several Lents most strictly, Leaving the common Diet for that, and that for the common, abruptly, without the least Inconvenience: So that I think there is little in the Advice of making those Changes by easy Gradations.——I went on pleasantly, but Poor Keimer suffer'd grievously, tir'd of the Project, long'd for the Flesh Pots of Egypt, and order'd a roast Pig; He invited me and two Women Friends to dine with him, but it being brought too soon upon table, he could not resist the Temptation, and ate it all up before we came.

I had made some Courtship during this time to Miss Read, I had a great Respect and Affection for her, and had some Reason to believe she had the same for me: but as I was about to take a long Voyage, and we were both very young, only a little above 18. it was thought most prudent by her Mother to prevent our going too far at present, as a Marriage if it was to take place would be more convenient after my Return, when I should be as I expected set up in my Business. Perhaps too she thought my Expectations not so wellfounded as I imagined them to be.——

My chief Acquaintances at this time were, Charles Osborne, Joseph Watson, and James Ralph; All Lovers of Reading. The two first were Clerks to an eminent Scrivener or Conveyancer in the Town, Charles Brogden; the other was Clerk to a Merchant. Watson was a pious sensible young Man, of great Integrity.——The others rather more lax in their Principles of Religion, particularly Ralph, who as well as Collins had been unsettled by me, for which they both made me suffer.——Osborne was sensible, candid, frank, sincere, and affectionate to his Friends; but in literary Matters too fond of Criticising. Ralph, was ingenious, genteel in his Manners, and extreamly eloquent; I think I never knew a prettier Talker. Both of them great Admirers of Poetry, and began to try their Hands in little Pieces. Many pleasant Walks we four had together on Sundays into the Woods near Skuylkill, where we read to one another and conferr'd on what we read. Ralph was inclin'd to pursue the Study of Poetry, not doubting but he might become eminent in it and make his Fortune by it, alledging that the best Poets must when they first began to write, make as many Faults as he did.——Osborne dissuaded him, assur'd him he had no Genius for Poetry, and advis'd him to think of nothing beyond the Business he was bred to; that in the mercantile way tho' he had no Stock, he might by his Diligence and Punctuality recommend himself to Employment as a Factor, and in time acquire wherewith to trade on his own Account. I approv'd the amusing one's self with Poetry now and then, so far as to improve one's Language, but no farther. On this it was propos'd that we should each of us at our next Meeting produce a Piece of our own Composing, in order to improve by our mutual Observations, Criticisms and Corrections. As Language and Expression was what we had in View, we excluded all Considerations of Invention, by agreeing that the Task should be a Version of the 18th Psalm, which describes the

Descent of a Deity. When the Time of our Meeting drew nigh, Ralph call'd on me first, and let me know his Piece was ready. I told him I had been busy, and having little Inclination had done nothing. He then show'd me his Piece for my Opinion; and I much approv'd it, as it appear'd to me to have great Merit. Now, says he, Osborne never will allow the least Merit in any thing of mine, but makes 1000 Criticisms out of mere Envy. He is not so jealous of you. I wish therefore you would take this Piece, and produce it as yours. I will pretend not to have had time, and so produce nothing: We shall then see what he will say to it. It was agreed, and I immediately transcrib'd it that it might appear in my own hand. We met. Watson's Performance was read: there were some Beauties in it: but many Defects. Osborne's was read: It was much better. Ralph did it Justice, remark'd some Faults, but applauded the Beauties. He himself had nothing to produce. I was backward, seem'd desirous of being excus'd, had not had sufficient Time to correct; &c. but no Excuse could be admitted, produce I must. It was read and repeated; Watson and Osborne gave up the Contest; and join'd in applauding it immoderately. Ralph only made some Criticisms and propos'd some Amendments, but I defended my Text. Osborne was against Ralph, and told him he was no better a Critic than Poet; so he dropt the Argument. As they two went home together, Osborne express'd himself still more strongly in favour of what he thought my Production, having restrain'd himself before as he said, lest I should think it Flattery. But who would have imagin'd, says he, that Franklin had been capable of such a Performance; such Painting, such Force! such Fire! he has even improv'd the Original! In his common Conversation, he seems to have no Choice of Words; he hesitates and blunders; and yet, good God, how he writes!——When we next met, Ralph discover'd the Trick, we had plaid him, and Osborne was a little laught at. This Transaction fix'd Ralph in his Resolution of becoming a Poet. I did all I could to dissuade him from it, but He continued scribbling Verses, till *Pope* cur'd him. He became however a pretty good Prose Writer. More of him hereafter. But as I may not have occasion again to mention the other two, I shall just remark here, that Watson died in my Arms a few Years after, much lamented, being the best of our Set. Osborne went to the West Indies, where he became an eminent Lawyer and made Money, but died young. He and I had made a serious Agreement, that the one who happen'd first to die, should if possible make a friendly Visit to the other, and acquaint him how he found things in that Separate State. But he never fulfill'd his Promise.

The Governor, seeming to like my Company, had me frequently to his House; and his Setting me up was always mention'd as a fix'd thing. I was to take with me Letters recommendatory to a Number of his Friends, besides the Letter of Credit to furnish me with the necessary Money for purchasing the Press and Types, Paper, &c. For these Letters I was appointed to call at different times, when they were to be ready, but a future time was still named.——Thus we went on till the Ship whose Departure too had been several times postponed was on the Point of sailing. Then when I call'd to take my Leave and receive the Letters, his Secretary, Dr. Baird, came out to me and said the Governor was extreamly busy, in writing, but would be down at New Castle before the Ship, and there the Letters would be delivered to me.

Ralph, tho' married and having one Child, had determined to accompany me in this Voyage. It was thought he intended to establish a Correspondence, and obtain Goods to sell on Commission. But I found afterwards, that thro' some Discontent with his Wife's Relations, he purposed to leave her on their Hands, and never return again.——Having taken leave of my Friends, and interchang'd some Promises with Miss Read, I left Philadelphia in the Ship, which anchor'd at New Castle. The Governor was there. But when I went to his Lodging, the Secretary came to me from him with the civillest Message in the World, that he could not then see me being engag'd in Business of the utmost Importance; but should send the Letters to me on board, wish'd me heartily a good Voyage and a speedy Return, &c. I return'd on board, a little puzzled, but still not doubting.——

Mr. Andrew Hamilton, a famous Lawyer of Philadelphia, had taken Passage in the same Ship for himself and Son: and with Mr. Denham a Quaker Merchant, and Messrs. Onion and Russel Masters of an iron Work in Maryland, had engag'd the Great Cabin; so that Ralph and I were forc'd to take up with a Birth in the Steerage: And none on board knowing us, were considered as ordinary Persons.——But Mr. Hamilton and his Son (it was James, since Governor) return'd from New Castle to Philadelphia, the Father being recall'd by a great Fee to plead for a seized Ship.——And just before we sail'd Col. French coming on board, and showing me great Respect, I was more taken Notice of, and with my Friend Ralph invited by the other Gentlemen to come into the Cabin, there being now Room. Accordingly we remov'd thither.

Understanding that Col. French had brought on board the Governor's Dispatches, I ask'd the Captain for those Letters that were to be under my Care. He said all were put into the Bag together; and he could not then come at them; but before we landed in England, I should have an Opportunity of picking them out. So I was satisfy'd for the present, and we proceeded on our Voyage. We had a sociable Company in the Cabin, and lived uncommonly well, having the Addition of all Mr. Hamilton's Stores, who had laid in plentifully. In this Passage Mr. Denham contracted a Friendship for me that continued during his Life. The Voyage was otherwise not a pleasant one, as we had a great deal of bad Weather.——

When we came into the Channel, the Captain kept his Word with me, and gave me an Opportunity of examining the Bag for the Governor's Letters. I found none upon which my Name was put, as under my Care; I pick'd out 6 or 7 that by the Hand writing I thought might be the promis'd Letters, especially as one of them was directed to Barket the King's Printer, and another to some Stationer. We arriv'd in London the 24th of December, 1724.——I waited upon the Stationer who came first in my Way, delivering the Letter as from Gov. Keith. I don't know such a Person, says he: but opening the Letter, O, this is from Riddlesden; I have lately found him to be a compleat Rascal, and I will have nothing to do with him, nor receive any Letters from him. So putting the Letter into my Hand, he turn'd on his Heel and left me to serve some Customer.——I was surprized to find these were not the Governor's Letters. And after recollecting and comparing Circumstances, I began to doubt his Sincerity.——I found my Friend Denham, and opened the whole Affair to him. He let me into Keith's Character, told me there was not the least Probability that he had written any Letters for me, that no one who knew him had the smallest Dependance on him, and he laught at the Notion of the Governor's giving me a Letter of Credit, having as he said no Credit to give. On my expressing some Concern about what I should do: He advis'd me to endeavour getting some Employment in the Way of my Business. Among the Printers here, says he, you will improve yourself; and when you return to America, you will set up to greater Advantage.——

We both of us happen'd to know, as well as the Stationer, that Riddlesden the Attorney, was a very Knave. He had half ruin'd Miss Read's Father by drawing him in to be bound for him. By his Letter it appear'd, there was a secret Scheme on foot to the Prejudice of Hamilton, (Suppos'd to be then coming over with us,) and that Keith was concern'd in it with Riddlesden. Denham, who was a Friend of Hamilton's, thought he ought to be acquainted with it. So when he arriv'd in England, which was soon after, partly from Resentment and Ill-Will to Keith and Riddlesden, and partly from Good Will to him: I waited on him, and gave him the Letter. He thank'd me cordially, the Information being of Importance to him. And from that time he became my Friend, greatly to my Advantage afterwards on many Occasions.

But what shall we think of a Governor's playing such pitiful Tricks, and imposing so grossly on a poor ignorant Boy! It was a Habit he had acquired. He wish'd to please every body; and having little to give, he gave Expectations.——He was otherwise an ingenious sensible Man, a pretty good Writer, and a good Governor for the People, tho' not for his Constituents the Proprietaries, whose Instructions he sometimes disregarded. Several of our best Laws were of his Planning, and pass'd during his Administration.——

Ralph and I were inseparable Companions. We took Lodgings together in Little Britain at 3s. 6d. per Week, as much as we could then afford. He found some Relations, but they were poor and unable to assist him. He now let me know his Intentions of remaining in London, and that he never meant to return to Philadelphia.——He had brought no Money with him, the whole he could muster having been expended in paying his Passage. I had 15 Pistoles: So he borrowed occasionally of me, to subsist while he was looking out for Business.——He first endeavoured to get into the Playhouse, believing himself qualify'd for an Actor; but Wilkes, to whom he apply'd, advis'd him candidly not to think of that, Employment, as it was impossible he should succeed in it.——Then he propos'd to Roberts, a Publisher in Paternoster Row, to write for him a Weekly Paper like the Spectator, on certain Conditions, which Roberts did not approve. Then he endeavour'd to get Employment as a Hackney Writer to copy for the Stationers and Lawyers about the Temple: but could find no Vacancy.——

I immediately got into Work at Palmer's then a famous Printing House in Bartholomew Close; and here I continu'd near a Year. I was pretty diligent; but spent with Ralph a good deal of my Earnings in going to Plays and other Places of Amusement. We had together consum'd all my Pistoles, and now just rubb'd on from hand to mouth. He seem'd quite to forget his Wife and Child, and I by degrees my Engagements with Miss Read, to whom I never wrote more than one Letter, and that was to let her know I was not likely soon to return. This was another of the great Errata of my Life, which I should wish to correct if I were to live it over again.——In fact, by our Expences, I was constantly kept unable to pay my Passage.

At Palmer's I was employ'd in composing for the second Edition of Wollaston's Religion of Nature. Some of his Reasonings not appearing to me well-founded, I wrote a little metaphysical Piece, in which I made Remarks on them. It was entitled, *A Dissertation on Liberty and Necessity, Pleasure and Pain*. I inscrib'd it to my Friend Ralph.——I printed a small Number. It occasion'd my being more consider'd by Mr. Palmer, as a young Man of some Ingenuity, tho' he seriously expostulated with me upon the Principles of my Pamphlet which to him appear'd abominable. My printing this Pamphlet was another Erratum.

While I lodg'd in Little Britain I made an Acquaintance with one Wilcox a Bookseller, whose Shop was at the next Door. He had an immense Collection of second-hand Books. Circulating Libraries were not then in Use; but we agreed that on certain reasonable Terms which I have now forgotten, I might take, read and return any of his Books. This I esteem'd a great Advantage, and I made as much use of it as I could.——

My Pamphlet by some means falling into the Hands of one Lyons, a Surgeon, Author of a Book intituled *The Infallibility of Human Judgment*, it occasioned an Acquaintance between us; he took great Notice of me, call'd on me often, to converse on those Subjects, carried me to the Horns a pale Ale-House in [ ] Lane, Cheapside, and introduc'd me to Dr. Mandeville, Author of the Fable of the Bees who had a Club there, of which he was the Soul, being a most facetious entertaining Companion.[12] Lyons too introduc'd me to Dr. Pemberton, at Batson's Coffee House, who promis'd to give me an Opportunity some time or other of seeing Sir Isaac Newton, of which I was extreamly desirous; but this never happened.

I had brought over a few Curiosities among which the principal was a Purse made of the Asbestos, which purifies by Fire. Sir Hans Sloane heard of it, came to see me, and invited me to his House in Bloomsbury Square, where he show'd me all his Curiosities, and persuaded me to let him add that to the Number, for which he paid me handsomely.——

In our House there lodg'd a young Woman; a Millener, who I think had a Shop in the Cloisters. She had been genteelly bred, was sensible and lively, and of most pleasing Conversation. Ralph read Plays to her in the Evenings, they grew intimate, she took another Lodging, and he follow'd her. They liv'd together some time, but he being still out of Business, and her Income not sufficient to maintain them with her Child, he took a Resolution of going from London, to try for a Country School, which he thought himself well qualify'd to undertake, as he wrote an

[12] [Bernard Mandeville, *The Fable of the Bees, or Private Vices, Public Benefits* (1714).]

excellent Hand, and was a Master of Arithmetic and Accounts.——This however he deem'd a Business below him, and confident of future better Fortune when he should be unwilling to have it known that he once was so meanly employ'd, he chang'd his Name, and did me the Honour to assume mine.——For I soon after had a Letter from him, acquainting me, that he was settled in a small Village in Berkshire, I think it was, where he taught reading and writing to 10 or a dozen Boys at 6 pence each per Week, recommending Mrs. T. to my Care, and desiring me to write to him directing for Mr. Franklin Schoolmaster at such a Place. He continu'd to write frequently, sending me large Specimens of an Epic Poem, which he was then composing, and desiring my Remarks and Corrections.——These I gave him from time to time, but endeavour'd rather to discourage his Proceeding. One of Young's Satires was then just publish'd. I copy'd and sent him a great Part of it, which set in a strong Light the Folly of pursuing the Muses with any Hope of Advancement by them. All was in vain. Sheets of the Poem continu'd to come by every Post. In the mean time Mrs. T. having on his Account lost her Friends and Business, was often in Distresses, and us'd to send for me, and borrow what I could spare to help her out of them. I grew fond of her Company, and being at this time under no Religious Restraints, and presuming on my Importance to her, I attempted Familiarities, (another Erratum) which she repuls'd with a proper Resentment, and acquainted him with my Behaviour. This made a Breach between us, and when he return'd again to London, he let me know he thought I had cancel'd all the Obligations he had been under to me.——So I found I was never to expect his Repaying me what I lent to him or advanc'd for him. This was however not then of much Consequence, as he was totally unable.——And in the Loss of his Friendship I found my self reliev'd from a Burthen. I now began to think of getting a little Money beforehand; and expecting better Work, I left Palmer's to work at Watts's near Lincoln's Inn Fields, a still greater Printing House. Here I continu'd all the rest of my Stay in London.

At my first Admission into this Printing House, I took to working at Press, imagining I felt a Want of the Bodily Exercise I had been us'd to in America, where Presswork is mix'd with Composing. I drank only Water; the other Workmen, near 50 in Number, were great Guzzlers of Beer. On occasion I carried up and down Stairs a large Form of Types in each hand, when others carried but one in both Hands. They wonder'd to see from this and several Instances that the Water-American as they call'd me was *stronger* than themselves who drank *strong* Beer. We had an

Alehouse Boy who attended always in the House to supply the Workmen. My Companion at the Press, drank every day a Pint before Breakfast, a Pint at Breakfast with his Bread and Cheese; a Pint between Breakfast and Dinner; a Pint at Dinner; a Pint in the Afternoon about Six o'Clock, and another when he had done his Day's-Work. I thought it a detestable Custom.——But it was necessary, he suppos'd, to drink *strong* Beer that he might be *strong* to labour. I endeavour'd to convince him that the Bodily Strength afforded by Beer could only be in proportion to the Grain or Flour of the Barley dissolved in the Water of which it was made; that there was more Flour in a Penny-worth of Bread, and therefore if he would eat that with a Pint of Water, it would give him more Strength than a Quart of Beer.——He drank on however, and had 4 or 5 Shillings to pay out of his Wages every Saturday Night for that muddling Liquor; an Expence I was free from.——And thus these poor Devils keep themselves always under.

Watts after some Weeks desiring to have me in the Composing Room, I left the Pressmen. A new *Bienvenu* or Sum for Drink, being 5 s., was demanded of me by the Compostors. I thought it an Imposition, as I had paid below. The Master thought so too, and forbad my Paying it. I stood out two or three Weeks, was accordingly considered as an Excommunicate, and had so many little Pieces of private Mischief done me, by mixing my Sorts, transposing my Pages, breaking my Matter, &c. &c. if I were ever so little out of the Room, and all ascrib'd to the Chapel Ghost, which they said ever haunted those not regularly admitted, that notwithstanding the Master's Protection, I found myself oblig'd to comply and pay the Money; convinc'd of the Folly of being on ill Terms with those one is to live with continually. I was now on a fair Footing with them, and soon acquir'd considerable Influence. I propos'd some reasonable Alterations in their Chapel[13] Laws, and carried them against all Opposition. From my Example a great Part of them, left their muddling Breakfast of Beer and Bread and Cheese, finding they could with me be supply'd from a neighbouring House with a large Porringer of hot Water-gruel, sprinkled with Pepper, crumb'd with Bread, and a Bit of Butter in it, for the Price of a Pint of Beer, viz, three halfpence. This was a more comfortable as well as cheaper Breakfast, and kept their Heads clearer.——Those who continu'd sotting with Beer all day, were often, by not paying, out of Credit at the Alehouse, and us'd to make Interest with me to get Beer, *their Light*, as they phras'd

[13] A Printing House is always called a Chappel by the Workmen.——

it, *being out.* I watch'd the Pay table on Saturday Night, and collected what I stood engag'd for them, having to pay some times near Thirty Shillings a Week on their Accounts.——This, and my being esteem'd a pretty good Riggite, that is a jocular verbal Satyrist, supported my Consequence in the Society.——My constant Attendance, (I never making a St. Monday), recommended me to the Master; and my uncommon Quickness at Composing, occasion'd my being put upon all Work of Dispatch which was generally better paid. So I went on now very agreably.——

My Lodging in Little Britain being too remote, I found another in Duke-street opposite to the Romish Chapel. It was two pair of Stairs backwards at an Italian Warehouse. A Widow Lady kept the House; she had a Daughter and a Maid Servant, and a Journeyman who attended the Warehouse, but lodg'd abroad.——After sending to enquire my Character at the House where I last lodg'd, she agreed to take me in at the same Rate, 3s. 6d. per Week, cheaper as she said from the Protection she expected in having a Man lodge in the House. She was a Widow, an elderly Woman, had been bred a Protestant, being a Clergyman's Daughter, but was converted to the Catholic Religion by her Husband, whose Memory she much revered, had lived much among People of Distinction, and knew a 1000 Anecdotes of them as far back as the Times of Charles the second. She was lame in her Knees with the Gout, and therefore seldom stirr'd out of her Room, so sometimes wanted Company; and hers was so highly amusing to me; that I was sure to spend an Evening with her whenever she desired it. Our Supper was only half an Anchovy each, on a very little Strip of Bread and Butter, and half a Pint of Ale between us. But the Entertainment was in her Conversation. My always keeping good Hours, and giving little Trouble in the Family, made her unwilling to part with me; so that when I talk'd of a Lodging I had heard of, nearer my Business, for 2s. a Week, which, intent as I now was on saving Money, made some Difference; she bid me not think of it, for she would abate me two Shillings a Week for the future, so I remain'd with her at 1s. 6d. as long as I staid in London.——

In a Garret of her House there lived a Maiden Lady of 70 in the most retired Manner, of whom my Landlady gave me this Account, that she was a Roman Catholic, had been sent abroad when young and lodg'd in a Nunnery with an Intent of becoming a Nun: but the Country not agreeing with her, she return'd to England, where there being no Nunnery, she had vow'd to lead the Life of a Nun as near as might be done in those Circumstances: Accordingly she had given all her Estate to charitable

Uses, reserving only Twelve Pounds a Year to live on, and out of this Sum she still gave a great deal in Charity, living her self on Watergruel only, and using no Fire but to boil it.——She had lived many Years in that Garret, being permitted to remain there gratis by successive Catholic Tenants of the House below, as they deem'd it a Blessing to have her there. A Priest visited her, to confess her every Day. I have ask'd her, says my Landlady, how she, as she liv'd, could possibly find so much Employment for a Confessor? O, says she, it is impossible to avoid *vain Thoughts*. I was permitted once to visit her: She was chearful and polite, and convers'd pleasantly. The Room was clean, but had no other Furniture than a Matras, a Table with a Crucifix and Book, a Stool, which she gave me to sit on, and a Picture over the Chimney of St. *Veronica*, displaying her Handkerchief with the miraculous Figure of Christ's bleeding Face on it, which she explain'd to me with great Seriousness. She look'd pale, but was never sick, and I give it as another Instance on how small an Income Life and Health may be supported.——

At Watts's Printinghouse I contracted an Acquaintance with an ingenious young Man, one Wygate, who having wealthy Relations, had been better educated than most Printers, was a tolerable Latinist, spoke French, and lov'd Reading. I taught him, and a Friend of his, to swim, at twice going into the River, and they soon became good Swimmers. They introduc'd me to some Gentlemen from the Country who went to Chelsea by Water to see the College and Don Saltero's Curiosities. In our Return, at the Request of the Company, whose Curiosity Wygate had excited, I stript and leapt into the River, and swam from near Chelsea to Blackfryars, performing on the Way many Feats of Activity both upon and under Water, that surpriz'd and pleas'd those to whom they were Novelties.——I had from a Child been ever delighted with this Exercise, had studied and practis'd all Thevenot's Motions and Positions, added some of my own, aiming at the graceful and easy, as well as the Useful. All these I took this Occasion of exhibiting to the Company, and was much flatter'd by their Admiration.——And Wygate, who was desirous of becoming a Master, grew more and more attach'd to me, on that account, as well as from the Similarity of our Studies. He at length propos'd to me travelling all over Europe together, supporting ourselves every where by working at our Business. I was once inclin'd to it. But mentioning it to my good Friend Mr. Denham, with whom I often spent an Hour, when I had Leisure. He dissuaded me from it, advising me to think only of returning to Pennsylvania, which he was now about to do.——

I must record one Trait of this good Man's Character. He had formerly been in Business at Bristol, but fail'd in Debt to a Number of People, compounded and went to America. There, by a close Application to Business as a Merchant, he acquir'd a plentiful Fortune in a few Years. Returning to England in the Ship with me, He invited his old Creditors to an Entertainment, at which he thank'd them for the easy Composition they had favour'd him with, and when they expected nothing but the Treat, every Man at the first Remove, found under his Plate an Order on a Banker for the full Amount of the unpaid Remainder with Interest.

He now told me he was about to return to Philadelphia, and should carry over a great Quantity of Goods in order to open a Store there: He propos'd to take me over as his Clerk, to keep his Books (in which he would instruct me), copy his Letters, and attend the Store. He added, that as soon as I should be acquainted with mercantile Business he would promote me by sending me with a Cargo of Flour and Bread &c. to the West Indies, and procure me Commissions from others; which would be profitable, and if I manag'd well, would establish me handsomely. The Thing pleas'd me, for I was grown tired of London, remember'd with Pleasure the happy Months I had spent in Pennsylvania, and wish'd again to see it. Therefore I immediately agreed, on the Terms of Fifty Pounds a Year, Pensylvania Money; less indeed than my then present Gettings as a Compostor, but affording a better Prospect.——

I now took Leave of Printing; as I thought for ever, and was daily employ'd in my new Business; going about with Mr. Denham among the Tradesmen, to purchase various Articles, and seeing them pack'd up, doing Errands, calling upon Workmen to dispatch, &c. and when all was on board, I had a few Days Leisure. On one of these Days I was to my Surprize sent for by a great Man I knew only by Name, a Sir William Wyndham and I waited upon him. He had heard by some means or other of my Swimming from Chelsey to Blackfryars, and of my teaching Wygate and another young Man to swim in a few Hours. He had two Sons about to set out on their Travels; he wish'd to have them first taught Swimming; and propos'd to gratify me handsomely if I would teach them.——They were not yet come to Town and my Stay was uncertain, so I could not undertake it. But from this Incident I thought it likely, that if I were to remain in England and open a Swimming School, I might get a good deal of Money. And it struck me so strongly, that had the Overture been sooner made me, probably I should not so soon have returned to America.——After many Years, you and I had something of more Importance to do with one of these Sons of Sir William Wyndham, become Earl of Egremont, which I shall mention in its Place.——

Thus I spent about 18 Months in London. Most Part of the Time, I work'd hard at my Business, and spent but little upon my self except in seeing Plays, and in Books.——My Friend Ralph had kept me poor. He owed me about 27 Pounds; which I was now never likely to receive; a great Sum out of my small Earnings. I lov'd him notwithstanding, for he had many amiable Qualities. Tho' I had by no means improv'd my Fortune. But I had pick'd up some very ingenious Acquaintance whose Conversation was of great Advantage to me, and I had read considerably.

We sail'd from Gravesend on the 23d of July 1726. For the Incidents of the Voyage, I refer you to my Journal, where you will find them all minutely related. Perhaps the most important Part of that journal is the *Plan* to be found in it which I formed at Sea, for regulating my future Conduct in Life. It is the more remarkable, as being form'd when I was so young, and yet being pretty faithfully adhered to quite thro' to old Age.——We landed in Philadelphia the 11th of October, where I found sundry Alterations. Keith was no longer Governor, being superceded by Major Gordon: I met him walking the Streets as a common Citizen. He seem'd a little asham'd at seeing me, but pass'd without saying any thing. I should have been as much asham'd at seeing Miss Read, had not her Friends despairing with Reason of my Return, after the Receipt of my Letter, persuaded her to marry another, one Rogers, a Potter, which was done in my Absence. With him however she was never happy, and soon parted from him, refusing to cohabit with him, or bear his Name It being now said that he had another Wife. He was a worthless Fellow tho' an excellent Workman which was the Temptation to her Friends. He got into Debt, and ran away in 1727 or 28, went to the West Indies, and died there. Keimer had got a better House, a Shop well supply'd with Stationary, plenty of new Types, a number of Hands tho' none good, and seem'd to have a great deal of Business.

Mr. Denham took a Store in Water Street, where we open'd our Goods. I attended the Business diligently, studied Accounts, and grew in a little Time expert at selling.——We lodg'd and boarded together, he counsell'd me as a Father, having a sincere Regard for me: I respected and lov'd him: and we might have gone on together very happily: But in the Beginning of February 1726/7 when I had just pass'd my 21st Year, we both were taken ill. My Distemper was a Pleurisy, which very nearly carried me off:——I suffered a good deal, gave up the Point in my own mind, and was rather disappointed when I found my Self recovering; regretting in some degree that I must now some time or other have all that disagreable Work to do over again.——I forget what his Distemper was. It held him a long time, and at length carried him off. He left me a small Legacy in a nuncupative Will, as a Token of his Kindness for me, and he left me once more to the wide World. For the Store was taken into the Care of his Executors, and my Employment under him ended:——My Brother-in-law Homes, being now at Philadelphia, advis'd my Return to my Business. And Keimer tempted me with an Offer of large Wages by the Year to come and take the Management of his Printing-House that he might better attend his Stationer's Shop.——I had heard a bad Character of him in London, from his Wife and her Friends, and was not fond of having any more to do with him. I try'd for farther Employment as a Merchant's Clerk; but not readily meeting with any, I clos'd again with Keimer.——

I found in *his* House these Hands; Hugh Meredith a Welsh-Pennsylvanian, 30 Years of Age, bred to Country Work: honest, sensible, had a great deal of solid Observation, was something of a Reader, but given to drink:——Stephen Potts, a young Country Man of full Age, bred to the Same: of uncommon natural Parts, and great Wit and Humour, but a little idle.——These he had agreed with at extream low Wages, per Week, to be rais'd a Shilling every 3 Months, as they would deserve by improving in their Business, and the Expectation of these high Wages to come on hereafter was what he had drawn them in with.——Meredith was to work at Press, Potts at Bookbinding, which he by Agreement, was to teach them, tho' he knew neither one nor t'other. John——a wild Irishman brought up to no Business, whose Service for 4 Years Keimer had purchas'd from the Captain of a Ship. He too was to be made a Pressman. George Webb, an Oxford Scholar, whose Time for 4 Years he had likewise bought, intending him for a Compositor: of whom more presently. And David Harry, a Country Boy, whom he had taken Apprentice. I soon perceiv'd that the Intention of engaging me at Wages so much higher than he had been us'd to give, was to have these raw cheap Hands form'd thro' me, and as soon as I had instructed them, then, they being all articled to him, he should be able to do without me.——I went on however, very chearfully; put his Printing House in Order, which had been in great Confusion, and brought his Hands by degrees to mind their Business and to do it better.

It was an odd Thing to find an Oxford Scholar in the Situation of a bought Servant. He was not more than 18 Years of Age, and gave me this Account of himself; that he was born in Gloucester, educated at a

Grammar School there, had been distinguish'd among the Scholars for some apparent Superiority in performing his Part when they exhibited Plays; belong'd to the Witty Club there, and had written some Pieces in Prose and Verse which were printed in the Gloucester Newspapers. Thence he was sent to Oxford; there he continu'd about a Year, but not well-satisfy'd, wishing of all things to see London and become a Player. At length receiving his Quarterly Allowance of 15 Guineas, instead of discharging his Debts, he walk'd out of Town, hid his Gown in a Furz Bush, and footed it to London, where having no Friend to advise him, he fell into bad Company, soon spent his Guineas, found no means of being introduc'd among the Players, grew necessitous, pawn'd his Cloaths and wanted Bread. Walking the Street very hungry, and not knowing what to do with himself, a Crimp's Bill was put into his Hand, offering immediate Entertainment and Encouragement to such as would bind themselves to serve in America. He went directly, sign'd the Indentures, was put into the Ship and came over; never writing a Line to acquaint his Friends what was become of him. He was lively, witty, good-natur'd, and a pleasant Companion, but idle, thoughtless and imprudent to the last Degree.

John the Irishman soon ran away. With the rest I began to live very agreably; for they all respected me, the more as they found Keimer incapable of instructing them, and that from me they learnt something daily. We never work'd on a Saturday, that being Keimer's Sabbath. So I had two Days for Reading. My Acquaintance with Ingenious People in the Town, increased. Keimer himself treated me with great Civility and apparent Regard; and nothing now made me uneasy but my Debt to Vernon, which I was yet unable to pay being hitherto but a poor Oeconomist.——He however kindly made no Demand of it.

Our Printing-House often wanted Sorts, and there was no Letter Founder in America. I had seen Types cast at James's in London, but without much Attention to the Manner: However I now contriv'd a Mould, made use of the Letters we had, as Puncheons, struck the Matrices in Lead, and thus supply'd in a pretty tolerable way all Deficiencies. I also engrav'd several Things on occasion. I made the Ink, I was Warehouseman and every thing, in short quite a Factotum.——

But however serviceable I might be, I found that my Services became every Day of less Importance, as the other Hands improv'd in the Business. And when Keimer paid my second Quarter's Wages, he let me know that he felt them too heavy, and thought I should make an Abatement. He grew by degrees less civil, put on more of the Master, frequently found Fault, was captious and seem'd ready for an Out-breaking. I went on nevertheless with a good deal of Patience, thinking that his incumber'd Circumstances were partly the Cause. At length a Trifle snapt our Connexion. For a great Noise happening near the Courthouse, I put my Head out of the Window to see what was the Matter. Keimer being in the Street look'd up and saw me, call'd out to me in a loud Voice and angry Tone to mind my Business, adding some reproachful Words, that nettled me the more for their Publicity, all the Neighbours who were looking out on the same Occasion being Witnesses how I was treated. He came up immediately into the Printing-House, continu'd the Quarrel, high Words pass'd on both Sides, he gave me the Quarter's Warning we had stipulated, expressing a Wish that he had not been oblig'd to so long a Warning: I told him his Wish was unnecessary for I would leave him that Instant; and so taking my Hat walk'd out of Doors; desiring Meredith whom I saw below to take care of some Things I left, and bring them to my Lodging.——

Meredith came accordingly in the Evening, when we talk'd my Affair over. He had conceiv'd a great Regard for me, and was very unwilling that I should leave the House while he remain'd in it. He dissuaded me from returning to my native Country which I began to think of. He reminded me that Keimer was in debt for all he possess'd, that his Creditors began to be uneasy, that he kept his Shop miserably, sold often without Profit for ready Money, and often trusted without keeping Accounts. That he must therefore fail; which would make a Vacancy I might profit of.——I objected my Want of Money. He then let me know, that his Father had a high Opinion of me, and from some Discourse that had pass'd between them, he was sure would advance Money to set us up, if I would enter into Partnership with him.——My Time, says he, will be out with Keimer in the Spring. By that time we may have our Press and Types in from London: I am sensible I am no Workman. If you like it, Your Skill in the Business shall be set against the Stock I furnish; and we will share the Profits equally.——The Proposal was agreable, and I consented. His Father was in Town, and approv'd of it, the more as he saw I had great Influence with his Son, had prevail'd on him to abstain long from Dramdrinking, and he hop'd might break him of that wretched Habit entirely, when we came to be so closely connected. I gave an Inventory to the Father, who carry'd it to a Merchant; the Things were sent for; the Secret was to be kept till they should arrive, and in the mean time I was to get work if I could at the other Printing House.——But I found no Vacancy there, and so remain'd idle a few Days, when Keimer, on a Prospect of being employ'd to print some

Paper-money, in New Jersey, which would require Cuts and various Types that I only could supply, and apprehending Bradford might engage me and get the Jobb from him, sent me a very civil Message, that old Friends should not part for a few Words the Effect of sudden Passion, and wishing me to return. Meredith persuaded me to comply, as it would give more opportunity for his Improvement under my daily Instructions.——So I return'd, and we went on more smoothly than for some time before.—— The New Jersey Jobb was obtain'd. I contriv'd a Copper-Plate Press for it, the first that had been seen in the Country. I cut several Ornaments and Checks for the Bills. We went together to Burlington, where I executed the Whole to Satisfaction, and he received so large a Sum for the Work, as to be enabled thereby to keep his Head much longer above Water.——

At Burlington I made an Acquaintance with many principal People of the Province. Several of them had been appointed by the Assembly a Committee to attend the Press, and take Care that no more Bills were printed than the Law directed. They were therefore by Turns constantly with us, and generally he who attended brought with him a Friend or two for Company. My Mind having been much more improv'd by Reading than Keimer's, I suppose it was for that Reason my Conversation seem'd to be more valu'd. They had me to their Houses, introduc'd me to their Friends and show'd me much Civility, while he, tho' the Master, was a little neglected. In truth he was an odd Fish, ignorant of common Life, fond of rudely opposing receiv'd Opinions, slovenly to extream dirtiness, enthusiastic in some Points of Religion, and a little Knavish withal. We continu'd there near 3 Months, and by that time I could reckon among my acquired Friends, Judge Allen, Samuel Bustill, the Secretary of the Province, Isaac Pearson, Joseph Cooper and several of the Smiths, Members of Assembly, and Isaac Decow the Surveyor General. The latter was a shrewd sagacious old Man, who told me that he began for himself when young by wheeling Clay for the Brickmakers, learnt to write after he was of Age, carry'd the Chain for Surveyors, who taught him Surveying, and he had now by his Industry acquired a good Estate; and says he, I foresee, that you will soon work this Man out of his Business and make a Fortune in it at Philadelphia. He had not then the least Intimation of my Intention to set up there or any where.——These Friends were afterwards of great Use to me, as I occasionally was to some of them. They all continued their Regard for me as long as they lived.——

Before I enter upon my public Appearance in Business it may be well to let you know the then State of my Mind, with regard to my Principles and

Morals, that you may see how far those influenc'd the future Events of my Life. My Parents had early given me religious Impressions, and brought me through my Childhood piously in the Dissenting Way. But I was scarce 15 when, after doubting by turns of several Points as I found them disputed in the different Books I read, I began to doubt of Revelation it self. Some Books against Deism fell into my Hands; they were said to be the Substance of Sermons preached at Boyle's Lectures. It happened that they wrought an Effect on me quite contrary to what was intended by them: For the Arguments of the Deists which were quoted to be refuted, appeared to me much stronger than the Refutations. In short I soon became a thorough Deist. My Arguments perverted some others, particularly Collins and Ralph: but each of them having afterwards wrong'd me greatly without the least Compunction and recollecting Keith's Conduct towards me, (who was another Freethinker) and my own towards Vernon and Miss Read which at Times gave me great Trouble, I began to suspect that this Doctrine tho' it might be true, was not very useful.——My London Pamphlet, which had for its Motto those Lines of Dryden

> —— W*hatever is, is right.*
> *Tho' purblind Man / Sees but a Part of*
> *the Chain, the nearest Link,*
> *His Eyes not carrying to the equal Beam,*
> *That poizes all, above.*[14]

And from the Attributes of God, his infinite Wisdom, Goodness and Power concluded that nothing could possibly be wrong in the World, and that Vice and Virtue were empty Distinctions, no such Things existing: appear'd now not so clever a Performance as I once thought it; and I doubted whether some Error had not insinuated itself unperceiv'd, into my Argument, so as to infect all that follow'd, as is common in metaphysical Reasonings.——I grew convinc'd that *Truth, Sincerity* and *Integrity* in Dealings between Man and Man, were of the utmost Importance to the Felicity of Life, and I form'd written Resolutions, (which still remain in my Journal Book) to practice them ever while I lived. Revelation had indeed no weight with me as such; but I entertain'd an Opinion, that tho' certain Actions might not be bad *because* they were forbidden by it, or good *because* it commanded them; yet probably those Actions might be forbidden *because* they were bad for us, or commanded *because* they were

[14] [The first line is from Alexander Pope, *Essay on Man* (1773), Epistle 1, line 284; the remainder is from John Dryden, *Oedipus* (1679), 3.1.244–8.]

beneficial to us, in their own Natures, all the Circumstances of things considered. And this Persuasion, with the kind hand of Providence, or some guardian Angel, or accidental favourable Circumstances and Situations, or all together, preserved me (thro' this dangerous Time of Youth and the hazardous Situations I was sometimes in among Strangers, remote from the Eye and Advice of my Father) without any *wilful* gross Immorality or Injustice that might have been expected from my Want of Religion.——I say *wilful*, because the Instances I have mentioned, had something of *Necessity* in them, from my Youth, Inexperience, and the Knavery of others.——I had therefore a tolerable Character to begin the World with, I valued it properly, and determin'd to preserve it.——

We had not been long return'd to Philadelphia, before the New Types arriv'd from London. We settled with Keimer, and left him by his Consent before he heard of it.——We found a House to hire near the Market, and took it. To lessen the Rent, (which was then but 24£ a Year tho' I have since known it let for 70) We took in Thomas Godfrey a Glazier and his Family, who were to pay a considerable Part of it to us, and we to board with them. We had scarce opened our Letters and put our Press in Order, before George House, an Acquaintance of Mine, brought a Countryman to us; whom he had met in the Street enquiring for a Printer. All our Cash was now expended in the Variety of Particulars we had been obliged to procure and this Countryman's Five Shillings being our First Fruits, and coming so seasonably, gave me more Pleasure than any Crown I have since earn'd; and from the Gratitude I felt towards House, has made me often more ready than perhaps I should otherwise have been to assist young Beginners.

There are Croakers in every Country always boding its Ruin. Such a one then lived in Philadelphia, a Person of Note, an elderly Man, with a wise Look, and very grave Manner of speaking. His Name was Samuel Mickle. This Gentleman, a Stranger to me, stopt one Day at my Door, and asked me if I was the young Man who had lately opened a new Printing House: Being answer'd in the Affirmative, he said he was sorry for me, because it was an expensive Undertaking and the Expence would be lost; for Philadelphia was a sinking Place, the People already half Bankrupts or near being so; all Appearances of the contrary, such as new Buildings and the Rise of Rents being to his certain Knowledge fallacious; for they were in fact among the Things that would soon ruin us.——And he gave me such a Detail of Misfortunes, now existing or that were soon to exist, that he left me half-melancholy. Had I known him before I engag'd in this Business, probably I never should have done it.——This Man continu'd to live in this decaying Place; and to declaim in the same Strain, refusing for many Years to buy a House there, because all was going to Destruction, and at last I had the Pleasure of seeing him give five times as much for one as he might have bought it for when he first began his Croaking.

I should have mention'd before, that in the Autumn of the preceding Year I had form'd most of my ingenious Acquaintance into a Club for mutual Improvement, which we call'd the Junto. We met on Friday Evenings. The Rules I drew up requir'd that every Member in his Turn should produce one or more Queries on any Point of Morals, Politics or Natural Philosophy, to be discuss'd by the Company, and once in three Months produce and read an Essay of his own Writing on any Subject he pleased. Our Debates were to be under the Direction of a President, and to be conducted in the sincere Spirit of Enquiry after Truth, without Fondness for Dispute, or Desire of Victory; and to prevent Warmth all Expressions of Positiveness in Opinions or of direct Contradiction, were after some time made contraband and prohibited under small pecuniary Penalties.——The first Members were Joseph Brientnal, a Copyer of Deeds for the Scriveners; a good-natur'd friendly middle-ag'd Man, a great Lover of Poetry, reading all he could meet with, and writing some that was tolerable; very ingenious in many little Nicknackeries, and of sensible Conversation. Thomas Godfrey, a self-taught Mathematician, great in his Way, and afterwards Inventor of what is now call'd Hadley's Quadrant. But he knew little out of his way, and was not a pleasing Companion, as like most Great Mathematicians I have met with, he expected unusual Precision in every thing said, or was forever denying or distinguishing upon Trifles, to the Disturbance of all Conversation.——He soon left us.——Nicholas Scull, a Surveyor, afterwards Surveyor-General, Who lov'd Books, and sometimes made a few Verses. William Parsons, bred a Shoemaker, but loving Reading, had acquir'd a considerable Share of Mathematics, which he first studied with a View to Astrology that he afterwards laught at. He also became Surveyor General.——William Maugridge, a Joiner, a most exquisite Mechanic and a solid sensible Man. Hugh Meredith, Stephen Potts, and George Webb, I have Characteris'd before. Robert Grace, a young Gentleman of some Fortune, generous, lively and witty, a Lover of Punning and of his Friends. And William Coleman, then a Merchant's Clerk, about my Age, who had the coolest clearest Head, the best Heart, and the exactest Morals, of almost any Man I ever met with. He became afterwards a Merchant of great Note, and one of our Provincial Judges: Our Friendship continued without Interruption to his Death upwards of 40 Years. And the club continu'd almost as long and was the best School of Philosophy, Morals and Politics that then existed in the Province; for our Queries which were read the Week preceding their Discussion, put us on Reading with Attention upon the several Subjects, that we might speak more to the purpose: and here too we acquired better Habits of Conversation, every thing being studied in our Rules which might prevent our disgusting each other. From hence the long Continuance of the Club, which I shall have frequent Occasion to speak farther of hereafter; But my giving this Account of it here, is to show something of the Interest I had, every one of these exerting themselves in recommending Business to us.——Brientnal particularly procur'd us from the Quakers, the Printing 40 Sheets of their History, the rest being to be done by Keimer: and upon this we work'd exceeding hard, for the Price was low. It was a Folio, Pro Patria Size, in Pica with Long Primer Notes. I compos'd of it a Sheet a Day, and Meredith work'd it off at Press. It was often 11 at Night and sometimes later, before I had finish'd my Distribution for the next days Work: For the little Jobbs sent in by our other Friends now and then put us back. But so determin'd I was to continue doing a Sheet a Day of the Folio, that one Night when having impos'd my Forms, I thought my Days Work over, one of them by accident was broken and two Pages reduc'd to Pie, I immediately distributed and compos'd it over again before I went to bed. And this Industry visible to our Neighbours began to give us Character and Credit; particularly I was told, that mention being made of the new Printing Office at the Merchants Every-night Club, the general Opinion was that it must fail, there being already two Printers in the Place, Keimer and Bradford; but Doctor Baird (whom you and I saw many Years after at his native Place, St. Andrews in Scotland) gave a contrary Opinion; for the Industry of that Franklin, says he, is superior to any thing I ever saw of the kind: I see him still at work when I go home from Club; and he is at Work again before his Neighbours are out of bed. This struck the rest, and we soon after had Offers from one of them to Supply us with Stationary. But as yet we did not chuse to engage in Shop Business.

I mention this Industry the more particularly and the more freely, tho' it seems to be talking in my own Praise, that those of my Posterity who shall read it, may know the Use of that Virtue, when they see its Effects in my Favour throughout this Relation.——

George Webb, who had found a Female Friend that lent him wherewith to purchase his Time of Keimer, now came to offer himself as a

Journeyman to us. We could not then imploy him, but I foolishly let him know, as a Secret, that I soon intended to begin a Newspaper, and might then have Work for him. My Hopes of Success as I told him were founded on this, that the then only Newspaper, printed by Bradford was a paltry thing, wretchedly manag'd, no way entertaining; and yet was profitable to him.——I therefore thought a good Paper could scarcely fail of good Encouragement. I requested Webb not to mention it, but he told it to Keimer, who immediately, to be beforehand with me, published Proposals for Printing one himself, on which Webb was to be employ'd.——I resented this, and to counteract them, as I could not yet begin our Paper, I wrote several Pieces of Entertainment for Bradford's Paper, under the Title of the Busy Body which Brientnal continu'd some Months. By this means the Attention of the Publick was fix'd on that Paper, and Keimers Proposals which we burlesqu'd and ridicul'd, were disregarded. He began his Paper however, and after carrying it on three Quarters of a Year, with at most only 90 Subscribers, he offer'd it to me for a Trifle, and I having been ready some time to go on with it, took it in hand directly, and it prov'd in a few Years extreamly profitable to me.——

I perceive that I am apt to speak in the singular Number, though our Partnership still continu'd. The Reason may be, that in fact the whole Management of the Business lay upon me. Meredith was no Compositor, a poor Pressman, and seldom sober. My Friends lamented my Connection with him, but I was to make the best of it.

Our first Papers made a quite different Appearance from any before in the Province, a better Type and better printed: but some spirited Remarks[15] of my Writing on the Dispute then going on between Gov.

[15] "His Excellency Governor *Burnet* died unexpectedly about two Days after the Date of this Reply to his last Message: And it was thought the Dispute would have ended with him, or at least have lain dormant till the Arrival of a new Governor from *England*, who possibly might, or might not be inclin'd to enter too rigorously into the Measures of his Precedessor. But our last Advices by the Post acquaint us, that his Honour the Lieutenant Governour (on whom the Government immediately devolves upon the Death or Absence of the Commander in Chief) has vigorously renew'd the Struggle on his own Account; of which the Particulars will be seen in our Next.

Perhaps some of our Readers may not fully understand the Original or Ground of this warm Contest between the Governour and Assembly.——It seems, that People have for these Hundred Years past, enjoyed the Privilege of Rewarding the Governour for the Time being, according to *their Sense* of his Merit and Services; and few or none of their Governors have hitherto complain'd, or had Reason to complain, of a too scanty Allowance. But the late Gov. *Burnet* brought with him Instructions to demand a *settled Salary* of 1000 *l. per Annum*, Sterling, on him and all his Successors, and the Assembly were required to fix it immediately. He insisted on it strenuously to the last, and they as constantly refused it. It

Burnet and the Massachusetts Assembly, struck the principal People, occasion'd the Paper and the Manager of it to be much talk'd of, and in a few Weeks brought them all to be our Subscribers. Their Example was follow'd by many, and our Number went on growing continually.——This was one of the first good Effects of my having learnt a little to scribble. Another was, that the leading Men, seeing a News Paper now in the hands of one who could also handle a Pen, thought it convenient to oblige and encourage me.——Bradford still printed the Votes and Laws and other Publick Business. He had printed an Address of the House to the Governor in a coarse blundering manner; We reprinted it elegantly and correctly, and sent one to every Member. They were sensible of the Difference, it strengthen'd the Hands of our Friends in the House, and they voted us their Printers for the Year ensuing.

Among my Friends in the House I must not forget Mr. Hamilton before mentioned, who was then returned from England and had a Seat in it. He interested himself for me strongly in that Instance, as he did in many others afterwards, continuing his Patronage till his Death.[16] Mr. Vernon

appears by their Votes and Proceedings, that they thought it an Imposition, contrarary to their own Charter, and to *Magna Charta*; and they judg'd that by the Dictates of Reason there should be a mutual Dependence between the *Governor* and the *Governed*, and that to make any Governour independent of his People, would be dangerous, and destructive of their Liberties, and the ready Way to establish Tyranny: They thought likewise, that the Province was not the less dependent on the Crown of *Great-Britain*, by the Governour's depending immediately on them and his own good Conduct for an ample Support, because all Acts and Laws which he might be induc'd to pass, must nevertheless be constantly sent Home for Approbation in Order to continue in Force. Many other Reasons were given and Arguments us'd in the Course of the Controversy, needless to particularize here, because all the material Papers relating to it, have been inserted already in our Publick News.

Much deserved Praise has the deceas'd Governour receiv'd, for his steady Integrity in adhering to his Instructions, notwithstanding the great Difficulty and Opposition he met with, and the strong Temptations offer'd from time to time to induce him to give up the Point.——And yet perhaps something is due to the *Assembly* (as the Love and Zeal of that Country for the present Establishment is too well known to suffer any Suspicion for Want of Loyalty) who continue thus resolutely to Abide by what *they Think* their Right, and that of the People they represent, maugre all the Arts and Menaces of a Governour fam'd for his Cunning and Politicks, back'd with Instructions from Home, and powerfully aided by the great Advantage such an Officer always has of engaging the principal Men of a Place in his Party, by conferring where he pleases so many Posts of Profit and Honour. Their happy Mother Country will perhaps observe with Pleasure, that tho' her gallant Cocks and matchless Dogs abate their native Fire and Intrepidity when transported to a Foreign Clime (as the common Notion is) yet her SONS in the remotest Part of the Earth, and even to the third and fourth Descent, still retain that ardent Spirit of Liberty, and that undaunted Courage in the Defence of it, which has in every Age so gloriously distinguished BRITONS and ENGLISHMEN from all the Rest of Mankind." [Gazette, 9 October 1729]

[16] I got his Son once 500£.

about this time put me in mind of the Debt I ow'd him: but did not press me. I wrote him an ingenuous Letter of Acknowledgments, crav'd his Forbearance a little longer which he allow'd me, and as soon as I was able I paid the Principal with Interest and many Thanks.——So that Erratum was in some degree corrected.——

But now another Difficulty came upon me, which I had never the least Reason to expect. Mr. Meredith's Father, who was to have paid for our Printing House according to the Expectations given me, was able to advance only one Hundred Pounds, Currency, which had been paid, and a Hundred more was due to the Merchant; who grew impatient and su'd us all. We gave Bail, but saw that if the Money could not be rais'd in time, the Suit must come to a Judgment and Execution, and our hopeful Prospects must with us be ruined, as the Press and Letters must be sold for Payment, perhaps at half Price.——In this Distress two true Friends whose Kindness I have never forgotten nor ever shall forget while I can remember any thing, came to me separately unknown to each other, and without any Application from me, offering each of them to advance me all the Money that should be necessary to enable me to take the whole Business upon my self if that should be practicable, but they did not like my continuing the Partnership with Meredith, who as they said was often seen drunk in the Streets, and playing at low Games in Alehouses, much to our Discredit. These two Friends were *William Coleman* and *Robert Grace*. I told them I could not propose a Separation while any Prospect remain'd of the Merediths fulfilling their Part of our Agreement. Because I thought my self under great Obligations to them for what they had done and would do if they could. But if they finally fail'd in their Performance, and our Partnership must be dissolv'd, I should then think myself at Liberty to accept the Assistance of my Friends. Thus the matter rested for some time. When I said to my Partner, perhaps your Father is dissatisfied at the Part you have under taken in this Affair of ours, and is unwilling to advance for you and me what he would for you alone: If that is the Case, tell me, and I will resign the whole to you and go about my Business. No says he, my Father has really been disappointed and is really unable; and I am unwilling to distress him farther. I see this is a Business I am not fit for. I was bred a Farmer, and it was a Folly in me to come to Town and put my Self at 30 Years of Age an Apprentice to learn a new Trade. Many of our Welsh People are going to settle in North Carolina where Land is cheap: I am inclin'd to go with them, and follow my old Employment. You may find Friends to assist you. If you will take the Debts of the Company upon you, return to my Father the hundred Pound he has advanc'd, pay my little personal Debts, and give me Thirty Pounds and a new Saddle, I will relinquish the Partnership and leave the whole in your Hands. I agreed to this Proposal. It was drawn up in Writing, sign'd and seal'd immediately. I gave him what he demanded and he went soon after to Carolina; from whence he sent me next Year two long Letters, containing the best Account that had been given of that Country, the Climate, Soil, Husbandry, &c. for in those Matters he was very judicious. I printed them in the Papers, and they gave grate Satisfaction to the Publick.

As soon as he was gone, I recurr'd to my two Friends; and because I would not give an unkind Preference to either, I took half what each had offered and I wanted, of one, and half of the other; paid off the Company Debts, and went on with the Business in my own Name, advertising that the Partnership was dissolved. I think this was in or about the Year 1729.——

About this Time there was a Cry among the People for more Paper-Money, only 15,000£ being extant in the Province and that soon to be sunk. The wealthy Inhabitants oppos'd any Addition, being against all Paper Currency, from an Apprehension that it would depreciate as it had done in New England to the Prejudice of all Creditors.——We had discuss'd this Point in our Junto, where I was on the Side of an Addition, being persuaded that the first small Sum struck in 1723 had done much good, by increasing the Trade Employment, and Number of Inhabitants in the Province, since I now saw all the old Houses inhabited, and many new ones building, where as I remember'd well, that when I first walk'd about the Streets of Philadelphia, eating my Roll, I saw most of the Houses in Walnut Street between Second and Front Streets with Bills on their Doors, to be let; and many likewise in Chesnut Street, and other Streets; which made me then think the Inhabitants of the City were one after another deserting it.——Our Debates possess'd me so fully of the Subject, that I wrote and printed an anonymous Pamphlet on it, entituled, *The Nature and Necessity of a Paper Currency*. It was well receiv'd by the common People in general; but the Rich Men dislik'd it; for it increas'd and strengthen'd the Clamour for more Money; and they happening to have no Writers among them that were able to answer it, their Opposition slacken'd, and the Point was carried by a Majority in the House. My Friends there, who conceiv'd I had been of some Service, thought fit to reward me, by employing me in printing the Money, a very profitable Jobb, and a great Help to me.——This was another Advantage gain'd by my being able to write. The Utility of this Currency became by Time and Experience so evident, as never afterwards to be much disputed, so that it grew soon to 55,000£, and in 1739 to 80,000£ since which it arose during War to upwards of 350,000£ Trade, Building and Inhabitants all the while increasing. Tho' I now think there are Limits beyond which the Quantity may be hurtful.——

I soon after obtain'd, thro' my Friend Hamilton, the Printing of the New Castle Paper Money, another profitable Jobb, as I then thought it; small Things appearing great to those in small Circumstances. And these to me were really great Advantages, as they were great Encouragements. He procured me also the Printing of the Laws and Votes of that Government which continu'd in my Hands as long as I follow'd the Business.——

I now open'd a little Stationer's Shop. I had in it Blanks of all Sorts the correctest that ever appear'd among us, being assisted in that by my Friend Brientnal; I had also Paper, Parchment, Chapmen's Books, &c. One Whitemash a Compositor I had known in London, an excellent Workman now came to me and work'd with me constantly and diligently, and I took an Apprentice the Son of Aquila Rose. I began now gradually to pay off the Debt I was under for the Printing-House.——In order to secure my Credit and Character as a Tradesman, I took care not only to be in *Reality* Industrious and frugal, but to avoid all *Appearances* of the Contrary. I drest plainly; I was seen at no Places of idle Diversion; I never went out a-fishing or shooting; a Book, indeed, sometimes debauch'd me from my Work; but that was seldom, snug, and gave no Scandal: and to show that I was not above my Business, I sometimes brought home the Paper I purchas'd at the Stores, thro' the Streets on a Wheelbarrow. Thus being esteem'd an industrious thriving young Man, and paying duly for what I bought, the Merchants who imported Stationary solicited my Custom, others propos'd supplying me with Books, and I went on swimmingly.——In the mean time Keimer's Credit and Business declining daily, he was at last forc'd to sell his Printing-house to satisfy his Creditors. He went to Barbadoes, and there lived some Years, in very poor Circumstances.

His Apprentice David Harry, whom I had instructed while I work'd with him, set up in his Place at Philadelphia, having bought his Materials. I was at first apprehensive of a powerful Rival in Harry, as his Friends were very able, and had a good deal of Interest. I therefore propos'd a Partnership to him; which he, fortunately for me, rejected with Scorn. He was very proud, dress'd like a Gentleman, liv'd expensively, took much Diversion and Pleasure abroad, ran in debt, and neglected his Business, upon which all Business left him; and finding nothing to do, he follow'd

Keimer to Barbadoes; taking the Printinghouse with him. There this Apprentice employ'd his former Master as a Journeyman. They quarrel'd often. Harry went continually behindhand, and at length was forc'd to sell his Types, and return to his Country Work in Pennsylvania. The Person that bought them, employ'd Keimer to use them, but in a few years he died. There remain'd now no Competitor with me at Philadelphia, but the old one, Bradford, who was rich and easy, did a little Printing now and then by straggling Hands, but was not very anxious about the Business. However, as he kept the Post Office, it was imagined he had better Opportunities of obtaining News, his Paper was thought a better Distributer of Advertisements than mine, and therefore had many more, which was a profitable thing to him and a Disadvantage to me. For tho' I did indeed receive and send Papers by Post, yet the publick Opinion was otherwise; for what I did send was by Bribing the Riders who took them privately: Bradford being unkind enough to forbid it: which occasion'd some Resentment on my Part; and I thought so meanly of him for it, that when I afterwards came into his Situation, I took care never to imitate it.

I had hitherto continu'd to board with Godfrey who lived in Part of my House with his Wife and Children, and had one Side of the Shop for his Glazier's Business, tho' he work'd little, being always absorb'd in his Mathematics.——Mrs. Godfrey projected a Match for me with a Relation's Daughter, took Opportunities of bringing us often together, till a serious Courtship on my Part ensu'd the Girl being in herself very deserving. The old Folks encourag'd me by continual Invitations to Supper, and by leaving us together, till at length it was time to explain. Mrs. Godfrey manag'd our little Treaty. I let her know that I expected as much Money with their Daughter as would pay off my Remaining Debt for the Printinghouse, which I believe was not then above a Hundred Pounds. She brought me Word they had no such Sum to spare. I said they might mortgage their House in the Loan Office. The Answer to this after some Days was, that they did not approve the Match; that on Enquiry of Bradford they had been inform'd the Printing Business was not a profitable one, the Types would soon be worn out and more wanted, that S. Keimer and D. Harry had fail'd one after the other, and I should probably soon follow them; and therefore I was forbidden the House, and the Daughter shut up.——Whether this was a real Change of Sentiment, or only Artifice, on a Supposition of our being too far engag'd in Affection to retract, and therefore that we should steal a Marriage, which would leave them at Liberty to give or withold what they pleas'd, I know not:

But I suspected the latter, resented it, and went no more. Mrs. Godfrey brought me afterwards some more favourable Accounts of their Disposition, and would have drawn me on again: but I declared absolutely my Resolution to have nothing more to do with that Family. This was resented by the Godfreys, we differ'd, and they removed, leaving me the whole House, and I resolved to take no more Inmates. But this Affair having turn'd my Thoughts to Marriage, I look'd round me, and made Overtures of Acquaintance in other Places; but soon found that the Business of a Printer being generally thought a poor one, I was not to expect Money with a Wife unless with such a one, as I should not otherwise think agreable.——In the mean time, that hard-to-be-govern'd Passion of Youth, had hurried me frequently into Intrigues with low Women that fell in my Way, which were attended with some Expence and great Inconvenience, besides a continual Risque to my Health by a Distemper which of all Things I dreaded, tho' by great good Luck I escaped it.——

A friendly Correspondence as Neighbours and old Acquaintances, had continued between me and Mrs. Read's Family, who all had a Regard for me from the time of my first Lodging in their House. I was often invited there and consulted in their Affairs, wherein I sometimes was of Service.——I pity'd poor Miss Read's unfortunate Situation, who was generally dejected, seldom chearful, and avoided Company. I consider'd my Giddiness and Inconstancy when in London as in a great degree the Cause of her Unhappiness; tho' the Mother was good enough to think the Fault more her own than mine, as she had prevented our Marrying before I went thither, and persuaded the other Match in my Absence.——Our mutual Affection was revived, but there were now great Objections to our Union. That Match was indeed look'd upon as invalid, a preceding Wife being said to be living in England; but this could not easily be prov'd, because of the Distance. And tho' there was a Report of his Death, it was not certain. Then tho' it should be true, he had left many Debts which his Successor might be call'd [on] to pay. We ventured however, over all these Difficulties, and I [took] her to Wife Sept. 1. 1730. None of the Inconveniencies happened that we had apprehended, she prov'd a good and faithful Helpmate, assisted me much by attending the Shop, we throve together, and have ever mutually endeavour'd to make each other happy.——Thus I corrected that great *Erratum* as well as I could.

About this Time our Club meeting, not at a Tavern, but in a little Room of Mr. Grace's set apart for that Purpose: a Proposition was made by me that since our Books were often referr'd to in our Disquisitions upon the

Queries, it might be convenient to us to have them all together where we met, that upon Occasion they might be consulted; and by thus clubbing our Books to a common Library, we should, while we lik'd to keep them together, have each of us the Advantage of using the Books of all the other Members, which would be nearly as beneficial as if each owned the whole. It was lik'd and agreed to, and we fill'd one End of the Room with such Books as we could best spare. The Number was not so great as we expected; and tho' they had been of great Use, yet some Inconveniencies occurring for want of due Care of them, the Collection after about a Year was separated, and each took his Books home again.

And now I set on foot my first Project of a public Nature, that for a Subscription Library. I drew up the Proposals, got them put into Form by our great Scrivener Brockden, and by the help of my Friends in the Junto, procur'd Fifty Subscribers of 40s. each to begin with and 10s. a Year for 50 Years, the Term our Company was to continue. We afterwards obtain'd a Charter, the Company being increas'd to 100. This was the Mother of all the North American Subscription Libraries now so numerous. It is become a great thing itself, and continually increasing.——These Libraries have improv'd the general Conversation of the Americans, made the common Tradesmen and Farmers as intelligent as most Gentlemen from other Countries, and perhaps have contributed in some degree to the Stand so generally made throughout the Colonies in Defence of their Privileges.——

Memorandum

Thus far was written with the Intention express'd in the Beginning and therefore contains several little family Anecdotes of no Importance to others. What follows was written many Years after in compliance with the Advice contain'd in these Letters, accordingly intended for the Publick. The Affairs of the Revolution occasion'd the Interruption.

Part Two

Letter from Mr. Abel James, with Notes on my Life, to be here inserted.[1]

My dear and honored Friend.

I have often been desirous of writing to thee, but could not be reconciled to the Thought that the Letter might fall into the Hands of the British, lest some Printer or busy Body should publish some Part of the Contents and give our Friends Pain and myself Censure.

Some Time since there fell into my Hands to my great Joy about 23 Sheets in thy own hand-writing containing all Account of the Parentage and Life of thyself, directed to thy Son ending in the Year 1730 with which there were Notes likewise in thy writing, a Copy of which I inclose in Hopes it may be a means if thou continuedst it up to a later period, that the first and latter part may be put together; and if it is not yet continued, I hope thou wilt not delay it, Life is uncertain as the Preacher tells us, and what will the World say if kind, humane and benevolent Ben Franklin should leave his Friends and the World deprived of so pleasing and profitable a Work, a Work which would be useful and entertaining not only to a few, but to millions.

The Influence Writings under that Class have on the Minds of Youth is very great, and has no where appeared so me so plain as in our public Friends' Journals. It almost insensibly leads the Youth into the Resolution of endeavouring to become as good and as eminent as the journalist. Should thine for Instance when published, and I think it could not fail of it, lead the Youth to equal the Industry and Temperance of thy early Youth, what a Blessing with that Class would such a Work be. I know of no Character living nor many of them put together, who has so much in his Power as Thyself to promote a greater Spirit of Industry and early Attention to Business, Frugality and Temperance with the American Youth. Not that I think the Work would have no other Merit and Use in the World, far from it, but the first is of such vast Importance, that I know nothing that can equal it.

The foregoing letter and the minutes accompanying it being shewn to a friend, I received from him the following:

[1] [Reprinted from *The Papers of Thomas Jefferson*, ed. Julian P. Boyd (Princeton, 1954), 9:483–95, and amended with reference to Temple 1:58–9 (following Lemay and Zall, *Genetic Text* 182–90).]

Letter from Mr. Vaughan to the same purpose.[2]

Paris, January 31, 1783.

My Dearest Sir,

When I had read over your sheets of minutes of the principal incidents of your life, recovered for you by your Quaker acquaintance; I told you I would send you a letter expressing my reasons why I thought it would be useful to complete and publish it as he desired. Various concerns have for some time past prevented this letter being written, and I do not know whether it was worth any expectation: happening to be at leisure however at present, I shall by writing at least interest and instruct myself; but as the terms I am inclined to use may tend to offend a person of your manners, I shall only tell you how I would address any other person, who was as good and as great as yourself, but less diffident. I would say to him, Sir, I solicit the history of your life from the following motives.

Your history is so remarkable, that if you do not give it, somebody else will certainly give it; and perhaps so as nearly to do as much harm, as your own management of the thing might do good.

It will moreover present a table of the internal circumstances of your country, which will very much tend to invite to it settlers of virtuous and manly minds. And considering the eagerness with which such information is sought by them, and the extent of your reputation, I do not know of a more efficacious advertisement than your Biography would give.

All that has happened to you is also connected with the detail of the manners and situation of *a rising* people; and in this respect I do not think that the writings of Caesar and Tacitus can be more interesting to a true judge of human nature and society.

But these, Sir, are small reasons in my opinion, compared with the chance which your life will give for the forming of future great men; and in conjunction with your *Art of Virtue*, (which you design to publish) of improving the features of private character, and consequently of aiding all happiness both public and domestic.

The two works I allude to, Sir, will in particular give a noble rule and example of *self-education*. School and other education constantly proceed upon false principles, and shew a clumsy apparatus pointed at a false mark; but your apparatus is simple, and the mark a true one; and while parents

[2] [Reprinted from Temple 1:59–62.]

and young persons are left destitute of other just means of estimating and becoming prepared for a reasonable course in life, your discovery that the thing is in many a man's private power, will be invaluable!

Influence upon the private character late in life, is not only an influence late in life, but a weak influence. It is in youth that we plant our chief habits and prejudices; it is in youth that we take our party as to profession, pursuits, and matrimony. In youth therefore the turn is given; in youth the education even of the next generation is given; in youth the private and public character is determined; and the term of life extending but from youth to age, life ought to begin well from youth; and more especially *before* we take our party as to our principal objects.

But your Biography will not merely teach self-education, but the education of *a wise man*; and the wisest man will receive lights and improve his progress, by seeing detailed the conduct of another wise man. And why are weaker men to be deprived of such helps, when we see our race has been blundering on in the dark, almost without a guide in this particular, from the farthest trace of time. Shew then, Sir, how much is to be done, *both to sons and fathers*; and invite all wise men to become like yourself; and other men to become wise.

When we see how cruel statesmen and warriors can be to the humble race, and how absurd distinguished men can be to their acquaintance, it will be instructive to observe the instances multiply of pacific acquiescing manners; and to find how compatible it is to be great and *domestic*; enviable and yet *good-humoured*.

The little private incidents which you will also have to relate, will have considerable use, as we want above all things, *rules of prudence in ordinary affairs*; and it will be curious to see how you have acted in these. It will be so far a sort of key to life, and explain many things that all men ought to have once explained to them, to give them a chance of becoming wise by foresight.

The nearest thing to having experience of one's own, is to have other people's affairs brought before us in a shape that is interesting; this is sure to happen from your pen. Your affairs and management will have an air of simplicity or importance that will not fail to strike; and I am convinced you have conducted them with as much originality as if you had been conducting discussions in politics or philosophy; and what more worthy of experiments and system, (its importance and its errors considered) than human life!

Some men have been virtuous blindly, others have speculated fantastically, and others have been shrewd to bad purposes; but you, Sir, I am sure, will give under your hand, nothing but what is at the same moment, wise, practical, and good.

Your account of yourself (for I suppose the parallel I am drawing for Dr. Franklin, will hold not only in point of character but of private history), will shew that you are ashamed of no origin; a thing the more important, as you prove how little necessary all origin is to happiness, virtue, or greatness.

As no end likewise happens without a means, so we shall find, Sir, that even you yourself framed a plan by which you became considerable; but at the same time we may see that though the event is flattering, the means are as simple as wisdom could make them; that is depending upon nature, virtue, thought, and habit.

Another thing demonstrated will be the propriety of every man's waiting for his time for appearing upon the stage of the world. Our sensations being very much fixed to the moment, we are apt to forget that more moments are to follow the first, and consequently that man should arrange his conduct so as to suit the *whole* of a life. Your attribution appears to have been applied to your *life*, and the passing moments of it have been enlivened with content and enjoyment, instead of being tormented with foolish impatience or regrets. Such a conduct is easy for those who make virtue and themselves their standard, and who try to keep themselves in countenance by examples of other truly great men, of whom patience is so often the characteristic.

Your Quaker correspondent, Sir, (for here again I will suppose the subject of my letter resembling Dr. Franklin,) praised your frugality, diligence, and temperance, which he considered as a pattern for all youth: but it is singular that he should have forgotten your modesty, and your disinterestedness, without which you never could have waited for your advancement, or found your situation in the mean time comfortable; which is a strong lesson to shew the poverty of glory, and the importance of regulating our minds.

If this correspondent had known the nature of your reputation as well as I do, he would have said; your former writings and measures would secure attention to your Biography, and Art of Virtue; and your Biography and Art of Virtue, in return, would secure attention to them. This is an advantage attendant upon a various character, and which brings all that belongs to it into greater play; and it is the more useful, as perhaps more persons are at a loss for the *means* of improving their minds and characters, than they are for the time or the inclination to do it.

But there is one concluding reflection, Sir, that will shew the use of your life as a mere piece of biography. This style of writing seems a little gone out of vogue, and yet it is a very useful one; and your specimen of it may be particularly serviceable, as it will make a subject of comparison with the lives of various public cut-throats and intriguers, and with absurd monastic self-tormentors, or vain literary triflers. If it encourages more writings of the same kind with your own, and induces more men to spend lives fit to be written; it will be worth all Plutarch's Lives put together.

But being tired of figuring to myself a character of which every feature suits only one man in the world, without giving him the praise of it; I shall end my letter, my dear Dr. Franklin, with a personal application to your proper self.

I am earnestly desirous then, my dear Sir, that you should let the world into the traits of your genuine character, as civil broils may otherwise tend to disguise or traduce it. Considering your great age, the caution of your character, and your peculiar style of thinking, it is not likely that any one besides yourself can be sufficiently master of the facts of your life, or the intentions of your mind.

Besides all this, the immense revolution of the present period, will necessarily turn our attention towards the author of it; and when virtuous principles have been pretended in it, it will be highly important to shew that such have really influenced; and, as your own character will be the principal one to receive a scrutiny, it is proper (even for its effects upon your vast and rising country, as well as upon England and upon Europe), that it should stand respectable and eternal. For the furtherance of human happiness, I have always maintained that it is necessary to prove that man is not even at present a vicious and detestable animal; and still more to prove that good management may greatly amend him; and it is for much the same reason, that I am anxious to see the opinion established, that there are fair characters existing among the individuals of the race; for the moment that all men, without exception, shall be conceived abandoned, good people will cease efforts deemed to be hopeless, and perhaps think of taking their share in the scramble of life, or at least of making it comfortable principally for themselves.

Take then, my dear Sir, this work most speedily into hand: shew yourself good as you are good, temperate as you are temperate; and above all things, prove yourself as one who from your infancy have loved justice, liberty, and concord, in a way that has made it natural and consistent for you to have acted, as we have seen you act in the last seventeen years of your life. Let Englishmen be made not only to respect, but even to love you. When they think well of individuals in your native country, they will go nearer to thinking well of your country; and when your countrymen see themselves well thought of by Englishmen, they will go nearer to thinking well of England. Extend your views even further; do not stop at those who speak the English tongue, but after having settled so many points in nature and politics, think of bettering the whole race of men.

As I have not read any part of the life in question, but know only the character that lived it, I write somewhat at hazard. I am sure however, that the life, and the treatise I allude to (on the *Art of Virtue*), will necessarily fulfil the chief of my expectations; and still more so if you take up the measure of suiting these performances to the several views above stated. Should they even prove unsuccessful in all that a sanguine admirer of yours hopes from them, you will at least have framed pieces to interest the human mind; and whoever gives a feeling of pleasure that is innocent to man, has added so much to the fair side of a life otherwise too much darkened by anxiety, and too much injured by pain.

In the hope therefore that you will listen to the prayer addressed to you in this letter, I beg to subscribe myself, my dearest Sir, &c. &c.

BENJ. VAUGHAN.

Continuation of the Account of my Life.
Begun at Passy 1784

It is some time since I receiv'd the above Letters, but I have been too busy till now to think of complying with the Request they contain. It might too be much better done if I were at home among my Papers, which would aid my Memory, and help to ascertain Dates. But my Return being uncertain, and having just now a little Leisure, I will endeavour to recollect and write what I can; If I live to get home, it may there be corrected and improv'd.

Not having any Copy here of what is already written, I know not whether an Account is given of the means I used to establish the Philadelphia publick Library, which from a small Beginning is now become so considerable, though I remember to have come down to near the Time of that Transaction, 1730. I will therefore begin here, with an Account of it, which may be struck out if found to have been already given.——

At the time I establish'd my self in Pennsylvania, there was not a good Bookseller's Shop in any of the Colonies to the Southward of Boston. In New-York and Philadelphia the Printers were indeed Stationers, they sold only Paper, &c. Almanacks, Ballads, and a few common School Books. Those who loved Reading were oblig'd to send for their Books from England.——The Members of the Junto had each a few. We had left the Alehouse where we first met, and hired a Room to hold our Club in. I propos'd that we should all of us bring our Books to that Room, where they would not only be ready to consult in our Conferences, but become a common Benefit, each of us being at Liberty to borrow such as he wish'd to read at home. This was accordingly done, and for some time contented us. Finding the Advantage of this little Collection, I propos'd to render the Benefit from Books more common by commencing a Public Subscription Library. I drew a Sketch of the Plan and Rules that would be necessary, and got a skilful Conveyancer Mr. Charles Brockden to put the whole in Form of Articles of Agreement to be subscribed, by which each Subscriber engag'd to pay a certain Sum down for the first Purchase of Books and an annual Contribution for encreasing them. So few were the Readers at that time in Philadelphia, and the Majority of us so poor, that I was not able with great Industry to find more than Fifty Persons, mostly young Tradesmen, willing to pay down for this purpose Forty shillings each, and Ten Shillings per Annum. On this little Fund we began. The Books were imported. The Library was open one Day in the Week for lending them to the Subscribers, on their Promisory Notes to pay Double the Value if not duly returned. The Institution soon manifested its Utility, was imitated by other Towns and in other Provinces, the Librarys were augmented by Donations, Reading became fashionable, and our People having no publick Amusements to divert their Attention from Study became better acquainted with Books, and in a few Years were observ'd by Strangers to be better instructed and more intelligent than People of the same Rank generally are in other Countries.——

When we were about to sign the above-mentioned Articles, which were to be binding on us, our Heirs, &c. for fifty Years, Mr. Brockden, the Scrivener, said to us, "You are young Men, but it is scarce probable that any of you will live to see the Expiration of the Term fix'd in this Instrument." A Number of us, however, are yet living: But the Instrument was after a few Years rendred null by a Charter that incorporated and gave Perpetuity to the Company.——

The Objections, and Reluctances I met with in Soliciting the Subscriptions, made me soon feel the Impropriety of presenting one's self as the Proposer of any useful Project that might be suppos'd to raise one's Reputation in the smallest degree above that of one's Neighbours, when one has need of their Assistance to accomplish that Project. I therefore put my self as much as I could out of sight, and stated it as a Scheme of *a Number of Friends*, who had requested me to go about and propose it to such as they thought Lovers of Reading. In this way my Affair went on more smoothly, and I ever after practis'd it on such Occasions; and from my frequent Successes, can heartily recommend it. The present little Sacrifice of your Vanity will afterwards be amply repaid. If it remains a while uncertain to whom the Merit belongs, some one more vain than yourself will be encourag'd to claim it, and then even Envy will be dispos'd to do you justice, by plucking those assum'd Feathers, and restoring them to their right Owner.

This Library afforded me the Means of Improvement by constant Study, for which I set apart an Hour or two each Day; and thus repair'd in some Degree the Loss of the Learned Education my Father once intended for me. Reading was the only Amusement I allow'd my self. I spent no time in Taverns, Games, or Frolicks of any kind. And my Industry in my Business continu'd as indefatigable as it was necessary. I was in debt for my Printing-house, I had a young Family coming on to be educated, and I had to contend with for Business two Printers who were establish'd in the Place before me. My Circumstances however grew daily easier: my original Habits of Frugality continuing. And My Father having among his Instructions to me when a Boy, frequently repeated a Proverb of Solomon, "*Seest thou a Man diligent in his Calling, he shall stand before Kings, he shall not stand before mean Men.*"[3] I from thence consider'd Industry as a

[3] [Proverbs 22:29.]

Means of obtaining Wealth and Distinction, which encourag'd me; tho' I did not think that I should ever literally stand before Kings, which however has since happened:—— for I have stood before five, and even had the honour of sitting down with one, the King of Denmark, to Dinner.

We have an English Proverb that says,

He that would thrive
Must ask his Wife;

it was lucky for me that I had one as much dispos'd to Industry and Frugality as my self. She assisted me chearfully in my Business, folding and stitching Pamphlets, tending Shop, purchasing old Linen Rags for the Paper-makers, &c &c. We kept no idle Servants, our Table was plain and simple, our Furniture of the cheapest. For instance my Breakfast was a long time Bread and Milk, (no Tea,) and I ate it out of a twopenny earthen Porringer with a Pewter Spoon. But mark how Luxury will enter Families, and make a Progress, in Spite of Principle. Being Call'd one Morning to Breakfast, I found it in a China Bowl with a Spoon of Silver. They had been bought for me without my Knowledge by my Wife, and had cost her the enormous Sum of three and twenty Shillings, for which she had no other Excuse or Apology to make, but that she thought *her* Husband deserv'd a Silver Spoon and China Bowl as well as any of his Neighbours. This was the first Appearance of Plate and China in our House, which afterwards in a Course of Years as our Wealth encreas'd, augmented gradually to several Hundred Pounds in Value.——

I had been religiously educated as a Presbyterian; and tho' some of the Dogmas of that Persuasion, such as the Eternal Decrees of God, Election, Reprobation, &c. appear'd to me unintelligible, others doubtful, and I early absented myself from the Public Assemblies of the Sect, Sunday being my Studying-Day, I never was without some religious Principles; I never doubted, for instance, the Existance of the Deity, that he made the World, and govern'd it by his Providence; that the most acceptable Service of God was the doing Good to Man; that our Souls are immortal; and that all Crime will be punished and Virtue rewarded either here or hereafter; these I esteem'd the Essentials of every Religion, and being to be found in all the Religions we had in our Country I respected them all, tho' with different degrees of Respect as I found them more or less mix'd with other Articles which without any Tendency to inspire, promote or confirm Morality, serv'd principally to divide us and make us unfriendly to one another.——This Respect to all, with an Opinion that the worst had some good Effects, induc'd me to avoid all Discourse that might tend to lessen the good Opinion another might have of his own Religion; and as our Province increas'd in People and new Places of worship were continually wanted, and generally erected by voluntary Contribution, my Mite for such purpose, whatever might be the Sect, was never refused.——

Tho' I seldom attended any Public Worship, I had still an Opinion of its Propriety, and of its Utility when rightly conducted, and I regularly paid my annual Subscription for the Support of the only Presbyterian Minister or Meeting we had in Philadelphia. He us'd to visit me sometimes as a Friend, and admonish me to attend his Administrations, and I was now and then prevail'd on to do so, once for five Sundays successively. Had he been, *in my Opinion*, a good Preacher perhaps I might have continued, notwithstanding the occasion I had for the Sunday's Leisure in my Course of Study: But his Discourses were chiefly either polemic Arguments, or Explications of the peculiar Doctrines of our Sect, and were all to me very dry, uninteresting and unedifying, since not a single moral Principle was inculcated or enforc'd, their Aim seeming to be rather to make us Presbyterians than good Citizens. At length he took for his Text that Verse of the 4th Chapter of Philippians, *Finally, Brethren, Whatsoever Things are true, honest, just, pure, lovely, or of good report, if there be any virtue, or any praise, think on these Things;*[4] and I imagin'd in a Sermon on such a Text, we could not miss of having some Morality: But he confin'd himself to five Points only as meant by the Apostle, viz. 1. Keeping holy the Sabbath Day. 2. Being diligent in Reading the Holy Scriptures. 3. Attending duly the Publick Worship. 4. Partaking of the Sacrament. 5. Paying a due Respect to God's Ministers.——These might be all good Things, but as they were not the kind of good Things that I expected from that Text, I despaired of ever meeting with them from any other, was disgusted, and attended his Preaching no more.——I had some Years before compos'd a little Liturgy or Form of Prayer for my own private Use, viz, in 1728. entitled,

[4] [Phil. 4:8.]

Articles of Belief and Acts of Religion. I return'd to the Use of this, and went no more to the public Assemblies.——My Conduct might be blameable, but I leave it without attempting farther to excuse it, my present purpose being to relate Facts, and not to make Apologies for them.——

It was about this time that I conceiv'd the bold and arduous Project of arriving at moral Perfection. I wish'd to live without committing any Fault at any time; I would conquer all that either Natural Inclination, Custom, or Company might lead me into. As I knew, or thought I knew, what was right and wrong, I did not see why I might not *always* do the one and avoid the other. But I soon found I had undertaken a Task of more Difficulty than I had imagined: While my Care was employ'd in guarding against one Fault, I was often surpriz'd by another. Habit took the Advantage of Inattention. Inclination was sometimes too strong for Reason. I concluded at length, that the mere speculative Conviction that it was our Interest to be compleatly virtuous, was not sufficient to prevent our Slipping, and that the contrary Habits must be broken and good Ones acquired and established, before we can have any Dependance on a steady uniform Rectitude of Conduct. For this purpose I therefore contriv'd the following Method.——

In the various Enumerations of the moral Virtues I had met with in my Reading, I found the Catalogue more or less numerous, as different Writers included more or fewer Ideas under the same Name. Temperance, for Example, was by some confin'd to Eating and Drinking, while by others it was extended to mean the moderating every other Pleasure, Appetite, Inclination or Passion, bodily or mental, even to our Avarice and Ambition. I propos'd to myself, for the sake of Clearness, to use rather more Names with fewer Ideas annex'd to each, than a few Names with more Ideas; and I included under Thirteen Names of Virtues all that at that time occurr'd to me as necessary or desirable, and annex'd to each a short Precept, which fully express'd the Extent I gave to its Meaning.——

These Names of Virtues with their Precepts were

1. Temperance.

Eat not to Dulness.

Drink not to Elevation.

2. Silence.

Speak not but what may benefit others or your self. Avoid trifling Conversation.

3. Order.

Let all your Things have their Places. Let each Part of your Business have its Time.

4. Resolution.

Resolve to perform what you ought. Perform without fail what you resolve.

5. Frugality.

Make no Expence but to do good to others or yourself: i.e. Waste nothing.

6. Industry.

Lose no Time.——Be always employ'd in something useful.——Cut off all unnecessary Actions.——

7. Sincerity.

Use no hurtful Deceit.

Think innocently and justly; and, if you speak, speak accordingly.

8. Justice.

Wrong none, by doing Injuries or omitting the Benefits that are your Duty.

9. Moderation.

Avoid Extreams. Forbear resenting Injuries so much as you think they deserve.

10. Cleanliness

Tolerate no Uncleanness in Body, Cloaths or Habitation.——

11. Tranquility

Be not disturbed at Trifles, or at Accidents common or unavoidable.

12. Chastity.

Rarely use Venery but for Health or Offspring; Never to Dulness, Weakness, or the Injury of your own or another's Peace or Reputation.——

13. Humility.

Imitate Jesus and Socrates.——

My intention being to acquire the *Habitude* of all these Virtues, I judg'd it would be well not to distract my Attention by attempting the whole at once, but to fix it on one of them at a time, and when I should be Master of that, then to proceed to another, and so on till I should have gone thro' the thirteen. And as the previous Acquisition of some might facilitate the Acquisition of certain others, I arrang'd them with that View as they stand above. *Temperance* first, as it tends to procure that Coolness and Clearness of Head, which is so necessary where constant Vigilance was to be kept up, and Guard maintained, against the unremitting Attraction of ancient Habits, and the Force of perpetual Temptations. This being acquir'd and establish'd, *Silence* would be more easy, and my Desire being to gain Knowledge at the same time that I improv'd in Virtue, and considering that in Conversation it was obtain'd rather by the Use of the Ears than of the Tongue, and therefore wishing to break a Habit I was getting into of Prattling, Punning and Joking, which only made me acceptable to trifling Company, I gave *Silence* the second Place. This, and the next, *Order*, I expected would allow me more Time for attending to my Project and my Studies; RESOLUTION once become habitual, would keep me firm in my Endeavours to obtain all the subsequent Virtues; *Frugality* and *Industry*, by freeing me from my remaining Debt, and producing Affluence and Independance would make more easy the Practice of *Sincerity* and *Justice*, &c. &c. Conceiving then that agreeable to the Advice of Pythagoras in his Golden Verses,[5] daily Examination would be necessary, I contriv'd the following Method for conducting that Examination.

I made a little Book in which I allotted a Page for each of the Virtues. I rul'd each Page with red Ink so as to have seven Columns, one for each Day of the Week, marking each Column with a Letter for the Day. I cross'd these Columns with thirteen red Lines, marking the Beginning of each Line with the first Letter of one of the Virtues, on which Line and in its proper Column I might mark by a little black Spot every Fault I found upon Examination, to have been committed respecting that Virtue upon that Day.

[5] [*Let not the stealing God of Sleep surprize,*
Nor creep in Slumbers on thy weary Eyes,
Ere ev'ry Action of the former Day,
Strictly thou dost, and righteously survey.
With Rev'rence at thy own Tribunal stand,
And answer justly to thy own Demand.
Where have I been? In what have I transgrest?
What Good or Ill has this Day's Life exprest?
Where have I fail'd in what I ought to do?
In what to GOD, to Man, or to myself I owe?
Inquire severe whate'er from first to last,
From Morning's Dawn till Ev'nings Gloom has past.
If Evil were thy Deeds, repenting mourn,
And let thy Soul with strong Remorse be torn:
If Good, the Good with Peace of Mind repay,
And to thy secret Self with Pleasure say,
Rejoice, my Heart, for all went well to Day.
Trans. Nicholas Rowe, and printed by Franklin in "Letter from Father Abraham," *The New-England Magazine* (August 1758), 22.]

Form of the Pages

	Temperance.						
	Eat not to Dulness. Drink not to Elevation.						
	S	M	T	W	T	F	S
T							
S	* *	*		*		*	
O	*	*	*		*	*	*
R			*			*	
F		*			*		
I			*				
S							
J							
M							
Cl.							
T							
Ch.							
H							

I determined to give a Week's strict Attention to each of the Virtues successively. Thus in the first Week my great Guard was to avoid every the least Offence against Temperance, leaving the other Virtues to their ordinary Chance, only marking every Evening the Faults of the Day. Thus if in the first Week I could keep my first Line marked T clear of Spots, I suppos'd the Habit of that Virtue so much strengthen'd and its opposite weaken'd, that I might venture extending my Attention to include the next, and for the following Week keep both Lines clear of Spots. Proceeding thus to the last, I could go thro' a Course compleat in Thirteen Weeks, and four Courses in a Year.——And like him who having a Garden to weed, does not attempt to eradicate all the bad Herbs at once, which would exceed his Reach and his Strength, but works on one of the Beds at a time, and having accomplish'd the first proceeds to a second; so I should have, (I hoped) the encouraging Pleasure of seeing on my Pages the Progress I made in Virtue, by clearing successively my

Lines of their Spots, till in the End by a Number of Courses, I should be happy in viewing a clean Book after a thirteen Weeks daily Examination.

This my little Book had for its Motto these Lines from *Addison's Cato*;

> *Here will I hold: If there is a Pow'r above us,*
> *(And that there is, all Nature cries aloud*
> *Thro' all her Works) he must delight in Virtue,*
> *And that which he delights in must be happy.*[6]

Another from Cicero.

> *O Vitae Philosophia Dux! O Virtutum indagatrix, expultrixque vitiorum! Unus dies bene, & ex preceptis tuis actus, peccanti immortalitati est anteponendus.*[7]

Another from the Proverbs of Solomon speaking of Wisdom or Virtue;

> Length of Days is in her right hand, and in her Left Hand Riches and Honours; Her Ways are Ways of Pleasantness, and all her Paths are Peace. III, 16, 17.

And conceiving God to be the Fountain of Wisdom, I thought it right and necessary to solicit his Assistance for obtaining it; to this End I form'd the following little Prayer, which was prefix'd to my Tables of Examination; for daily Use.

> *O Powerful Goodness! bountiful Father! merciful Guide! Increase in me that Wisdom which discovers my truest Interests; Strengthen my Resolutions to perform what that Wisdom dictates. Accept my kind Offices to thy other Children, as the only Return in my Power for thy continual Favours to me.*

I us'd also sometimes a little Prayer which I took from *Thomson's* Poems. viz

> *Father of Light and Life, thou Good supreme,*
> *O teach me what is good, teach me thy self!*
> *Save me from Folly, Vanity and Vice,*
> *From every low Pursuit, and fill my Soul*
> *With Knowledge, conscious Peace, and Virtue pure,*
> *Sacred, substantial, neverfading Bliss!*[8]

[6] [Joseph Addison, *Cato, A Tragedy* (1713), 5.1.15–18.]

[7] [*Tusculan Disputations* 5.2.5: "Oh philosophy, guide of life! Oh searcher out of virtues and expeller of vices! . . . One day lived well and according to thy precepts is to be preferred to an eternity of sin."]

[8] [James Thomson, *The Seasons* (1726), "Winter," lines 218–23.]

The Precept of *Order* requiring that *every Part of my Business should have its allotted Time*, one Page in my little Book contain'd the following Scheme of Employment for the Twenty-four Hours of a natural Day,

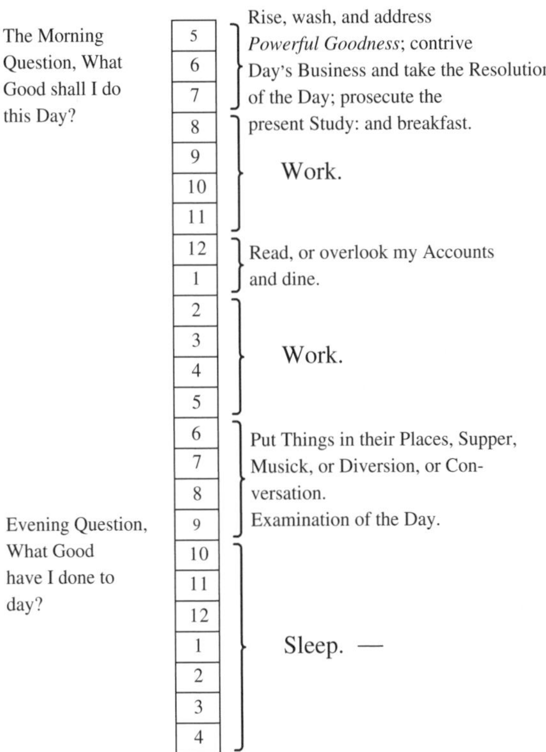

I enter'd upon the Execution of this Plan for Self Examination, and continu'd it with occasional Intermissions for some time. I was surpriz'd to find myself so much fuller of Faults than I had imagined, but I had the Satisfaction of seeing them diminish. To avoid the Trouble of renewing now and then my little Book, which by scraping out the Marks on the Paper of old Faults to make room for new Ones in a new Course, became full of Holes: I transferr'd my Tables and Precepts to the Ivory Leaves of a Memorandum Book, on which the Lines were drawn with red Ink that made a durable Stain, and on those Lines I mark'd my Faults with a black Lead Pencil, which Marks I could easily wipe out with a wet Sponge. After a while I went thro' one Course only in a Year, and afterwards only one in several Years; till at length I omitted them entirely, being employ'd in Voyages and Business abroad with a Multiplicity of Affairs, that interfered. But I always carried my little Book with me. My Scheme of ORDER, gave me the most Trouble, and I found, that tho' it might be practicable where a Man's Business was such as to leave him the Disposition of his Time, that of a Journey-man Printer for instance, it was not possible to be exactly observ'd by a Master, who must mix with the World, and often receive People of Business at their own Hours.——*Order* too, with regard to Places for Things, Papers, &c. I found extreamly difficult to acquire. I had not been early accustomed to it, and having an exceeding good Memory, I was not so sensible of the Inconvenience attending Want of Method. This Article therefore cost me so much painful Attention and my Faults in it vex'd me so much, and I made so little Progress in Amendment, and had such frequent Relapses, that I was almost ready to give up the Attempt, and content my self with a faulty Character in that respect. Like the Man who in buying an Ax of a Smith my Neighbour, desired to have the whole of its Surface as bright as the Edge; the Smith consented to grind it bright for him if he would turn the Wheel. He turn'd while the Smith press'd the broad Face of the Ax hard and heavily on the Stone, which made the Turning of it very fatiguing. The Man came every now and then from the Wheel to see how the Work went on; and at length would take his Ax as it was without farther Grinding. No, says the Smith, Turn on, turn on; we shall have it bright by and by; as yet 'tis only speckled. Yes, says the Man; but——*I think I like a speckled Ax best*.——And I believe this may have been the Case with many who having for want of some such Means as I employ'd found the Difficulty of obtaining good, and breaking bad Habits, in other Points of Vice and Virtue, have given up the Struggle, and concluded that *a speckled Ax was best*. For something that pretended to be Reason was every now and then suggesting to me, that such extream Nicety as I exacted of my self might be a kind of Foppery in Morals, which if it were known would make me ridiculous; that a perfect Character might be attended with the Inconvenience of being envied and hated; and that a benevolent Man should allow a few Faults in himself, to keep his Friends in Countenance. In Truth I found myself incorrigible with respect to *Order*; and now I am grown old, and my Memory bad, I feel very sensibly the want of it. But on the whole, tho' I never arrived at the Perfection I had been so ambitious of obtaining, but fell far short of it, yet I was by the Endeavour a better and a happier Man than I otherwise should have been, if I had not attempted it; As those who aim at perfect Writing by imitating the engraved Copies, tho' they never reach the wish'd for Excellence of those Copies, their Hand is mended by the Endeavour, and is tolerable while it continues fair and legible.——

And it may be well my Posterity should be informed, that to this little Artifice, with the Blessing of God, their Ancestor ow'd the constant Felicity of his Life down to his 79th Year in which this is written. What Reverses may attend the Remainder is in the Hand of Providence: But if they arrive the Reflection on past Happiness enjoy'd ought to help his Bearing them with more Resignation. To *Temperance* he ascribes his long-continued Health, and what is still left to him of a good Constitution. To *Industry* and *Frugality* the early Easiness of his Circumstances, and Acquisition of his Fortune, with all that Knowledge which enabled him to be an useful Citizen, and obtain'd for him some degree of Reputation among the Learned. To *Sincerity* and *Justice* the Confidence of his Country, and the honourable Employs it conferr'd upon him. And to the joint Influence of the whole Mass of the Virtues, even in the imperfect State he was able to acquire them, all that Evenness of Temper, and that Chearfulness in Conversation which makes his Company still sought for, and agreable even to his younger Acquaintance. I hope therefore that some of my Descendants may follow the Example and reap the Benefit.——

It will be remark'd that, tho' my Scheme was not wholly without Religion there was in it no Mark of any of the distinguishing Tenets of any particular Sect.——I had purposely avoided them; for being fully persuaded of the Utility and Excellency of my Method, and that it might be serviceable to People in all Religions, and intending some time or other to publish it, I would not have any thing in it that should prejudice any one of any Sect against it. I purposed writing a little Comment on each Virtue, in which I would have shown the Advantages of possessing it, and the Mischiefs attending its opposite Vice;[9] and I should have called my Book the ART of *VIRTUE*, because it would have shown the *Means and Manner* of obtaining Virtue; which would have distinguish'd it from the mere Exhortation to be good, that does not instruct and indicate the Means; but is like the Apostle's Man of verbal Charity, who only, without showing to the Naked and the Hungry *how* or where they might get Cloaths or Victuals, exhorted them to be fed and clothed. *James* II, 15, 16.——

But it so happened that my Intention of writing and publishing this Comment was never fulfilled. I did indeed, from time to time put down

[9] Nothing so likely to make a Man's fortune as Virtue.——[marginal note]

short Hints of the Sentiments, Reasonings, &c. to be made use of in it; some of which I have still by me: But the necessary close Attention to private Business in the earlier part of Life, and public Business since, have occasioned my postponing it. For it being connected in my Mind with a *great and extensive Project* that required the whole Man to execute, and which an unforeseen Succession of Employs prevented my attending to, it has hitherto remain'd unfinish'd.——

In this Piece it was my Design to explain and enforce this Doctrine, that vicious Actions are not hurtful because they are forbidden, but forbidden because they are hurtful, the Nature of Man alone consider'd: That it was therefore every ones Interest to be virtuous, who wish'd to be happy even in this World. And I should from this Circumstance, there being always in the World a Number of rich Merchants, Nobility, States and Princes, who have need of honest Instruments for the Management of their Affairs, and such being so rare, have endeavoured to convince young Persons, that no Qualities were so likely to make a poor Man's Fortune as those of Probity and Integrity.

My List of Virtues contain'd at first but twelve: But a Quaker Friend having kindly inform'd me that I was generally thought proud; that my Pride show'd itself frequently in Conversation; that I was not content with being in the right when discussing any Point, but was overbearing and rather insolent; of which he convinc'd me by mentioning several Instances;——I determined endeavouring to cure myself if I could of this Vice or Folly among the rest, and I added *Humility* to my List, giving an extensive Meaning to the Word.——I cannot boast of much Success in acquiring the *Reality* of this Virtue; but I had a good deal with regard to the *Appearance* of it.——I made it a Rule to forbear all direct Contradiction to the Sentiments of others, and all positive Assertion of my own. I even forbid myself agreable to the old Laws of our Junto, the Use of every Word or Expression in the Language that imported a fix'd Opinion; such as *certainly*, *undoubtedly*, &c. and I adopted instead of them, *I conceive, I apprehend*, or *I imagine* a thing to be so or so, or it so appears to me at present.——When another asserted something that I thought an Error, I deny'd my self the Pleasure of contradicting him abruptly, and of showing immediately some Absurdity in his Proposition; and in answering I began by observing that in certain Cases or Circumstances his Opinion would be right, but that in the present case there *appear'd* or *seem'd* to me some Difference, &c. I soon found the Advantage of this Change in my Manners. The Conversations I engag'd in went on more pleasantly. The modest way in which I propos'd my Opinions, procur'd them a readier Reception and less Contradiction; I had less Mortification when I was found to be in the wrong, and I more easily prevail'd with others to give up their Mistakes and join with me when I happen'd to be in the right. And this Mode, which I at first put on, with some violence to natural Inclination, became at length so easy and so habitual to me, that perhaps for these Fifty Years past no one has ever heard a dogmatical Expression escape me. And to this Habit (after my Character of Integrity) I think it principally owing, that I had early so much Weight with my Fellow Citizens, when I proposed new Institutions, or Alterations in the old; and so much Influence in public Councils when I became a Member. For I was but a bad Speaker, never eloquent, subject to much Hesitation in my choice of Words, hardly correct in Language, and yet I generally carried my Points.——

In reality there is perhaps no one of our natural Passions so hard to subdue as *Pride*. Disguise it, struggle with it, beat it down, stifle it, mortify it as much as one pleases, it is still alive, and will every now and then peep out and show itself. You will see it perhaps often in this History. For even if I could conceive that I had compleatly overcome it, I should probably be proud of my Humility.——

Thus far written at Passy 1784

Part Three

I am now about to write at home, August 1788.——but cannot have the help expected from my Papers, many of them being lost in the War. I have however found the following.

Having mentioned *a great and extensive Project* which I had conceiv'd, it seems proper that some Account should be here given of that Project and its Object. Its first Rise in my Mind appears in the following little Paper, accidentally preserv'd, viz.

OBSERVATIONS on my Reading History in Library, May 9. 1731.

"That the great Affairs of the World, the Wars, Revolutions, &c. are carried on and effected by Parties.——

"That the View of these Parties is their present general Interest, or what they take to be such.——

"That the different Views of these different Parties, occasion all Confusion.

"That while a Party is carrying on a general Design, each Man has his particular private Interest in View.

"That as soon as a Party has gain'd its general Point, each Member becomes intent upon his particular Interest, which thwarting others, breaks that Party into Divisions, and occasions more Confusion.

"That few in Public Affairs act from a meer View of the Good of their Country, whatever they may pretend; and tho' their Actings bring real Good to their Country, yet Men primarily consider'd that their own and their Country's Interest was united, and did not act from a Principle of Benevolence.

"That fewer still in public Affairs act with a View to the Good of Mankind.

"There seems to me at present to be great Occasion for raising an united Party for Virtue, by forming the Virtuous and good Men of all Nations into a regular Body, to be govern'd by suitable good and wise Rules, which good and wise Men may probably be more unanimous in their Obedience to, than common People are to common Laws.

"I at present think, that whoever attempts this aright, and is well qualified, cannot fail of pleasing God, and of meeting with Success.——"

B F.——

Revolving this Project in my Mind, as to be undertaken hereafter when my Circumstances should afford me the necessary Leisure, I put down from time to time on Pieces of Paper such Thoughts as occur'd to me respecting it. Most of these are lost; but I find one purporting to be the Substance of an intended Creed, containing as I thought the Essentials of every known Religion, and being free of every thing that might shock the Professors of any Religion. It is express'd in these Words. viz.

> "That there is one God who made all things.
> "That he governs the World by his Providence.——
> "That he ought to be worshipped by Adoration, Prayer and Thanksgiving.
> "But that the most acceptable Service of God is doing Good to Man.
> "That the Soul is immortal.
> "And that God will certainly reward Virtue and punish Vice either here or hereafter."——

My Ideas at that time were, that the Sect should be begun and spread at first among young and single Men only; that each Person to be initiated should not only declare his Assent to such Creed, but should have exercis'd himself with the Thirteen Weeks Examination and Practice of the Virtues as in the before-mention'd Model; that the Existence of such a Society should be kept a Secret till it was become considerable, to prevent Solicitations for the Admission of improper Persons; but that the Members should each of them search among his Acquaintance for ingenuous well-disposed Youths, to whom with prudent Caution the Scheme should be gradually communicated: That the Members should engage to afford their Advice Assistance and Support to each other in promoting one another's Interest Business and Advancement in Life: That for Distinction we should be call'd the Society of the *Free and Easy*; Free, as being by the general Practice and Habit of the Virtues, free from the Dominion of Vice, and particularly by the Practice of Industry and Frugality, free from Debt, which exposes a Man to Confinement and a Species of Slavery to his Creditors. This is as much as I can now recollect of the Project, except that I communicated it in part to two young Men, who adopted it with some Enthusiasm. But my then narrow Circumstances, and the Necessity I was under of sticking close to my Business, occasion'd my Postponing the farther Prosecution of it at that time, and my multifarious Occupations public and private induc'd me to continue postponing, so that it has been omitted till I have no longer Strength or Activity left sufficient for such an Enterprize: Tho' I am still of Opinion that it was a practicable Scheme, and might have been very useful, by forming a great Number of good Citizens: And I was not discourag'd by the seeming Magnitude of the Undertaking, as I have always thought that one Man of tolerable Abilities may work great Changes, and accomplish great Affairs among Mankind, if he first forms a good Plan, and, cutting off all Amusements or other Employments that would divert his Attention, makes the Execution of that same Plan his sole Study and Business.——

In 1732 I first published my Almanack, under the Name of *Richard Saunders*; it was continu'd by me about 25 Years, commonly call'd *Poor Richard's* Almanack. I endeavour'd to make it both entertaining and useful, and it accordingly came to be in such Demand that I reap'd considerable Profit from it, vending annually near ten Thousand. And observing that it was generally read, scarce any Neighbourhood in the Province being without it, I consider'd it as a proper Vehicle for conveying Instruction among the common People, who bought scarce any other Books. I therefore filled all the little Spaces that occur'd between the Remarkable Days in the Calendar, with Proverbial Sentences, chiefly such as inculcated Industry and Frugality, as the Means of procuring Wealth and thereby securing Virtue, it being more difficult for a Man in Want to act always honestly, as (to use here one of those Proverbs) *it is hard* for *an empty Sack to stand upright*. These Proverbs, which contained the Wisdom of many Ages and Nations, I assembled and form'd into a connected Discourse prefix'd to the Almanack of 1757, as the Harangue of a wise old Man to the People attending an Auction. The bringing all these scatter'd Counsels thus into a Focus, enabled them to make greater Impression. The Piece being universally approved was copied in all the Newspapers of the Continent, reprinted in Britain on a Broadside to be stuck up in Houses, two Translations were made of it in French, and great Numbers bought by the Clergy and Gentry to distribute gratis among their poor Parishioners and Tenants. In Pennsylvania, as it discouraged useless Expence in foreign Superfluities, some thought it had its share of Influence in producing that growing Plenty of Money which was observable for several Years after its Publication.——

I consider'd my Newspaper also as another Means of communicating Instruction, and in that View frequently reprinted in it Extracts from the Spectator and other moral Writers, and sometimes publish'd little Pieces of my own which had been first compos'd for Reading in our Junto. Of these are a Socratic Dialogue tending to prove, that, whatever might be his Parts and Abilities, a vicious Man could not properly be called a Man of Sense. And a Discourse on Self denial, showing that Virtue was not Secure, till its Practice became a Habitude, and was free from the Opposition of contrary Inclinations.——These may be found in the Papers about the beginning of 1735.——In the Conduct of my Newspaper I carefully excluded all Libelling and Personal Abuse, which is of late Years become so disgraceful to our Country. Whenever I was solicited to insert any thing of that kind, and the Writers pleaded as they generally did, the Liberty of the Press, and that a Newspaper was like a Stage Coach in which any one who would pay had a Right to a Place, my Answer was, that I would print the Piece separately if desired, and the Author might have as many Copies as he pleased to distribute himself, but that I would not take upon me to spread his Detraction, and that having contracted with my Subscribers to furnish them with what might be either useful or entertaining, I could not fill their Papers with private Altercation in which they had no Concern without doing them manifest Injustice. Now many of our Printers make no scruple of gratifying the Malice of Individuals by false Accusations of the fairest Characters among ourselves, augmenting Animosity even to the producing of Duels, and are moreover so indiscreet as to print scurrilous Reflections on the Government of neighbouring States, and even on the Conduct of our best national Allies, which may be attended with the most pernicious Consequences.——These Things I mention as a Caution to young Printers, and that they may be encouraged not to pollute their Presses and disgrace their Profession by such infamous Practices, but refuse steadily; as they may see by my Example, that such a Course of Conduct will not on the whole be injurious to their Interests.——

In 1733, I sent one of my Journeymen to Charleston South Carolina where a Printer was wanting. I furnish'd him with a Press and Letters, on an Agreement of Partnership, by which I was to receive One Third of the Profits of the Business, paying One Third of the Expence. He was a Man of Learning and honest, but ignorant in Matters of Account; and tho' he sometimes made me Remittances, I could get no Account from him, nor any satisfactory State of our Partnership while he lived. On his Decease, the Business was continued by his Widow, who being born and bred in Holland, where as I have been inform'd the Knowledge of Accompts makes a Part of Female Education, she not only sent me as clear a State as she could find of the Transactions past, but continued to account with the greatest Regularity and Exactitude every Quarter afterwards; and manag'd the Business with such Success that she not only brought up reputably a Family of Children, but at the Expiration of the Term was able to purchase of me the Printing-House and establish her Son in it. I mention this Affair chiefly for the Sake of recommending that Branch of Education for our young Females, as likely to be of more Use to them and their Children in Case of Widowhood than either Music or Dancing, by preserving them from Losses by Imposition of crafty Men, and enabling them to continue perhaps a profitable mercantile House with establish'd Correspondence till a Son is grown up fit to undertake and go on with It, to the lasting Advantage and enriching of the Family.——

About the Year 1734. there arrived among us from Ireland, a young Presbyterian Preacher named Hemphill, who delivered with a good Voice, and apparently extempore, most excellent Discourses, which drew together considerable Numbers of different Persuasions, who join'd in admiring them. Among the rest I became one of his constant Hearers, his Sermons pleasing me as they had little of the dogmatical kind, but inculcated strongly the Practice of Virtue, or what in the religious Stile are called Good Works. Those however, of our Congregation, who considered themselves as orthodox Presbyterians, disapprov'd his Doctrine, and were join'd by most of the old Clergy, who arraign'd him of Heterodoxy before the Synod, in order to have him silenc'd. I became his zealous Partisan, and contributed all I could to raise a Party in his Favour; and we combated for him a while with some Hopes of Success. There was much Scribbling pro and con upon the Occasion; and finding that tho' an elegant Preacher he was but a poor Writer, I lent him my Pen and wrote for him two or three Pamphlets, and one Piece in the Gazette of April 1735. Those Pamphlets, as is generally the Case with controversial Writings, tho' eagerly read at the time, were soon out of Vogue, and I question whether a single Copy of them now exists. During the Contest an unlucky Occurrence hurt his Cause exceedingly. One of our Adversaries having heard him preach a Sermon that was much admired, thought he had somewhere read that Sermon before, or at least a part of it. On Search he found that Part quoted at length in one of the British Reviews, from a Discourse of Dr. Forster's. This Detection gave many of our Party Disgust, who accordingly abandoned his Cause, and occasion'd our more speedy Discomfiture in the Synod. I stuck by him however, as I rather approv'd his giving us good Sermons compos'd by others, than bad ones of his own Manufacture; tho' the latter was the Practice of our common Teachers. He afterwards acknowledg'd to me that none of those he preach'd were his own; adding that his Memory was such as enabled him to retain and repeat any Sermon after one Reading only——On our Defeat he left us, in search elsewhere of better Fortune, and I quitted the Congregation, never joining it after, tho' I continu'd many Years my Subscription for the Support of its Ministers.——

I had begun in 1733 to study Languages. I soon made myself so much a Master of the French as to be able to read the Books with Ease. I then undertook the Italian. An Acquaintance who was also learning it, us'd often to tempt me to play Chess with him. Finding this took up too much of the Time I had to spare for Study, I at length refus'd to play any more, unless on this Condition, that the Victor in every Game, should have a Right to impose a Task, either in Parts of the Grammar to be got by heart, or in Translation, &c. which Tasks the Vanquish'd was to perform upon Honour before our next Meeting. As we play'd pretty equally we thus beat one another into that Language.——I afterwards with a little Pains-taking acquir'd as much of the Spanish as to read their Books also. I have already mention'd that I had only one Years Instruction in a Latin School, and that when very young, after which I neglected that Language entirely.——But when I had attained an Acquaintance with the French, Italian and Spanish, I was surpriz'd to find, on looking over a Latin Testament, that I understood so much more of that Language than I had imagined; which encouraged me to apply my self again to the Study of it, and I met with the more Success, as those preceding Languages had greatly smooth'd my Way. From these Circumstances I have thought, that there is some Inconsistency in our common Mode of Teaching Languages. We are told that it is proper to begin first with the Latin, and having acquir'd that it will be more easy to attain those modern Languages which are deriv'd from it; and yet we do not begin with the Greek in order more easily to acquire the Latin. It is true, that if you can clamber and get to the Top of a Stair-Case without using the Steps, you will more easily gain them in descending: but certainly if you begin with the lowest you will with more Ease ascend to the Top. And I would therefore offer it to the Consideration of those who superintend the Educating of our Youth, whether, since many of those who begin with the Latin, quit the same after spending some Years, without having made any great Proficiency, and what they have learnt becomes almost useless, so that their time has been lost, it would not have been better to have begun them with the French, proceeding to the Italian &c. for tho' after spending the same time they should quit the

Study of Languages, and never arrive at the Latin, they would however have acquir'd another Tongue or two that being in modern Use might be serviceable to them in common Life.

After ten Years Absence from Boston, and having become more easy in my Circumstances, I made a Journey thither to visit my Relations, which I could not sooner well afford. In returning I call'd at Newport, to see my Brother then settled there with his Printing-House. Our former Differences were forgotten, and our Meeting was very cordial and affectionate. He was fast declining in his Health, and requested of me that in case of his Death which he apprehended not far distant, I would take home his Son, then but 10 Years of Age, and bring him up to the Printing Business. This I accordingly perform'd, sending him a few Years to School before I took him into the Office. His Mother carry'd on the Business till he was grown up, when I assisted him with an Assortment of new Types, those of his Father being in a Manner worn out.——Thus it was that I made my Brother ample Amends for the Service I had depriv'd him of by leaving him so early.——

In 1736 I lost one of my Sons a fine Boy of 4 Years old, by the Small Pox taken in the common way. I long regretted bitterly and still regret that I had not given it to him by Inoculation; This I mention for the Sake of Parents, who omit that Operation on the Supposition that they should never forgive themselves if a Child died under it; my Example showing that the Regret may be the same either way, and that therefore the safer should be chosen.——

Our Club, the Junto, was found so useful, and afforded such Satisfaction to the Members, that several were desirous of introducing their Friends, which could not well be done without exceeding what we had settled as a convenient Number, viz. Twelve. We had from the Beginning made it a Rule to keep our Institution a Secret, which was pretty well observ'd. The Intention was, to avoid Applications of improper Persons for Admittance, some of whom perhaps we might find it difficult to refuse. I was one of those who were against any Addition to our Number, but instead of it made in Writing a Proposal, that every Member separately should endeavour to form a subordinate Club, with the same Rules respecting Queries, &c. and without informing them of the Connexion with the Junto. The Advantages propos'd were the Improvement of so many more young Citizens by the Use of our Institutions; Our better Acquaintance with the general Sentiments of the Inhabitants on any Occasion, as the Junto-Member might propose what Queries we should desire, and was to report to Junto what pass'd in his separate Club; the Promotion of our particular Interests in Business by more extensive Recommendations; and the Increase of our Influence in public Affairs and our Power of doing Good by spreading thro' the several Clubs the Sentiments of the Junto. The Project was approv'd, and every Member undertook to form his Club: but they did not all succeed. Five or six only were compleated, which were call'd by different Names, as the Vine, the Union, the Band, &c. they were useful to themselves, and afforded us a good deal of Amusement, Information and Instruction, besides answering in some considerable Degree our Views of influencing the public Opinion on particular Occasions, of which I shall give some Instances in course of time as they happened.——

My first Promotion was my being chosen in 1736 Clerk of the General Assembly. The Choice was made that Year without Opposition; but the Year following when I was again propos'd (the Choice, like that of the Members being annual) a new Member made a long Speech against me in order to favour some other Candidate. I was however chosen; which was the more agreable to me, as besides the Pay for immediate Service as Clerk, the Place gave me a better Opportunity of keeping up an Interest among the Members, which secur'd to me the Business of Printing the Votes, Laws, Paper Money, and other occasional Jobbs for the Public, that on the whole were very profitable. I therefore did not like the Opposition of this new Member, who was a Gentleman of Fortune, and Education, with Talents that were likely to give him in time great Influence in the House, which indeed afterwards happened. I did not however aim at gaining his Favour by paying any servile Respect to him, but after some time took this other Method. Having heard that he had in his Library a certain very scarce and curious Book, I wrote a Note to him expressing my Desire of perusing that Book, and requesting he would do me the Favour of lending it to me for a few Days. He sent it immediately; and I return'd it in about a Week, with another Note expressing strongly my Sense of the Favour. When we next met in the House he spoke to me, (which he had never done before) and with great Civility. And he ever afterwards manifested a Readiness to serve me on all Occasions, so that we became great Friends, and our Friendship continu'd to his Death. This is another Instance of the Truth of an old Maxim I had learnt, which says, *He that has once done you a Kindness will be more ready to do you another, than he whom you yourself have obliged*. And it shows how much more profitable it is prudently to remove, than to resent, return and continue inimical Proceedings.——

In 1737, Col. Spotswood, late Governor of Virginia, and then Postmaster, General, being dissatisfied with the Conduct of his Deputy at Philadelphia, respecting some Negligence in rendering, and Inexactitude of his Accounts, took from him the Commission and offered it to me. I accepted it readily, and found it of great Advantage; for tho' the Salary was small, it facilitated the Correspondence that improv'd my Newspaper, encreas'd the Number demanded, as well as the Advertisements to be inserted, so that it came to afford me a very considerable Income. My old Competitor's Newspaper declin'd proportionably, and I was satisfy'd without retaliating his Refusal, while Postmaster, to permit my Papers being carried by the Riders. Thus He suffer'd greatly from his Neglect in due Accounting; and I mention it as a Lesson to those young Men who may be employ'd in managing Affairs for others that they should always render Accounts and make Remittances, with great Clearness and Punctuality.——The Character of observing such a Conduct is the most powerful of all Recommendations to new Employments and Increase of Business.

I began now to turn my Thoughts a little to public Affairs, beginning however with small Matters. The City Watch was one of the first Things that I conceiv'd to want Regulation. It was managed by the Constables of the respective Wards in Turn. The Constable warn'd a Number of Housekeepers to attend him for the Night. Those who chose never to attend paid him Six Shillings a Year to be excus'd, which was suppos'd to be for hiring Substitutes; but was in Reality much more than was necessary for that purpose, and made the Constableship a Place of Profit. And the Constable for a little Drink often got such Ragamuffins about him as a Watch, that reputable Housekeepers did not chuse to mix with. Walking the Rounds too was often neglected, and most of the Night spent in Tippling. I thereupon wrote a Paper to be read in Junto, representing these Irregularities, but insisting more particularly on the Inequality of this Six Shilling Tax of the Constables, respecting the Circumstances of those who paid it, since a poor Widow Housekeeper, all whose Property to be guarded by the Watch did not perhaps exceed the Value of Fifty Pounds, paid as much as the wealthiest Merchant who had Thousands of Pounds-worth of Goods in his Stores. On the whole I proposed as a more effectual Watch, the Hiring of proper Men to serve constantly in that Business; and as a more equitable Way of supporting the Charge, the levying a Tax that should be proportion'd to Property. This Idea being approv'd by the Junto, was communicated to the other Clubs, but as arising in each of them. And tho' the Plan was not immediately carried into Execution, yet by preparing the Minds of People for the Change, it paved the Way for the Law obtain'd a few Years after, when the Members of our Clubs were grown into more Influence.——

About this time I wrote a Paper, (first to be read in Junto but it was afterwards publish'd) on the different Accidents and Carelessnesses by which Houses were set on fire, with Cautions against them, and Means proposed of avoiding them. This was much spoken of as a useful Piece, and gave rise to a Project, which soon followed it, of forming a Company for the more ready Extinguishing of Fires, and mutual Assistance in Removing and Securing of Goods when in Danger. Associates in this Scheme were presently found amounting to Thirty. Our Articles of Agreement oblig'd every Member to keep always in good Order and fit for Use, a certain Number of Leather Buckets, with strong Bags and Baskets (for packing and transporting of Goods), which were to be brought to every Fire; and we agreed to meet once a Month and spend a social Evening together, in discoursing, and communicating such Ideas as occur'd to us upon the Subject of Fires as might be useful in our Conduct on such Occasions. The Utility of this Institution soon appear'd, and many more desiring to be admitted than we thought convenient for one Company, they were advised to form another; which was accordingly done. And this went on, one new Company being formed after another, till they became so numerous as to include most of the Inhabitants who were Men of Property; and now at the time of my Writing this, tho' upwards of Fifty Years since its Establishment, that which I first formed, called the Union Fire Company, still subsists and flourishes, tho' the first Members are all deceas'd but myself and one who is older by a Year than I am.——The small Fines that have been paid by Members for Absence at the Monthly Meetings, have been apply'd to the Purchase of Fire Engines, Ladders, Firehooks, and other useful Implements for each Company, so that I question whether there is a City in the World better provided with the Means of putting a Stop to beginning Conflagrations; and in fact since these Institutions, the City has never lost by Fire more than one or two Houses at a time, and the Flames have often been extinguish'd before the House in which they began has been half-consumed.——

In 1739 arriv'd among us from England the Rev. Mr. Whitefield, who had made himself remarkable there as an itinerant Preacher. He was at first permitted to preach in some of our Churches; but the Clergy taking a Dislike to him, soon refus'd him their Pulpits and he was oblig'd to preach in the Fields. The Multitudes of all Sects and Denominations that attended his Sermons were enormous and it was matter of Speculation to me who was one of the Number, to observe the extraordinary Influence of his Oratory on his Hearers, and how much they admir'd and respected him, notwithstanding his common Abuse of them, by assuring them they were naturally *half Beasts and half Devils.* It was wonderful to see the Change soon made in the Manners of our Inhabitants; from being thoughtless or indifferent about Religion, it seem'd as if all the World were growing Religious; so that one could not walk thro' the Town in an Evening without Hearing Psalms sung in different Families of every Street. And it being found inconvenient to assemble in the open Air, subject to its Inclemencies, the Building of a House to meet-in was no sooner propos'd and Persons appointed to receive Contributions, but sufficient Sums were soon receiv'd to procure the Ground and erect the Building which was 100 feet long and 70 broad, about the Size of Westminster-hall; and the Work was carried on with such Spirit as to be finished in a much shorter time than could have been expected. Both House and Ground were vested in Trustees, expressly for the Use of any Preacher of any religious Persuasion who might desire to say something to the People of Philadelphia, the Design in building not being to accommodate any particular Sect, but the Inhabitants in general, so that even if the Mufti of Constantinople were to send a Missionary to preach Mahometanism to us, he would find a Pulpit at his Service.——

Mr. Whitefield, in leaving us, went preaching all the Way thro' the Colonies to Georgia. The Settlement of that Province had lately been begun; but instead of being made with hardy industrious Husbandmen accustomed to Labour, the only People fit for such an Enterprise, it was with Families of broken Shopkeepers and other insolvent Debtors, many of indolent and idle habits, taken out of the Gaols, who being set down in the Woods, unqualified for clearing Land, and unable to endure the Hardships of a new Settlement, perished in Numbers, leaving many helpless Children unprovided for. The Sight of their miserable Situation inspired the benevolent Heart of Mr. Whitefield with the Idea of building an Orphan House there, in which they might be supported and educated. Returning northward he preach'd up this Charity, and made large Collections;——for his Eloquence had a wonderful Power over the Hearts and Purses of his Hearers, of which I myself was an Instance. I did not disapprove of the Design, but as Georgia was then destitute of Materials and Workmen, and it was propos'd to send them from Philadelphia at a great Expence, I thought it would have been better to have built the House here and brought the Children to it. This I advis'd, but he was resolute in his first Project, and rejected my Counsel, and I thereupon refus'd to contribute. I happened soon after to attend one of his Sermons, in the Course of which I perceived he intended to finish with a Collection, and I silently resolved he should get nothing from me. I had in my Pocket a Handful of Copper Money, three or four silver Dollars, and five Pistoles in Gold. As he proceeded I began to soften, and concluded to give the Coppers. Another Stroke of his Oratory made me asham'd of that, and determin'd me to give the Silver; and he finish'd so admirably, that I empty'd my Pocket wholly into the Collector's Dish, Gold and all. At this Sermon there was also one of our Club, who being of my Sentiments respecting the Building in Georgia, and suspecting a Collection might be intended, had by Precaution emptied his Pockets before he came from home; towards the Conclusion of the Discourse however, he felt a strong Desire to give, and apply'd to a Neighbour who stood near him to borrow some Money for the Purpose. The Application was unfortunately to perhaps the only Man in the Company who had the firmness not to be affected by the Preacher. His Answer was, *At any other time, Friend Hopkinson, I would lend to thee freely; but not now; for thee seems to be out of thy right Senses.——*

Some of Mr. Whitefield's Enemies affected to suppose that he would apply these Collections to his own private Emolument; but I, who was intimately acquainted with him, (being employ'd in printing his Sermons and Journals, &c.) never had the least Suspicion of his Integrity, but am to this day decidedly of Opinion that he was in all his Conduct, a perfectly *honest Man.* And methinks my Testimony in his Favour ought to have the more Weight, as we had no religious Connection. He us'd indeed sometimes to pray for my Conversion, but never had the Satisfaction of believing that his Prayers were heard. Ours was a mere civil Friendship, sincere on both Sides, and lasted to his Death.

The following Instance will show something of the Terms on which we stood. Upon one of his Arrivals from England at Boston, he wrote to me that he should come soon to Philadelphia, but knew not where he could lodge when there, as he understood his old kind Host Mr. Benezet was remov'd to Germantown. My Answer was; You know my House, if you can make shift with its scanty Accommodations you will be most heartily welcome. He reply'd, that if I made that kind Offer for Christ's sake, I should not miss of a Reward.——And I return'd, *Don't let me be mistaken; it was not for Christ's sake, but for your sake.* One of our common Acquaintance jocosely remark'd, that knowing it to be the Custom of the Saints, when they receiv'd any favour, to shift the Burthen of the Obligation from off their own Shoulders, and place it in Heaven, I had contriv'd to fix it on Earth.——

The last time I saw Mr. Whitefield was in London, when he consulted me about his Orphan House Concern, and his Purpose of appropriating it to the Establishment of a College.

He had a loud and clear Voice, and articulated his Words and Sentences so perfectly that he might be heard and understood at a great Distance, especially as his Auditories, however numerous, observ'd the most exact Silence. He preach'd one Evening from the Top of the Court House Steps, which are in the Middle of Market Street, and on the West Side of Second Street which crosses it at right angles. Both Streets were fill'd with his Hearers to a considerable Distance. Being among the hindmost in Market Street, I had the Curiosity to learn how far he could be heard, by retiring backwards down the Street towards the River, and I found his Voice distinct till I came near Front-Street, when some Noise in that Street, obscur'd it. Imagining then a Semi-Circle, of which my Distance should be the Radius, and that it were fill'd with Auditors, to each of whom I allow'd two square feet, I computed that he might well be heard by more than Thirty-Thousand. This reconcil'd me to the Newspaper Accounts of his having preach'd to 25,000 People in the Fields, and to the antient Histories of Generals haranguing whole Armies, of which I had sometimes doubted.——

By hearing him often I came to distinguish easily between Sermons newly compos'd, and those which he had often preach'd in the Course of his Travels. His Delivery of the latter was so improv'd by frequent Repetitions, that every Accent, every Emphasis, every Modulation of Voice, was so perfectly well turn'd and well plac'd, that without being interested in the Subject, one could not help being pleas'd with the Discourse, a Pleasure of much the same kind with that receiv'd from an excellent Piece of Musick. This is an Advantage itinerant Preachers have over those who are stationary: as the latter cannot well improve their Delivery of a Sermon by so many Rehearsals.——

His Writing and Printing from time to time gave great Advantage to his Enemies. Unguarded Expressions and even erroneous Opinions delivered in Preaching might have been afterwards explain'd, or qualify'd by supposing others that might have accompany'd them; or they might have been deny'd; But *litera scripta manet.*[1] Critics attack'd his Writings violently, and with so much Appearance of Reason as to diminish the Number of his Votaries, and prevent their Encrease: So that I am of Opinion, if he had never written any thing he would have left behind him a much more numerous and important Sect. And his Reputation might in that case have been still growing, even after his Death; as there being nothing of his Writing on which to found a Censure; and give him a lower Character, his Proselites would be left at Liberty to feign for him as great a Variety of Excellencies, as their enthusiastic Admiration might wish him to have possessed.

My Business was now continually augmenting, and my Circumstances growing daily easier, my Newspaper having become very profitable, as being for a time almost the only one in this and the neighbouring Provinces.——I experienc'd too the Truth of the Observation, that *after getting the first hundred Pound, it is more easy to get the second*: Money itself being of a prolific Nature: The Partnership at Carolina having succeeded, I was encourag'd to engage in others, and to promote several of my Workmen who had behaved well, by establishing them with Printing-Houses in different Colonies, on the same Terms with that in Carolina. Most of them did well, being enabled at the End of our Term, Six Years, to purchase the Types of me; and go on working for themselves, by which means several Families were raised. Partnerships often finish in Quarrels, but I was happy in this, that mine were all carry'd on and ended amicably; owing I think a good deal to the Precaution of having very explicitly settled in our Articles every thing to be done by or expected from each Partner, so that there was nothing to dispute, which Precaution I would therefore recommend to all who enter into Partnerships, for whatever Esteem Partners may have for and Confidence in each other at the time of the Contract, little Jealousies and Disgusts may arise, with Ideas of Inequality in the Care and Burthen of the Business, &c. which are attended often with Breach of Friendship and of the Connection, perhaps with Lawsuits and other disagreable Consequences.

I had on the whole abundant Reason to be satisfied with my being established in Pennsylvania. There were however two things that I regretted: There being no Provision for Defence, nor for a compleat Education of Youth. No Militia nor any College. I therefore in 1743, drew up a Proposal for establishing an Academy; and at that time thinking the Rev. Mr. Peters,

[1] ["The written letter remains."]

who was out of Employ, a fit Person to superintend such an Institution, I communicated the Project to him. But he having more profitable Views in the Service of the Proprietor, which succeeded, declin'd the Undertaking. And not knowing another at that time suitable for such a Trust, I let the Scheme lie a while dormant.——I succeeded better the next Year, 1744, in proposing and establishing a Philosophical Society. The Paper I wrote for that purpose will be found among my Writings when collected.——

With respect to Defence, Spain having been several Years at War against Britain, and being at length join'd by France, which brought us into greater Danger; and the laboured and long-continued Endeavours of our Governor Thomas to prevail with our Quaker Assembly to pass a Militia Law, and make other Provisions for the Security of the Province having proved abortive, I determined to try what might be done by a voluntary Association of the People. To promote this I first wrote and published a Pamphlet, intitled, PLAIN TRUTH, in which I stated our defenceless Situation in strong Lights, with the Necessity of Union and Discipline for our Defence, and promis'd to propose in a few Days an Association to be generally signed for that purpose. The Pamphlet had a sudden and surprizing Effect. I was call'd upon for the Instrument of Association: And having settled the Draft of it with a few Friends, I appointed a Meeting of the Citizens in the large Building before mentioned. The House was pretty full. I had prepared a Number of printed Copies, and provided Pens and Ink dispers'd all over the Room. I harangu'd them a little on the Subject, read the Paper and explain'd it, and then distributed the Copies which were eagerly signed, not the least Objection being made. When the Company separated, and the Papers were collected we found above Twelve hundred Hands; and other Copies being dispers'd in the Country the Subscribers amounted at length to upwards of Ten Thousand. These all furnish'd themselves as soon as they could with Arms; form'd themselves into Companies, and Regiments, chose their own Officers, and met every Week to be instructed in the manual Exercise, and other Parts of military Discipline. The Women, by Subscriptions among themselves, provided Silk Colours, which they presented to the Companies, painted with different Devices and Motto's which I supplied. The Officers of the Companies composing the Philadelphia Regiment, being met, chose me for their Colonel; but conceiving myself unfit, I declin'd that Station, and recommended Mr. Lawrence, a fine Person and Man of Influence, who was accordingly appointed. I then propos'd a Lottery to defray the Expence of Building a Battery below the Town, and furnishing it with Cannon. It filled expeditiously and the Battery was soon erected, the Merlons being fram'd of Logs and fill'd with Earth. We bought some old Cannon from Boston, but these not being sufficient, we wrote to England for more, soliciting at the same Time our Proprietaries for some Assistance, tho' without much Expectation of obtaining it. Mean while Colonel Lawrence, William Allen, Abraham Taylor, Esquires, and myself were sent to New York by the Associators, commission'd to borrow some Cannon of Governor Clinton. He at first refus'd us peremptorily: but at a Dinner with his Council where there was great Drinking of Madeira Wine, as the Custom at that Place then was, he soften'd by degrees, and said he would lend us Six. After a few more Bumpers he advanc'd to Ten. And at length he very good-naturedly conceded Eighteen. They were fine Cannon, 18 pounders, with their Carriages, which we soon transported and mounted on our Battery, where the Associators kept a nightly Guard while the War lasted: And among the rest I regularly took my Turn of Duty there as a common Soldier.——

My Activity in these Operations was agreable to the Governor and Council; they took me into Confidence, and I was consulted by them in every Measure wherein their Concurrence was thought useful to the Association. Calling in the Aid of Religion, I propos'd to them the Proclaiming a Fast, to promote Reformation, and implore the Blessing of Heaven on our Undertaking. They embrac'd the Motion, but as it was the first Fast ever thought of in the Province, the Secretary had no Precedent from which to draw the Proclamation. My Education in New England, where a Fast is proclaim'd every Year, was here of some Advantage. I drew it in the accustomed Stile, it was translated into German, printed in both Languages and divulg'd thro' the Province. This gave the Clergy of the different Sects an Opportunity of Influencing their Congregations to join in the Association; and it would probably have been general among all but Quakers if the Peace had not soon interven'd.

It was thought by some of my Friends that by my Activity in these Affairs, I should offend that Sect, and thereby lose my Interest in the Assembly where they were a great Majority. A young Gentleman who had likewise some Friends in the House, and wish'd to succeed me as their Clerk, acquainted me that it was decided to displace me at the next Election, and he therefore in good Will advis'd me to resign, as more consistent with my Honour than being turn'd out. My Answer to him was, that I had read or heard of some Public Man, who made it a Rule never to ask for an Office, and never to refuse one when offer'd to him.

I approve, says I, of his Rule, and will practise it with a small Addition; I shall never *ask*, never *refuse*, nor ever *resign* an Office. If they will have my Office of Clerk to dispose of to another, they shall take it from me. I will not by giving it up, lose my Right of some time or other making Reprisals on my Adversaries. I heard however no more of this. I was chosen again, unanimously as usual, at the next Election. Possibly as they dislik'd my late Intimacy with the Members of Council, who had join'd the Governors in all the Disputes about military Preparations with which the House had long been harass'd, they might have been pleas'd if I would voluntarily have left them; but they did not care to displace me on Account merely of my Zeal for the Association; and they could not well give another Reason.——Indeed I had some Cause to believe, that the Defence of the Country was not disagreeable to any of them, provided they were not requir'd to assist in it. And I found that a much greater Number of them than I could have imagined, tho' against offensive War, were clearly for the defensive. Many Pamphlets *pro* and *con* were publish'd on the Subject, and some by good Quakers in favour of Defence, which I believe convinc'd most of their younger People. A Transaction in our Fire Company gave me some Insight into their prevailing Sentiments. It had been propos'd that we should encourage the Scheme for building a Battery by laying out the present Stock, then about Sixty Pounds, in Tickets of the Lottery. By our Rules no Money could be dispos'd of but at the next Meeting after the Proposal. The Company consisted of Thirty Members, of which Twenty-two were Quakers, and Eight only of other Persuasions. We eight punctually attended the Meeting; but tho' we thought that some of the Quakers would join us, we were by no means sure of a Majority. Only one Quaker, Mr. James Morris, appear'd to oppose the Measure: He express'd much Sorrow that it had ever been propos'd, as he said *Friends* were all against it, and it would create such Discord as might break up the Company. We told him, that we saw no Reason for that; we were the Minority, and if *Friends* were against the Measure and outvoted us, we must and should, agreable to the Usage of all Societies, submit. When the Hour for Business arriv'd, it was mov'd to put the Vote. He allow'd we might then do it by the Rules, but as he could assure us that a Number of Members intended to be present for the purpose of opposing it, it would be but candid to allow a little time for their appearing. While we were disputing this, a Waiter came to tell me two Gentlemen below desir'd to speak with me. I went down, and found they were two of our Quaker Members. They told me there were eight of them assembled at a

Tavern just by; that they were determin'd to come and vote with us if there should be occasion, which they hop'd would not be the Case; and desir'd we would not call for their Assistance if we could do without it, as their Voting for such a Measure might embroil them with their Elders and Friends; Being thus secure of a Majority, I went up, and after a little seeming Hesitation, agreed to a Delay of another Hour. This Mr. Morris allow'd to be extreamly fair. Not one of his opposing Friends appear'd, at which he express'd great Surprize; and at the Expiration of the Hour, we carry'd the Resolution Eight to one; And as of the 22 Quakers, Eight were ready to vote with us and, Thirteen by their Absence manifested that they were not inclin'd to oppose the Measure, I afterwards estimated the Proportion of Quakers sincerely against Defence as one to twenty one only. For these were all regular Members, of that Society, and in good Reputation among them, and had due Notice of what was propos'd at that Meeting.

The honourable and learned Mr. Logan, who had always been of that Sect, was one who wrote an Address to them, declaring his Approbation of defensive War, and supporting his Opinion by many strong Arguments: He put into my Hands Sixty Pounds, to be laid out in Lottery Tickets for the Battery, with Directions to apply what Prizes might be drawn wholly to that Service. He told me the following Anecdote of his old Master William Penn respecting Defence. He came over from England, when a young Man, with that Proprietary, and as his Secretary. It was War Time, and their Ship was chas'd by an armed Vessel suppos'd to be an Enemy. Their Captain prepar'd for Defence, but told William Penn and his Company of Quakers, that he did not expect their Assistance, and they might retire into the Cabin; which they did, except James Logan, who chose to stay upon Deck, and was quarter'd to a Gun. The suppos'd Enemy prov'd a Friend; so there was no Fighting. But when the Secretary went down to communicate the Intelligence, William Penn rebuk'd him severely for staying upon Deck and undertaking to assist in defending the Vessel, contrary to the Principles of *Friends*, especially as it had not been required by the Captain. This Reproof being before all the Company, piqu'd the Secretary, who answer'd, *I being thy Servant, why did thee not order me to come down: but thee was willing enough that I should stay and help to fight the Ship when thee thought there was Danger.*

My being many Years in the Assembly, the Majority of which were constantly Quakers, gave me frequent Opportunities of seeing the Embarassment given them by their Principle against War, whenever Application was made to them by Order of the Crown to grant Aids for military

Purposes. They were unwilling to offend Government on the one hand, by a direct Refusal, and their Friends the Body of Quakers on the other, by a Compliance contrary to their Principles. Hence a Variety of Evasions to avoid Complying, and Modes of disguising the Compliance when it became unavoidable. The common Mode at last was to grant Money under the Phrase of its being *for the King's Use*, and never to enquire how it was applied. But if the Demand was not directly from the Crown, that Phrase was found not so proper, and some other was to be invented. As when Powder was wanting, (I think it was for the Garrison at Louisburg,) and the Government of New England solicited a Grant of some from Pennsylvania, which was much urg'd on the House by Governor Thomas, they could not grant Money to buy Powder, because that was an Ingredient of War, but they voted an Aid to New England, of Three Thousand Pounds, to be put into the hands of the Governor, and appropriated it for the Purchasing of Bread, Flour, Wheat, *or other Grain.* Some of the Council desirous of giving the House still farther Embarassment, advis'd the Governor not to accept Provision, as not being the Thing he had demanded. But he reply'd, "I shall take the Money, for I understand very well their Meaning; *Other Grain*, is Gunpowder;" which he accordingly bought; and they never objected to it. It was in Allusion to this Fact, that when in our Fire Company we feared the Success of our Proposal in favour of the Lottery, and I had said to my Friend Mr. Syng, one of our Members, if we fail, let us move the Purchase of a Fire Engine with the Money; the Quakers can have no Objection to that: and then if you nominate me, and I you, as a Committee for that purpose, we will buy a great Gun, which is certainly a *Fire-Engine*: I see, says he, you have improv'd by being so long in the Assembly; your equivocal Project would be just a Match for their Wheat *or other Grain.*

These Embarassments that the Quakers suffer'd from having establish'd and published it as one of their Principles, that no kind of War was lawful, and which being once published, they could not afterwards, however they might change their minds, easily get rid of, reminds me of what I think a more prudent Conduct in another Sect among us; that of the Dunkers. I was acquainted with one of its Founders, Michael Welfare, soon after it appear'd.——He complain'd to me that they were grievously calumniated by the Zealots of other Persuasions, and charg'd with abominable Principles and Practices to which they were utter Strangers. I told him this had always been the case with new Sects; and that to put a Stop to such Abuse, I imagin'd it might be well to publish the Articles of their

Belief and the Rules of their Discipline. He said that it had been propos'd among them, but not agreed to, for this Reason; "When we were first drawn together as a Society, says he, it had pleased God to inlighten our Minds so far, as to see that some Doctrines which we once esteemed Truths were Errors, and that others which we had esteemed Errors were real Truths. From time to time he has been pleased to afford us farther Light, and our Principles have been improving, and our Errors diminishing. Now we are not sure that we are arriv'd at the End of this Progression, and at the Perfection of Spiritual or Theological Knowledge; and we fear that if we should once print our Confession of Faith, we should feel ourselves as if bound and confin'd by it, and perhaps be unwilling to receive farther Improvement; and our Successors still more so, as conceiving what we their Elders and Founders had done, to be something sacred, never to be departed from."——This Modesty in a Sect is perhaps a singular Instance in the History of Mankind, every other Sect supposing itself in Possession of all Truth, and that those who differ are so far in the Wrong: Like a Man travelling in foggy Weather: Those at some Distance before him on the Road he sees wrapt up in the Fog, as well as those behind him, and also the People in the Fields on each side; but neer him all appears clear.——Tho' in truth he is as much in the Fog as any of them. To avoid this kind of Embarrassment the Quakers have of late Years been gradually declining the public Service in the Assembly and in the Magistracy. Chusing rather to quit their Power than their Principle.

In Order of Time I should have mentioned before, that having in 1742 invented an open Stove, for the better warming of Rooms and at the same time saving Fuel, as the fresh Air admitted was warmed in Entring, I made a Present of the Model to Mr. Robert Grace, one of my early Friends, who having an Iron Furnace, found the Casting of the Plates for these Stoves a profitable Thing, as they were growing in Demand. To promote that Demand I wrote and published a Pamphlet Intitled, *An Account of the New-Invented* PENNSYLVANIA FIRE PLACES: *Wherein their Construction and manner of Operation is particularly explained; their Advantages above every other Method of warming Rooms demonstrated; and all Objections that have been raised against the Use of them answered and obviated, &c.* This Pamphlet had a good Effect, Governor Thomas was so pleas'd with the Construction of this Stove, as describ'd in it that he offer'd to give me a Patent for the sole Vending of them for a Term of Years; but I declin'd it from a Principle which has ever weigh'd with me on such Occasions, viz. *That as we enjoy great Advantages from the Inventions of others, we should be glad of an Opportunity to serve others by any Invention of ours, and this we should do freely and generously*. An Ironmonger in London, however, after assuming a good deal of my Pamphlet and working it up into his own, and making some small Changes in the Machine, which rather hurt its Operation, got a Patent for it there, and made as I was told a little Fortune by it.——And this is not the only Instance of Patents taken out for my Inventions by others, tho' not always with the same Success: which I never contested, as having no Desire of profiting by Patents my self, and hating Disputes.——The Use of these Fireplaces in very many Houses both of this and the neighbouring Colonies, has been and is a great Saving of Wood to the Inhabitants.——

Peace being concluded, and the Association Business therefore at an End, I turn'd my Thoughts again to the Affair of establishing an Academy. The first Step I took was to associate in the Design a Number of active Friends, of whom the Junto furnished a good Part; the next was to write and publish a Pamphlet intitled, *Proposals relating to the Education of Youth in Pennsylvania*.——This I distributed among the principal Inhabitants gratis; and as soon as I could suppose their Minds a little prepared by the Perusal of it, I set on foot a Subscription for Opening and Supporting an Academy; it was to be paid in Quotas yearly for Five Years; by so dividing it I judg'd the Subscription might be larger, and I believe it was so, amounting to no less (if I remember right) than Five thousand Pounds.——In the Introduction to these Proposals, I stated their Publication not as an Act of mine, but of some *publick-spirited Gentlemen*; avoiding as much as I could, according to my usual Rule, the presenting myself to the Publick as the Author of any Scheme for their Benefit.——

The Subscribers, to carry the Project into immediate Execution chose out of their Number Twenty-four Trustees, and appointed Mr. Francis, then Attorney General, and myself, to draw up Constitutions for the Government of the Academy, which being done and signed, an House was hired, Masters engag'd and the Schools opened I think in the same Year 1749. The Scholars encreasing fast, the House was soon found too small, and we were looking out for a Piece of Ground properly situated, with Intention to build, when Providence threw into our way a large House ready built, which with a few Alterations might well serve our purpose, this was the Building before mentioned erected by the Hearers of Mr. Whitefield, and was obtain'd for us in the following Manner.

It is to be noted, that the Contributions to this Building being made by People of different Sects, Care was taken in the Nomination of Trustees, in whom the Building and Ground was to be vested, that a Predominancy should not be given to any Sect, lest in time that Predominancy might be a means of appropriating the whole to the Use of such Sect, contrary to the original Intention; it was therefore that one of each Sect was appointed, viz. one Church-of-England-man, one Presbyterian, one Baptist, one Moravian, &c. Those in case of Vacancy by Death were to fill it by Election from among the Contributors. The Moravian happen'd not to please his Colleagues, and on his Death, they resolved to have no other of that Sect. The Difficulty then was, how to avoid having two of some other Sect, by means of the new Choice. Several Persons were named and for that Reason not agreed to. At length one mention'd me, with the Observation that I was merely an honest Man, and of no Sect at all; which prevail'd with them to chuse me. The Enthusiasm which existed when the House was built, had long since abated, and its Trustees had not been able to procure fresh Contributions for paying the Ground Rent, and discharging some other Debts the Building had occasion'd, which embarrass'd them greatly. Being now a Member of both Sets of Trustees, that for the Building and that for the Academy, I had good Opportunity of negociating with both, and brought them finally to an Agreement, by which the Trustees for the Building were to cede it to those of the Academy, the latter undertaking to discharge the Debt, to keep forever open in the Building a large Hall for occasional Preachers according to the original Intention, and maintain a Free School for the Instruction of poor Children. Writings were accordingly drawn, and on paying the Debts the Trustees of the Academy were put in Possession of the Premises, and by dividing the great and lofty Hall into Stories, and different Rooms above and below for the several Schools, and purchasing some additional Ground, the whole was soon made fit for our purpose, and the Scholars remov'd into the Building. The Care and Trouble of agreeing with the Workmen, purchasing Materials, and superintending the Work fell upon me, and I went thro' it the more chearfully, as it did not then interfere with my private Business, having the Year before taken a very able, industrious and honest Partner, Mr. David Hall, with whose Character I was well acquainted, as he had work'd for me four Years. He took off my Hands all Care of the Printing-Office, paying me punctually my Share of the Profits. This Partnership continued Eighteen Years, successfully for us both.——

The Trustees of the Academy after a while were incorporated by a Charter from the Governor; their Funds were increas'd by Contributions in Britain, and Grants of Land from the Proprietaries, to which the Assembly has since made considerable Addition, and thus was established the present University of Philadelphia. I have been continued one of its Trustees from the Beginning, now near forty Years, and have had the very great Pleasure of seeing a Number of the Youth who have receiv'd their Education in it, distinguish'd by their improv'd Abilities, serviceable in public Stations, and Ornaments to their Country.

When I disengag'd myself as above mentioned from private Business, I flatter'd myself that, by the sufficient tho' moderate Fortune I had acquir'd, I had secur'd Leisure during the rest of my Life, for Philosophical Studies and Amusements; I purchas'd all Dr. Spence's Apparatus, who had come from England to lecture here; and I proceeded in my Electrical Experiments with great Alacrity; but the Publick now considering me as a Man of Leisure, laid hold of me for their Purposes; every Part of our Civil Government, and almost at the same time, imposing some Duty upon me. The Governor put me into the Commission of the Peace; the Corporation of the City chose me of the Common Council, and soon after an Alderman; and the Citizens at large chose me a Burgess to represent them in Assembly. This latter Station was the more agreable to me, as I was at length tired with sitting there to hear Debates in which as Clerk I could take no part, and which were often so unentertaining, that I was induc'd to amuse myself with making magic Squares, or Circles, or any thing to avoid Weariness. And I conceiv'd my becoming a Member would enlarge my Power of doing Good. I would not however insinuate that my Ambition was not flatter'd by all these Promotions. It certainly was. For considering my low Beginning they were great Things to me. And they were still more pleasing, as being so many spontaneous Testimonies of the public's good Opinion, and by me entirely unsolicited.

The Office of Justice of the Peace I try'd a little, by attending a few Courts, and sitting on the Bench to hear Causes. But finding that more Knowledge of the Common Law than I possess'd, was necessary to act in that Station with Credit, I gradually withdrew from it, excusing myself by my being oblig'd to attend the higher Dutys of a Legislator in the Assembly. My Election to this Trust was repeated every Year for Ten Years, without my ever asking any Elector for his Vote, or signifying either directly or indirectly any Desire of being chosen.——On taking my Seat in the House, my Son was appointed their Clerk.

The Year following, a Treaty being to be held with the Indians at Carlisle, the Governor sent a Message to the House, proposing that they should nominate some of their Members to be join'd with some Members of Council as Commissioners for that purpose. The House nam'd the Speaker (Mr. Norris) and my self; and being commission'd we went to Carlisle, and met the Indians accordingly.——As those People are extreamly apt to get drunk, and when so are very quarrelsome and disorderly, we strictly forbad the selling any Liquor to them; and when they complain'd of this Restriction, we told them that if they would continue sober during the Treaty, we would give them Plenty of Rum when Business was over. They promis'd this; and they kept their Promise——because they could get no Liquor——and the Treaty was conducted very orderly, and concluded to mutual Satisfaction. They then claim'd and receiv'd the Rum. This was in the Afternoon. They were near 100 Men, Women and Children, and were lodg'd in temporary Cabins built in the Form of a Square just without the Town. In the Evening, hearing a great Noise among them, the Commissioners walk'd out to see what was the Matter. We found they had made a great Bonfire in the Middle of the Square. They were all drunk Men and Women, quarrelling and fighting. Their dark-colour'd Bodies, half naked, seen only by the gloomy Light of the Bonfire, running after and beating one another with Firebrands, accompanied by their horrid Yellings, form'd a Scene the most resembling our Ideas of Hell that could well be imagin'd. There was no appeasing the Tumult, and we retired to our Lodging. At Midnight a Number of them came thundering at our Door, demanding more Rum; of which we took no Notice. The next Day, sensible they had misbehav'd in giving us that Disturbance, they sent three of their old Counsellors to make their Apology. The Orator acknowledg'd the Fault, but laid it upon the Rum; and then endeavour'd to excuse the Rum, by saying, "*The great Spirit who made all things made every thing for some Use, and whatever Use he design'd any thing for, that Use it should always be put to; Now, when he made Rum, he said*, LET THIS BE FOR INDIANS TO GET DRUNK WITH. *And it must be so*."——And indeed if it be the Design of Providence to extirpate these Savages in order to make room for Cultivators of the Earth, it seems not improbable that Rum may be the appointed Means. It has already annihilated all the Tribes who formerly inhabited the Seacoast.——

In 1751. Dr. Thomas Bond, a particular Friend of mine, conceiv'd the Idea of establishing a Hospital in Philadelphia, for the Reception and Cure of poor sick Persons, whether Inhabitants of the Province or Strangers. A very beneficent Design, which has been ascrib'd to me, but was originally his. He was zealous and active in endeavouring to procure Subscriptions for it; but the Proposal being a Novelty in America, and at first not well understood, he met with small Success. At length he came to me, with the Compliment that he found there was no such thing as carrying a public Spirited Project through, without my being concern'd in it; "for, says he, I am often ask'd by those to whom I propose Subscribing, Have you consulted Franklin upon this Business? and what does he think of it?——And when I tell them that I have not, (supposing it rather out of your Line,) they do not subscribe, but say they will consider of it." I enquir'd into the Nature, and probable Utility of his Scheme, and receiving from him a very satisfactory Explanation, I not only subscrib'd to it myself, but engag'd heartily in the Design of Procuring Subscriptions from others. Previous however to the Solicitation, I endeavoured to prepare the Minds of the People by writing on the Subject in the Newspapers, which was my usual Custom in such Cases, but which he had omitted. The Subscriptions afterwards were more free and generous, but beginning to flag, I saw they would be insufficient without some Assistance from the Assembly, and therefore propos'd to petition for it, which was done. The Country Members did not at first relish the Project. They objected that it could only be serviceable to the City, and therefore the Citizens should alone be at the Expence of it; and they doubted whether the Citizens themselves generally approv'd of it: My Allegation on the contrary, that it met with such Approbation as to leave no doubt of our being able to raise 2000£ by voluntary Donations, they considered as a most extravagant Supposition, and utterly impossible. On this I form'd my Plan; and asking Leave to bring in a Bill, for incorporating the Contributors, according to the Prayers of their Petition, and granting them a blank Sum of Money, which Leave was obtain'd chiefly on the Consideration that the House could throw the Bill out if they did not like it, I drew it so as to make the important Clause a conditional One, viz. "And be it enacted by the Authority aforesaid That when the said Contributors shall have met and chosen their Managers and Treasurer, *and shall have raised by their Contributions a Capital Stock of 2000£ Value*, (the yearly Interest of which is to be applied to the Accommodating of the Sick Poor in the said Hospital, free of Charge for Diet, Attendance, Advice and Medicines) and *shall make the same appear to the Satisfaction of the Speaker of the Assembly* for the time being; that *then* it shall and may be lawful for the said Speaker, and he is hereby required to sign an Order on the Provincial Treasurer for the Payment of Two Thousand Pounds in two yearly Payments, to the Treasurer of the said Hospital, to be applied to the Founding, Building and Finishing of the same."——This Condition carried the Bill through; for the Members who had oppos'd the Grant, and now conceiv'd they might have the Credit of being charitable without the Expence, agreed to its Passage; And then in soliciting Subscriptions among the People we urg'd the conditional Promise of the Law as an additional Motive to give, since every Man's Donation would be doubled. Thus the Clause work'd both ways. The Subscriptions accordingly soon exceeded the requisite Sum, and we claim'd and receiv'd the Public Gift, which enabled us to carry the Design into Execution. A convenient and handsome Building was soon erected, the Institution has by constant Experience been found useful, and flourishes to this Day.——And I do not remember any of my political Maneuvres, the Success of which gave me at the time more Pleasure. Or that in after-thinking of it, I more easily excus'd my-self for having made some Use of Cunning.——

It was about this time that another Projector, the Rev. Gilbert Tennent, came to me, with a Request that I would assist him in procuring a Subscription for erecting a new Meeting-house. It was to be for the Use of a Congregation he had gathered among the Presbyterians who were originally Disciples of Mr. Whitefield. Unwilling to make myself disagreable to my fellow Citizens, by too frequently soliciting their Contributions, I absolutely refus'd. He then desir'd I would furnish him with a List of the Names of Persons I knew by Experience to be generous and public-spirited. I thought it would be unbecoming in me, after their kind Compliance with my Solicitations, to mark them out to be worried by other Beggars, and therefore refus'd also to give such a List.——He then desir'd I would at least give him my Advice. That I will readily do, said I; and, in the first Place, I advise you to apply to all those whom you know will give something; next to those whom you are uncertain whether they will give any thing or not; and show them the List of those who have given: and lastly, do not neglect those who you are sure will give nothing; for in some of them you may be mistaken.——He laugh'd, and thank'd me, and said he would take my Advice. He did so, for he ask'd of *every body*; and he obtain'd a much larger Sum than he expected, with which he erected the capacious and very elegant Meeting-house that stands in Arch Street.——

Our City, tho' laid out with a beautifull Regularity, the Streets large, strait, and crossing each other at right Angles, had the Disgrace of suffering those Streets to remain long unpav'd, and in wet Weather the Wheels of heavy Carriages plough'd them into a Quagmire, so that it was difficult to cross them. And in dry Weather the Dust was offensive. I had liv'd near the Jersey Market, and saw with Pain the Inhabitants wading in Mud while purchasing their Provisions. A Strip of Ground down the middle of that Market was at length pav'd with Brick, so that being once in the Market they had firm Footing, but were often over Shoes in Dirt to get there.——By talking and writing on the Subject, I was at length instrumental in getting the Street pav'd with Stone between the Market and the brick'd Foot-Pavement that was on each Side next the Houses. This for some time gave an easy Access to the Market, dry-shod. But the rest of the Street not being pav'd, whenever a Carriage came out of the Mud upon this Pavement, it shook off and left its Dirt on it, and it was soon cover'd with Mire, which was not remov'd, the City as yet having no Scavengers.——After some Enquiry I found a poor industrious Man, who was willing to undertake keeping the Pavement clean, by sweeping it twice a week and carrying off the Dirt from before all the Neighbours Doors, for the Sum of Sixpence per Month, to be paid by each House. I then wrote and printed a Paper, setting forth the Advantages to the Neighbourhood that might be obtain'd by this small Expence; the greater Ease in keeping our Houses clean, so much Dirt not being brought in by People's Feet; the Benefit to the Shops by more Custom, as Buyers could more easily get at them, and by not having in windy Weather the Dust blown in upon their Goods, &c. &c. I sent one of these Papers to each House, and in a Day or two went round to see who would subscribe an Agreement to pay these Sixpences. It was unanimously sign'd, and for a time well executed. All the Inhabitants of the City were delighted with the Cleanliness of the Pavement that surrounded the Market; it being a Convenience to all; and this rais'd a general Desire to have all the Streets paved; and made the People more willing to submit to a Tax for that purpose. After some time I drew a Bill for Paving the City, and brought it into the Assembly. It was just before I went to England in 1757. and did not pass till I was gone, and then with an Alteration in the Mode of Assessment, which I thought not for the better, but with an additional Provision for lighting as well as Paving the Streets, which was a great Improvement.——It was by a private Person, the late Mr. John Clifton, his giving a Sample of the Utility of Lamps by placing one at his Door, that the People were first impress'd with the Idea of enlightning all the City. The Honour of this public Benefit has also been ascrib'd to me, but it belongs truly to that Gentleman. I did but follow his Example; and have only some Merit to claim respecting the Form of our Lamps as differing from the Globe Lamps we at first were supply'd with from London. Those we found inconvenient in these respects; they admitted no Air below, the Smoke therefore did not readily go out above, but circulated in the Globe, lodg'd on its Inside, and soon obstructed the Light they were intended to afford; giving, besides, the daily Trouble of wiping them clean: and an accidental Stroke on one of them would demolish it, and render it totally useless. I therefore suggested the composing them of four flat Panes, with a long Funnel above to draw up the Smoke, and Crevices admitting Air below, to facilitate the Ascent of the Smoke. By this means they were kept clean, and did not grow dark in a few Hours as the London Lamps do, but continu'd bright till Morning; and an accidental Stroke would generally break but a single Pane, easily repair'd. I have sometimes wonder'd that the Londoners did not, from the Effect Holes in the Bottom of the Globe Lamps us'd at Vauxhall, have in keeping them clean, learn to have such Holes in their Street Lamps. But those Holes being made for another purpose, viz. to communicate Flame more suddenly to the Wick, by a little Flax hanging down thro' them, the other Use of letting in Air seems not to have been thought of. And therefore, after the Lamps have been lit a few Hours, the Streets of London are very poorly illuminated.——

The Mention of these Improvements puts me in mind of one I propos'd when in London, to Dr. Fothergill, who was among the best Men I have known, and a great Promoter of useful Projects. I had observ'd that the Streets when dry were never swept and the light Dust carried away, but it was suffer'd to accumulate till wet Weather reduc'd it to Mud, and then after lying some Days so deep on the Pavement that there was no Crossing but in Paths kept clean by poor People with Brooms, it was with great Labour rak'd together and thrown up into Carts open above, the Sides of which suffer'd some of the Slush at every jolt on the Pavement to shake out and fall, some times to the Annoyance of Foot-Passengers. The Reason given for not sweeping the dusty Streets was, that the Dust would fly into the Windows of Shops and Houses. An accidental Occurrence had instructed me how much Sweeping might be done in a little Time. I found at my Door in Craven Street one Morning a poor Woman sweeping my Pavement with a birch Broom. She appeared very pale and feeble as just come out of a Fit of Sickness. I ask'd who employ'd her to sweep there. She said, "Nobody; but I am very poor and in Distress, and I sweeps before Gentlefolkeses Doors, and hopes they will give me something." I bid her sweep the whole Street clean and I would give her a Shilling. This was at 9 aClock. At 12 she came for the Shilling. From the Slowness I saw at first in her Working, I could scarce believe that the Work was done so soon, and sent my Servant to examine it, who reported that the whole Street was swept perfectly clean, and all the Dust plac'd in the Gutter which was in the Middle. And the next Rain wash'd it quite away, so that the Pavement and even the Kennel were perfectly clean.——I then judg'd that if that feeble Woman could sweep such a Street in 3 Hours, a strong active Man might have done it in half the time. And here let me remark the Convenience of having but one Gutter in such a narrow Street, running down its Middle, instead of two, one on each Side near the Footway. For when all the Rain that falls on a Street runs from the Sides and meets in the middle, it forms there a Current strong enough to wash away all the Mud it meets with: But when divided into two Channels, it is often too weak to cleanse either, and only makes the Mud it finds more fluid, so that the Wheels of Carriages and Feet of Horses throw and dash it up on the Foot Pavement which is thereby rendred foul and slippery, and sometimes splash it upon those who are walking.——My Proposal communicated to the good Doctor, was as follows.

"For the more effectual cleaning and keeping clean the Streets of London and Westminster, it is proposed,

"That the several Watchmen be contracted with to have the Dust swept up in dry Seasons, and the Mud rak'd up at other Times, each in the several Streets and Lanes of his Round.

"That they be furnish'd with Brooms and other proper Instruments for these purposes, to be kept at their respective Stands, ready to furnish the poor People they may employ in the Service.

"That in the dry Summer Months the Dust be all swept up into Heaps at proper Distances, before the Shops and Windows of Houses are usually opened: when the Scavengers with close-covered Carts shall also carry it all away.——

"That the Mud when rak'd up be not left in Heaps to be spread abroad again by the Wheels of Carriages and Trampling of Horses; but that the Scavengers be provided with Bodies of Carts, not plac'd high upon Wheels, but low upon Sliders; with Lattice Bottoms, which being cover'd with Straw, will retain the Mud thrown into them, and permit the Water to drain from it, whereby it will become much lighter, Water making the greatest Part of its Weight. These Bodies of Carts to be plac'd at convenient Distances, and the Mud brought to them in Wheelbarrows, they remaining where plac'd till the Mud is drain'd, and then Horses brought to draw them away."——

I have since had Doubts of the Practicability of the latter Part of this Proposal, on Account of the Narrowness of some Streets, and the Difficulty of placing the Draining Sleds so as not to encumber too much the Passage: But I am still of Opinion that the former, requiring the Dust, to be swept up and carry'd away before the Shops are open, is very practicable in the Summer, when the Days are long. For in walking thro' the Strand and Fleetstreet one Morning at 7 aClock I observ'd there was not one shop open tho' it had been Day-light and the Sun up above three Hours. The Inhabitants of London chusing voluntarily to live much by Candle Light, and sleep by Sunshine; and yet often complain a little absurdly, of the Duty on Candles and the high Price of Tallow.——

Some may think these trifling Matters not worth minding or relating: But when they consider, that tho' Dust blown into the Eyes of a single Person or into a single Shop on a windy Day, is but of small Importance, yet the great Number of the Instances in a populous City, and its frequent Repetitions give it Weight and Consequence; perhaps they will not censure very severely those who bestow some of Attention to Affairs of this seemingly low Nature. Human Felicity is produc'd not so much by great Pieces of good Fortune that seldom happen, as by little Advantages that occur every Day. Thus if you teach a poor young Man to shave himself and keep his Razor in order, you may contribute more to the Happiness of his Life than in giving him a 1000 Guineas. The Money may be soon spent, the Regret only remaining of having foolishly consum'd it. But in the other Case he escapes the frequent Vexation of waiting for Barbers, and of their sometimes dirty Fingers, offensive Breaths and dull Razors. He shaves when most convenient to him, and enjoys daily the Pleasure of its being done with a good Instrument.——With these Sentiments I have hazarded the few preceding Pages, hoping they may afford Hints which some time or other may be useful to a City I love, having lived many Years in it very happily; and perhaps to some of our Towns in America.——

Having been for some time employed by the Postmaster General of America, as his Comptroller, in regulating the several Offices, and bringing the Officers to account, I was upon his Death in 1753 appointed jointly with Mr. William Hunter to succeed him by a Commission from the Postmaster General in England. The American Office had never hitherto paid any thing to that of Britain. We were to have 600£ a Year between us if we could make that Sum out of the Profits of the Office. To do this, a Variety of Improvements were necessary; some of these were inevitably at first expensive; so that in the first four Years the Office became above 900£ in debt to us.——But it soon after began to repay us, and before I was displac'd, by a Freak of the Minister's, of which I shall speak hereafter, we had brought it to yield *three times* as much clear Revenue to the Crown as the Post-Office of Ireland. Since that imprudent Transaction, they have receiv'd from it,——Not one Farthing.——

The Business of the Post-Office occasion'd my taking a Journey this Year to New England, where the College of Cambridge of their own Motion, presented me with the Degree of Master of Arts. Yale College in Connecticut, had before made me a similar Compliment. Thus without studying in any College I came to partake of their Honours. They were confer'd in Consideration of my Improvements and Discoveries in the electric Branch of Natural Philosophy.——

In 1754, War with France being again apprehended, a Congress of Commissioners from the different Colonies, was by an Order of the Lords of Trade, to be assembled at Albany, there to confer with the Chiefs of the Six Nations, concerning the Means of defending both their Country and ours. Governor Hamilton, having receiv'd this Order, acquainted the House with it, requesting they would furnish proper Presents for the Indians to be given on this Occasion; and naming the Speaker (Mr. Norris) and my self, to join Mr. Thomas Penn and Mr. Secretary Peters, as Commissioners to act for Pennsylvania. The House approv'd the Nomination, and provided the Goods for the Present, tho' they did not much like treating out of the Province, and we met the other Commissioners and met at Albany about the Middle of June. In our Way thither, I projected and drew up a Plan for the Union of all the Colonies, under one Government so far as might be necessary for Defence, and other important general Purposes. As we pass'd thro' New York, I had there shown my Project to Mr. James Alexander and Mr. Kennedy, two Gentlemen of great Knowledge in public Affairs, and being fortified by their Approbation I ventur'd to lay it before the Congress. It then appear'd that several of the Commissioners had form'd Plans of the same kind. A previous Question was first taken whether a Union should be established, which pass'd in the Affirmative unanimously. A Committee was then appointed one Member from each Colony, to consider the several Plans and report. Mine happen'd to be prefer'd, and with a few Amendments was accordingly reported. By this Plan, the general Government was to be administred by a President General appointed and supported by the Crown, and a Grand Council to be chosen by the Representatives of the People of the several Colonies met in their respective Assemblies. The Debates upon it in Congress went on daily hand in hand with the Indian Business. Many Objections and Difficulties were started, but at length they were all overcome, and the Plan was unanimously agreed to, and Copies ordered to be transmitted to the Board of Trade and to the Assemblies of the several Provinces. Its Fate was singular. The Assemblies did not adopt it as they all thought there was too much *Prerogative* in it; and in England it was judg'd to have too much of the *Democratic*: The Board of Trade therefore did not approve of it; nor recommend it for the Approbation of his Majesty; but another Scheme was form'd (suppos'd better to answer the same Purpose) whereby the Governors of the Provinces with some Members of their respective Councils were to meet and order the raising of Troops, building of Forts, &c. &c to draw on the Treasury of Great Britain for the Expence, which was afterwards to be refunded by an Act of Parliament laying a Tax on America. My Plan, with my Reasons in support of it, is to be found among my political Papers that are printed. Being the Winter following in Boston, I had much Conversation with Governor Shirley upon both the Plans. Part of what pass'd between us on the Occasion may also be seen among those Papers.——The different and contrary Reasons of dislike to my Plan, makes me suspect that it was really the true Medium; and I am still of Opinion it would have been happy for both Sides the Water if it had been adopted. The Colonies so united would have been sufficiently strong to have defended themselves; there would then have been no need of Troops from England; of course the subsequent Pretence for Taxing America, and the bloody Contest it occasioned, would have been avoided. But such Mistakes are not new; History is full of the Errors of States and Princes.

> *"Look round the habitable World, how few*
> *Know their own Good, or knowing it pursue."*[2]

Those who govern, having much Business on their hands, do not generally like to take the Trouble of considering and carrying into Execution new Projects. The best public Measures are therefore seldom *adopted from previous Wisdom*, but *forc'd by the Occasion*.

The Governor of Pennsylvania in sending it down to the Assembly, express'd his Approbation of the Plan "as appearing to him to be drawn

[2] [Juvenal's tenth *Satire*, lines 1–3, trans. John Dryden.]

up with great Clearness and Strength of Judgment, and therefore recommended it as well worthy their closest and most serious Attention." The House however, by the Managemt of a certain Member, took it up when I happen'd to be absent, which I thought not very fair, and reprobated it without paying any Attention to it at all, to my no small Mortification.

In my Journey to Boston this Year I met at New York with our new Governor, Mr. Morris, just arriv'd there from England, with whom I had been before intimately acquainted. He brought a Commission to supersede Mr. Hamilton, who, tir'd with the Disputes his Proprietary Instructions subjected him to, had resigned. Mr. Morris ask'd me, if I thought he must expect as uncomfortable an Administration. I said, No; you may on the contrary have a very comfortable one, if you will only take care not to enter into any Dispute with the Assembly; "My dear Friend, says he, pleasantly, how can you advise my avoiding Disputes. You know I love Disputing; it is one of my greatest Pleasures: However, to show the Regard I have for your Counsel, I promise you I will if possible avoid them." He had some Reason for loving to dispute, being eloquent, an acute Sophister, and therefore generally successful in argumentative Conversation. He had been brought up to it from a Boy, his Father (as I have heard) accustoming his Children to dispute with one another for his Diversion while sitting at Table after Dinner. But I think the Practice was not wise, for in the Course of my Observation, these disputing, contradicting and confuting People are generally unfortunate in their Affairs. They get Victory sometimes, but they never get Good Will, which would be of more use to them. We parted, he going to Philadelphia, and I to Boston. In returning, I met at New York with the Votes of the Assembly, by which it appear'd that notwithstanding his Promise to me, he and the House were already in high Contention, and it was a continual Battle between them, as long as he retain'd the Government. I had my Share of it; for as soon as I got back to my Seat in the Assembly, I was put on every Committee for answering his Speeches and Messages, and by the Committees always desired to make the drafts. Our Answers as well as his Messages were often tart, and sometimes indecently abusive. And as he knew I wrote for the Assembly, one might have imagined that when we met we could hardly avoid cutting Throats. But he was so good natur'd a Man, that no personal Difference between him and me was occasion'd by the Contest, and we often din'd together. One Afternoon in the height of this public Quarrel, we met in the Street. "Franklin, says he, you must go home with me and spend the Evening. I am to have some Company that you will like;" and taking me by the Arm he led me to his House. In gay Conversation over our Wine after Supper he told us Jokingly that he much admir'd the Idea of Sancho Panza, who when it was propos'd to give him a Government, requested it might be a Government of *Blacks*, as then, if he could not agree with his People he might sell them. One of his Friends who sat next me, says, "Franklin, why do you continue to side with these damn'd Quakers? had not you better sell them? the Proprietor would give you a good Price." The Governor, says I, has not yet *black'd* them enough. He had indeed labour'd hard to blacken the Assembly in all his Messages, but they wip'd off his Colouring as fast as he laid it on, and plac'd it in return thick upon his own Face; so that finding he was likely to be negrify'd himself, he as well as Mr. Hamilton, grew tir'd of the Contest, and quitted the Government.

These public Quarrels were all at bottom owing to the Proprietaries, our hereditary Governors; who when any Expence was to be incurr'd for the Defence of their Province, with incredible Meanness instructed their Deputies to pass no Act for levying the necessary Taxes, unless their vast Estates were in the same Act expresly excused; and they had even taken Bonds of those Deputies to observe such Instructions. The Assemblies for three Years held out against this Injustice, Tho' constrain'd to bend at last. At length Capt. Denny, who was Governor Morris's Successor, ventur'd to disobey those Instructions; how that was brought about I shall show hereafter.

But I am got forward too fast with my Story; there are still some Transactions to be mentioned that happened during the Administration of Governor Morris.——

War being, in a manner, commenced with France, the Government of Massachusetts Bay projected an Attack upon Crown Point, and sent Mr. Quincy to Pennsylvania, and Mr. Pownall, afterwards Governor Pownall, to New York to sollicit Assistance. As I was in the Assembly, knew its Temper, and was Mr. Quincy's Countryman, he apply'd to me for my Influence and Assistance. I dictated his Address to them which was well receiv'd. They voted an Aid of Ten Thousand Pounds, to be laid out in Provisions. But the Governor refusing his Assent to their Bill, (which included this with other Sums granted for the Use of the Crown) unless a Clause were inserted exempting the Proprietary Estate from bearing any Part of the Tax that would be necessary, the Assembly, tho' very desirous of making their Grant to New England effectual, were at a Loss how to accomplish it. Mr. Quincy laboured hard with the Governor to obtain his Assent, but he was obstinate. I then suggested a Method of doing the Business without the Governor, by Orders on the Trustees of the Loan-Office, which by Law the Assembly had the Right of Drawing. There was indeed little or no Money at that time in the Office, and therefore I propos'd that the Orders should be payable in a Year and to bear an Interest of Five percent. With these Orders I suppos'd the Provisions might easily be purchas'd. The Assembly with very little Hesitation adopted the Proposal. The Orders were immediately printed, and I was one of the Committee directed to sign and dispose of them. The Fund for Paying them was the Interest of all the Paper Currency then extant in the Province upon Loan, together with the Revenue arising from the Excise which being known to be more than sufficient, they obtain'd instant Credit, and were not only receiv'd in Payment for the Provisions, but many money'd People who had Cash lying by them, vested it in those Orders, which they found advantageous, as they bore Interest while upon hand, and might on any Occasion be used as Money: So that they were eagerly all bought up, and in a few Weeks none of them were to be seen. Thus this important Affair was by my means compleated, Mr. Quincy return'd Thanks to the Assembly in a handsome Memorial, went home highly pleas'd with the Success of his Embassy, and ever after bore for me the most cordial and affectionate Friendship.——

The British Government not chusing to permit the Union of the Colonies, as propos'd at Albany, and to trust that Union with their Defence, lest they should thereby grow too military, and feel their own Strength, Suspicions and Jealousies at this time being entertain'd of them; sent over General Braddock with two Regiments of Regular English Troops for that purpose. He landed at Alexandria in Virginia, and thence march'd to Frederic Town in Maryland, where he halted for Carriages. Our Assembly apprehending, from some Information, that he had conceived violent Prejudices against them, as averse to the Service, wish'd me to wait upon him, not as from them, but as Postmaster General, under the guise of proposing to settle with him the Mode of conducting with most Celerity and Certainty the Dispatches between him and the Governors of the several Provinces, with whom he must necessarily have continual Correspondence, and of which they propos'd to pay the Expence. My Son accompanied me on this Journey. We found the General at Frederic Town, waiting impatiently for the Return of those he had sent thro' the back Parts of Maryland and Virginia to collect Waggons. I staid with him several Days, din'd with him daily, and had full Opportunity of removing all his Prejudices, by the Information of what the Assembly had before his Arrival actually done and were still willing to do to facilitate his Operations. When I was about to depart, the Returns of Waggons to be obtain'd were brought in, by which it appear'd that they amounted only to twenty-five, and not all of those were in serviceable Condition. The General and all the Officers were surpriz'd, declar'd the Expedition was then at an End, being impossible, and exclaim'd against the Ministers for ignorantly landing them in a Country destitute of the Means of conveying their Stores, Baggage, &c. not less than 150 Waggons being necessary. I happen'd to say, I thought it was pity they had not been landed rather in Pennsylvania, as in that Country almost every Farmer had his Waggon. The General eagerly laid hold of my Words, and said, "Then you, Sir, who are a Man of Interest there, can probably procure them for us; and I beg you will undertake it." I ask'd what Terms were to be offer'd the Owners of the Waggons; and I was desir'd to put on Paper the Terms that appear'd to me necessary. This I did, and they were agreed to, and a Commission and Instructions accordingly prepar'd immediately. What those Terms were will appear in the Advertisement I publish'd as soon as I arriv'd at Lancaster; which being, from the great and sudden Effect it produc'd, a Piece of some Curiosity, I shall insert at length, as follows.

Advertisement.[3]

Lancaster, April 26, 1755.

Whereas 150 Waggons, with 4 Horses to each Waggon, and 1500 Saddle or Pack-Horses are wanted for the Service of his Majesty's Forces now about to rendezvous at *Wills*'s Creek; and his Excellency General *Braddock* hath been pleased to impower me to contract for the Hire of the same; I hereby give Notice, that I shall attend for that Purpose at *Lancaster* from this Time till next *Wednesday* Evening; and at *York* from next *Thursday* Morning 'till *Friday* Evening; where I shall be ready to agree for Waggons and Teams, or single Horses, on the following Terms, *viz.*

1*st*. That there shall be paid for each Waggon with 4 good Horses and a Driver, *Fifteen Shillings* per *Diem:* And for each able Horse with a Pack-Saddle or other Saddle and Furniture, *Two Shillings* per *Diem*. And for each able Horse without a Saddle, *Eighteen Pence* per *Diem*.

[3] [Lancaster: (William Dunlap), 26 April 1755.]

2dly, That the Pay commence from the Time of their joining the Forces at *Wills*'s Creek (which must be on or before the twentieth of *May* ensuing) and that a reasonable Allowance be made over and above for the Time necessary for their travelling to *Wills*'s Creek and home again after their Discharge.

3dly, Each Waggon and Team, and every Saddle or Pack Horse is to be valued by indifferent Persons, chosen between me and the Owner, and in Case of the Loss of any Waggon, Team or other Horse in the Service, the Price according to such Valuation, is to be allowed and paid.

4thly, Seven Days Pay is to be advanced and paid in hand by me to the Owner of each Waggon and Team, or Horse, at the Time of contracting, if required; and the Remainder to be paid by General *Braddock*, or by the Paymaster of the Army, at the Time of their Discharge, or from time to time as it shall be demanded.

5thly, No Drivers of Waggons, or Persons taking care of the hired Horses, are on any Account to be called upon to do the Duty of Soldiers, or be otherwise employ'd than in conducting or taking Care of their Carriages and Horses.

6thly, All Oats, Indian Corn or other Forage, that Waggons or Horses bring to the Camp more than is necessary for the Subsistence of the Horses, is to be taken for the Use of the Army, and a reasonable Price paid for it.

Note. My Son *William Franklin*, is impowered to enter into like Contracts with any Person in *Cumberland* County.

B. FRANKLIN.

To the Inhabitants of the Counties of
Lancaster, York, *and* Cumberland.

Friends and Countrymen,

BEING occasionally at the Camp at *Frederic* a few Days since, I found the General and Officers of the Army extreamly exasperated, on Account of their not being supply'd with Horses and Carriages, which had been expected from this Province as most able to furnish them; but thro' the Dissensions between our Governor and Assembly, Money had not been provided nor any Steps taken for that Purpose.

It was proposed to send an armed Force immediately into these Counties, to seize as many of the best Carriages and Horses as should be wanted, and compel as many Persons into the Service as would be necessary to drive and take care of them.

I apprehended that the Progress of a Body of Soldiers thro' these Counties on such an Occasion, especially considering the Temper they are in, and their Resentment against us, would be attended with many and great Inconveniencies to the Inhabitants; and therefore more willingly undertook the Trouble of trying first what might be done by fair and equitable Means.

The People of these back Counties have lately complained to the Assembly that a sufficient Currency was wanting; you have now an Opportunity of receiving and dividing among you a very considerable Sum; for if the Service of this Expedition should continue (as it's more than probable it will) for 120 Days, the Hire of these Waggons and Horses will amount to upwards of *Thirty thousand Pounds*, which will be paid you in Silver and Gold of the King's Money.

The Service will be light and easy, for the Army will scarce march above 12 Miles per Day, and the Waggons and Baggage Horses, as they carry those Things that are absolutely necessary to the Welfare of the Army, must march with the Army and no faster, and are, for the Army's sake, always plac'd where they can be most secure, whether on a March or in Camp.

If you are really, as I believe you are, good and loyal Subjects to His Majesty, you may now do a most acceptable Service, and make it easy to yourselves; for three or four of such as cannot separately spare from the Business of their Plantations a Waggon and four Horses and a Driver, may do it together, one furnishing the Waggon, another one or two Horses, and another the Driver, and divide the Pay proportionably between you. But if you do not this Service to your King and Country voluntarily, when such good Pay and reasonable Terms are offered you, your Loyalty will be strongly suspected; the King's Business must be done; so many brave Troops, come so far for your Defence, must not stand idle, thro' your backwardness to do what may be reasonably expected from you; Waggons and Horses must be had; violent Measures will probably be used; and you will be to seek for a Recompence where you can find it, and your Case perhaps be little pitied or regarded.

I have no particular Interest in this Affair; as (except the Satisfaction of endeavouring to do Good and prevent Mischief) I shall have only my Labour for my Pains. If this Method of obtaining the Waggons and Horses is not like to succeed, I am oblig'd to send Word to the General in fourteen Days; and I suppose Sir *John St. Clair* the Hussar, with a Body of Soldiers, will immediately enter the Province, for the Purpose aforesaid, of which I shall be sorry to hear, because *I am*,

very sincerely and truly
your Friend and Well-wisher,

B. FRANKLIN

I receiv'd of the General about 800£ to be disburs'd in Advance-money to the Waggon-Owners &c: but that Sum being insufficient, I advanc'd upwards of 200£ more, and in two Weeks, the 150 Waggons with 259 carrying Horses were on their March for the Camp.——The Advertisement promised Payment according to the Valuation, in case any Waggon or Horse should be lost. The Owners however, alledging they did not know General Braddock, or what Dependance might be had on his Promise, insisted on my Bond for the Performance, which I accordingly gave them.

While I was at the Camp, supping one Evening with the Officers of Col. Dunbar's Regiment, he represented to me his Concern for the Subalterns, who he said were generally not in Affluence, and could ill afford in this dear Country to lay in the Stores that might be necessary in so long a March thro' a Wilderness where nothing was to be purchas'd. I commisserated their Case, and resolved to endeavour procuring them some Relief. I said nothing however to him of my Intention, but wrote the next Morning to the Committee of Assembly, who had the Disposition of some public Money, warmly recommending the Case of these Officers to their Consideration, and proposing that a Present should be sent them of Necessaries and Refreshments. My Son, who had had some Experience of a Camp Life, and of its Wants, drew up a List for me, which I inclos'd in my Letter. The Committee approv'd, and used such Diligence, that conducted by my Son, the Stores arrived at the Camp as soon as the Waggons. They consisted of 20 Parcels, each containing

6 lb Loaf Sugar
6 lb good Muscovado D°
1 lb good Green Tea
1 lb good Bohea D°
6 lb good ground Coffee
6 lb Chocolate
1/2 Cwt best white Biscuit
1/2 lb Pepper
1 Quart best white Wine Vinegar

1 Gloucester Cheese
1 Kegg containing 20 lb good Butter
2 Doz. old Madeira Wine
2 Gallons Jamaica Spirits
1 Bottle Flour of Mustard
2 well-cur'd Hams
1/2 Doz dry'd Tongues
6 lb Rice
6 lb Raisins.

These 20 Parcels well pack'd were plac'd on as many Horses, each Parcel with the Horse, being intended as a Present for one Officer. They were very thankfully receiv'd, and the Kindness acknowledg'd by Letters to me from the Colonels of both Regiments in the most grateful Terms. The General too was highly satisfied with my Conduct in procuring him the Waggons, &c. and readily paid my Account of Disbursements; thanking me repeatedly and requesting my farther Assistance in sending Provisions after him. I undertook this also, and was busily employ'd in it till we heard of his Defeat, advancing, for the Service, of my own Money, upwards of 1000£ Sterling, of which I sent him an Account. It came to his Hands luckily for me a few Days before the Battle, and he return'd me immediately an Order on the Paymaster for the round Sum of 1000£ leaving the Remainder to the next Account. I consider this Payment as good Luck; having never been able to obtain that Remainder; of which more hereafter.

This General was I think a brave Man, and might probably have made a Figure as a good Officer in some European War. But he had too much self-confidence, too high an Opinion of the Validity of Regular Troops, and too mean a One of both Americans and Indians. George Croghan, our Indian Interpreter, join'd him on his March with 100 of those People, who might have been of great Use to his Army as Guides, Scouts, &c. if he had treated them kindly;——but he slighted and neglected them, and they gradually left him. In Conversation with him one day, he was giving me some Account of his intended Progress. "After taking Fort Duquesne, says he, I am to proceed to Niagara; and having taken that, to Frontenac, if the Season will allow time; and I suppose it will; for Duquesne can hardly detain me above three or four Days; and then I see nothing that can obstruct my March to Niagara."——Having before revolv'd in my Mind the long Line his Army must make in their March, by a very narrow

Road to be cut for them thro' the Woods and Bushes; and also what I had read of a former Defeat of 1500 French who invaded the Iroquois Country, I had conceiv'd some Doubts,——and some Fears for the Event of the Campaign. But I ventur'd only to say, To be sure, Sir, if you arrive well before Duquesne, with these fine Troops so well provided with Artillery, that Place, not yet compleatly fortified, and as we hear with no very strong Garrison, can probably make but a short Resistance. The only Danger I apprehend of Obstruction to your March, is from Ambuscades of Indians, who by constant Practice are dextrous in laying and executing them. And the slender Line near four Miles long, which your Army must make, may expose it to be attack'd by Surprize in its Flanks, and to be cut like a Thread into several Pieces, which from their Distance cannot come up in time to support each other. He smil'd at my Ignorance, and reply'd, "These Savages may indeed be a formidable Enemy to your raw American Militia; but, upon the King's regular and disciplin'd Troops, Sir, it is impossible they should make any Impression." I was conscious of an Impropriety in my Disputing with a military Man in Matters of his Profession, and said no more.——The Enemy however did not take the Advantage of his Army which I apprehended its long Line of March expos'd it to, but let it advance without Interruption till within 9 Miles of the Place; and then when more in a Body, (for it had just pass'd a River, where the Front had halted till all were come over) and in a more open Part of the Woods than any it had pass'd, attack'd its advanc'd Guard, by a heavy Fire from behind Trees and Bushes; which was the first Intelligence the General had of an Enemy's being near him. This Guard being disordered, the General hurried the Troops up to their Assistance, which was done in great Confusion thro' Waggons, Baggage and Cattle; and presently the Fire came upon their Flank; the Officers being on Horseback were more easily distinguish'd, picked out as Marks, and fell very fast; and the Soldiers were crowded together in a Huddle, having or hearing no Orders, and standing to be shot at till two thirds of them were killed, and then being seiz'd with a Pannick the whole fled with Precipitation. The Waggoners took each a Horse out of his Team, and scamper'd; their Example was immediately follow'd by others, so that all the Waggons, Provisions, Artillery and Stores were left to the Enemy. The General being wounded was brought off with Difficulty, his Secretary Mr. Shirley was killed by his Side, and out of 86 Officers 63 were killed or wounded, and 714 Men killed out of 1100. These 1100 had been picked Men, from the whole Army, the Rest had been left behind with Col. Dunbar, who was to follow with the heavier Part of the

Stores, Provisions and Baggage. The Flyers, not being pursu'd, arriv'd at Dunbar's Camp, and the Pannick they brought with them Instantly seiz'd him and all his People. And tho' he had now above 1000 Men, and the Enemy who had beaten Braddock did not at most exceed 400, Indians and French together; instead of Proceeding and endeavouring to recover some of the lost Honour, he order'd all the Stores Ammunition, &c to be destroy'd, that he might have more Horses to assist his Flight towards the Settlements and less Lumber to remove. He was there met with Requests from the Governor's of Virginia, Maryland and Pennsylvania, that he would post his Troops on the Frontiers so as to afford some Protection to the Inhabitants; but he continu'd his hasty March thro' all the Country, not thinking himself safe till he arriv'd at Philadelphia, where the Inhabitants could protect him. This whole Transaction gave us Americans the first Suspicion that our exalted Ideas of the Prowess of British Regulars had not been well founded.——

In their first March too, from their Landing till they got beyond the Settlements, they had plundered and stript the Inhabitants, totally ruining some poor Families, besides insulting, abusing and confining the People if they remonstrated.——This was enough to put us out of Conceit of such Defenders if we had really wanted any. How different was the Conduct of Our French Friends in 1781, who during a March thro' the most inhabited Part of our Country, from Rhode Island to Virginia, near 700 Miles, occasion'd not the smallest Complaint, for the Loss of a Pig, a Chicken, or even an Apple!

Capt. Orme, who was one of the General's Aid de Camps, and being grievously wounded was brought off with him, and continu'd with him to his Death, which happen'd in a few Days, told me, that he was totally silent, all the first Day, and at Night only said, *Who'd have thought it?* that he was silent again the following Days, only saying at last, *We shall better know how to deal with them another time;* and dy'd a few Minutes after.

The Secretary's Papers with all the General's Orders, Instructions and Correspondence falling into the Enemy's Hands, they selected and translated into French a Number of the Articles, which they printed to prove the hostile Intentions of the British Court before the Declaration of War. Among these I saw some Letters of the General to the Ministry speaking highly of the great Service I had rendred the Army, and recommending me to their Notice. David Hume too, who was some Years after Secretary to Lord Harcourt when Minister in France, and afterwards to General Conway when Secretary of State, told me he had seen among the Papers in that Office Letters from Braddock highly recommending me. But the Expedition having been unfortunate, my Service it seems was not thought of much Value, for those Recommendations were never of any Use to me.——

As to Rewards from himself, I ask'd only one, which was, that he would give Orders to his Officers not to enlist any more of our bought Servants, and that he would discharge such as had been already enlisted. This he readily granted, and several were accordingly return'd to their Masters on my Application.——Dunbar, when the Command devolv'd on him, was not so generous. He Being at Philadelphia on his Retreat, or rather Flight, I apply'd to him for the Discharge of the Servants of three poor Farmers of Lancaster County that he had inlisted, reminding him of the late General's Orders on that head. He promis'd me, that if the Masters would come to him at Trenton, where he should be in a few Days on his March to New York, he would there deliver their Men to them. They accordingly were at the Expence and Trouble of going to Trenton,——and there he refus'd to perform his Promise, to their great Loss and Disappointment.——

As soon as the Loss of the Waggons and Horses was generally known, all the Owners came upon me for the Valuation which I had given Bond to pay. Their Demands gave me a great deal of Trouble, my acquainting them that the Money was ready in the Paymaster's Hands, but that Orders for paying it must first be obtained from General Shirley, and my assuring them that I had apply'd to that General by Letter, but he being at a Distance an Answer could not soon be receiv'd, and they must have Patience; all this was not sufficient to satisfy, and some began to sue me. General Shirley at length reliev'd me from this terrible Situation, by appointing Commissioners to examine the Claims and ordering Payment. They amounted to near twenty Thousand Pound, which to pay would have ruined me.

Before we had the News of this Defeat, the two Doctors Bond came to me with a Subscription Paper, for raising Money to defray the Expence of a grand Fire Work, which it was intended to exhibit at a Rejoicing on receipt of the News of our Taking Fort Duquesne. I looked grave and said, "it would, I thought, be time enough to prepare for the Rejoicing when we knew we should have occasion to rejoice."——They seem'd surpriz'd that I did not immediately comply with their Proposal. "Why, the D__l," says one of them, "you surely don't suppose that the Fort will not be taken?" "I don't know that it will not be taken; but I know that the Events of War are subject to great Uncertainty."——I gave them the Reasons of my doubting. The Subscription was dropt, and the Projectors thereby miss'd that Mortification they would have undergone if the Firework had been prepared.——Dr. Bond on some other Occasions afterwards said, that he did not like Franklin's forebodings.——

Governor Morris who had continually worried the Assembly with Message after Message before the Defeat of Braddock, to beat them into the making of Acts to raise Money for the Defence of the Province without Taxing among others the Proprietary Estates, and had rejected all their Bills for not having such an exempting Clause, now redoubled his Attacks, with more hope of Success, the Danger and Necessity being greater. The Assembly however continu'd firm, believing they had Justice on their side, and that it would be giving up an essential Right, if they suffered the Governor to amend their Money-Bills. In one of the last, indeed, which was for granting 50,000£ his propos'd Amendment was only of a single Word; the Bill express'd that all Estates real and personal were to be taxed, those of the Proprietaries *not* excepted. His Amendment was; for *not* read *only*. A small but very material Alteration!——However, when the News of this Disaster reach'd England, our Friends there whom we had taken care to furnish with all the Assembly's Answers to the Governor's Messages, rais'd a Clamour against the Proprietaries for their Meanness and Injustice in giving their Governor such Instructions, some going so far as to say that by obstructing the Defence of their Province, they forfeited their Right to it. They were intimidated by this, and sent Orders to their Receiver General to add 5000£ of their Money to whatever Sum might be given by the Assembly, for such Purpose. This being notified to the House, was accepted in Lieu of their Share of a general Tax, and a new Bill was form'd with an exempting Clause which pass'd accordingly. By this Act I was appointed one of the Commissioners for disposing of the Money, 60,000£. I had been active in modelling it, and procuring its Passage: and had at the same time drawn a Bill for establishing and disciplining a voluntary Militia, which I carried thro' the House without much Difficulty, as Care was taken in it, to leave the Quakers at their Liberty. To promote the Association necessary to form the Militia, I wrote a Dialogue,[4] stating and answering all the Objections I could think of to such a Militia, which was printed and had as I thought great Effect. While the several Companies in the City and Country were forming and learning their Exercise, the

[4] This Dialogue and the Militia Act, are in the Gentleman's Magazine for February and March 1756.

Governor prevail'd with me to take Charge of our Northwestern Frontier, which was infested by the Enemy, and provide for the Defence of the Inhabitants by raising Troops, and building a Line of Forts. I undertook this military Business, tho' I did not conceive myself well-qualified for it. He gave me a Commission with full Powers and a Parcel of blank Commissions for Officers to be given to whom I thought fit. I had but little Difficulty in raising Men, having soon 560 under my Command. My Son who had in the preceding War been an Officer in the Army rais'd against Canada, was my Aid de Camp, and of great Use to me. The Indians had burnt Gnadenhut, a Village settled by the Moravians, and massacred the Inhabitants, but the Place was thought a good Situation for one of the Forts. In order to march thither, I assembled the Companies at Bethlehem, the chief Establishment of those People. I was surprized to find it in so good a Posture of Defence. The Destruction of Gnadenhut had made them apprehend Danger. The principal Buildings were defended by a Stockade: They had purchased a Quantity of Arms and Ammunition from New York, and had even plac'd Quantities of small Paving Stones between the Windows of their high Stone Houses, for their Women to throw down upon the Heads of any Indians that should attempt to force into them. The armed Bretheren too, kept Watch, and reliev'd as methodically as in any Garrison Town. In Conversation with Bishop Spangenberg, I mention'd this my Surprize; for knowing they had obtain'd an Act of Parliament exempting them from military Duties in the Colonies, I had suppos'd they were conscienciously scrupulous of bearing Arms. He answer'd me, "That it was not one of their establish'd Principles; but that at the time of their obtaining that Act, it was thought to be a Principle with many of their People. On this Occasion, however, they to their Surprize found it adopted by but a few." It seems they were either deceiv'd in themselves, or deceiv'd the Parliament. But Common Sense aided by present Danger, will sometimes be too strong for whimsicall Opinions.

It was the Beginning of January when we set out upon this Business of Building Forts. I sent one Detachment towards the Minisinks, with Instructions to erect one for the Security of that upper Part of the Country; and another to the lower Part, with similar Instructions. And I concluded to go myself with the rest of my Force to Gnadenhut, where a Fort was tho't more immediately necessary. The Moravians procur'd me five Waggons for our Tools, Stores, Baggage, &c. Just before we left Bethlehem, Eleven Farmers who had been driven from their Plantations by the Indians, came to me, requesting a supply of Fire Arms, that they might go back and fetch off their Cattle. I gave them each a Gun with suitable Ammunition. We had not march'd many Miles before it began to rain, and it continu'd raining all Day. There were no Habitations on the Road, to shelter us, till we arriv'd near Night, at the House of a German, where and in his Barn we were all huddled together as wet as Water could make us. It was well we were not attack'd in our March, for Our Arms were of the most ordinary Sort and our Men could not keep their Gunlocks dry. The Indians are dextrous in Contrivances for that purpose, which we had not. They met that Day the eleven poor Farmers above-mentioned and kill'd Ten of them. The one who escap'd inform'd that his and his Companions Guns would not go off, the Priming being wet with the Rain. The next Day being fair, we continu'd our March and arriv'd at the desolated Gnadenhut. There was a Saw Mill near, round which were left several Piles of Boards, with which we soon hutted ourselves; an Operation the more necessary at that inclement Season, as we had no Tents. Our first Work was to bury more effectually the Dead we found there, who had been half interr'd by the Country People. The next Morning our Fort was plann'd and mark'd out, the Circumference measuring 455 feet, which would require as many Palisades to be made of Trees one with another of a Foot Diameter each. Our Axes, of which we had 70 were immediately set to work, to cut down Trees; and our Men being dextrous in the Use of them, great Dispatch was made. Seeing the Trees fall so fast, I had the Curiosity to look at my Watch when two Men began to cut at a Pine. In 6 Minutes they had it upon the Ground; and I found it of 14 Inches Diameter. Each Pine made three Palisades of 18 Feet long, pointed at one End. While these were preparing, our other Men, dug a Trench all round of three feet deep in which the Palisades were to be planted, and our Waggons, the Body being taken off, and the fore and hind Wheels separated by taking out the Pin which united the two Parts of the Perch, we had 10 Carriages with two Horses each, to bring the Palisades from the Woods to the Spot. When they were set up, our Carpenters built a Stage of Boards all round within, about 6 Feet high, for the Men to stand on when to fire thro' the Loopholes. We had one swivel Gun which we mounted on one of the Angles; and fired it as soon as fix'd, to let the Indians know, if any were within hearing, that we had such Pieces; and thus our Fort, (if such a magnificent Name may be given to so miserable a Stockade) was finished in a Week, tho' it rain'd so hard every other Day that the Men could not work.

This gave me occasion to observe, that when Men are employ'd they are best contented. For on the Days they work'd they were good-natur'd and chearful; and with the consciousness of having done a good Days work they spent the Evenings jollily; but on the idle Days they were mutinous and quarrelsome, finding fault with their Pork, the Bread, &c. and in continual ill-humour: which put me in mind of a Sea-Captain, whose Rule it was to keep his Men constantly at Work; and when his Mate once told him that they had done every thing, and there was nothing farther to employ them about; O, says he, *make them scour the Anchor*.

This kind of Fort, however contemptible, is a sufficient Defence against Indians who have no Cannon. Finding our selves now posted securely, and having a Place to retreat to on Occasion, we ventur'd out in Parties to scour the adjacent Country. We met with no Indians, but we found the Places on the neighbouring Hills where they had lain to watch our Proceedings. There was an Art in their Contrivance of these Places that seems worth mention. It being Winter, a Fire was necessary for them. But a common Fire on the Surface of the Ground would by its Light have discover'd their Position at a Distance. They had therefore dug Holes in the Ground about three feet Diameter, and some what deeper. We saw where they had with their Hatchets cut off the Charcoal from the Sides of burnt Logs lying in the Woods. With these Coals they had made small Fires in the Bottom of the Holes, and we observ'd among the Weeds and Grass the Prints of their Bodies made by their laying all round with their Legs hanging down in the Holes to keep their Feet warm, which with them is an essential Point. This kind of Fire, so manag'd, could not discover them either by its Light, Flame; Sparks or even Smoke. It appear'd that their Number was not great, and it seems they saw we were too many to be attack'd by them with Prospect of Advantage.

We had for our Chaplain a zealous Presbyterian Minister, Mr. Beatty, who complain'd to me that the Men did not generally attend his Prayers and Exhortations. When they enlisted, they were promis'd, besides Pay and Provisions, a Gill of Rum a Day, which was punctually serv'd out to them half in the Morning and the other half in the Evening, and I observ'd they were as punctual in attending to receive it. Upon which I said to Mr. Beatty, "It is perhaps below the Dignity of your Profession to act as Steward of the Rum. But if you were to deal it out, and only just after Prayers, you would have them all about you." He lik'd the Thought, undertook the Office, and with the help of a few hands to measure out the Liquor executed it to Satisfaction; and never were Prayers more generally and more punctually attended. So that I thought this Method preferable to the Punishments inflicted by some military Laws for Non-Attendance on Divine Service.

I had hardly finish'd this Business, and got my Fort well stor'd with Provisions, when I receiv'd a Letter from the Governor, acquainting me that he had called the Assembly, and wish'd my Attendance there, if the Posture of Affairs on the Frontiers was such that my remaining there was no longer necessary. My Friends too of the Assembly pressing me by their Letters to be if possible at the Meeting, and my three intended Forts being now compleated, and the Inhabitants contented to remain on their Farms under that Protection, I resolved to return. The more willingly as a New England Officer, Col. Clapham, experienc'd in Indian War, being on a Visit to our Establishment, consented to accept the Command. I gave him a Commission, and parading the Garrison had it read before them, and introduc'd him to them as an Officer who from his Skill in Military Affairs, was much more fit to command them than myself; and giving them a little Exhortation took my Leave. I was escorted as far as Bethlehem, where I rested a few Days, to recover from the Fatigue I had undergone. The first Night being in a good Bed, I could hardly sleep, it was so different from my hard Lodging on the Floor of our Hut at Gnaden, wrapt only in a Blanket or two.——

While at Bethlehem, I enquir'd a Little into the Practices of the Moravians. Some of them had accompanied me, and all were very kind to me. I found they work'd for a common Stock, eat at common Tables, and slept in common Dormitorys, great Numbers together. In the Dormitories I observ'd Loopholes at certain Distances all along just under the Ceiling, which I thought judiciously plac'd for Change of Air. I was at their Church, where I was entertain'd with good Musick, the Organ being accompanied with Violins, Hautboys, Flutes, Clarinets, &c. I understood that their Sermons were not usually preached to mix'd Congregations, of Men Women and Children, as is our common Practice; but that they assembled sometimes the married Men, at other times their Wives, then the Young Men, the young Women, and the little Children, each Division by itself. The Sermon I heard was to the latter, who came in and were plac'd in Rows on Benches, the Boys under the Conduct of a young Man their Tutor, and the Girls conducted by a young Woman. The Discourse seem'd well adapted to their Capacities, and was delivered in a pleasing familiar Manner, coaxing them as it were to be good. They behav'd very orderly, but look'd pale and unhealthy, which made me suspect they were kept too much within-doors, or not allow'd sufficient Exercise. I enquir'd concerning the Moravian Marriages, whether the Report was true that they were by Lot? I was told that Lots were us'd only in particular Cases. That generally when a young Man found himself dispos'd to marry, he inform'd the Elders of his Class, who consulted the Elder Ladies that govern'd the young Women. As these Elders of the different Sexes were well acquainted with the Tempers and Dispositions of their respective Pupils, they could best judge what Matches were suitable, and their Judgments were generally acquiesc'd in. But if for example it should happen that two or three young Women were found to be *equally* proper for the young Man, the Lot was then recurr'd to. I objected, If the Matches are not made by the mutual Choice of the Parties, some of them may chance to be very unhappy. And so they may, answer'd my Informer, if you let the Parties chose for themselves.——Which indeed I could not deny.

Being return'd to Philadelphia, I found the Association went on swimmingly, the Inhabitants that were not Quakers having pretty generally come into it, form'd themselves into Companies, and chosen their Captains, Lieutenants and Ensigns according to the new Law. Dr. Bond visited me, and gave me an Account of the Pains he had taken to spread a general good Liking to the Law, and ascrib'd much to those Endeavours. I had had the Vanity to ascribe all to my Dialogue; However, not knowing but that he might be in the right, I let him enjoy his Opinion, which I take to be generally the best way in such Cases.——The Officers meeting chose me to be Colonel of the Regiment; which I this time accepted. I forget how many Companies we had, but We paraded about 1200 well-looking Men, with a Company of Artillery who had been furnish'd with 6 brass Field Pieces, which they had become so expert in the Use of as to fire twelve times in a Minute. The first Time I review'd my Regiment, they accompanied me to my House, and would salute me with some Rounds fired before my Door, which shook down and broke several Glasses of my Electrical Apparatus. And my new Honour prov'd not much less brittle; for all our Commissions were soon after broke by a Repeal of the Law in England.——

During the short time of my Colonelship, being about to set out on a Journey to Virginia, the Officers of my Regiment took it into their heads that it would be proper for them to escort me out of town as far as the Lower Ferry. Just as I was getting on Horseback, they came to my door, between 30 and 40, mounted, and all in their Uniforms. I had not been previously acquainted with the Project, or I should have prevented it, being naturally averse to the assuming of State on any Occasion, and I was a good deal chagrin'd at their Appearance, as I could not avoid their accompanying me. What made it worse, was, that as soon as we began to move, they drew their Swords, and rode with them naked all the way. Somebody wrote an Account of this to our Proprietor, and it gave him great Offence. No such Honour had been paid him when in the Province; nor to any of his Governors; and he said it was only proper to Princes of the Blood Royal; which may be true for aught I know, who was, and still am, ignorant of the Etiquette, in such Cases. This silly Affair, however greatly increas'd his Rancour against me, which was before not a little, on account of my Conduct in the Assembly, respecting the Exemption of his Estate from Taxation, which I had always oppos'd very warmly, and not without severe Reflections on his Meanness and Injustice in contending for it. He accus'd me to the Ministry as being the great Obstacle to the King's Service, preventing by my Influence in the House the proper Forming of the Bills for raising Money; and he instanc'd this Parade with my Officers as a Proof of my having an Intention to take the Government of the Province out of his Hands by Force. He also apply'd to Sir Everard Fauckener, then Post Master General, to deprive me of my Office. But this had no other Effect, than to procure from Sir Everard a gentle Admonition.

Notwithstanding the continual Wrangle between the Governor and the House, in which I as a Member had so large a Share, there still subsisted a civil Intercourse between that Gentleman and myself, and we never had any personal Difference. I have sometimes since thought that his little or no Resentment against me for the Answers it was known I drew up to his Messages, might be the Effect of professional Habit, and that, being bred a Lawyer, he might consider us both as merely Advocates for contending Clients in a Suit, he for the Proprietaries and I for the Assembly, He would therefore sometimes call in a friendly way to advise with me on difficult Points, and sometimes, tho' not often, take my Advice. We acted in Concert to supply Braddock's Army with Provisions, and when the shocking News arriv'd of his Defeat, the Governor sent in haste for me, to consult with him on Measures for preventing the Desertion of the back Counties. I forget now the Advice I gave, but I think it was, that Dunbar should be written to and prevail'd with if possible to post his Troops on the Frontiers for their Protection, till by Reinforcements from the Colonies he might be able to proceed on the Expedition.——And after my Return from the Frontier, he would have had me undertake the Conduct of such an Expedition with Provincial Troops, for the Reduction of Fort Duquesne, Dunbar and his Men being otherwise employ'd; and he propos'd to commission me as General. I had not so good an Opinion of my military Abilities as he profess'd to have; and I believe his Professions must have exceeded his real Sentiments: but probably he might think that my Popularity would facilitate the Raising of the Men, and my Influence in Assembly the Grant of Money to pay them;——and that perhaps without taxing the Proprietary Estate. Finding me not so forward to engage as he expected, the Project was dropt: and he soon after left the Government, being superseded by Capt. Denny.——

Before I proceed in relating the Part I had in public Affairs under this new Governor's Administration, it may not be amiss here to give some Account of the Rise and Progress of my Philosophical Reputation.

In 1746 being at Boston, I met there with a Dr. Spence, who was lately arrived from Scotland, and show'd me some electric Experiments. They were imperfectly perform'd, as he was not very expert; but being on a Subject quite new to me, they equally surpriz'd and pleas'd me. Soon after my Return to Philadelphia, our Library Company receiv'd from Mr. Peter Collinson, F. R. S. of London a Present of a Glass Tube, with some Account of the Use of it in making such Experiments. I eagerly seiz'd the Opportunity of repeating what I had seen at Boston, and by much Practice acquir'd great Readiness in performing those also which we had an Account of from England, adding a Number of new Ones.——I say much Practice, for my House was continually full for some time, with People who came to see these new Wonders. To divide a little this Incumbrance among my Friends, I caused a Number of similar Tubes to be blown at our Glass-House, with which they furnish'd themselves, so that we had at length several Performers. Among these the principal was Mr. Kinnersley, an ingenious Neighbour, who being out of Business, I encouraged to undertake showing the Experiments for Money, and drew up for him two Lectures, in which the Experiments were rang'd in such Order and accompanied with Explanations, in such Method, as that the foregoing should assist in Comprehending the following. He procur'd an elegant Apparatus for the purpose, in which all the little Machines that I had roughly made for myself, were nicely form'd by Instrument-makers. His Lectures were well attended and gave great Satisfaction; and after some time he went thro' the Colonies exhibiting them in every capital Town, and pick'd up some Money. In the West India Islands indeed it was with Difficulty the Experiments could be made, from the general Moisture of the Air.

Oblig'd as we were to Mr. Collinson for his Present of the Tube, &c. I thought it right he should be inform'd of our Success in using it, and wrote him several Letters containing Accounts of our Experiments. He got them read in the Royal Society, where they were not at first thought worth so much Notice as to be printed in their Transactions. One Paper which I wrote for Mr. Kinnersley, on the Sameness of Lightning with Electricity, I sent to Dr. Mitchel, an Acquaintance of mine, and one of the Members also of that Society; who wrote me word that it had been read but was laught at by the Connoisseurs: The Papers however being shown to Dr. Fothergill, he thought them of too much value to be stifled, and advis'd the Printing of them. Mr. Collinson then gave them to *Cave* for publication in his Gentleman's Magazine; but he chose to print them separately in a Pamphlet, and Dr. Fothergill wrote the Preface. Cave it seems judg'd rightly for his Profit; for by the Additions that arriv'd afterwards they swell'd to a Quarto Volume, which has had five Editions, and cost him nothing for Copy-money.

It was however some time before those Papers were much taken Notice of in England. A Copy of them happening to fall into the Hands of the Count de Buffon, a Philosopher deservedly of great Reputation in France, and indeed all over Europe he prevail'd with M. Dalibard to translate them into French; and they were printed at Paris. The Publication offended the Abbé Nollet, Preceptor in Natural Philosophy to the Royal Family, and an able Experimenter, who had form'd and publish'd a Theory of Electricity, which then had the general Vogue. He could not at first believe that such a Work came from America, and said it must have been fabricated by his Enemies at Paris, to decry his System. Afterwards having been assur'd that there really existed such a Person as Franklin of Philadelphia, which he had doubted, he wrote and published a Volume of Letters, chiefly address'd to me, defending his Theory, and denying the Verity of my Experiments and of the Positions deduc'd from them. I once purpos'd answering the Abbé, and actually began the Answer. But on Consideration that my Writings contain'd only a Description of Experiments, which any one might repeat and verify, and if not to be verify'd could not be defended; or of Observations, offer'd as Conjectures, and not deliver'd dogmatically, therefore not laying me under any Obligation to defend them; and reflecting that a Dispute between two Persons writing in different Languages might be lengthend greatly by mis-translations, and thence misconceptions of one anothers Meaning, much of one of the Abbé's Letters being founded on an Error in the Translation; I concluded to let my Papers shift for themselves; believing it was better to spend what time I could spare from public Business in making new Experiments, than in Disputing about those already made. I therefore never answer'd M. Nollet; and the Event gave me no Cause to repent my Silence; for my friend M. le Roy of the Royal Academy of Sciences took up my Cause and refuted him, my Book was translated into the Italian, German and Latin Languages, and the Doctrine it contain'd was by degrees universally adopted by the Philosophers of Europe in preference to that of the Abbé, so that he liv'd to see himself the last of his Sect; except Mr. B___ his Elève and immediate Disciple.

What gave my Book the more sudden and general Celebrity, was the Success of one of its propos'd Experiments, made by Messrs Dalibard and Delor, at Marly; for drawing Lightning from the Clouds. This engag'd the public Attention every where. M. Delor, who had an Apparatus for experimental Philosophy, and lectur'd in that Branch of Science, undertook to repeat what he call'd the *Philadelphia Experiments*, and after they were performed before the King and Court, all the Curious of Paris flock'd to see them. I will not swell this Narrative with an Account of that capital Experiment, nor of the infinite Pleasure I receiv'd in the Success of a similar one I made soon after with a Kite at Philadelphia, as both are to be found in the Histories of Electricity.——Dr. Wright, an English Physician then at Paris, wrote to a Friend who was of the Royal Society an Account of the high Esteem my Experiments were in among the Learned abroad, and of their Wonder that my Writings had been so little noticed in England. The Society on this resum'd the Consideration of the Letters that had been read to them, and the celebrated Dr. Watson drew up a summary Account of them, and of all I had afterwards sent to England on the Subject, which he accompanied with some Praise of the Writer. This Summary was then printed in their Transactions: And some Members of the Society in London, particularly the very ingenious Mr. Canton, having verified the Experiment of procuring Lightning from the Clouds by a Pointed Rod, and acquainting them with the Success, they soon made me more than Amends for the Slight with which they had before treated me. Without my having made any Application for that Honour, they chose me a Member, and voted that I should be excus'd the customary Payments, which would have amounted to twenty-five Guineas, and ever since have given me their Transactions gratis.——They also presented me with the Gold Medal of Sir Godfrey Copley for the Year 1753, the Delivery of which was accompanied by a very handsome Speech of the President Lord Macclesfield, wherein I was highly honoured.——

Our new Governor, Captain Denny, brought over for me the before mentioned Medal from the Royal Society, which he presented to me at an Entertainment given him by the City. He accompanied it with very polite Expressions of his Esteem for me, having, as he said been long acquainted with my Character. After Dinner, when the Company as was customary at that time, were engag'd in Drinking, he took me aside into another Room, and acquainted me that he had been advis'd by his Friends in England to cultivate a Friendship with me, as one who was capable of giving him the best Advice, and of contributing most effectually to the making his Administration easy. That he therefore desired of all things to have a good Understanding with me; and he begg'd me to be assur'd of his Readiness on all Occasions to render me every Service that might be in his Power. He said much to me also of the Proprietor's good Dispositions towards the Province, and of the Advantage it might be to us all, and to me in particular, if the Opposition that had been so long continu'd to his Measures, were dropt, and Harmony restor'd between him and the People, in effecting which it was thought no one could be more serviceable than my self, and I might depend on adequate Acknowledgements and Recompences, &c. &c. The Drinkers finding we did not return immediately to the Table, sent us a Decanter of Madeira, which the Governor made liberal Use of, and in proportion became more profuse of his Solicitations and Promises. My Answers were to this purpose, that my Circumstances, Thanks to God, were such as to make Proprietary Favours unnecessary to me; and that being a Member of the Assembly I could not possibly accept of any; that however I had no personal Enmity to the Proprietary, and that whenever the public Measures he propos'd should appear to be for the Good of the People, no one should espouse and forward them more zealously than myself, my past Opposition having been founded on this, that the Measures which had been urg'd were evidently intended to serve the Proprietary Interest with great Prejudice to that of the People. That I was much obliged to him (the Governor) for his Professions of Regard to me, and that he might rely on every thing in my Power to make his Administration as easy to him as possible, hoping at the same time that he had not brought with him the same unfortunate Instructions his Predecessor had been hamper'd with. On this he did not then explain himself. But when he afterwards came to do Business with the Assembly they appear'd again, the Disputes were renewed, and I was as active as ever in the Opposition, being the Penman first of the Request to have a Communication of the Instructions, and then of the Remarks upon them, which may be found in the Votes of the Time, and in the Historical Review I afterwards publish'd; but between us personally no Enmity arose; we were often together, he was a Man of Letters, had seen much of the World, and was very entertaining and pleasing in Conversation. He gave me the first Information that my old Friend James Ralph was still alive, that he was esteem'd one of the best political Writers in England, had been employ'd in the Dispute between Prince Frederic and the King, and had obtain'd a Pension of Three Hundred a Year; that his Reputation was indeed small as a Poet, *Pope* having damn'd his Poetry in the Dunciad, but his Prose was thought as good as any Man's.——

The Assembly finally, finding the Proprietaries obstinately persisted in manacling their Deputies with Instructions inconsistent not only with the Privileges of the People, but with the Service of the Crown, to petition the King against them, and appointed me their Agent to go over to England to present and support the Petition. The House had sent up a Bill to the Governor granting a Sum of Sixty Thousand Pounds for the King's Use, (10,000£ of which was subjected to the Orders of the then General Lord Loudon,) which the Governor absolutely refus'd to pass in Compliance with his Instructions. I had agreed with Captain Morris of the Packet at New York for my Passage, and my Stores were put on board, when Lord Loudon arriv'd at Philadelphia, expresly, as he told me to endeavour an Accomodation between the Governor and Assembly, that his Majesty's Service might not be obstructed by their Dissensions: Accordingly he desired the Governor and myself to meet him, that he might hear what was to be said on both sides. We met and discuss'd the Business. In behalf of the Assembly I urg'd all the Arguments that may be found in the publick Papers of that Time, which were of my Writing, and are printed with the Minutes of the Assembly and the Governor pleaded his Instructions, the Bond he had given to observ them, and his Ruin if he disobey'd: Yet seem'd not unwilling to hazard himself if Lord Loudon would advise it. This his Lordship did not chose to do, tho' I once thought I had nearly prevail'd with him to do it; but finally he rather chose to urge the Compliance of the Assembly; and he intreated me to use my Endeavours with them for that purpose; declaring he could spare none of the King's Troops for the Defence of our Frontiers, and that if we did not continue to provide for that Defence ourselves they must remain expos'd to the Enemy.

I acquainted the House with what had pass'd, and presenting them with a Set of Resolutions I had drawn up, declaring our Rights, and that we did not relinquish our Claim to those Rights but only suspended the Exercise of them on this Occasion thro' *Force*, against which we protested, they at length agreed to drop that Bill and frame another conformable to the Proprietary Instructions. This of course the Governor pass'd, and I was then at Liberty to proceed on my Voyage: but in the meantime the Pacquet had sail'd with my Sea-Stores, which was some Loss to me, and my only Recompence was his Lordship's Thanks for my Service, all the Credit of obtaining the Accommodation falling to his Share.

He set out for New York before me; and as the Time for dispatching the Pacquet Boats, was in his Disposition, and there were two then remaining there, one of which he said was to sail very soon, I requested to know the precise time, that I might not miss her by any Delay of mine. His Answer was, I have given out that she is to sail on Saturday next, but I may let you know *entre nous*, that if you are there by Monday morning you will be in time, but do not delay longer. By some Accidental Hindrance at a Ferry, it was Monday Noon before I arrived, and I was much afraid she might have sailed as the Wind was fair, but I was soon made easy by the Information that she was still in the Harbour, and would not move till the next Day.——

One would imagine that I was now on the very point of Departing for Europe. I thought so; but I was not then so well acquainted with his Lordship's Character, of which *Indecision* was one of the Strongest Features. I shall give some Instances. It was about the Beginning of April that I came to New York, and I think it was near the End of June before we sail'd. There were then two of the Pacquet Boats which had been long in Port, but were detain'd for the General's Letters, which were always to be ready to-morrow. Another Pacquet arrived, and she too was detain'd, and before we sail'd a fourth was expected. Ours was the first to be dispatch'd, as having been there longest. Passengers were engag'd in all, and some extreamly impatient to be gone, and the Merchants uneasy about their Letters, and the Orders they had given for Insurance (it being War-time) and for Fall Goods. But their Anxiety avail'd nothing; his Lordships Letters were not ready. And yet whoever waited on him found him always at his Desk, Pen in hand, and concluded he must needs write abundantly. Going my self one Morning to pay my Respects, I found in his Antechamber one Innis, a Messenger of Philadelphia, who had come from thence express, with a Pacquet from Governor Denny for the General. He deliver'd to me some Letters from my Friends there, which occasion'd my enquiring when he was to return and where he lodg'd, that I might send some Letters by him. He told me he was order'd to call to-morrow at nine for the General's Answer to the Governor, and should set off immediately. I put my Letters into his Hands the same Day. A Fortnight after I met him again in the same Place. So you are soon return'd, Innis! *Return'd*; No, I am not *gone* yet.——How so?——I have call'd here by Order every Morning these two Weeks past for his Lordship's Letter, and it is not yet ready.——Is it possible, when he is so great a Writer, for I see him constantly at his Scritore. Yes, says Innis, but he is like St. George on the Signs, *always on horseback, and never rides on*. This Observation of the Messenger was it seems well founded; for when in England, I understood that Mr. Pitt gave it as one Reason for Removing this General, and sending Amherst and Wolfe, *that the Ministers never heard from him, and could not know what he was doing*.

This daily Expectation of Sailing, and all the three Packets going down Sandy hook, to join the Fleet there the Passengers, thought it best to be on board, lest by a sudden Order the Ships should sail, and they be left behind. There if I remember right we were about Six Weeks, consuming our Sea Stores, and oblig'd to procure more. At length the Fleet sail'd, the General and all his Army on board, bound to Lewisburg with Intent to besiege and take that Fortress; all the Packet Boats in Company, ordered to attend the General's Ship, ready to receive his Dispatches when those should be ready. We were out 5 Days before we got a Letter with Leave to part; and then our Ship quitted the Fleet and steered for England. The other two Packets he still detain'd, carry'd them with him to Halifax, where he staid some time to exercise the Men in sham Attacks upon sham Forts, then alter'd his Mind as to besieging Louisburg, and return'd to New York with all his Troops, together with the two Packets abovementioned and all their Passengers. During his Absence the French and Savages had taken Fort George on the Frontier of that Province, and the Savages had massacred many of the Garrison after Capitulation. I saw afterwards in London, Capt. Bonnell, who commanded one of those Packets. He told me, that when he had been detain'd a Month, he acquainted his Lordship that his Ship was grown foul, to a degree that must necessarily hinder her fast Sailing, a Point of consequence for a Packet Boat, and requested an Allowance of Time to heave her down and clean her Bottom. He was ask'd how long time that would require. He answer'd Three Days. The General reply'd, If you can do it in one Day, I give leave; otherwise not;

for you must certainly sail the Day after to-morrow. So he never obtain'd leave tho' detain'd afterwards from day to day during full three Months. I saw also in London one of Bonell's Passengers, who was so enrag'd against his Lordship for deceiving and detaining him so long at New York, and then carrying him to Halifax, and back again, that he swore he would sue him for Damages. Whether he did or not I never heard; but as he represented the Injury to his Affairs it was very considerable. On the whole I then wonder'd much, how such a Man came to be entrusted with so important a Business as the Conduct of a great Army: but having since seen more of the great World, and the means of obtaining and Motives for giving Places, and Employments my Wonder is diminished. General Shirley, on whom the Command of the Army devolved upon the Death of Braddock, would in my Opinion if continued in Place, have made a much better Campaign than that of Loudon in 1757, which was frivolous, expensive and disgraceful to our Nation beyond Conception: For tho' Shirley was not a bred Soldier, he was sensible and sagacious in himself, and attentive to good Advice from others, capable of forming judicious Plans, quick and active in carrying them into Execution. Loudon, instead of defending the Colonies with his great Army, left them totally expos'd while he paraded it idly at Halifax, by which means Fort George was lost;——besides he derang'd all our mercantile Operations, and distress'd our Trade by a long Embargo on the Exportation of Provisions, on pretence of keeping Supplies from being obtain'd by the Enemy, but in Reality for beating down their Price in Favour of the Contractors, in whose Profits it was said, perhaps from Suspicion only, he had a Share. And when at length the Embargo was taken off, by neglecting to send Notice of it to Charlestown, the Carolina Fleet was detain'd near three Months longer, whereby their Bottoms were so much damag'd by the Worm, that a great Part of them founder'd in the Passage home. Shirley was I believe sincerely glad of being reliev'd from so burthensom a Charge as the Conduct of an Army must be to a Man unacquainted with military Business. I was at the Entertainment given by the City of New York, to Lord Loudon on his taking upon him the Command. Shirley, tho' thereby superseded, was present also. There was a great Company of Officers, Citizens and Strangers, and some Chairs having been borrowed in the Neighbourhood, there was one among them very low which fell to the Lot of Mr. Shirley. Perceiving it as I sat by him, I said, they have given you, Sir, too low a Seat.——No Matter, says he; Mr. Franklin, I find *a low Seat* the easiest!

While I was, as aforemention'd, detain'd at New York, I receiv'd all the Accounts of the Provisions, &c. that I had furnish'd to Braddock, some of which Accounts could not sooner be obtain'd from the different Persons I had employ'd to assist in the Business. I presented them to Lord Loudon, desiring to be paid the Ballance. He caus'd them to be regularly examin'd by the proper Officer, who, after comparing every Article with its Voucher, certified them to be right, and the Ballance due, for which his Lordship promis'd to give me an Order on the Paymaster. This, however, was put off from time to time, and tho' I called often for it by Appointment, I did not get it. At length, just before my Departure, he told me he had on better Consideration concluded not to mix his Accounts with those of his Predecessors. And you, says he, when in England, have only to exhibit your Accounts at the Treasury, and you will be paid immediately. I mention'd, but without Effect, the great and unexpected Expence I had been put to by being detain'd so long at New York, as a Reason for my desiring to be presently paid; and on my observing that it was not right I should be put to any farther Trouble or Delay in obtaining the Money I had advanc'd, as I charg'd no Commissions for my Service. O, Sir, says he, you must not think of persuading us that you are no Gainer. We understand better those Affairs, and know that every one concern'd in supplying the Army finds means in the doing it to fill his own Pockets. I assur'd him that was not my Case, and that I had not pocketed a Farthing: but he appear'd clearly not to believe me; and indeed I have since learnt that immense Fortunes are often made in such Employments.——As to my Ballance, I am not paid it to this Day, of which more hereafter.——

Our Captain of the Pacquet had boasted much before we sail'd, of the Swiftness of his Ship. Unfortunately when we came to Sea, she proved the dullest of 96 Sail, to his no small Mortification. After many Conjectures respecting the Cause, when we were near another Ship almost as dull as ours, which however gain'd upon us, the Captain order'd all hands to come aft and stand as near the Ensign Staff as possible. We were, Passengers included, about forty Persons. While we stood there the Ship mended her Pace, and soon left our Neighbour far behind, which proved clearly what our Captain suspected, that she was loaded too much by the Head. The Casks of Water it seems had been all plac'd forward. These he therefore order'd to be remov'd farther aft; on which the Ship recover'd her Character, and proved the best Sailer in the Fleet. The Captain said she had once gone at the Rate of 13 Knots, which is accounted 13 Miles per hour. We had on board as a Passenger Captain Kennedy of the Navy, who contended that it was impossible, that no Ship ever sailed so fast, and that there must have been some Error in the Division of the Log-Line, or some Mistake in heaving the Log. A Wager ensu'd between the two Captains, to be decided when there should be sufficient Wind. Kennedy thereupon examin'd rigorously the Log-line, and being satisfy'd with that, he determin'd to throw the Log himself. Accordingly some Days after when the Wind blew very fair and fresh, and the Captain of the Packet (Lutwidge) said he believ'd she then went at the Rate of 13 Knots, Kennedy made the Experiment, and own'd his Wager lost. The above Fact I give for the sake of the following Observation. It has been remark'd as an Imperfection in the Art of Ship-building, that it can never be known 'till she is try'd, whether a new Ship will or will not be a good Sailer; for that the Model of a good sailing Ship has been exactly follow'd in a new One, which has prov'd on the contrary remarkably dull. I apprehend this may be partly occasion'd by the different Opinions of Seamen respecting the Modes of lading, rigging and sailing of a Ship. Each has his System. And the same Vessel laden by the judgment and Orders of one Captain shall sail better or worse than when by the Orders of another. Besides, it scarce ever happens that a Ship is form'd, fitted for the Sea, and sail'd by the same Person. One Man builds the Hull, another riggs her, a third lades and sails her. No one of these has the Advantage of knowing all the Ideas and Experience of the others, and therefore cannot draw just Conclusions from a Combination of the whole. Even in the simple Operation of Sailing when at Sea, I have often observ'd different Judgments in the Officers who commanded the successive Watches, the Wind being the same, One would have the Sails trimm'd sharper or flatter than another, so that they seem'd to have no certain Rule to govern by. Yet I think a Set of Experiments might be instituted, first to determine the most proper Form of the Hull for swift sailing; next the best Dimensions and properest Place for the Masts; then the Form and Quantity of Sail, and their Position as the Winds may be; and lastly the Disposition of her Lading. This is the Age of Experiments; and such a Set accurately made and combin'd would be of great Use. I am therefore persuaded that ere long some ingenious Philosopher will undertake it:——to whom I wish Success——

We were several times chas'd on our Passage, but outsail'd every thing, and in thirty Days had Soundings. We had a good Observation, and the Captain judg'd himself so near our Port, (Falmouth) that if we made a good Run in the Night we might be off the Mouth of that Harbour in the Morning, and by running in the Night might escape the Notice of the

Enemy's Privateers, who often cruis'd near the Entrance of the Channel. Accordingly all the Sail was set that we could possibly make, and the Wind being very fresh and fair, we went right before it, and made great Way. The Captain after his Observation, shap'd his Course as he thought so as to pass wide of the Scilly Isles: but it seems there is sometimes a strong Indraught setting up St. George's Channel which deceives Seamen, and caus'd the Loss of Sir Cloudsley Shovel's Squadron. This Indraught was probably the Cause of what happen'd to us. We had a Watchman plac'd in the Bow to whom they often call'd, *Look well out before, there*; and he as often answer'd *Aye, Aye!* But perhaps had his Eyes shut, and was half asleep at the time: they sometimes answering as is said mechanically: For he did not see a Light just before us, which had been hid by the Studding Sails from the Man at Helm and from the rest of the Watch; but by an accidental Yaw of the Ship was discover'd, and occasion'd a great Alarm, we being very near it, the light appearing to me as big as a Cart Wheel. It was Midnight, and Our Captain fast asleep. But Capt. Kennedy jumping upon Deck, and seeing the Danger, ordered the Ship to wear round, all Sails standing. An Operation dangerous to the Masts, but it carried us clear, and we escap'd Shipwreck, for we were running right upon the Rocks on which the Lighthouse was erected. This Deliverance impress'd me strongly with the Utility of Lighthouses, and made me resolve to encourage the building more of them in America, if I should live to return there.

In the Morning it was found by the Soundings, &c. that we were near our Port, but a thick fog hid the Land from our Sight. About 9 aClock the Fog began to rise, and seem'd to be lifted up from the Water like the Curtain at a Play-house, discovering underneath the Town of Falmouth, the Vessels in its Harbour, and the Fields that surrounded it. A most pleasing Spectacle to those who had been so long without any other Prospects, than the uniform View of a vacant Ocean!——And it gave us the more Pleasure, as we were now freed from the Anxieties which the State of War occasion'd.——

I set out immediately with my Son for London, and we only stopt a little by the Way to view Stonehenge on Salisbury Plain, and Lord Pembroke's House and Gardens, with his very curious Antiquities at Wilton.

We arriv'd in London the 27th of July 1757.[5]

[5] [This sentence concludes Part Three of *The Autobiography* in the Temple edition. The holograph manuscript, however, continues without break.]

Part Four

As soon as I was settled in a Lodging Mr. Charles had provided for me, I went to visit Dr. Fothergill, to whom I was strongly recommended, and whose Counsel respecting my Proceedings I was advis'd to obtain. He was against an immediate Complaint to Government, and thought the Proprietaries should first be personally apply'd to, who might possibly be induc'd by the Interposition and Persuasion of some private Friends to accommodate Matters amicably. I then waited on my old Friend and Correspondent Mr. Peter Collinson; who told me that John Hanbury, the great Virginia Merchant, had requested to be informed when I should arrive, that he might carry me to Lord Granville's, who was then President of the Council, and wish'd to see me as soon as possible. I agreed to go with him the next Morning. Accordingly Mr. Hanbury called for me and took me in his Carriage to that Nobleman's, who receiv'd me with great Civility; and after some Questions respecting the present State of Affairs in America, and Discourse thereupon, he said to me, "You Americans have wrong Ideas of the Nature of your Constitution; you contend that the King's Instructions to his Governors are not Laws, and think yourselves at Liberty to regard or disregard them at your own Discretion. But those Instructions are not like the Pocket Instructions given to a Minister going abroad, for regulating his Conduct in some trifling Point of Ceremony. They are first drawn up by Judges learned in the Laws; they are then considered, debated and perhaps amended in Council, after which they are signed by the King. They are then so far as relates to you, the *Law of the Land*; for THE KING IS THE LEGISLATOR OF THE COLONIES." I told his Lordship this was new Doctrine to me. I had always understood from our Charters, that our Laws were to be made by our Assemblies, to be presented indeed to the King for his Royal Assent, but that being once given the King could not repeal or alter them. And as the Assemblies could not make permanent Laws without his Assent, so neither could he make a Law for them without theirs. He assur'd me I was totally mistaken. I did not think so however. And his Lordship's Conversation having a little alarm'd me as to what might be the Sentiments of the Court concerning us, I wrote it down as soon as I return'd to my Lodgings.——I recollected that about 20 Years before, a Clause in a Bill brought into Parliament by the Ministry, had propos'd to make the King's Instructions Laws in the Colonies; but the Clause was thrown out by the Commons, for which we ador'd them as our Friends and Friends of Liberty, till by their Conduct towards us in 1765, it seem'd that they had refus'd that Point of Sovereignty to the King, only that they might reserve it for themselves.

After some Days, Dr. Fothergill having spoken to the Proprietaries, they agreed to a Meeting with me at Mr. Thomas Penn's House in Spring Garden. The Conversation at first consisted of mutual Declarations of Disposition to reasonable Accommodation; but I suppose each Party had its own Ideas of what should be meant by *reasonable*. We then went into Consideration of our several Points of Complaint which I enumerated. The Proprietaries justify'd their Conduct as well as they could, and I the Assembly's. We now appeared very wide, and so far from each other in our Opinions, as to discourage all Hope of Agreement. However, it was concluded that I should give them the Heads of our Complaints in Writing, and they promis'd then to consider them.——I did so soon after; but they put the Paper into the Hands of their Solicitor Ferdinando John Paris, who manag'd for them all their Law Business in their great Suit with the neighbouring Proprietary of Maryland, Lord Baltimore, which had subsisted 70 Years, and wrote for them all their Papers and Messages in their Dispute with the Assembly. He was a proud angry Man; and as I had occasionally in the Answers of the Assembly treated his Papers with some Severity, they being really weak in point of Argument, and haughty in Expression, he had conceiv'd a mortal Enmity to me, which discovering itself whenever we met, I declin'd the Proprietary's Proposal that he and I should discuss the Heads of Complaint between our two selves, and refus'd treating with any one but them. They then by his Advice put the Paper into the Hands of the Attorney and Solicitor General for their Opinion and Counsel upon it, where it lay unanswered a Year wanting eight Days, during which time I made frequent Demands of an Answer from the Proprietaries but without obtaining any other than that they had not yet receiv'd the Opinion of the Attorney and Solicitor General: What it was when they did receive it I never learnt, for they did not communicate it to me, but sent a long Message to the Assembly drawn and signed by Paris reciting my Paper, complaining of its want of Formality as a Rudeness on my part, and giving a flimsey Justification of their Conduct, adding that they should be willing to accomodate Matters, if the Assembly would send over *some Person of Candour* to treat with them for that purpose, intimating thereby that I was not such. The want of Formality or Rudeness, was probably my not having address'd the Paper to them with their assum'd Titles of true and absolute Proprietaries of the Province of Pennsylvania, which I omitted as not thinking it necessary in a

Paper the Intention of which was only to reduce to a Certainty by writing what in Conversation I had delivered *vivâ voce*. But during this Delay, the Assembly having prevail'd with Gov. Denny to pass an Act taxing the Proprietary Estate in common with the Estates of the People, which was the grand Point in Dispute, they omitted answering the Message.

When this Act however came over, the Proprietaries counsell'd by Paris determin'd to oppose its receiving the Royal Assent. Accordingly they petition'd the King in Council, and a Hearing was appointed, in which two Lawyers were employ'd by them against the Act, and two by me in Support of it. They alledg'd that the Act was intended to load the Proprietary Estate in order to spare those of the People, and that if it were suffer'd to continue in force, and the Proprietaries who were in Odium with the People, left to their Mercy in proportioning the Taxes, they would inevitably be ruined. We reply'd that the Act had no such Intention and would have no such Effect. That the Assessors were honest and discreet Men, under an Oath to assess fairly and equitably, and that any Advantage each of them might expect in lessening his own Tax by augmenting that of the Proprietaries was too trifling to induce them to perjure themselves. This is the purport of what I remember as urg'd by both Sides, except that we insisted strongly on the mischievous Consequences that must attend a Repeal; for that the Money, 100,000£, being printed and given to the King's Use, expended in his Service, and now spread among the People, the Repeal would strike it dead in their Hands to the Ruin of many, and the total Discouragement of future Grants, and the Selfishness of the Proprietors in soliciting such a general Catastrophe, merely from a groundless Fear of their Estate being taxed too highly, was insisted on in the strongest Terms. On this Lord Mansfield, one of the Council rose, and beckoning to me, took me into the Clerk's Chamber, while the Lawyers were pleading, and ask'd me if I was really of Opinion that no Injury would be done the Proprietary Estate in the Execution of the Act. I said, Certainly. Then says he, you can have little Objection to enter into an Engagement to assure that Point. I answer'd None, at all. He then call'd in Paris, and after some Discourse his Lordship's Proposition was accepted on both Sides; a Paper to the purpose was drawn up by the Clerk of the Council, which I sign'd with Mr. Charles, who was also an Agent of the Province for their ordinary Affairs; when Lord Mansfield return'd to the Council Chamber where finally the Law was allowed to pass. Some Changes were however recommended and we also engag'd they should be made by a subsequent Law; but the Assembly did not think them necessary. For one Year's Tax having been levied by the

Act, before the Order of Council arrived, they appointed a Committee to examine the Percedings of the Assessors, and On this Committee they put several particular Friends of the Proprietaries. After a full Enquiry they unanimously sign'd a Report that they found the Tax had been assess'd with perfect Equity. The Assembly look'd on my entring into the first Part of the Engagement as an essential Service to the Province, since it secur'd the Credit of the Paper Money then spread over all the Country; and they gave me their Thanks in form when I return'd.——But the Proprietaries were enrag'd at Governor Denny for having pass'd the Act, and turn'd him out, with Threats of suing him for Breach of Instructions which he had given Bond to observe. He however having done it the Instance of the General and for his Majesty's Service, and having some powerful Interest at Court, despis'd the Threats, and they were never put in Execution.

CHAPTER 2
Plan of Conduct
(July–October 1726)

Those who write of the art of poetry teach us that if we would write what may be worth the reading, we ought always, before we begin, to form a regular plan and design of our piece: otherwise, we shall be in danger of incongruity. I am apt to think it is the same as to life. I have never fixed a regular design in life; by which means it has been a confused variety of different scenes. I am now entering upon a new one: let me, therefore, make some resolutions, and form some scheme of action, that, henceforth, I may live in all respects like a rational creature.

1. It is necessary for me to be extremely frugal for some time, till I have paid what I owe.

2. To endeavour to speak truth in every instance; to give nobody expectations that are not likely to be answered, but aim at sincerity in every word and action — the most amiable excellence in a rational being.

3. To apply myself industriously to whatever business I take in hand, and not divert my mind from my business by any foolish project of growing suddenly rich; for industry and patience are the surest means of plenty.

4. I resolve to speak ill of no man whatever, not even in a matter of truth; but rather by some means excuse the faults I hear charged upon others, and upon proper occasions speak all the good I know of every body.

[Robert Walsh, "Life of Benjamin Franklin," *Delaplaine's Repository of the Lives and Portraits of Distinguished Americans* (Philadelphia, 1815–17), 2:51–2.]

CHAPTER 3

A Modest Enquiry into the Nature and Necessity of a Paper-Currency

(3 April 1729)

——*Quid asper*
Utile Nummus babet; patriae, charisq; propinquis
Quantum elargiri deceat.——

Pers.[1]

There is no Science, the Study of which is more useful and commendable than the Knowledge of the true Interest of one's Country; and perhaps there is no Kind of Learning more abstruse and intricate, more difficult to acquire in any Degree of Perfection than This, and therefore none more generally neglected. Hence it is, that we every Day find Men in Conversation contending warmly on some Point in Politicks, which, altho' it may nearly concern them both, neither of them understand any more than they do each other.

Thus much by way of Apology for this present *Enquiry into the Nature and Necessity of a Paper Currency*. And if any Thing I shall say, may be a Means of fixing a Subject that is now the chief Concern of my Countrymen, in a clearer Light, I shall have the Satisfaction of thinking my Time and Pains well employed.

To proceed, then,

There is a certain proportionate Quantity of Money requisite to carry on the Trade of a Country freely and currently; More than which would be of no Advantage in Trade, and Less, if much less, exceedingly detrimental to it.

This leads us to the following general Considerations.

First, *A great Want of Money in any Trading Country, occasions Interest to be at a very high Rate*. And here it may be observed, that it is impossible by

[1] [Persius, *Satires* 3:69–71: "What good there is in fresh-minted coin; how much should be spent on country and on your dear kin."]

any Laws to restrain Men from giving and receiving exorbitant Interest, where Money is suitably scarce: For he that wants Money will find out Ways to give 10 *per Cent.* when he cannot have it for less, altho' the Law forbids to take more than *6 per Cent.* Now the Interest of Money being high is prejudicial to a Country several Ways: It makes Land bear a low Price, because few Men will lay out their Money in Land, when they can make a much greater Profit by lending it out upon Interest: And much less will Men be inclined to venture their Money at Sea, when they can, without Risque or Hazard, have a great and certain Profit by keeping it at home; thus Trade is discouraged. And if in two Neighbouring Countries the Traders of one, by Reason of a greater Plenty of Money, can borrow it to trade with at a lower Rate than the Traders of the other, they will infallibly have the Advantage, and get the greatest Part of that Trade into their own Hands; For he that trades with Money he hath borrowed at 8 or 10 *per Cent.* cannot hold Market with him that borrows his Money at 6 or 4.——On the contrary, *A plentiful Currency will occasion Interest to be low*: And this will be an Inducement to many to lay out their Money in Lands, rather than put it out to Use, by which means Land will begin to rise in Value and bear a better Price: And at the same Time it will tend to enliven Trade exceedingly, because People will find more Profit in employing their Money that Way than in Usury; and many that understand Business very well, but have not a Stock sufficient of their own, will be encouraged to borrow Money to trade with, when they can have it at moderate Interest.

Secondly, *Want of Money in a Country reduces the Price of that Part of its Produce which is used in Trade*: Because Trade being discouraged by it as above, there is a much less Demand for that Produce. And this is another Reason why Land in such a Case will be low, especially where the Staple Commodity of the Country is the immediate Produce of the Land, because that Produce being low, fewer People find an Advantage in Husbandry, or the Improvement of Land.——On the contrary, *A Plentiful Currency will occasion the Trading Produce to bear a good Price*: Because Trade being encouraged and advanced by it, there will be a much greater Demand for that Produce; which will be a great Encouragement of Husbandry and Tillage, and consequently make Land more valuable, for that many People would apply themselves to Husbandry, who probably might otherwise have sought some more profitable Employment.

As we have already experienced how much the Increase of our Currency by what Paper Money has been made, has encouraged our Trade;

particularly to instance only in one Article, *Ship-Building*, it may not be amiss to observe under this Head, what a great Advantage it must be to us as a Trading Country, that has Workmen and all the Materials proper for that Business within itself, to have *Ship-Building* as much as possible advanced: For every Ship that is built here for the English Merchants, gains the Province her clear Value in Gold and Silver, which must otherwise have been sent Home for Returns in her Stead; and likewise, every Ship built in and belonging to the Province, not only saves the Province her first Cost, but all the Freight, Wages and Provisions she ever makes or requires as long as she lasts; provided Care is taken to make This her *Pay Port*, and that she always takes Provisions with her for the whole Voyage, which may easily be done. And how considerable an Article this is yearly in our Favour, even one, the least acquainted with mercantile Affairs, must needs be sensible; for if we could not Build our selves, we must either purchase so many Vessels as we want from other Countries, or else Hire them to carry our Produce to Market, which would be more expensive than Purchasing, and on many other Accounts exceedingly to our Loss. Now as Trade in general will decline where there is not a plentiful Currency, so *Ship-Building* must certainly of Consequence decline where Trade is declining.

Thirdly, *Want of Money in a Country discourages Labouring and Handicrafts Men (which are the chief Strength and Support of a People) from coming to settle in it, and induces many that were settled to leave the Country, and seek Entertainment and Employment in other Places, where they can be better paid.* For what can be more disheartning to an industrious labouring Man, than this, that after he hath earned his Bread with the Sweat of his Brows, he must spend as much Time, and have near as much Fatigue in getting it, as he had to earn it. *And nothing makes more bad Paymasters than a general Scarcity of Money.* And here again is a Third Reason for Land's bearing a low Price in such a Country, because Land always increases in Value in Proportion with the Increase of the People settling on it, there being so many more Buyers; and its Value will infallibly be diminished, if the Number of its Inhabitants diminish.——On the contrary, *A Plentiful Currency will encourage great Numbers of Labouring and Handicrafts Men to come and Settle in the Country*, by the same Reason that a Want of it will discourage and drive them out. Now the more Inhabitants, the greater Demand for Land (as is said above) upon which it must necessarily rise in Value, and bear a better Price. The same may be said of the Value of House-Rent, which will be advanced for the same Reasons; and by the

Increase of Trade and Riches People will be enabled to pay greater Rents. Now the Value of House-Rent rising, and Interest becoming low, many that in a Scarcity of Money practised Usury, will probably be more inclined to Building; which will likewise sensibly enliven Business in any Place; it being an Advantage not only to *Brickmakers, Bricklayers, Masons, Carpenters, Joiners, Glaziers*, and several other Trades immediately employ'd by Building, but likewise to *Farmers, Brewers, Bakers, Taylors, Shoemakers, Shop-keepers*, and in short to every one that they lay their Money out with.

Fourthly, *Want of Money in such a Country as ours, occasions a greater Consumption of* English *and* European *Goods, in Proportion to the Number of the People, than there would otherwise be*. Because Merchants and Traders, by whom abundance of Artificers and labouring Men are employed, finding their other Affairs require what Money they can get into their hands, oblige those who work for them to take one half, or perhaps two thirds Goods in Pay. By this Means a greater Quantity of Goods are disposed of, and to a greater Value; because Working Men and their Families are thereby induced to be more profuse and extravagant in fine Apparel and the like, than they would be if they were obliged to pay ready Money for such Things after they had earn'd and received it, or if such Goods were not imposed upon them, of which they can make no other Use: For such People cannot send the Goods they are paid with to a Foreign Market, without losing considerably by having them sold for less than they stand 'em in here; neither can they easily dispose of them at Home, because their Neighbours are generally supplied in the same Manner; But how unreasonable would it be, if some of those very Men who *have been a Means* of thus forcing People into unnecessary Expence, should be the first and most earnest in accusing them of *Pride and Prodigality*. Now tho' this extraordinary Consumption of Foreign Commodities may be a Profit to particular Men, yet the Country in general grows poorer by it apace.——On the contrary, As *A plentiful Currency will occasion a less Consumption of* European *Goods, in Proportion to the Number of the People*, so it will be a means of making the Balance of our Trade more equal than it now is, if it does not give it in our Favour; because our own Produce will be encouraged at the same Time. And it is to be observed, that tho' less Foreign Commodities are consumed in Proportion to the Number of People, yet this will be no Disadvantage to the Merchant, because the Number of People increasing, will occasion an increasing Demand of more Foreign Goods in the Whole.

Thus we have seen some of the many heavy Disadvantages a Country (especially such a Country as ours) must labour under, when it has not a sufficient Stock of running Cash to manage its Trade currently. And we have likewise seen some of the Advantages which accrue from having Money sufficient, or a Plentiful Currency.

The foregoing Paragraphs being well considered, we shall naturally be led to draw the following Conclusions with Regard to what Persons will probably be for or against Emitting a large Additional Sum of Paper Bills in this Province.

1. Since Men will always be powerfully influenced in their Opinions and Actions by what appears to be their particular Interest: Therefore all those, who wanting Courage to venture in Trade, now practise Lending Money on Security for exorbitant Interest, which in a Scarcity of Money will be done notwithstanding the Law, I say all such will probably be against a large Addition to our present Stock of Paper-Money; because a plentiful Currency will lower Interest, and make it common to lend on less Security.

2. All those who are Possessors of large Sums of Money, and are disposed to purchase Land, which is attended with a great and sure Advantage in a growing Country as this is; I say, the Interest of all such Men will encline them to oppose a large Addition to our Money. Because their Wealth is now continually increasing by the large Interest they receive, which will enable them (if they can keep Land from rising) to purchase More some time hence than they can at present; and in the mean time all Trade being discouraged, not only those who borrow of them, but the Common People in general will be impoverished, and consequently obliged to sell More Land for less Money than they will do at present. And yet, after such Men are possessed of as much Land as they can purchase, it will then be their Interest to have Money made Plentiful, because that will immediately make Land rise in Value in *their* Hands. Now it ought not to be wonder'd at, if People from the Knowledge of a Man's Interest do sometimes make a true Guess at his Designs; for, *Interest*, they say, *will not Lie*.

3. Lawyers, and others concerned in Court Business, will probably many of them be against a plentiful Currency; because People in that Case will have less Occasion to run in Debt, and consequently less Occasion to go to Law and Sue one another for their Debts. Tho' I know some even among these Gentlemen, that regard the Publick Good before their own apparent private Interest.

4. All those who are any way Dependants on such Persons as are above mentioned, whether as holding Offices, as Tenants, or as Debtors, must at least *appear* to be against a large Addition; because if they do not, they must sensibly feel their present Interest hurt. And besides these, there are, doubtless, many well-meaning Gentlemen and Others, who, without any immediate private Interest of their own in View, are against making such an Addition, thro' an Opinion they may have of the Honesty and sound Judgment of some of their Friends that oppose it, (perhaps for the Ends aforesaid) without having given it any thorough Consideration themselves. And thus it is no Wonder if there is a *powerful* Party on that Side.

On the other Hand, Those who are Lovers of Trade, and delight to see Manufactures encouraged, will be for having a large Addition to our Currency: For they very well know, that People will have little Heart to advance Money in Trade, when what they can get is scarce sufficient to purchase Necessaries, and supply their Families with Provision. Much less will they lay it out in advancing new Manufactures; nor is it possible new Manufactures should turn to any Account, where there is not Money to pay the Workmen, who are discouraged by being paid in Goods, because it is a great Disadvantage to them.

Again, Those who are truly for the Proprietor's Interest (and have no separate Views of their own that are predominant) will be heartily for a large Addition: Because, as I have shewn above, Plenty of Money will for several Reasons make Land rise in Value exceedingly: And I appeal to those immediately concerned for the Proprietor in the Sale of his Lands, whether Land has not risen very much since the first Emission of what Paper Currency we now have, and even by its Means. Now we all know the Proprietary has great Quantities to sell.

And since a Plentiful Currency will be so great a Cause of advancing this Province in Trade and Riches, and increasing the Number of its People; which, tho' it will not sensibly lessen the Inhabitants of *Great Britain*, will occasion a much greater Vent and Demand for their Commodities here; and allowing that the Crown is the more powerful for its Subjects increasing in Wealth and Number, I cannot think it the Interest of *England* to oppose us in making as great a Sum of Paper Money here, as we, who are the best Judges of our own Necessities, find convenient. And if I were not sensible that the Gentlemen of Trade in *England*, to whom we have already parted with our Silver and Gold, are misinformed of our

Circumstances, and therefore endeavour to have our Currency stinted to what it now is, I should think the Government at Home had some Reasons for discouraging and impoverishing this Province, which we are not acquainted with.

It remains now that we enquire, *Whether a large Addition to our Paper Currency will not make it sink in Value very much*; And here it will be requisite that we first form just Notions of the Nature and Value of Money in general.

As Providence has so ordered it, that not only different Countries, but even different Parts of the same Country, have their peculiar most suitable Productions; and likewise that different Men have Genius's adapted to Variety of different Arts and Manufactures, Therefore *Commerce*, or the Exchange of one Commodity or Manufacture for another, is highly convenient and beneficial to Mankind. As for Instance, *A* may be skilful in the Art of making Cloth, and *B* understand the raising of Corn; *A* wants Corn, and *B* Cloth; upon which they make an Exchange with each other for as much as each has Occasion, to the mutual Advantage and Satisfaction of both.

But as it would be very tedious, if there were no other Way of general Dealing, but by an immediate Exchange of Commodities; because a Man that had Corn to dispose of, and wanted Cloth for it, might perhaps in his Search for a Chapman to deal with, meet with twenty People that had Cloth to dispose of, but wanted no Corn; and with twenty others that wanted his Corn, but had no Cloth to suit him with. To remedy such Inconveniences, and facilitate Exchange, Men have invented MONEY, properly called a *Medium of Exchange*, because through or by its Means Labour is exchanged for Labour, or one Commodity for another. And whatever particular Thing Men have agreed to make this Medium of, whether Gold, Silver, Copper, or Tobacco; it is, to those who possess it (if they want any Thing) that very Thing which they want, because it will immediately procure it for them. It is Cloth to him that wants Cloth, and Corn to those that want Corn; and so of all other Necessaries, it *is* whatsoever it will procure. Thus he who had Corn to dispose of, and wanted to purchase Cloth with it, might sell his Corn for its Value in this general Medium, to one who wanted Corn but had no Cloth; and with this Medium he might purchase Cloth of him that wanted no Corn, but perhaps some other Thing, as Iron it may be, which this Medium will immediately procure, and so he may be said to have exchanged his

Cloth for Iron; and thus the general Exchange is soon performed, to the Satisfaction of all Parties, with abundance of Facility.

For many Ages, those Parts of the World which are engaged in Commerce, have fixed upon Gold and Silver as the chief and most proper Materials for this Medium; they being in themselves valuable Metals for their Fineness, Beauty, and Scarcity. By these, particularly by Silver, it has been usual to value all Things else: But as Silver it self is of no certain permanent Value, being worth more or less according to its Scarcity or Plenty, therefore it seems requisite to fix upon Something else, more proper to be made a *Measure of Values*, and this I take to be *Labour*.

By Labour may the Value of Silver be measured as well as other Things. As, Suppose one Man employed to raise Corn, while another is digging and refining Silver; at the Year's End, or at any other Period of Time, the compleat Produce of Corn, and that of Silver, are the natural Price of each other; and if one be twenty Bushels, and the other twenty Ounces, then an Ounce of that Silver is worth the Labour of raising a Bushel of that Corn. Now if by the Discovery of some nearer, more easy or plentiful Mines, a Man may get Forty Ounces of Silver as easily as formerly he did Twenty, and the same Labour is still required to raise Twenty Bushels of Corn, then Two Ounces of Silver will be worth no more than the same Labour of raising One Bushel of Corn, and that Bushel of Corn will be as cheap at two Ounces, as it was before at one; *cæteris paribus*.

Thus the Riches of a Country are to be valued by the Quantity of Labour its Inhabitants are able to purchase, and not by the Quantity of Silver and Gold they possess; which will purchase more or less Labour, and therefore is more or less valuable, as is said before, according to its Scarcity or Plenty. As those Metals have grown much more plentiful in *Europe* since the Discovery of *America*, so they have sunk in Value exceedingly; for, to instance in *England*, formerly one Penny of Silver was worth a Days Labour, but now it is hardly worth the sixth Part of a Days Labour; because not less than Six-pence will purchase the Labour of a Man for a Day in any Part of that Kingdom; which is wholly to be attributed to the much greater Plenty of Money now in *England* than formerly. And yet perhaps *England* is in Effect no richer now than at that Time; because as much Labour might be purchas'd, or Work got done of almost any kind, for 100 *l.* then, as will now require or is now worth 600 *l.*

In the next Place let us consider the Nature of *Banks* emitting *Bills of Credit*, as they are at this Time used in *Hamburgh, Amsterdam, London* and *Venice*.

Those Places being Seats of vast Trade, and the Payment of great Sums being for that Reason frequent, *Bills of Credit* are found very convenient in Business; because a great Sum is more easily counted in Them, lighter in Carriage, concealed in less Room, and therefore safer in Travelling or Laying up, and on many other Accounts they are very much valued. The Banks are the general Cashiers of all Gentlemen, Merchants and great Traders in and about those Cities; there they deposite their Money, and may take out Bills to the Value, for which they can be certain to have Money again at the Bank at any Time: This gives the Bills a Credit; so that in *England* they are never less valuable than Money, and in *Venice* and *Amsterdam* they are generally worth more. And the Bankers always reserving Money in hand to answer more than the common Run of Demands (and some People constantly putting in while others are taking out) are able besides to lend large Sums, on good Security, to the Government or others, for a reasonable Interest, by which they are paid for their Care and Trouble; and the Money which otherwise would have lain dead in their Hands, is made to circulate again thereby among the People: And thus the Running Cash of the Nation is as it were doubled; for all great Payments being made in Bills, Money in lower Trade becomes much more plentiful: And this is an exceeding great Advantage to a Trading Country, that is not over-stock'd with Gold and Silver.

As those who take Bills out of the Banks in *Europe*, put in Money for Security; so here, and in some of the neighbouring Provinces, we engage our Land. Which of these Methods will most effectually secure the Bills from actually sinking in Value, comes next to be considered.

Trade in general being nothing else but the Exchange of Labour for Labour, the Value of all Things is, as I have said before, most justly measured by Labour. Now suppose I put my Money into a Bank, and take out a Bill for the Value; if this Bill at the Time of my receiving it, would purchase me the Labour of one hundred Men for twenty Days; but some time after will only purchase the Labour of the same Number of Men for fifteen Days; it is plain the Bill has sunk in Value one fourth Part. Now Silver and Gold being of no permanent Value; and as this Bill is founded on Money, and therefore to be esteemed as such, it may be that the Occasion of this Fall is the increasing Plenty of Gold and Silver, by which Money is one fourth Part less valuable than before, and therefore one fourth more is given of it for the same Quantity of Labour; and if Land is not become more plentiful by some proportionate Decrease of the People, one fourth Part more of Money is given for the same Quantity of Land, whereby it appears that it would have been more profitable to me to have laid that Money out in Land which I put into the Bank, than to place it there and take a Bill for it. And it is certain that the Value of Money has been continually sinking in *England* for several Ages past, because it has been continually increasing in Quantity. But if Bills could be taken out of a Bank in *Europe* on a Land Security, it is probable the Value of such Bills would be more certain and steady, because the Number of Inhabitants continue to be near the same in those Countries from Age to Age.

For as Bills issued upon Money Security are Money, so Bills issued upon Land, are in Effect *Coined Land.*

Therefore (to apply the Above to our own Circumstances) If Land in this Province was falling, or any way likely to fall, it would behove the Legislature most carefully to contrive how to prevent the Bills issued upon Land from falling with it. But as our People increase exceedingly, and will be further increased, as I have before shewn, by the Help of a large Addition to our Currency; and as Land in consequence is continually rising, So, in case no Bills are emitted but what are upon Land Security, the Money-Acts in every Part punctually enforced and executed, the Payments of Principal and Interest being duly and strictly required, and the Principal *bona fide* sunk according to Law, it is absolutely impossible such Bills should ever sink below their first Value, or below the Value of the Land on which they are founded. In short, there is so little Danger of their sinking, that they would certainly rise as the Land rises, if they were not emitted in a proper Manner for preventing it; That is, by providing in the Act *That Payment may be made, either in those Bills, or in any other Bills made current by any Act of the Legislature of this Province*; and that the Interest, as it is received, may be again emitted in Discharge of Publick Debts; whereby circulating it returns again into the Hands of the Borrowers, and becomes Part of their future Payments; and thus as it is likely there will not be any Difficulty for want of Bills to pay the Office, they are hereby kept from rising above their first Value: For else, supposing there should be emitted upon mortgaged Land its full present Value in Bills; as in the Banks in *Europe* the full Value of the Money deposited is given out in Bills; and supposing the Office would take nothing but the same Sum in those Bills in Discharge of the Land; as in the Banks aforesaid, the same Sum in their

Bills must be brought in, in order to receive out the Money: In such Case the Bills would most surely rise in Value as the Land rises; as certainly as the Bank Bills founded on Money would fall if that Money was falling. Thus if I were to mortgage to a Loan-Office, or Bank, a Parcel of Land now valued at 100 *l*. in Silver, and receive for it the like Sum in Bills, to be paid in again at the Expiration of a certain Term of Years; before which, my Land rising in Value, becomes worth 150 *l*. in Silver: 'Tis plain, that if I have not these Bills in Possession, and the Office will take nothing but these Bills, or else what it is now become worth in Silver, in Discharge of my Land; I say it appears plain, that those Bills will now be worth 150 *l*. in Silver to the Possessor; and if I can purchase them for less, in order to redeem my Land, I shall by so much be a Gainer.

I need not say any Thing to convince the Judicious that our Bills have not yet sunk, tho' there is and has been some Difference between them and Silver; because it is evident that that Difference is occasioned by the Scarcity of the latter, which is now become a Merchandize, rising and falling, like other Commodities, as there is a greater or less Demand for it, or as it is more or less Plenty.

Yet farther, in order to make a true Estimate of the Value of Money, we must distinguish between Money as it is Bullion, which is Merchandize, and as by being coin'd it is made a Currency: For its Value as a Merchandize, and its Value as a Currency, are two distinct Things; and each may possibly rise and fall in some Degree independent of the other. Thus if the Quantity of Bullion increases in a Country, it will proportionably decrease in Value; but if at the same Time the Quantity of current Coin should decrease, (supposing Payments may not be made in Bullion) what Coin there is will rise in Value as a Currency, *i.e.* People will give more Labour in Manufactures for a certain Sum of ready Money.

In the same Manner must we consider a *Paper Currency* founded on Land; as it is Land, and as it is a Currency.

Money as Bullion, or as Land, is valuable by so much Labour as it costs to procure that Bullion or Land.

Money, as a Currency, has an Additional Value by so much Time and Labour as it saves in the Exchange of Commodities.

If, as a Currency, it saves one Fourth Part of the Time and Labour of a Country; it has, on that Account, one Fourth added to its original Value.

When there is no Money in a Country, all Commerce must be by Exchange. Now if it takes one fourth Part of the Time and Labour of a Country, to exchange or get their Commodities exchanged; then, in computing their Value, that Labour of Exchanging must be added to the Labour of manufacturing those Commodities: But if that Time or Labour is saved by introducing Money sufficient, then the additional Value on Account of the Labour of Exchanging may be abated, and Things sold for only the Value of the Labour in making them; because the People may now in the same Time make one Fourth more in Quantity of Manufactures than they could before.

From these Considerations it may be gathered, that in all the Degrees between having no Money in a Country, and Money sufficient for the Trade, it will rise and fall in Value as a Currency, in Proportion to the Decrease or Increase of its Quantity: And if there may be at some Time more than enough, the Overplus will have no Effect towards making the Currency, as a Currency, of less Value than when there was but enough; because such Overplus will not be used in Trade, but be some other way disposed of.

If we enquire, *How much* per Cent. *Interest ought to be required upon the Loan of these Bills*; we must consider what is the Natural Standard of Usury: And this appears to be, where the Security is undoubted, at least the Rent of so much Land as the Money lent will buy: For it cannot be expected that any Man will lend his Money for less than it would fetch him in as Rent if he laid it out in Land, which is the most secure Property in the World. But if the Security is casual, then a kind of Ensurance must be enterwoven with the simple natural Interest, which may advance the Usury very conscionable to any height below the Principal it self. Now among us, if the Value of Land is twenty Years Purchase, Five *per Cent.* is the just Rate of Interest for Money lent on undoubted Security. Yet if Money grows scarce in a Country, it becomes more difficult for People to make punctual Payments of what they borrow, Money being hard to be raised; likewise Trade being discouraged, and Business impeded for want of a Currency, abundance of People must be in declining Circumstances, and by these Means Security is more precarious than where Money is plenty. On such Accounts it is no wonder if People ask a greater Interest for their Money than the natural Interest; and what is above is to be look'd upon as a kind of *Præmium* for the Ensurance of those Uncertainties, as they are greater or less. Thus we always see, that where Money is scarce, Interest is high, and low where it is plenty. Now it is certainly the Advantage of a Country to make Interest as low as possible, as I have already shewn; and this can be done no other way than by making Money plentiful. And since, in Emitting Paper Money among us, the Office has the best of Security, the Titles to the Land being all skilfully and strictly examined and ascertained; and as it is only permitting the People by Law to coin their own Land, which costs the Government nothing, the Interest being more than enough to pay the Charges of Printing, Officers Fees, *&c.* I cannot see any good Reason why Four *per Cent.* to the Loan-Office should not be thought fully sufficient. As a low Interest may incline more to take Money out, it will become more plentiful in Trade; and this may bring down the common Usury, in which Security is more dubious, to the Pitch it is determined at by Law.

If it should be objected, *That Emitting It at so low an Interest, and on such easy Terms, will occasion more to be taken out than the Trade of the Country really requires*: It may be answered, That, as has already been shewn, there can never be so much of it emitted as to make it fall below the Land it is founded on; because no Man in his Senses will mortgage his Estate for what is of no more Value to him than That he has mortgaged, especially if the Possession of what he receives is more precarious than of what he mortgages, as that of Paper Money is when compared to Land: And if it should ever become so plenty by indiscreet Persons continuing to take out a large Overplus, above what is necessary in Trade, so as to make People imagine it would become by that Means of less Value than their mortgaged Lands, they would immediately of Course begin to pay it in again to the Office to redeem their Land, and continue to do so till there was no more left in Trade than was absolutely necessary. And thus the Proportion would find it self, (tho' there were a Million too much in the Office to be let out) without giving any one the Trouble of Calculation.

It may perhaps be objected to what I have written concerning the Advantages of a large Addition to our Currency, *That if the People of this Province increase, and Husbandry is more followed, we shall overstock the Markets with our Produce of Flower*, &c. To this it may be answered, that we can never have too many People (nor too much Money) For when one Branch of Trade or Business is overstocked with Hands, there are the more to spare to be employed in another. So if raising Wheat proves dull, more may (if there is Money to support and carry on new Manufactures) proceed to the raising and manufacturing of *Hemp*, *Silk*, *Iron*, and many other Things the Country is very capable of, for which we only want People to work, and Money to pay them with.

Upon the Whole it may be observed, That it is the highest Interest of a Trading Country in general to make Money plentiful; and that it can be a Disadvantage to none that have honest Designs. It cannot hurt even the Usurers, tho' it should sink what they receive as Interest; because they will be proportionably more secure in what they lend; or they will have an Opportunity of employing their Money to greater Advantage, to themselves as well as to the Country. Neither can it hurt those Merchants who have great Sums out-standing in Debts in the Country, and seem on that Account to have the most plausible Reason to fear it; *to wit*, because a large Addition being made to our Currency, will increase the Demand of our Exporting Produce, and by that Means raise the Price of it, so that they will not be able to purchase so much Bread or Flower with 100 *l*. when they shall receive it after such an Addition, as they now can, and may if there is no Addition: I say it cannot hurt even such, because they will get in their Debts just in exact Proportion so much the easier and sooner as the Money becomes plentier; and therefore, considering the Interest and Trouble saved, they will not be Losers; because it only sinks in Value as a Currency, proportionally as it becomes more plenty. It cannot hurt the Interest of *Great Britain*, as has been shewn; and it will greatly advance the Interest of the Proprietor. It will be an Advantage to every industrious Tradesman, *&c.* because his Business will be carried on more freely, and Trade be universally enlivened by it. And as more Business in all Manufactures will be done, by so much as the Labour and Time spent in Exchange is saved, the Country in general will grow so much the richer.

It is nothing to the Purpose to object the wretched Fall of the Bills in *New-England* and *South-Carolina*, unless it might be made evident that their Currency was emitted with the same Prudence, and on such good Security as ours is; and it certainly was not.

As this Essay is wrote and published in Haste, and the Subject in it self intricate, I hope I shall be censured with Candour, if, for want of Time carefully to revise what I have written, in some Places I should appear to have express'd my self too obscurely, and in others am liable to Objections I did not foresee. I sincerely desire to be acquainted with the Truth, and on that Account shall think my self obliged to any one, who will take the Pains to shew me, or the Publick, where I am mistaken in my Conclusions, And as we all know there are among us several Gentlemen of acute parts and profound Learning, who are very much against any Addition to our Money, it were to be wished that they would favour the Country with their Sentiments on this Head in Print; which, supported with Truth and good Reasoning, may probably be very convincing. And this is to be desired the rather, because many People knowing the Abilities of those Gentlemen to manage a good Cause, are apt to construe their Silence in This, as an

Argument of a bad One. Had any Thing of that Kind ever yet appeared, perhaps I should not have given the Publick this Trouble: But as those ingenious Gentlemen have not yet (and I doubt never will) think it worth their Concern to enlighten the Minds of their erring Countrymen in this Particular, I think it would be highly commendable in every one of us, more fully to bend our Minds to the Study of *What is the true Interest of* P*ENNSYLVANIA*; whereby we may be enabled, not only to reason pertinently with one another; but, if Occasion requires, to transmit Home such clear Representations, as must inevitably convince our Superiors of the Reasonableness and Integrity of our Designs.

B. B.

Philadelphia, April 3. 1729.

[Philadelphia: New Printing-Office, 1729]

CHAPTER 4
Apology for Printers
(10 June 1731)

Being frequently censur'd and condemn'd by different Persons for printing Things which they say ought not to be printed, I have sometimes thought it might be necessary to make a standing Apology for my self, and publish it once a Year, to be read upon all Occasions of that Nature. Much Business has hitherto hindered the execution of this Design; but having very lately given extraordinary Offence by printing an Advertisement with a certain *N.B.* at the End of it, I find an Apology more particularly requisite at this juncture, tho' it happens when I have not yet Leisure to write such a thing in the proper Form, and can only in a loose manner throw those Considerations together which should have been the Substance of it.

I request all who are angry with me on the Account of printing things they don't like, calmly to consider these following Particulars

1. That the Opinions of Men are almost as various as their Faces; an Observation general enough to become a common Proverb, *So many Men so many Minds.*

2. That the Business of Printing has chiefly to do with Mens Opinions; most things that are printed tending to promote some, or oppose others.

3. That hence arises the peculiar Unhappiness of that Business, which other Callings are no way liable to; they who follow Printing being scarce able to do any thing in their way of getting a Living, which shall not probably give Offence to some, and perhaps to many; whereas the Smith, the Shoemaker, the Carpenter, or the Man of any other Trade, may work indifferently for People of all Persuasions, without offending any of them: and the Merchant may buy and sell with Jews, Turks, Hereticks and Infidels of all sorts, and get Money by every one of them, without giving Offence to the most orthodox, of any sort; or suffering the least Censure or Ill-will on the Account from any Man whatever.

4. That it is as unreasonable in any one Man or Set of Men to expect to be pleas'd with every thing that is printed, as to think that nobody ought to be pleas'd but themselves.

5. Printers are educated in the Belief, that when Men differ in Opinion, both Sides ought equally to have the Advantage of being heard by the Publick; and that when Truth and Error have fair Play, the former is always an overmatch for the latter: Hence they chearfully serve all contending Writers that pay them well, without regarding on which side they are of the Question in Dispute.

6. Being thus continually employ'd in serving all Parties, Printers naturally acquire a vast Unconcernedness as to the right or wrong Opinions contain'd in what they print; regarding it only as the Matter of their daily labour: They print things full of Spleen and Animosity, with the utmost Calmness and Indifference, and without the least Ill-will to the Persons reflected on; who nevertheless unjustly think the Printer as much their Enemy as the Author, and join both together in their Resentment.

7. That it is unreasonable to imagine Printers approve of every thing they print, and to censure them on any particular thing accordingly; since in the way of their Business they print such great variety of things opposite and contradictory. It is likewise as unreasonable what some assert, *That Printers ought not to print any Thing but what they approve*; since if all of that Business should make such a Resolution, and abide by it, an End would thereby be put to Free Writing, and the World would afterwards have nothing to read but what happen'd to be the Opinions of Printers.

8. That if all Printers were determin'd not to print any thing till they were sure it would offend no body, there would be very little printed.

9. That if they sometimes print vicious or silly things not worth reading, it may not be because they approve such things themselves, but because the People are so viciously and corruptly educated that good things are not encouraged. I have known a very numerous Impression of *Robin Hood's Songs* go off in this Province at 2 *s.* per Book, in less than a Twelvemonth; when a small Quantity of *David's Psalms* (an excellent Version) have lain upon my Hands above twice the Time.

10. That notwithstanding what might be urg'd in behalf of a Man's being allow'd to do in the Way of his Business whatever he is paid for, yet Printers do continually discourage the Printing of great Numbers of bad things, and stifle them in the Birth. I my self have constantly refused to print any thing that might countenance Vice, or promote Immorality; tho' by complying in such Cases with the corrupt Taste of the Majority,

I might have got much Money. I have also always refus'd to print such things as might do real Injury to any Person, how much soever I have been solicited, and tempted with Offers of great Pay; and how much soever I have by refusing got the Ill-will of those who would have employ'd me. I have heretofore fallen under the Resentment of large Bodies of Men, for refusing absolutely to print any of their Party or Personal Reflections. In this Manner I have made my self many Enemies, and the constant Fatigue of denying is almost insupportable. But the Publick being unacquainted with all this, whenever the poor Printer happens either through Ignorance or much Persuasion, to do any thing that is generally thought worthy of Blame, he meets with no more Friendship or Favour on the above Account, than if there were no Merit in't at all. Thus, as *Waller* says,

> *Poets loose half the Praise they would have got*
> *Were it but known what they discreetly blot;*[1]

Yet are censur'd for every bad Line found in their Works with the utmost Severity.

I come now to the particular Case of the *N.B.* above-mention'd, about which there has been more Clamour against me, than ever before on any other Account.——In the Hurry of other Business an Advertisement was brought to me to be printed; it signified that such a Ship lying at such a Wharff, would sail for *Barbadoes* in such a Time, and that Freighters and Passengers might agree with the Captain at such a Place; so far is what's common: But at the Bottom this odd Thing was added, N.B. *No Sea Hens nor Black Gowns will be admitted on any Terms.* I printed it, and receiv'd my Money; and the Advertisement was stuck up round the Town as usual. I had not so much Curiosity at that time as to enquire the Meaning of it, nor did I in the least imagine it would give so much Offence. Several good Men are very angry with me on this Occasion; they are pleas'd to say I have too much Sense to do such things ignorantly; that if they were Printers they would not have done such a thing on any Consideration; that it could proceed from nothing but my abundant Malice against Religion and the Clergy: They therefore declare they will not take any more of my Papers, nor have any farther Dealings with me; but will hinder me of all the Custom they can. All this is very hard!

I believe it had been better if I had refused to print the said Advertisement. However, 'tis done and cannot be revok'd. I have only the following

[1] [Edmund Waller, *Works* (London, 1729), 238.]

few Particulars to offer, some of them in my Behalf, by way of Mitigation, and some not much to the Purpose; but I desire none of them may be read when the Reader is not in a very good Humour.

1. That I really did it without the least Malice, and imagin'd the *N.B.* was plac'd there only to make the Advertisement star'd at, and more generally read.

2. That I never saw the Word *Sea-Hens* before in my Life; nor have I yet ask'd the meaning of it; and tho' I had certainly known that *Black Gowns* in that Place signified the Clergy of the Church of *England*, yet I have that confidence in the generous good Temper of such of them as I know, as to be well satisfied such a trifling mention of their Habit gives them no Disturbance.

3. That most of the Clergy in this and the neighbouring Provinces, are my Customers, and some of them my very good Friends; and I must be very malicious indeed, or very stupid, to print this thing for a small Profit, if I had thought it would have given them just Cause of Offence.

4. That if I have much Malice against the Clergy, and withal much Sense; 'tis strange I never write or talk against the Clergy my self. Some have observed that 'tis a fruitful Topic, and the easiest to be witty upon of all others. I can print any thing I write at less Charge than others; yet I appeal to the Publick that I am never guilty this way, and to all my Acquaintance as to my Conversation.

5. That if a Man of Sense had Malice enough to desire to injure the Clergy, this is the foolishest Thing he could possibly contrive for that Purpose.

6. That I got Five Shillings by it.

7. That none who are angry with me would have given me so much to let it alone.

8. That if all the People of different Opinions in this Province would engage to give me as much for not printing things they don't like, as I can get by printing them, I should probably live a very easy Life; and if all Printers were every where so dealt by, there would be very little printed.

9. That I am oblig'd to all who take my Paper, and am willing to think they do it out of meer Friendship. I only desire they would think the same when I deal with them. I thank those who leave off, that they have taken it so long. But I beg they would not endeavour to dissuade others, for that will look like Malice.

10. That 'tis impossible any Man should know what he would do if he was a Printer.

11. That notwithstanding the Rashness and Inexperience of Youth, which is most likely to be prevail'd with to do things that ought not to be done; yet I have avoided printing such Things as usually give Offence either to Church or State, more than any Printer that has followed the Business in this Province before.

12. And lastly, That I have printed above a Thousand Advertisements which made not the least mention of *Sea-Hens* or *Black Gowns*; and this being the first Offence, I have the more Reason to expect Forgiveness.

I take leave to conclude with an old Fable, which some of my Readers have heard before, and some have not.

"A certain well-meaning Man and his Son, were travelling towards a Market Town, with an Ass which they had to sell. The Road was bad; and the old Man therefore rid, but the Son went a-foot. The first Passenger they met, asked the Father if he was not ashamed to ride by himself, and suffer the poor Lad to wade along thro' the Mire; this induced him to take up his Son behind him: He had not travelled far, when he met others, who said, they were two unmerciful Lubbers to get both on the Back of that poor Ass, in such a deep Road. Upon this the old Man gets off, and let his Son ride alone. The next they met called the Lad a graceless, rascally young Jackanapes, to ride in that Manner thro' the Dirt, while his aged Father trudged along on Foot; and they said the old Man was a Fool, for suffering it. He then bid his Son come down, and walk with him, and they travell'd on leading the Ass by the Halter; 'till they met another Company, who called them a Couple of sensless Blockheads, for going both on Foot in such a dirty Way, when they had an empty Ass with them, which they might ride upon. The old Man could bear no longer; My Son, said he, it grieves me much that we cannot please all these People: Let us throw the Ass over the next Bridge, and be no farther troubled with him."

Had the old Man been seen acting this last Resolution, he would probably have been call'd a Fool for troubling himself about the different Opinions of all that were pleas'd to find Fault with him: Therefore, tho' I have a Temper almost as complying as his, I intend not to imitate him in this last Particular. I consider the Variety of Humours among Men, and despair of pleasing every Body; yet I shall not therefore leave off Printing. I shall continue my Business. I shall not burn my Press and melt my Letters.

[Gazette, 10 June 1731]

CHAPTER 5
Rules for a Club Formerly Established at Philadelphia
(1732)

Previous question, to be answer'd at every meeting.

Have you read over these queries this morning, in order to consider what you might have to offer the Junto [touching] any one of them? viz.

1. Have you met with any thing in the author you last read, remarkable, or suitable to be communicated to the Junto? particularly in history, morality, poetry, physic, travels, mechanic arts, or other parts of knowledge.

2. What new story have you lately heard agreeable for telling in conversation?

3. Hath any citizen in your knowledge failed in his business lately, and what have you heard of the cause?

4. Have you lately heard of any citizen's thriving well, and by what means?

5. Have you lately heard how any present rich man, here or elsewhere, got his estate?

6. Do you know of any fellow citizen, who has lately done a worthy action, deserving praise and imitation? or who has committed an error proper for us to be warned against and avoid?

7. What unhappy effects of intemperance have you lately observed or heard? of imprudence? of passion? or of any other vice or folly?

8. What happy effects of temperance? of prudence? of moderation? or of any other virtue?

9. Have you or any of your acquaintance been lately sick or wounded? If so, what remedies were used, and what were their effects?

10. Who do you know that are shortly going voyages or journies, if one should have occasion to send by them?

11. Do you think of any thing at present, in which the Junto may be serviceable to *mankind*? to their country, to their friends, or to themselves?

12. Hath any deserving stranger arrived in town since last meeting, that you heard of? and what have you heard or observed of his character or merits? and whether think you, it lies in the power of the Junto to oblige him, or encourage him as he deserves?

13. Do you know of any deserving young beginner lately set up, whom it lies in the power of the Junto any way to encourage?

14. Have you lately observed any defect in the laws of your *country*, [of] which it would be proper to move the legislature for an amendment? Or do you know of any beneficial law that is wanting?

15. Have you lately observed any encroachment on the just liberties of the people?

16. Hath any body attacked your reputation lately? and what can the Junto do towards securing it?

17. Is there any man whose friendship you want, and which the Junto or any of them, can procure for you?

18. Have you lately heard any member's character attacked, and how have you defended it?

19. Hath any man injured you, from whom it is in the power of the junto to procure redress?

20. In what manner can the Junto, or any of them, assist you in any of your honourable designs?

21. Have you any weighty affair in hand, in which you think the advice of the Junto may be of service?

22. What benefits have you lately received from any man not present?

23. Is there any difficulty in matters of opinion, of justice, and injustice, which you would gladly have discussed at this time?

24. Do you see any thing amiss in the present customs or proceedings of the Junto, which might be amended?

Any person to be qualified, to stand up, and lay his hand on his breast, and be asked these questions; viz

1. Have you any particular disrespect to any present members?——*Answer*. I have not.

2. Do you sincerely declare that you love mankind in general; of what profession or religion soever?——*Answ*. I do.

3. Do you think any person ought to be harmed in his body, name or goods, for mere speculative opinions, or his external way of worship?——*Ans*. No.

4. Do you love truth for truth's sake, and will you endeavour impartially to find and receive it yourself and communicate it to others?——*Answ*. Yes.

[Vaughan 533–6]

CHAPTER 6

Dialogue Between Two Presbyterians

(10 April 1735)

MR. FRANKLIN,

You are desired by several of *your Readers to print the following* DIALOGUE. *It is between Two of the Presbyterian Meeting in this City. We cannot tell whether it may not be contrary to your Sentiments, but hope, if it should, you will not refuse publishing it on that Account: nor shall we be offended if you print any thing in Answer to it. We are yours, &c.*

A.B.C.D.

S. Good Morrow! I am glad to find you well and abroad; for not having seen you at Meeting lately, I concluded you were indispos'd.

T. *Tis true I have not been much at Meeting lately, but that was not occasion'd by any Indisposition. In short, I stay at home, or else go to Church, because I do not like Mr.* H. *your newfangled Preacher.*

S. I am sorry we should differ in Opinion upon any Account; but let us reason the Point calmly; what Offence does Mr. *H.* give you?

T. *Tis his Preaching disturbs me: He talks of nothing but the Duties of Morality: I do not love to hear so much of Morality: I am sure it will carry no Man to Heaven, and I do not think it fit to be preached in a Christian Congregation.*

S. I suppose you think no Doctrine fit to be preached in a Christian Congregation, but such as Christ and his Apostles used to preach.

T. *To be sure I think so.*

S. I do not conceive then how you can dislike the Preaching of Morality, when you consider, that Morality made the principal Part of their Preaching as well as of Mr. *H's.* What is Christ's Sermon on the Mount but an excellent moral Discourse, towards the End of which, (as foreseeing that People might in time come to depend more upon their *Faith* in him, than upon *Good Works*, for their Salvation) he tells the Hearers plainly, that their saying to him, *Lord*, *Lord*, (that is, professing themselves his Disciples or *Christians*) should give them no Title to Salvation, but their *Doing* the Will of his Father; and that tho' they have prophesied in his Name, yet he will declare to them, as Neglecters of Morality, that he never knew them.

T. *But what do you understand by that Expression of Christ's,* Doing the Will of my Father.

S. I understand it to be the Will of God, that we should live virtuous, upright, and good-doing Lives; as the Prophet understood it, when he said, *What doth the Lord require of thee, O Man, but to do justly, love Mercy, and walk humbly with the Lord thy God.*[1]

T. *But is not Faith recommended in the New Testament as well as Morality?*

S. Tis true, it is. Faith is recommended as a Means of producing Morality: Our Saviour was a Teacher of Morality or Virtue, and they that were deficient and desired to be taught, ought first to *believe* in him as an able and faithful Teacher. Thus Faith would be a Means of producing Morality, and Morality of Salvation. But that from such Faith alone Salvation may be expected, appears to me to be neither a Christian Doctrine nor a reasonable one. And I should as soon expect, that my bare Believing Mr. *Grew* to be an excellent Teacher of the Mathematicks, would make me a Mathematician, as that Believing in Christ would of it self make a Man a Christian.

T. *Perhaps you may think, that tho' Faith alone cannot save a Man, Morality or Virtue alone, may.*

S. Morality or Virtue is the End, Faith only a Means to obtain that End: And if the End be obtained, it is no matter by what Means. What think you of these Sayings of Christ, when he was reproached for conversing chiefly with gross Sinners, *The whole*, says he, *need not a Physician, but they that are sick*; and, *I come not to call the Righteous, but Sinners, to Repentance*: Does not this imply, that there were good Men, who, without Faith in him, were in a State of Salvation? And moreover, did he not say of *Nathanael*, while he was yet an Unbeliever in him, and thought no Good could possibly come out of Nazareth, *Behold an Israelite indeed, in whom there is no Guile*! that is, *behold a virtuous upright Man*. Faith in Christ, however, may be and is of great Use to produce a good Life, but that it can conduce nothing towards Salvation where it does not conduce to

[1] [Micah 6:8.]

Virtue, is, I suppose, plain from the Instance of the Devils, who are far from being Infidels, *they believe*, says the Scripture, *and tremble*. There were some indeed, even in the Apostle's Days, that set a great Value upon Faith, distinct from Good Works, they meerly idolized it, and thought that a Man ever so righteous could not be saved without it: But one of the Apostles, to show his Dislike of such Notions, tells them, that not only those heinous Sins of Theft, Murder, and Blasphemy, but even *Idleness*, or the Neglect of a Man's Business, was more pernicious than meer harmless Infidelity, *He that neglects to provide for them of his own House*, says he, *is WORSE than an Infidel*. St. *James*, in his second Chapter, is very zealous against these Cryers-up of Faith, and maintains that Faith without Virtue is useless, *Wilt thou know, O vain Man*, says he, *that Faith without Works is dead*; and, *shew me your Faith without your Works, and I will shew you mine by my Works*. Our Saviour, when describing the last Judgment, and declaring what shall give Admission into Bliss, or exclude from it, says nothing of *Faith* but what he says against it, that is, that those who cry *Lord, Lord*, and profess to have *believed* in his Name, have no Favour to expect on that Account; but declares that 'tis the Practice, or the omitting the Practice of the Duties of Morality, *Feeding the Hungry, cloathing the Naked, visiting the Sick*, &c. in short, 'tis the Doing or not Doing all the Good that lies in our Power, that will render us the Heirs of Happiness or Misery.[2]

T. *But if Faith is of great Use to produce a good Life, why does not Mr.* H. *preach up Faith as well as Morality?*

S. Perhaps it may [be] this, that as the good Physician suits his Physick to the Disease he finds in the Patient, so Mr. *H.* may possibly think, that though Faith in Christ be properly first preach'd to Heathens and such as are ignorant of the Gospel, yet since he knows that we have been baptized in the Name of Christ, and educated in his Religion, and call'd after his Name, it may not be so immediately necessary to preach *Faith* to us who abound in it, as *Morality* in which we are evidently deficient: For our late Want of Charity to each other, our Heart-burnings and Bickerings are notorious. St. *James* says, *Where Envying and Strife is, there is Confusion and every evil Work*: and where Confusion and every evil Work is, *Morality* and Good-will to Men, can, I think, be no unsuitable Doctrine.[3] But surely *Morality* can do us no harm. Upon a Supposition that we all have Faith in Christ already, as I think we have, where can be the Damage of being

[2] [Matthew 9:12–13; John 1:47; James 2:19; I Timothy 5:8; James 2:20; Matthew 7:21.]

[3] [James 3:16.]

exhorted to Good Works? Is Virtue Heresy; and Universal Benevolence False Doctrine, that any of us should keep away from Meeting because it is preached there.

T. *Well, I do not like it, and I hope we shall not long be troubled with it. A Commission of the Synod will sit in a short Time, and try this Sort* of *Preaching.*

S. I am glad to hear that the Synod are to take it into Consideration. There are Men of unquestionable Good Sense as well as Piety among them, and I doubt not but they will, by their Decision, deliver our Profession from the satyrical Reflection, which a few uneasy People of our Congregation have of late given Occasion for, *to wit*, That the *Presbyterians* are going to persecute, silence and condemn a good Preacher, for exhorting them to be honest and charitable to one another and the rest of Mankind.

T. *If Mr.* H. *is a Presbyterian Teacher, he ought to preach as Presbyterians use to preach; or else he may justly be condemn'd and silenced by our Church Authority. We ought to abide by the* Westminster *Confession of Faith; and he that does not, ought not to preach in our Meetings.*

S. The Apostacy of the Church from the primitive Simplicity of the Gospel, came on by Degrees; and do you think that the Reformation was of a sudden perfect, and that the first Reformers knew at once all that was right or wrong in Religion? Did not *Luther* at first preach only against selling of Pardons, allowing all the other Practices of the *Romish* Church for good? He afterwards went further, and *Calvin*, some think, yet further. The Church of *England* made a Stop, and fix'd her Faith and Doctrine by 39 Articles; with which the Presbyterians not satisfied, went yet farther; but being too self-confident to think, that as their Fathers were mistaken in some Things, they also might be in some others; and fancying themselves infallible in *their* Interpretations, they also ty'd themselves down by the *Westminster Confession*. But has not a Synod that meets in King GEORGE the Second's Reign, as much Right to interpret Scripture, as one that met in *Oliver's* Time? And if any Doctrine then maintain'd is, or shall hereafter be found not altogether orthodox, why must we be for ever confin'd to that, or to any, *Confession?*

T. *But if the Majority of the Synod be against any Innovation, they may justly hinder the Innovator from Preaching.*

S. That is as much as to say, if the Majority of the Preachers be in the wrong, they may justly hinder any Man from setting the People right; for a *Majority* may be in the wrong as well as the *Minority*, and frequently are. In the beginning of the Reformation, the *Majority* was vastly against the Reformers, and continues so to this Day; and, if, according to your Opinion, they had a Right to silence the *Minority*, I am sure the *Minority* ought to have been silent. But tell me, if the *Presbyterians* in this Country, being charitably enclin'd, should send a Missionary into *Turky*, to propagate the Gospel, would it not be unreasonable in the *Turks* to prohibit his Preaching?

T. *It would, to be sure, because he comes to them for their good.*

S. And if the *Turks*, believing us in the wrong, as we think them, should out of the same charitable Disposition, send a Missionary to preach *Mahometanism* to us, ought we not in the same manner to give him free Liberty of preaching his Doctrine?

T. *It may be so; but what would you infer from that?*

S. I would only infer, that if it would be thought reasonable to suffer a *Turk* to preach among us a Doctrine diametrically opposite to *Christianity*, it cannot be reasonable to silence one of our own Preachers, for preaching a Doctrine exactly agreeable to *Christianity*, only because he does not perhaps zealously propagate all the Doctrines of an old *Confession*. And upon the whole, though the *Majority* of the Synod should not in all respects approve of Mr. *H*'s Doctrine, I do not however think they will find it proper to condemn him. We have justly deny'd the Infallibility of the *Pope* and his *Councils* and *Synods* in their Interpretations of Scripture, and can we modestly claim *Infallibility* for our selves or our *Synods* in our way of Interpreting? Peace, Unity and Virtue in any Church are more to be regarded than Orthodoxy. In the present weak State of humane Nature, surrounded as we are on all sides with Ignorance and Error, it little becomes poor fallible Man to be positive and dogmatical in his Opinions. No Point of Faith is so plain, as that *Morality* is our Duty, for all Sides agree in that. A virtuous Heretick shall be saved before a wicked Christian: for there is no such Thing as voluntary Error. Therefore, since 'tis an Uncertainty till we get to Heaven what true Orthodoxy in all points is, and since our Congregation is rather too small to be divided, I hope this Misunderstanding will soon be got over, and that we shall as heretofore unite again in mutual *Christian Charity*.

T. *I wish we may. I'll consider of what you've said, and wish you well.*

S. Farewell.

[Gazette, 10 April 1735]

CHAPTER 7
To Josiah and Abiah Franklin
(13 April 1738)

Honour'd Father and Mother

I have your Favour of the 21st of March in which you both seem concern'd lest I have imbib'd some erroneous Opinions. Doubtless I have my Share, and when the natural Weakness and Imperfection of Human Understanding is considered, with the unavoidable Influences of Education, Custom, Books and Company, upon our Ways of thinking, I imagine a Man must have a good deal of Vanity who believes, and a good deal of Boldness who affirms, that all the Doctrines he holds, are true; and all he rejects, are false. And perhaps the same may be justly said of every Sect, Church and Society of men when they assume to themselves that Infallibility which they deny to the Popes and Councils.——I think Opinions should be judg'd of by their Influences and Effects; and if a Man holds none that tend to make him less Virtuous or more vicious, it may be concluded he holds none that are dangerous; which I hope is the Case with me.——I am sorry you should have any Uneasiness on my Account, and if it were a thing possible for one to alter his Opinions in order to please others, I know none whom I ought more willingly to oblige in that respect than your selves: But since it is no more in a Man's Power *to think* than *to look* like another, methinks all that should be expected from me is to keep my Mind open to Conviction, to hear patiently and examine attentively whatever is offered me for that end; and if after all I continue to the same Errors, I believe your usual Charity will induce you rather to pity and excuse than blame me. In the mean time your Care and Concern for me is what I am very thankful for.

As to the Freemasons, unless she will believe me when I assure her that they are in general a very harmless sort of People; and have no principles or Practices that are inconsistent with Religion or good Manners, I know no Way of giving my Mother a better Opinion of them than she seems to have at present, (since it is not allow'd that Women should be admitted into that secret Society). She has, I must confess, on that Account, some reason to be displeas'd with it; but for any thing else, I must entreat her to suspend her Judgment till she is better inform'd, and in the mean time exercise her Charity.

My Mother grieves that one of her Sons is an Arian, another an Arminian. What an Arminian or an Arian is, I cannot say that I very well know; the Truth is, I make such Distinctions very little my Study; I think vital Religion has always suffer'd, when Orthodoxy is more regarded than Virtue. And the Scripture assures me, that at the last Day, we shall not be examin'd what we *thought*, but what we *did*; and our Recommendation will not be that we said *Lord, Lord*, but that we did GOOD to our Fellow Creatures. See Matth. 26.

We have had great Rains here lately, which with the Thawing of Snow in the Mountains back of our Country has made vast Floods in our Rivers, and by carrying away Bridges, Boats, &c. made travelling almost impracticable for a Week past, so that our Post has entirely mist making one Trip.

I know nothing of Dr. Crook, nor can I learn that any such Person has ever been here.

I hope my Sister Janey's Child is by this time recovered. I am Your dutiful Son

[Papers 2:202–4]

CHAPTER 8

A Proposal for Promoting Useful Knowledge Among the British Plantations in America

(14 May 1743)

The *English* are possess'd of a long Tract of Continent, from *Nova Scotia* to *Georgia*, extending North and South thro' different Climates, having different Soils, producing different Plants, Mines and Minerals, and capable of different Improvements, Manufactures, *&c.*

The first Drudgery of Settling new Colonies, which confines the Attention of People to mere Necessaries, is now pretty well over; and there are many in every Province in Circumstances that set them at Ease, and afford Leisure to cultivate the finer Arts, and improve the common Stock of Knowledge. To such of these who are Men of Speculation, many Hints must from time to time arise, many Observations occur, which if well-examined, pursued and improved, might produce Discoveries to the Advantage of some or all of the *British* Plantations, or to the Benefit of Mankind in general.

But as from the Extent of the Country such Persons are widely separated, and seldom can see and converse or be acquainted with each other, so that many useful Particulars remain uncommunicated, die with the Discoverers, and are lost to Mankind; it is, to remedy this Inconvenience for the future, proposed,

That One Society be formed of Virtuosi or ingenious Men residing in the several Colonies, to be called *The American Philosophical Society*; who are to maintain a constant Correspondence.

That *Philadelphia* being the City nearest the Centre of the Continent-Colonies, communicating with all of them northward and southward by Post, and with all the Islands by Sea, and having the Advantage of a good growing Library, be the Centre of the Society.

That at *Philadelphia* there be always at least seven Members, *viz.* a Physician, a Botanist, a Mathematician, a Chemist, a Mechanician, a Geographer, and a general Natural Philosopher, besides a President, Treasurer and Secretary.

That these Members meet once a Month, or oftner, at their own Expence, to communicate to each other their Observations, Experiments, *&c.* to receive, read and consider such Letters, Communications, or Queries as shall be sent from distant Members; to direct the Dispersing of Copies of such Communications as are valuable, to other distant Members, in order to procure their Sentiments thereupon, *&c.*

That the Subjects of the Correspondence be, All new-discovered Plants, Herbs, Trees, Roots, *&c.* their Virtues, Uses, *&c.* Methods of Propagating them, and making such as are useful, but particular to some Plantations, more general. Improvements of vegetable juices, as Cyders, Wines, *&c.* New Methods of Curing or Preventing Diseases. All new-discovered Fossils in different Countries, as Mines, Minerals, Quarries, *&c.* New and useful Improvements in any Branch of Mathematicks. New Discoveries in Chemistry, such as Improvements in Distillation, Brewing, Assaying of Ores, *&c.* New Mechanical Inventions for saving Labour; as Mills, Carriages, *&c.* and for Raising and Conveying of Water, Draining of Meadows, *&c.* All new Arts, Trades, Manufactures, *&c.* that may be proposed or thought of. Surveys, Maps and Charts of particular Parts of the Sea-coasts, or Inland Countries; Course and Junction of Rivers and great Roads, Situation of Lakes and Mountains, Nature of the Soil and Productions, *&c.* New Methods of Improving the Breed of useful Animals, Introducing other Sorts from foreign Countries. New Improvements in Planting, Gardening, Clearing Land, *&c.* And all philosophical Experiments that let Light into the Nature of Things, tend to increase the Power of Man over Matter, and multiply the Conveniencies or Pleasures of Life.

That a Correspondence already begun by some intended Members, shall be kept up by this Society with the ROYAL SOCIETY of *London*, and with the DUBLIN SOCIETY.

That every Member shall have Abstracts sent him Quarterly, of every Thing valuable communicated to the Society's Secretary at *Philadelphia*; free of all Charge except the Yearly Payment hereafter mentioned.

That by Permission of the Postmaster-General, such Communications pass between the Secretary of the Society and the Members, Postage-free.

That for defraying the Expence of such Experiments as the Society shall judge proper to cause to be made, and other contingent Charges for the common Good, every Member send a Piece of Eight *per Annum* to the Treasurer, at *Philadelphia*, to form a Common Stock, to be disburs'd by Order of the President with the Consent of the Majority of the Members that can conveniently be consulted thereupon, to such Persons and Places where and by whom the Experiments are to be made, and otherwise as there shall be Occasion; of which Disbursements an exact Account shall be kept, and communicated yearly to every Member.

That at the first Meetings of the Members at *Philadelphia*, such Rules be formed for Regulating their Meetings and Transactions for the General Benefit, as shall be convenient and necessary; to be afterwards changed and improv'd as there shall be Occasion, wherein due Regard is to be had to the Advice of distant Members.

That at the End of every Year, Collections be made and printed, of such Experiments, Discoveries, Improvements, *&c.* as may be thought of publick Advantage: And that every Member have a Copy sent him.

That the Business and Duty of the Secretary be, To receive all Letters intended for the Society, and lay them before the President and Members at their Meetings; to abstract, correct and methodize such Papers, *&c.* as require it, and as he shall be directed to do by the President, after they have been considered, debated and digested in the Society; to enter Copies thereof in the Society's Books, and make out Copies for distant Members; to answer their Letters by Direction of the President, and keep Records of all material Transactions of the Society, &c.

Benjamin Franklin, the Writer of this Proposal, offers himself to serve the Society as their Secretary, 'till they shall be provided with one more capable.

Philadelphia, *May* 14. 1743.

[Philadelphia, 1743]

CHAPTER 9
The Speech of Miss Polly Baker
(15 April 1747)

The SPEECH *of Miss* Polly Baker, *before a Court of Judicature, at* Connecticut *near Boston in* New-England*; where she was prosecuted the Fifth Time, for having a Bastard Child; Which influenced the Court to dispense with her Punishment, and induced one of her Judges to marry her the next Day.*

MAY it please the Honourable Bench to indulge me in a few Words: I am a poor unhappy Woman, who have no Money to fee Lawyers to plead for me, being hard put to it to get a tolerable Living. I shall not trouble your Honours with long Speeches; for I have not the Presumption to expect, that you may, by any Means, be prevailed on to deviate in your Sentence from the Law, in my Favour. All I humbly hope is, That your Honours would charitably move the Governor's Goodness on my Behalf, that my Fine may be remitted. This is the Fifth Time, Gentlemen, that I have been dragg'd before your Court on the same Account; twice I have paid heavy Fines, and twice have been brought to publick Punishment, for want of Money to pay those Fines. This may have been agreeable to the Laws, and I do not dispute it: but since Laws are sometimes unreasonable in themselves, and therefore repealed, and others bear too hard on the Subject in particular Circumstances; and therefore there is left a Power somewhat to dispense with the Execution of them; I take the Liberty to say, That I think this Law, by which I am punished, is both unreasonable in itself, and particularly severe with regard to me, who have always lived an inoffensive Life in the Neighbourhood where I was born, and defy my Enemies (if I have any) to say I ever wrong'd Man, Woman, or Child. Abstracted from the Law, I cannot conceive (may it please your Honours) what the Nature of my Offence is. I have brought Five fine Children into the World, at the Risque of my Life; I have maintain'd them well by my own Industry, without burthening the Township, and would have done it better, if it had not been for the heavy Charges and Fines I have paid. Can it be a Crime (in the Nature of Things I mean) to add to the Number of the King's Subjects, in a new Country that really wants People? I own it should think it a Praise-worthy, rather than a punishable Action. I have debauched no other Woman's Husband, nor enticed any innocent Youth; these Things I never was charg'd with, nor has any one the least cause of Complaint against me, unless, perhaps the Minister, or Justice, because I have had Children without being married, by which they have missed a Wedding Fee. But, can ever this be a Fault of mine? I appeal to your Honours. You are pleased to allow I don't want Sense; but I must be stupid to the last Degree, not to prefer the Honourable State of Wedlock, to the Condition I have lived in. I always was, and still am willing to enter into it; and doubt not my behaving well in it, having all the Industry, Frugality, Fertility, and Skill in Oeconomy, appertaining to a good Wife's Character. I defy any Person to say, I ever refused an Offer of that Sort: On the contrary, I readily Consented to the only Proposal of Marriage that ever was made me, which was when I was a Virgin; but too easily confiding in the Person's Sincerity that made it, I unhappily lost my own Honour, by trusting to his; for he got me with Child, and then forsook me: That very Person you all know; he is now become a Magistrate of this Country; and I had hopes he would have appeared this Day on the Bench, and have endeavoured to moderate the Court in my Favour; then I should have scorn'd to have mention'd it; but I must now complain of it, as unjust and unequal, That my Betrayer and Undoer, the first Cause of all my Faults and Miscarriages (if they must be deemed such) should be advanc'd to Honour and Power in the Government, that punishes my Misfortunes with Stripes and Infamy. I should be told, 'tis like, That were there no Act of Assembly in the Case, the Precepts of Religion are violated by my Transgressions. If mine, then, is a religious Offence, leave it to religious Punishments. You have already excluded me from the Comforts of your Church-Communion. Is not that sufficient? You believe I have offended Heaven, and must suffer eternal Fire: Will not that be sufficient? What Need is there, then, of your additional Fines and Whipping? I own, I do not think as you do; for, if I thought what you call a Sin, was really such, I could not presumptuously commit it. But, how can it be believed, that Heaven is angry at my having Children, when to the little done by me towards it, God has been pleased to add his Divine Skill and admirable Workmanship in the Formation of their Bodies, and crown'd it, by furnishing them with rational and immortal Souls. Forgive me Gentlemen, if I talk a little extravagantly on these Matters; I am no Divine, but if you, Gentlemen, must be making Laws, do not turn natural and useful Actions into Crimes, by your Prohibitions. But take into your wise Consideration, the great and growing Number of Batchelors in the Country, many of whom from the mean Fear of the Expence of a Family, have never sincerely and honourably Courted a Woman in their Lives; and by their Manner of Living, leave unproduced (which I think is little better than Murder) Hundreds of their Posterity to the Thousandth Generation. Is not this a greater Offence against the Publick Good, than mine? Compel them, then, by Law, either to Marriage, or to pay double the Fine of Fornication every Year. What must poor young Women do, whom Custom have forbid to solicit the Men, and who cannot force themselves upon Husbands, when the Laws take no Care to provide them any; and yet severely punish them if they do their Duty without them; the Duty of the first and great Command of Nature, and of Nature's God, *Encrease and Multiply*. A Duty, from the steady Performance of which, nothing has been able to deter me; but for its Sake, I have hazarded the Loss of the Publick Esteem, and have frequently endured Publick Disgrace and Punishment; and therefore ought, in my humble Opinion, instead of a Whipping, to have a Statue erected to my Memory.

[*The General Advertiser* (London), 15 April 1747]

CHAPTER 10

Plain Truth: or, Serious Considerations On the Present State of the City of Philadelphia, and Province of Pennsylvania

(17 November 1747)

> "*Capta urbe, nihil sit reliqui victis. Sed, per Deos immortales, vos ego appello, qui semper domos, villas, signa, tabulas vestras, tantæ æstimationis secistis; si ista, cujuscumque modi sint, quæ amplexamini, retinere, si voluptatibus vestris otium præbere vultis; expergiscimini aliquando, & capessite rempublicam. Non agitur nunc de sociorum injuriis;* LIBERTAS & ANIMA *nostra in dubio est. Dux hostium cum exercitu supra caput est. Vos cunctamini ætam nunc, & dubitatis quid faciatis? Scilicet, res ipsa asperæ est, sed vos non timetis eam. Imo vero maxume; sed inertia & mollitia animi, alius alium expectantes, cunctamini; videlicet, Diis immortalibus consisi, qui hanc rempublicam in maxumis periculis servavere.* NON VOTIS, NEQUE SUPPLICIIS MULIBRIBUS, AUXILIA DEORUM PARANTUR: *vigilando, agendo, bene consulendo, prospere omnia cedunt. Ubi socordiæ tete atque ignaviæ tradideris, nequicquam Deos implores; irati, infestique sunt.*" M. POR. CAT. *in* SALLUST[1]

[1] [Sallust, *De Conjuratione Catilinae*, 52:4–6, 24–5, 28–9. Franklin printed a translation in the second edition at the end of the text: "Should the City be taken, all will be lost to the Conquered. Therefore if you desire to preserve your Buildings, Houses and Country Seats, your Statues, Paintings, and all your other Possessions, which you so highly esteem; if you wish to continue in the Enjoyment of them, or have Leisure for any future Pleasures; I beseech you by the immortal Gods, *rouse* at last, *awake* from your Lethargy, and save the Common-Wealth. It is not the trifling Concern of Injuries from your Allies that demands your Attention; your *Liberties, Lives* and *Fortunes*, with every Thing that is interesting and dear to you, are in the most imminent *Danger*.

Can you doubt of, or delay what you ought to do, *now*, when the Enemies Swords are unsheathed, and descending on your Heads?——The Affair is shocking and horrid! Yet, perhaps you are not afraid.——Yes——You are terrified to the highest Degree. But thro' *Indolence* and *Supineness* of Soul, gazing at each other, to see who shall first rise to your

Non Votis, &c.

[Franklin first used this woodcut in his edition of Thomas Dilworth's *A New Guide to the English Tongue* (Philadelphia, 1747). The picture accompanies the fable "Of the Waggoner and Hercules": "As a Waggoner was driving his Team, his Waggon sunk into a Hole, and stuck fast. The poor Man immediately fell upon his Knees, and prayed to Hercules, that he would get his Waggon out of the Hole again. Thou Fool, says *Hercules*, whip thy Horses, and set thy shoulder to the Wheels; and then if thou wilt call upon *Hercules*, he will help thee. The Interpretation. *Lazy Wishes never do a Man any Service; but if he would have Help from God in the Time of Need, let him not only implore his Assistance, but make use of his own best Endeavours.*"]

It is said the wise *Italians* make this proverbial Remark on our Nation, *viz. The English* FEEL, *but they do not* SEE. That is, they are sensible of Inconveniencies when they are present, but do not take sufficient Care to prevent them: Their natural Courage makes them too little apprehensive of Danger, so that they are often surpriz'd by it, unprovided of the proper Means of Security. When 'tis too late they are sensible of their Imprudence: After great Fires, they provide Buckets and Engines: After a Pestilence

Succour; and a *presumptuous Dependence* on the immortal *Gods*, who have indeed preserv'd this Republick in many dangerous Seasons; you *delay* and *neglect* every Thing necessary for your Preservation. Be not deceived – *Divine Assistance and Protection are not to be obtain'd by timorous Prayers, and womanish Supplications.* To succeed, you must *join salutary Counsels, Vigilence*, and *couragious Actions.* If you sink into Effeminacy and Cowardice; if you *desert* the *Tender* and *Helpless*, by Providence committed to your Charge; *never presume* to implore the Gods:——It will provoke them, and raise their *Indignation* against you."]

they think of keeping clean their Streets and common Shores: and when a Town has been sack'd by their Enemies, they provide for its Defence, *&c*. This Kind of AFTER-WISDOM is indeed so common with us, as to occasion the vulgar, tho' very significant Saying, *When the Steed is stolen, you shut the Stable Door*.

But the more insensible we generally are of publick Danger, and indifferent when warn'd of it, so much the more freely, openly, and earnestly, ought such as apprehend it, to speak their Sentiments; that if possible, those who seem to sleep, may be awaken'd, to think of some Means of Avoiding or Preventing the Mischief before it be too late.

Believing therefore that 'tis my DUTY, I shall honestly speak my Mind in the following Paper.

War, at this Time, rages over a great Part of the known World; our News-Papers are Weekly filled with fresh Accounts of the Destruction it every where occasions. *Pennsylvania*, indeed, situate in the Center of the Colonies, has hitherto enjoyed profound Repose; and tho' our Nation is engag'd in a bloody War, with two great and powerful Kingdoms, yet, defended, in a great Degree, from the *French* on the one Hand by the Northern Provinces, and from the *Spaniards* on the other by the Southern, at no small Expence to each, our People have, till lately, slept securely in their Habitations.

There is no *British* Colony excepting this, but has made some Kind of Provision for its Defence; many of them have therefore never been attempted by an Enemy; and others that were attack'd, have generally defended themselves with Success. The Length and Difficulty of our Bay and River has been thought so effectual a Security to us, that hitherto no Means have been entered into that might discourage an Attempt upon us, or prevent its succeeding.

But whatever Security this might have been while both Country and City were poor, and the Advantage to be expected scarce worth the Hazard of an Attempt, it is now doubted whether we can any longer safely depend upon it. Our Wealth, of late Years much encreas'd, is one strong Temptation, our defenceless State another, to induce an Enemy to attack us; while the Acquaintance they have lately gained with our Bay and River, by Means of the Prisoners and Flags of Truce they have had among us; by Spies which they almost every where maintain, and perhaps from Traitors among ourselves; with the Facility of getting Pilots to conduct them; and the known Absence of Ships of War, during the greatest Part of the Year, from both *Virginia and New-York*, ever since the War began, render the Appearance of Success to the Enemy far more promising, and therefore highly encrease our DANGER.

That our Enemies may have Spies abroad, and some even in these Colonies, will not be made much doubt of, when 'tis considered, that such has been the Practice of all Nations in all Ages, whenever they were engaged, or intended to engage in War. Of this we have an early Example in the Book of *Judges* (too too pertinent to our Case, and therefore I must beg leave a little to enlarge upon it) where we are told, *Chap.* xviii, *v.* 2. That *the Children of Dan sent of their Family five Men from their Coasts to spie out the Land, and search it, saying, Go, search the* LAND. These *Danites* it seems were at this Time not very orthodox in their Religion, and their Spies met with a certain idolatrous Priest of their own Persuasion, *v.* 3. and they said to him, *Who brought thee hither! what makest thou in this Place? and what host thou here?* [would to God no such Priests were to be found among us.][2] And they said unto him, *verse* 5. *Ask Counsel of God, that we may know whether our Way which we go shall be prosperous? And the Priest said unto them, Go in Peace; before the Lord is your Way wherein you go.* [Are there no Priests among us, think you, that might, in the like Case, give an Enemy as good Encouragement? 'Tis well known, that we have Numbers of the same Religion with those who of late encouraged the *French* to invade our Mother-Country.] *And they came*, Verse 7. *to Laish, and saw the People that were therein, how they dwelt* CARELESS, *after the Manner of the Zidonians*, QUIET *and* SECURE. They *thought* themselves secure, no doubt; and as they *never had been* disturbed, vainly imagined they *never should.* 'Tis not unlikely that some might see the Danger they were exposed to by living in that *careless* Manner; but that if these publickly expressed their Apprehensions, the rest reproached them as timorous Persons, wanting Courage or Confidence in their Gods, who (they might say) had hitherto protected them. But the Spies, Verse 8. returned, and said to their Countrymen, Verse 9. *Arise that we may go up against them; for we have seen the Land, and behold it is very good! And are ye still? Be not slothful to go.* Verse 10. *When ye go, ye shall come unto a People* SECURE; [that is, a People that apprehend no Danger, and therefore have made no Provision against it; great Encouragement this!] *and to a large Land, and a Place where there is no Want of any Thing.* What could they desire more? Accordingly we find, in the following Verses, that *Six hundred Men* only, *appointed with Weapons of War*, undertook the Conquest of this *large Land;*

[2] [Brackets in this paragraph in the original.]

knowing that 600 Men, armed and disciplined, would be an Over-match perhaps for 60,000, unarmed, undisciplined, and off their Guard. And when they went against it, the idolatrous Priest, Verse 17. *with his graven Image, and his Ephod, and his Teraphim, and his molten Image*, [Plenty of superstitious Trinkets] joined with them, and, no doubt, gave them all the Intelligence and Assistance in his Power; his Heart, as the Text assures us, *being glad*, perhaps for Reasons more than one. And now, what was the Fate of poor *Laish*! The 600 Men being arrived, found, as the Spies had reported, a People QUIET and SECURE, Verse 20, 21. *And they smote them with the Edge of the Sword, and burnt the City with* FIRE; *and there was no* DELIVERER, *because it was far from Zidon.*——Not so far from *Zidon*, however, as *Pennsylvania* is from *Britain*; and yet we are, if possible, more *careless* than the People of *Laish*!——As the Scriptures are given for our Reproof, Instruction and Warning, may we make a due Use Of this Example, before it be too late!

And is our *Country*, any more than our City, altogether free from Danger? Perhaps not. We have, 'tis true, had a long Peace with the *Indians*: But it is a long Peace indeed, as well as a long Lane, that has no Ending. The *French* know the Power and Importance of the *Six Nations*, and spare no Artifice, Pains or Expence, to gain them to their Interest. By their Priests they have converted many to their Religion, and these[3] have openly espoused their Cause. The rest appear irresolute which Part to take; no Persuasions, tho' enforced with costly Presents, having yet been able to engage them generally on our Side, tho' we had numerous Forces on their Borders, ready to second and support them. What then may be expected, now those Forces are, by Orders from the Crown, to be disbanded; when our boasted Expedition is laid aside, thro' want (as it may appear to them) either of Strength or Courage; when they see that the *French*, and their *Indians*, boldly, and with Impunity, ravage the Frontiers of *New-York*, and scalp the Inhabitants; when those few *Indians* that engaged with us against the *French*, are left exposed to their Resentment: When they consider these Things, is there no Danger that, thro' Disgust at our Usage, joined with Fear of the *French* Power, and greater Confidence in their Promises and Protection than in ours, they may be wholly gained over by our Enemies, and join in the War against us? If such should be the Case, which God forbid, how soon may the Mischief spread to our Frontier

[3] The Praying Indians.

Counties? And what may we expect to be the Consequence, but deserting of Plantations, Ruin, Bloodshed and Confusion!

Perhaps some in the City, Towns and Plantations near the River, may say to themselves, *An* Indian *War on the Frontiers will not affect us; the Enemy will never come near our Habitations; let those concern'd take Care of themselves.* And others who live in the Country, when they are told of the Danger the City is in from Attempts by Sea, may say, *What is that to us? The Enemy will be satisfied with the Plunder of the Town, and never think it worth his while to visit our Plantations: Let the Town take care of itself.* These are not mere Suppositions, for I have heard some talk in this strange Manner. But are these the Sentiments of true *Pennsylvanians*, of Fellow-Countrymen, or even of Men that have common Sense or Goodness? Is not the whole Province one Body, united by living under the same Laws, and enjoying the same Priviledges? Are not the People of City and Country connected as Relations both by Blood and Marriage, and in Friendships equally dear? Are they not likewise united in Interest, and mutually useful and necessary to each other? When the Feet are wounded, shall the Head say, *It is not me; I will not trouble myself to contrive Relief!* Or if the Head is in Danger, shall the Hands say, *We are not affected, and therefore will lend no Assistance!* No. For so would the Body be easily destroyed: But when all Parts join their Endeavours for its Security, it is often preserved. And such should be the Union between the Country and the Town; and such their mutual Endeavours for the Safety of the Whole. When *New-England*, a distant Colony, involv'd itself in a grievous Debt to reduce *Cape-Breton*, we freely gave *Four Thousand Pounds* for *their* Relief. And at another Time, remembring that *Great Britain*, still more distant, groan'd under heavy Taxes in Supporting the War, we threw in our Mite to their Assistance, by a free Gift of *Three Thousand Pounds*: And shall Country and Town join in helping Strangers (as those comparatively are) and yet refuse to assist each other?

But whatever different Opinions we have of our Security in other Respects, our TRADE, all seem to agree, is in Danger of being ruin'd in another Year. The great Success of our Enemies, in two different Cruizes this last Summer in our Bay, must give them the greatest Encouragement to repeat more frequently their Visits, the Profit being almost certain, and the Risque next to nothing. Will not the first Effect of this be, an Enhauncing of the Price of all foreign Goods to the Tradesman and Farmer, who use or consume them? For the Rate of Insurance will increase in Proportion to the Hazard of Importing them; and in the same Proportion will the Price of those Goods increase.——If the Price of the Tradesman's Work and the Farmer's Produce would encrease equally with the Price of foreign Commodities, the Damage would not be so great: But the direct contrary must happen. For the same Hazard, or Rate of Insurance, that raises the Price of what is imported, must be deducted out of, and lower the Price of what is exported. Without this Addition and Deduction, as long as the Enemy cruize at our Capes, and take those Vessels that attempt to *go out*, as well as those that endeavour to *come in*, none can afford to trade, and Business must be soon at a Stand. And will not the Consequences be, A discouraging of many of the Vessels that us'd to come from other Places to purchase our Produce, and thereby a Turning of the Trade to Ports that can be entered with less Danger, and capable of furnishing them with the same Commodities, as *New-York*, &c? A Lessening of Business to every Shopkeeper, together with Multitudes of bad Debts; the high Rate of Goods discouraging the Buyers, and the low Rates of their Labour and Produce rendering them unable to pay for what they had bought: Loss of Employment to the Tradesman, and bad Pay for what little he does: And lastly, Loss of many Inhabitants, who will retire to other Provinces not subject to the like Inconveniencies; whence a Lowering of the Value of Lands, Lots, and Houses.

The Enemy, no doubt, have been told, That the People of *Pennsylvania* are *Quakers*, and against all Defence, from a Principle of Conscience; this, tho' true of a Part, and that a small Part only of the Inhabitants, is commonly said of the Whole; and what may make it look probable to Strangers, is, that in Fact, nothing is done by any Part of the People towards their Defence. But to refuse Defending one's self or one's Country, is so unusual a Thing among Mankind, that possibly they may not believe it, till by Experience they find, they can come higher and higher up our River, seize our Vessels, land and plunder our Plantations and Villages, and retire with their Booty unmolested. Will not this confirm the Report, and give them the greatest Encouragement to strike one bold Stroke for the City, and for the whole Plunder of the River?

It is said by some, that the Expence of a Vessel to guard our Trade, would be very heavy, greater than perhaps all the Enemy can be supposed to take from us at Sea would amount to; and that it would be cheaper for the Government to open an Insurance-Office, and pay all Losses.——But is this right Reasoning?——I think not: For what the Enemy takes is clear Loss to us, and Gain to him; encreasing his Riches and Strength as much as it diminishes ours, so making the Difference double; whereas the Money paid our own Tradesmen for Building and Fitting out a Vessel of Defence, remains in the Country, and circulates among us; what is paid to the Officers and Seamen that navigate her, is also spent ashore, and soon gets into other Hands; the Farmer receives the Money for her Provisions; and on the whole, nothing is clearly lost to the Country but her Wear and Tear, or so much as she sells for at the End of the War less than her first Cost. This Loss, and a trifling one it is, is all the Inconvenience; But how many and how great are the Conveniencies and Advantages! And should the Enemy, thro' our Supineness and Neglect to provide for the Defence both of our Trade and Country, be encouraged to attempt this City, and after plundering us of our Goods, either *burn it*, or put it to Ransom; how great would that Loss be! Besides the Confusion, Terror, and Distress, so many Hundreds of Families would be involv'd in!

The Thought of this latter Circumstance so much affects me, that I cannot forbear expatiating somewhat more upon it. You have, my dear Countrymen, and Fellow Citizens, Riches to tempt a considerable Force to unite and attack you, but are under no Ties or Engagements to unite for your Defence. Hence, on the first Alarm, *Terror* will spread over All; and as no Man can with Certainty depend that another will stand by him, beyond Doubt very many will seek Safety by a speedy Flight. Those that are reputed rich, will flee, thro' Fear of Torture, to make them produce more than they are able. The Man that has a Wife and Children, will find them hanging on his Neck, beseeching him with Tears to quit the City, and save his Life, to guide and protect them in that Time of general Desolation and Ruin. All will run into Confusion, amidst Cries and Lamentations, and the Hurry and Disorder of Departers, carrying away their Effects. The Few that remain will be unable to resist.——*Sacking* the City will be the first, and *Burning* it, in all Probability, the last Act of the Enemy.——This, I believe, will be the Case, if you have timely Notice. But what must be your Condition, if suddenly surprized, without previous Alarm, perhaps in the Night! Confined to your Houses, you will have nothing to trust to but the Enemy's Mercy. Your best Fortune will be, to fall under the Power of Commanders of King's Ships, able to controul the Mariners; and not into the Hands of *licentious Privateers*. Who can, without the utmost Horror, conceive the Miseries of the Latter! when your Persons, Fortunes, Wives and Daughters, shall be subject to the wanton and unbridled Rage, Rapine and Lust, of *Negroes, Molattoes*, and others, the vilest and most abandoned of Mankind.[4] A dreadful Scene! which some may represent as exaggerated.——I think it my Duty to warn you: Judge for yourselves.

'Tis true, with very little Notice, the Rich may shift for themselves. The Means of speedy Flight are ready in their Hands; and with some previous Care to lodge Money and Effects in distant and secure Places, tho' they should lose much, yet enough may be left them, and to spare. But most unhappily circumstanced indeed are we, the middling People, the Tradesmen, Shopkeepers, and Farmers of this Province and City! We cannot all fly with our Families; and if we could, how shall we subsist?——No; we and they, and what little we have gained by hard Labour and Industry, must bear the Brunt: The Weight of Contributions, extorted by the Enemy (as it is of Taxes among ourselves) must be surely borne by us. Nor can it be avoided as we stand at present; for tho' we are numerous, we are quite defenceless, having neither Forts, Arms, Union, nor Discipline. And tho' it were true, that our Trade might be protected at no great Expence, and our Country and our City easily defended, if proper Measures were but taken; yet who shall take these Measures? Who shall pay that Expence? On whom may we fix our Eyes with the least Expectation that they will do any one Thing for our Security?——Should we address that wealthy and powerful Body of People, who have ever since the War governed our Elections, and filled almost every Seat in our Assembly; should we intreat them to consider, if not as Friends, at least as Legislators, that *Protection* is as truly due from the Government to the People, as *Obedience* from the People to the Government; and that if on account of their religious Scruples, they themselves could do no Act for our Defence, yet they might retire, relinquish their Power for a Season, quit the Helm to freer Hands during the present Tempest, to Hands chosen by their own Interest too, whose Prudence and Moderation, with regard to them, they might safely confide in; secure, from their own native Strength, of resuming again their present Stations, whenever it shall please them: Should we remind them, that the Publick Money, raised *from All*, belongs

[4] By Accounts, the ragged Crew of the *Spanish* Privateer that plundered Mr. *Liston's*, and another Plantation, a little below *Newcastle*, was composed of such as these. The *Honour* and *Humanity* of their Officers may be judg'd of, by the Treatment they gave poor Capt. *Brown*, whom they took with *Martin's* Ship in Returning from their Cruize. Because he bravely defended himself and Vessel longer than they expected, for which every generous Enemy would have esteem'd him, did they, after he had struck and submitted, barbarously *stab* and *murder* him, tho' on his Knees begging Quarter!

to All; that since they have, for their own Ease, and to secure themselves in the quiet Enjoyment of their Religious Principles (and may they long enjoy them) expended such large Sums to oppose Petitions, and engage favourable Representations of their Conduct, if they themselves could by no Means be free to appropriate any Part of the Publick Money for our Defence; yet it would be no more than Justice to spare us a reasonable Sum for that Purpose, which they might easily give to the King's Use as heretofore, leaving all the Appropriation to others, who would faithfully apply it as we desired: Should we tell them, that tho' the Treasury be at present empty, it may soon be filled by the outstanding Publick Debts collected; or at least Credit might be had for such a Sum, on a single Vote of the Assembly: That tho' *they* themselves may be resigned and easy under this naked, defenceless State of the Country, it is far otherwise with a very great Part of the People; with *us*, who can have no Confidence that God will protect those that neglect the Use of rational Means for their Security; nor have any Reason to hope, that our Losses, if we should suffer any, may be made up by Collections in our Favour at Home. Should we conjure them by all the Ties of Neighbourhood, Friendship, Justice and Humanity, to consider these Things; and what Distraction, Misery and Confusion, what Desolation and Distress, may possibly be the Effect of their *unseasonable* Predominancy and Perseverance; yet all would be in vain: For they have already been by great Numbers of the People petitioned in vain. Our late Governor did for Years sollicit, request, and even threaten them in vain. The Council have since twice remonstrated to them in vain. Their religious Prepossessions are unchangeable, their Obstinacy invincible. Is there then the least Hope remaining, that from that Quarter any Thing should arise for our Security?

And is our Prospect better, if we turn our Eyes to the Strength of the *opposite Party*, those Great and rich Men, Merchants and others, who are ever railing at *Quakers* for doing what their Principles seem to require, and what in Charity we ought to believe they think their Duty, but take no one Step themselves for the Publick Safety? They have so much Wealth and Influence, if they would use it, that they might easily, by their Endeavours and Example, raise a military Spirit among us, make us fond, studious of, and expert in Martial Discipline, and effect every Thing that is necessary, under God, for our Protection. But ENVY seems to have taken Possession of their Hearts, and to have eaten out and destroyed every generous, noble, Publick-spirited Sentiment. *Rage* at the Disappointment of their little Schemes for Power, gnaws their Souls, and fills them with such cordial Hatred to their Opponents, that every Proposal, by the Execution of which *those* may receive Benefit as well as themselves, is rejected with Indignation. *What*, say they, *shall we lay out our Money to protect the Trade of Quakers? Shall we fight to defend Quakers? No; Let the Trade perish, and the City burn; let what will happen, we shall never lift a Finger to prevent it.*——Yet the Quakers have *Conscience* to plead for their Resolution not to fight, which these Gentlemen have not: *Conscience* with you, Gentlemen, is on the other Side of the Question: *Conscience* enjoins it as a DUTY on you (and indeed I think it such on every Man) to defend your Country, your Friends, your aged Parents, your Wives, and helpless Children: And yet you resolve not to perform this Duty, but act *contrary* to *your own* Consciences, because the Quakers act *according* to *theirs*. 'Till of late I could scarce believe the Story of him who refused to pump in a sinking Ship, because one on board, whom he hated, would be saved by it as well as himself. But such, it seems, is the Unhappiness of human Nature, that our Passions, when violent, often are too hard for the united Force of *Reason, Duty* and *Religion*.

Thus unfortunately are we circumstanc'd at this Time, my dear Countrymen and Fellow-Citizens; we, I mean, the middling People, the Farmers, Shopkeepers and Tradesmen of this City and Country. Thro' the Dissensions of our Leaders, thro' *mistaken Principles* of *Religion*, join'd with a Love of Worldly Power, on the one Hand; thro' *Pride, Envy* and *implacable Resentment* on the other; our Lives, our Families and little Fortunes, dear to us as any Great Man's can be to him, are to remain continually expos'd to Destruction, from an enterprizing, cruel, now well-inform'd, and by Success encourag'd Enemy. It seems as if Heaven, justly displeas'd at our growing Wickedness, and determin'd to[5] punish this once favour'd Land, had suffered our Chiefs to engage in these foolish and mischievous Contentions, for *little Posts* and *paltry Distinctions*, that our Hands might be bound up, our Understandings darkned and misled, and every Means of our Security neglected. It seems as if our greatest Men, our *Cives nobilissimi*[6] of both Parties, had *sworn the Ruin of the*

[5] When God determined to punish his chosen People, the Inhabitants of *Jerusalem*, who, tho' Breakers of his other Laws, were scrupulous Observers of that ONE which required keeping holy the Sabbath Day; he suffered even the strict Observation of that Command to be their Ruin: For *Pompey* observing that they *then* obstinately refused to fight, made a general Assault on that Day, took the Town, and butcher'd them with as little Mercy as he found resistance. JOSEPHUS.

[6] Conjuravere cives nobilissimi Patriam incendere; GALLORUM GENTEM, infestissimam nomini Romano, ad Bellum arcessunt. CAT. in SALLUST. [Sallust, *De Conjuratione Catilinae*

Country, and invited the French, our most inveterate Enemy, to destroy it. Where then shall we seek for Succour and Protection? The Government we are immediately under denies it to us; and if the Enemy comes, we are *far from* ZIDON, *and there is no Deliverer near.*——Our Case indeed is dangerously bad; but perhaps there is yet a Remedy, if we have but the Prudence and the Spirit to apply it.

If this now flourishing City, and greatly improving Colony, is destroy'd and ruin'd, it will not be for want of Numbers of Inhabitants able to bear Arms in its Defence. 'Tis computed that we have at least (exclusive of the Quakers) 60,000 Fighting Men, acquainted with Fire-Arms, many of them Hunters and Marksmen, hardy and bold. All we want is Order, Discipline, and a few Cannon. At present we are like the separate Filaments of Flax before the Thread is form'd, without Strength because without Connection; but UNION would make us strong and even formidable: Tho' the *Great* should neither help nor join us; tho' they should even oppose our Uniting, from some mean Views of their own, yet, if we resolve upon it, and it please GOD to inspire us with the necessary Prudence and Vigour, it *may* be effected.——Great Numbers of our People are of BRITISH RACE, and tho' the fierce fighting Animals of those happy Islands, are said to abate their native Fire and Intrepidity, when removed to a Foreign Clime, yet with the People 'tis not so; Our Neighbours of *New-England* afford the World a convincing Proof, that BRITONS, tho' a Hundred Years transplanted, and to the remotest Part of the Earth, may yet retain, even to the third and fourth Descent, that *Zeal* for the *Publick Good*, that *military Prowess*, and that *undaunted Spirit*, which has in every Age distinguished their Nation. What Numbers have we likewise of *those brave People*, whose Fathers in the last Age made so glorious a Stand for our Religion and Liberties, when invaded by a powerful *French* Army, join'd by *Irish* Catholicks, under a bigotted *Popish* King! Let the memorable SIEGE of LONDONDERRY, and the signal Actions of the INISKILLINGERS, by which the Heart of that Prince's Schemes was broken, be perpetual Testimonies of the *Courage* and *Conduct* of those *noble Warriors!*——Nor are there wanting amongst us, Thousands of *that Warlike Nation*, whose Sons have ever since the Time of Caesar maintained the Character he gave their Fathers, of joining the most *obstinate Courage* to all the other military Virtues. I mean the *brave* and *steady*

52: "Certain citizens, of the highest rank, have conspired to ruin their country; they are engaging the Gauls, the bitterest foes of the Roman name, to join in a war against us."]

Germans. Numbers of whom have actually borne Arms in the Service of their respective Princes; and if they fought well for their Tyrants and Oppressors, would they refuse to unite with us in Defence of their *newly acquired* and most precious *Liberty* and *Property*? Were this Union form'd, were we once united, thoroughly arm'd and disciplin'd, was every Thing in our Power done for our Security, as far as human Means and Foresight could provide, we might then, *with more Propriety*, humbly ask the Assistance of Heaven, and a Blessing on our lawful Endeavours. The very Fame of our Strength and Readiness would be a Means of Discouraging our Enemies; for 'tis a wise and true Saying, that *One Sword often keeps another in the Scabbard.* The Way to secure Peace is to be prepared for War. They that are on their Guard, and appear ready to receive their Adversaries, are in much less Danger of being attack'd, than the supine, secure and negligent. We have yet a Winter before us, which may afford a good and almost sufficient Opportunity for this, if we seize and improve it with a becoming Vigour. And if the Hints contained in this Paper are so happy as to meet with a suitable Disposition of Mind in his Countrymen and Fellow Citizens, the Writer of it will, in a few Days, lay before them a Form of an Association for the Purposes herein mentioned, together with a practicable Scheme for raising the Money necessary for the Defence of our Trade, City, and Country, without laying a Burthen on any Man.

May the God of Wisdom, Strength *and* Power, *the Lord of the Armies of Israel, inspire us with Prudence in this Time of* Danger; *take away from us all the Seeds of Contention and Division, and unite the Hearts and Counsels of all of us, of whatever* Sect *or* Nation, *in one Bond of Peace, Brotherly Love, and generous Publick Spirit; May he give us Strength and Resolution to amend our Lives, and remove from among us every Thing that is displeasing to him; afford us his most gracious Protection, confound the Designs of our Enemies, and give* Peace *in all our Borders, is the sincere Prayer of*

A Tradesman of *Philadelphia.*

[Philadelphia: 1747]

CHAPTER II

Form of the Association into which Numbers are daily entering, for the Defence of this City and Province——With Remarks on each Paragraph

(3 December 1747)

WE whose Names are hereunto subscribed, Inhabitants of the Province of *Pennsylvania* in *America*, taking into serious Consideration, that *Great Britain*, to which we are subject, is now engag'd in a War with two powerful Nations: That it is become too well known to our Enemies, that this Colony is in a naked, defenceless State, without Fortifications or Militia of any Sort, and is therefore exposed daily to Destruction from the Attacks of a very small Force: That we are at a great Distance from our Mother Country, and cannot, on any Emergency, receive Assistance from thence: That thro' the Multiplicity of other Affairs of greater Importance (as we presume) no particular Care hath hitherto been taken by the Government at Home of our Protection, an humble Petition to the Crown for that purpose, sign'd by a great Number of Hands, having yet had no visible Effect: That the Assemblies of this Province, by Reason of their religious Principles, have not done, nor are likely to do any Thing for our Defence, notwithstanding repeated Applications to them for that Purpose: That being thus unprotected by the Government under which we live, against our foreign Enemies that may come to invade us, As we think it absolutely necessary, WE DO HEREBY, for our mutual Defence and Security, and for the Security of our Wives, Children and Estates, and the Preservation of the Persons and Estates of others, our Neighbours and Fellow-Subjects, form ourselves into an ASSOCIATION, and imploring the Blessing of

Heaven on our Undertaking, do agree *solemnly* with each other in Manner following; that is to say;

First, THAT we will each of us, before the first Day of *January* next, or as soon as possible, provide ourselves with a good Firelock, Cartouch Box, and at least twelve Charges of Powder and Ball, and as many of us as conveniently can, with a good Sword, Cutlass or Hanger, to be kept always in our respective Dwellings, in Readiness, and good Order.

Secondly, THAT we will before the said Day, form ourselves into Companies, from Fifty to One Hundred Men each, consisting of such as are situated most conveniently for meeting together.

Thirdly, THAT at the first Meetings of each Company, which shall be on the Day aforesaid, three Persons shall be chosen by Ballot out of, and by each Company, to be Captain, Lieutenant and Ensign of the same, whose Names shall be presented to the Governor for the Time being, or in his Absence to the President and Council of this Province, in order to obtain Commissions accordingly.——Which Persons, so commissioned, shall be the Captains, Lieutenants and Ensigns, of each Company, respectively, for the ensuing Year.

Fourthly, THAT after the Election of the said Captains, Lieutenants and Ensigns, they who are chosen within each County shall immediately meet, and they, or the Majority of them, shall form the said Companies into a Regiment or Regiments, and shall elect Colonels, Lieutenant-Colonels, Majors, and other superior Officers, whose Names shall be likewise presented to the Governor for the Time being, or, in his Absence, to the President and Council, to receive Commissions as above mentioned, for one Year. To all which Officers (who shall serve *gratis*, without Wages, Salary or Pay) we will, in our several Stations, respectively, pay due Obedience. And the superior Officers so chosen, shall, on the third *Monday* in *March* next, meet together at *Philadelphia*, and frame such general Regulations as shall be necessary for Uniting our whole Force on any Occasion, or such Part of it as shall be requisite; which Regulations shall continue and be observed, until the Meeting of our General Military Council hereafter mentioned.

Fifthly, THAT we will meet in our respective Companies, to improve ourselves in military Discipline, at the Times and Places appointed by our said superior Officers, and hereafter to be fixed by the General Military Council hereinafter mentioned, not exceeding four Times in one Year, unless called together on some Emergency by the Governor, or, in his

Absence, the President and Council. And on the third *Monday* in *August* yearly, all the Regiments in each County shall meet at the County Town, for a general Exercise and Review.

Sixthly, THAT at the said annual Meetings, we will chuse, by Ballot, in the fairest Manner, four Deputies for each County, from among such of our Association as shall be of most Note for their Virtue, Prudence and Ability, who shall meet together at *Philadelphia*, in fourteen Days after their Election, at their own Expence, and form a GENERAL MILITARY COUNCIL, to consult upon and frame such *Regulations* as shall be requisite for the better ordering our military Affairs, improving us in military Knowledge, and uniting and ordering our Strength, so as to make it of the most Service for our common Security. And whatever Orders and Regulations shall be so made by the said Council, or the Majority of them, shall have the Force of LAWS with us, and we promise to pay them all the Obedience in our Power, until they shall be altered or repealed by the same Authority.

Seventhly, PROVIDED ALWAYS, that our said General Military Council shall not, by any Laws made as aforesaid, subject us to any Pecuniary Mulcts, Fines, or Corporal Penalties, on any Account whatever; We being determined, in this whole Affair, to act *only* on Principles of REASON, DUTY and HONOUR. Nor shall they lay any Tax upon us, nor shall we be obliged, by their Authority, to contribute towards any Batteries or Fortifications; but whatever of that kind is judg'd necessary to be done, and recommended by them, shall be left to voluntary Subscription.

Eighthly, THIS Association shall continue firm, and every Part of this Agreement be faithfully observed by us (unless the KING'S MAJESTY shall order otherwise) until some more effectual Provision be made to answer the same good Ends and Purposes, or until Peace shall be established between *Great Britain*, and *France* and *Spain*, and no longer.

Remarks on the Preamble

This contains the Reasons and the Necessity of our associating. Where a Government takes proper Measures to protect the People under its Care, such a Proceeding might have been thought both unnecessary and unjustifiable: But here it is quite the Reverse. For in our State (and perhaps if you search the World through, you will find it in ours only) the Government, that Part of it at least that holds the Purse, has always, from religious

Considerations, refused to use the common Means for the Defence of the Country against an Enemy.

Remarks on Article I

As *Use* is in our Case more to be regarded than *Uniformity*, and it would be difficult so suddenly to procure such a Number of Arms, exactly of the same Kind, the general Word *Firelock* is used (rather than *Musket*, which is the Name of a particular kind of Gun) most People having a Firelock of some kind or other already in their Hands. If the Cartouch Box should not contain the 12 Charges, the rest may be ready in the Pocket. It is said by some military Writers, that one fourth Part of the Weight of the Ball, is Powder sufficient for a Charge; an Over-quantity, that makes a Gun violently recoil, rendering the Shot less certain. They add, that the nicest Care ought to be taken in casting Bullets so much less than the Bore, that they may slip down with Ease, when rolled in Cartridges, even into a foul Gun, otherwise there is great Loss of Time and Fire in an Engagement, to the no small Advantage of the Enemy. Tho' Bayonets are not required, it would be well enough for some to provide them; for they may be as useful against a violent Onset from irregular Foot, as against Horse. Those who on Account of their Age or Infirmities ought to be excused from the common Exercises, yet will do well to keep Arms and Ammunition ready in their Houses, that when Occasion calls, they may either use them if they can, or lend them to those who happen to be unprovided. The Expence of providing these Arms is small, and may be saved in some other Article; and they will always fetch near the Money they cost.

Remarks on Article II

This Article is intended to prevent People's sorting themselves into Companies, according to their Ranks in Life, their Quality or Station. 'Tis designed to mix the Great and Small together, for the sake of Union and Encouragement. Where Danger and Duty are equal to All, there should be no Distinction from Circumstances, but All be on the Level.

Remarks on Article III

Where the Officers of a Militia are appointed by the Governor (as in some Colonies) it often happens, that Persons absolutely disagreeable to the People are impower'd to command them. This is attended with very ill Consequences, rendering the Meetings for military Exercise, instead of a Pleasure, a most grievous Burthen, and by Degrees discouraging them even to a total Disuse. But where those to be commanded chuse those that are to command, it is to be presumed the Choice will naturally fall on Men of the best Character for their military Skill; on such too, from whose Prudence and Good-nature there may be no Fear of Injustice or military Oppression: And as the Ballot prevents all Resentments, so the Choice for one Year only, will keep all Officers within the Bounds of Moderation and Decorum in the Exercise of their Power, and excite an Emulation in All to qualify themselves for being chosen in their Turn. The Rotation of military Offices may be objected to, as contrary to modern Practice; but the wonderful Success of the Old *Romans* proves it absolutely right. The *Romans*, without Doubt, affected Glory and Command as much as other People; but yet they disdained not to obey in their Armies the same Persons whom they had formerly commanded; and to serve as private Soldiers, where they had been formerly Generals. The Application to the Governor, &c. for Commissions, preserves the Prerogative, at the same time that these frequent Elections secure the Liberty of the People. And what can give more Spirit and martial Vigour to an Army of FREEMEN, than to be led by those of whom they have the best Opinion.

Remarks on Article IV

If it is reasonable for the People to chuse those Officers who are immediately over *them*, it is no less so for the Officers themselves to chuse their immediate Superiors. The whole Choice, indeed, may, in one Sense, be said to be in the People, as it takes its Rise from them. Without some general Regulations for uniting our Force, or such Part of it as may be requisite, our general arming would be to little Purpose. And as every Neighbourhood would be glad of Assistance if attacked, so it ought to be willing to give Assistance where it is needed. The great Number of Horses in this Province are in this Respect a vast Advantage; for tho' perhaps we may not form Regiments of Horse, yet those who are to fight on Foot, may, by *their* Means, be suddenly assembled in great Numbers where wanted, even from very distant Places. The *Romans*, in sudden Expeditions, sometimes put two Men to a Horse. One on Foot was greatly assisted in his March by holding on the Horse's Mane, while the other rid; and they alternately relieved each other. The modern Horsemen, on the like Occasions, sometimes take up each a Foot Soldier behind them.

Remarks on Article v

Those who from their Years or Infirmity of Body, are not able to undergo the military Exercises, would do well, notwithstanding, to attend the Meetings of the Companies, and observe what the others do, that they may not on Occasion be wholly at a Loss: Their Presence and Approbation may encourage younger Men; and the gravest and wisest among us need not be ashamed to countenance Exercises so manifestly tending to the publick Good. The Number of Meetings for Exercise is limited to four in one Year, that People may not be called too often from their Business. 4 Exercisings in a Year are sufficient to keep what we have learnt in Memory; but more frequent Meetings may be necessary at first, till we are become expert in the Discipline.——On any Emergency, that is, on an actual Invasion by our Enemies, we agree to assemble on the Governor's Call; but when 'tis known that we are all prepared, well armed and disciplined., &c. there is Reason to hope such an Emergency may never happen.——That there should be Meetings of Regiments, as well as of particular Companies, is necessary, there being Parts of the military Discipline best learnt when great Bodies are together: The 3d *Monday* in *August* is chosen for these Meetings, as a Time of most Leisure, being after Harvest, the Days of a middling Length, and the Heats chiefly over. To make these Meetings more entertaining and useful, Prizes may be set up for the best Marksmen, and others most expert in any of the martial Exercises.

Remarks on Article vi

There are a Number of Regulations necessary to be made, which could not well be particulariz'd in these Articles; and which, as Circumstances change, may often want Amendment or Alteration. To form these Regulations, this Article provides a *Military Council*, to be compos'd of prudent, good and able Men. The old and wise, unfit for personal Duty, may here be of Service; many being good at contriving, that are not so fit to put what is contriv'd, in Execution, as younger and more vigorous Spirits. This General Military Council is the Common-Band that unites all Parts of the whole Association in one Body. The Regulations they shall make, we promise to observe as Laws; and it will behove our Lawgivers to see that they are reasonable Ones, since, by the subsequent Article, they cannot annex any Penalty to the Breach of them. But however that be, it will certainly be reasonable to observe them till repealed or altered.

Remarks on Article VII

A Militia of FREEMEN, ought not to be subject to any corporal Penalties. In worthy Minds, the Principles of *Reason, Duty* and *Honour*, work more strongly than the Fears of Punishment. The Military Council therefore is not impowered to appoint any such, nor yet even pecuniary Mulcts or Fines; that it may clearly appear we act only on the most honourable Motives.——If the Persons who compose the several Companies should think fit (as Juries sometimes do) to make a temporary Agreement, to pay little Fines when they do not appear in good Time, or the like, to be apply'd to the Purchasing of Drums, Colours, &c. or to be given in Prizes, or to refresh their weary Spirits after Exercise; they are not hereby restrain'd from doing so, but left to their Liberty.

Remarks on Article VIII

This Article, as well as several of the others, expresses a dutiful Regard to the Government we are under. As to the Continuance of the Association, 'tis certainly necessary no longer than the War continues; and 'tis heartily to be wish'd, that a safe and honourable Peace may the very next Year render it useless.

'Tis hoped this whole Affair will be conducted with *good Order* and *Sobriety*, and that no *ill-natured* Reflections, no *Injuries* or *Insults* will be offered our *peaceable Friends, Neighbours* and *Fellow-subjects*, who, from their *religious Scruples*, cannot allow themselves to join us. Such Proceedings tending rather to give them an *Aversion* to the proper Method of Defence, than to *engage* them to *unite* in it.——

[Gazette, 3 December 1747]

CHAPTER 12

Advice to a Young Tradesman, Written by an Old One

(21 July 1748)

To my Friend *A. B.*

As you have desired it of me, I write the following Hints, which have been of Service to me, and may, if observed, be so to you.

Remember that TIME is Money. He that can earn Ten Shillings a Day by his Labour, and goes abroad, or sits idle one half of that Day, tho' he spends but Sixpence during his Diversion or Idleness, ought not to reckon That the only Expence; he has really spent or rather thrown away Five Shillings besides.

Remember that CREDIT is Money. If a Man lets his Money lie in my Hands after it is due, he gives me the Interest, or so much as I can make of it during that Time. This amounts to a considerable Sum where a Man has good and large Credit, and makes good Use of it.

Remember that Money is of a prolific generating Nature. Money can beget Money, and its Offspring can beget more, and so on. Five Shillings turn'd, is *Six*: Turn'd again, 'tis Seven and Three Pence; and so on 'til it becomes an Hundred Pound. The more there is of it, the more it produces every Turning, so that the Profits rise quicker and quicker. He that kills a breeding Sow, destroys all her Offspring to the thousandth Generation. He that murders a Crown, destroys all it might have produc'd, even Scores of Pounds.

Remember that Six Pounds a Year is but a Groat a Day. For this little Sum (which may be daily wasted either in Time or Expence unperceiv'd) a Man of Credit may on his own Security have the constant Possession and Use of an Hundred Pounds. So much in Stock briskly turn'd by an industrious Man, produces great Advantage.

Remember this Saying, *That the good Paymaster is Lord of another Man's Purse*. He that is known to pay punctually and exactly to the Time he promises, may at any Time, and on any Occasion, raise all the Money his Friends can spare. This is sometimes of great Use: Therefore never keep borrow'd Money an Hour beyond the Time you promis'd, lest a Disappointment shuts up your Friends Purse forever.

The most trifling Actions that affect a Man's Credit, are to be regarded. The Sound of your Hammer at Five in the Morning or Nine at Night, heard by a Creditor, makes him easy Six Months longer. But if he sees you at a Billiard Table, or hears your Voice in a Tavern, when you should be at Work, he sends for his Money the next Day. Finer Cloaths than he or his Wife wears, or greater Expence in any particular than he affords himself, shocks his Pride, and he duns you to humble you. Creditors are a kind of People, that have the sharpest Eyes and Ears, as well as the best Memories of any in the World.

Good-natur'd Creditors (and such one would always chuse to deal with if one could) feel Pain when they are oblig'd to ask for Money. Spare 'em that Pain, and they will love you. When you receive a Sum of Money, divide it among 'em in Proportion to your Debts. Don't be asham'd of paying a small Sum because you owe a greater. Money, more or less, is always welcome; and your Creditor had rather be at the Trouble of receiving Ten Pounds voluntarily brought him, tho' at ten different Times or Payments, than be oblig'd to go ten Times to demand it before he can receive it in a Lump. It shews, besides, that you are mindful of what you owe; it makes you appear a careful as well as an honest Man; and that still encreases your Credit.

Beware of thinking all your own that you possess, and of living accordingly. 'Tis a Mistake that many People who have Credit fall into. To prevent this, keep an exact Account for some Time of both your Expences and your Incomes. If you take the Pains at first to mention Particulars, it will have this good Effect; you will discover how wonderfully small trifling Expences mount up to large Sums, and will discern what might have been, and may for the future be saved, without occasioning any great Inconvenience.

In short, the Way to Wealth, if you desire it, is as plain as the Way to Market. It depends chiefly on two Words, INDUSTRY and FRUGALITY; *i.e.* Waste neither Time nor Money, but make the best Use of both. He that gets all he can honestly, and saves all he gets (necessary Expences excepted) will certainly become RICH; If that Being who governs the World, to whom all should look for a Blessing on their honest Endeavours, doth not in his wise Providence otherwise determine.

[George Fisher, *The American Instructor: or Young Man's Best Companion*, 9th edn, rev. and corr. (Philadelphia: B. Franklin and D. Hall, 1748), 375–7]

CHAPTER 13

Proposals Relating to the Education of Youth in Pennsylvania

(October 1749)

Advertisement to the Reader

It has long been regretted as a Misfortune to the Youth of this Province, that we have no ACADEMY, *in which they might receive the Accomplishments of a regular Education.*

The following Paper of Hints *towards forming a Plan for that Purpose, is so far approv'd by some publick-spirited Gentlemen, to whom it has been privately communicated, that they have directed a Number of Copies to be made by the Press, and properly distributed, in order to obtain the Sentiments and Advice of Men of Learning, Understanding, and Experience in these Matters; and have determin'd to use their Interest and best Endeavours, to have the Scheme, when compleated, carried gradually into Execution; in which they have Reason to believe they shall have the hearty Concurrence and Assistance of many who are Wellwishers to their Country.*

Those who incline to favour the Design with their Advice, either as to the Parts of Learning to be taught, the Order of Study, the Method of Teaching, the Oeconomy of the School, or any other Matter of Importance to the Success of the Undertaking, are desired to communicate their Sentiments as soon as may be, by Letter directed to B. Franklin, *Printer, in* Philadelphia.

Authors *quoted in this* Paper[1]

1. The famous *Milton*, whose Learning and Abilities are well known and who had practised some Time the Education of Youth, so could speak from Experience.

2. The great Mr. Locke, who wrote a Treatise on Education, well known, and much esteemed, being translated into most of the modern Languages of *Europe*.

3. *Dialogues on Education*, 2 Vols. Octavo, that are much esteem'd, having had two Editions in 3 Years. Suppos'd to be wrote by the ingenuous Mr. *Hutcheson* (Author of *A Treatise on the Passions*, and another on the *Ideas of Beauty and Virtue)* who has had much Experience in Educating of Youth, being a Professor in the College at *Glasgow*, &c.

4. The learned Mr. *Obadiah Walker*, who had been many Years a Tutor to young Noblemen, and wrote a Treatise *on the Education of a young Gentleman*; of which the Fifth Edition was printed 1687.

5. The much admired Mons. *Rollin*, whose whole Life was spent in a College; and wrote 4 Vols. on Education, under the Title of, *The Method of Teaching and Studying the Belles Lettres*; which are translated into *English*, *Italian*, and most of the modern Languages.

6. The learned and ingenious Dr. *George Turnbull*, Chaplain to the present Prince of *Wales*; who has had much Experience in the Educating of Youth, and publish'd a Book, Octavo, intituled, *Observations on Liberal Education, in all its Branches*, 1742. With some others.

The good Education of Youth has been esteemed by wise Men in all Ages, as the surest Foundation of the Happiness both of private Families and of Common-wealths.[2] Almost all Governments have therefore made

[1] [Franklin's sources are: John Milton, *Paradise Regain'd . . . With a Tractate of Education*, 5th edn (1721); John Locke, *Some Thoughts concerning Education*, 11th edn (1745); [David Fordyce], *Dialogues concerning Education*, 2 vols. (1745–48), erroneously attributed to Francis Hutcheson; Obadiah Walker, *Of Education* (1687); Charles Rollin, *The Method of Studying and Teaching in Belles Lettres*, 4 vols., 4th edn (1749); George Turnbull, *Observations upon Liberal Education* (1742).]

[2] As some Things here propos'd may be found to differ a little from the Forms of Education in common Use, the following Quotations are to shew the opinions of several learned Men, who have carefully considered and wrote expresly on the Subject; such as *Milton*, *Locke*, *Rollin*, *Turnbull*, and others. They generally complain, that the *old Method* is in many Respects wrong; but long settled Forms are not easily changed. For us, who are now to make a Beginning, 'tis, at least, as easy to set out right as wrong; and therefore their Sentiments are on this Occasion well worth our Consideration . . .

it a principal Object of their Attention, to establish and endow with proper Revenues, such Seminaries of Learning, as might supply the succeeding Age with Men qualified to serve the Publick with Honour to themselves, and to their Country.

Many of the first Settlers of these Provinces, were Men who had received a good Education in *Europe*, and to their Wisdom and good Management we owe much of our present Prosperity. But their Hands were full, and they could not do all Things. The present Race are not thought to be generally of equal Ability: For though the *American* Youth are allow'd not to want Capacity; yet the best Capacities require Cultivation, it being truly with them, as with the best Ground, which unless well tilled and sowed with profitable Seed, produces only ranker Weeds.

That we may obtain the Advantages arising from an Increase of Knowledge, and prevent as much as may be the mischievous Consequences that would attend a general Ignorance among us, the following *Hints* are offered towards forming a Plan for the Education of the Youth of *Pennsylvania*, viz.

It is propos'd,

THAT some Persons of Leisure and publick Spirit, apply for a CHARTER, by which they may be incorporated, with Power to erect an ACADEMY for the Education of Youth, to govern the same, provide Masters, make Rules, receive Donations, purchase Lands, *&c.* and to add to their Number, from Time to Time such other Persons as they shall judge suitable.

That the Members of the Corporation make it their Pleasure, and in some Degree their Business, to visit the Academy often, encourage and[3] countenance the Youth, countenance and assist the Masters, and by all Means in their Power advance the Usefulness and Reputation of the Design; that they look on the Students as in some Sort their Children, treat them with Familiarity and Affection, and when they have behav'd well, and gone through their Studies, and are to enter the World, zealously unite, and make all the Interest that can be made to establish them,[4]

[3] [. . .]

[4] Something seems wanting in America to incite and stimulate Youth to Study. In Europe the Encouragements to Learning are of themselves much greater than can be given here. Whoever distinguishes himself there, in either of the three learned Professions, gains Fame, and often Wealth and Power: A poor Man's Son has a Chance, if he studies hard, to rise, either in the Law or the Church, to gainful Offices or Benefices; to an extraordinary Pitch of Grandeur; to have a Voice in Parliament, a Seat among the Peers; as a Statesman or first Minister to govern Nations, and even to mix his Blood with Princes.

whether in Business, Offices, Marriages, or any other Thing for their Advantage, preferably to all other Persons whatsoever even of equal Merit.

And if Men may, and frequently do, catch such a Taste for cultivating Flowers, or Planting, Grafting, Inoculating, and the like, as to despise all other Amusements for their Sake, why may not we expect they should acquire a Relish for that *more useful* Culture of young Minds. *Thomson* says,

> *'Tis Joy to see the human Blossoms blow,*
> *When infant Reason grows apace, and calls*
> *For the kind Hand of an assiduous Care;*
> *Delightful Task! to rear the tender Thought,*
> *To teach the young Idea how to shoot,*
> *To pour the fresh Instruction o'er the Mind,*
> *To breathe th' enliv'ning Spirit, and to fix*
> *The generous Purpose in the glowing Breast.*[5]

That a House be provided for the ACADEMY, if not in the Town, not many Miles from it; the Situation high and dry, and if it may be, not far from a River, having a Garden, Orchard, Meadow, and a Field or two.

That the House be furnished with a Library (if in the Country, if in the Town, the Town[6] Libraries may serve) with Maps of all Countries, Globes, some mathematical Instruments, an Apparatus for Experiments in Natural Philosophy, and for Mechanics; Prints, of all Kinds, Prospects, Buildings, Machines, *&c.*[7]

That the RECTOR be a Man of good Understanding, good Morals, diligent and patient, learn'd in the Languages and Sciences, and a correct pure Speaker and Writer of the *English* Tongue; to have such Tutors under him as shall be necessary.

That the boarding Scholars diet[8] together, plainly, temperately, and frugally.

[5] [James Thomson, *The Seasons*, "Spring" (1726), 1143–4, 1147–53.]

[6] Besides the English Library begun and carried on by Subscription in Philadelphia, we may expect the Benefit of another much more valuable in the Learned Languages, which has been many Years collecting with the greatest Care, by a Gentleman distinguish'd for his universal Knowledge, no less than for his judgment in Books . . .

[7] [. . .]

[8] Perhaps it would be best if none of the Scholars were to diet abroad. Milton is of that Opinion (*Tractate of Education*) for that much Time would else be lost, and many ill Habits got.

That to keep them in Health, and to strengthen and render active their Bodies, they be frequently[9] exercis'd in Running, Leaping, Wrestling, and Swimming,[10] *&c.*

That they have peculiar Habits to distinguish them from other Youth, if the Academy be in or near the Town; for this, among other Reasons, that their Behaviour may be the better observed.

As to their STUDIES, it would be well if they could be taught *every Thing* that is useful, and *every Thing* that is ornamental: But Art is long, and their Time is short. It is therefore propos'd that they learn those Things that are likely to be *most useful* and *most ornamental*, Regard being had to the several Professions for which they are intended.

All should be taught to write a *fair Hand*, and swift, as that is useful to All. And with it may be learnt something of *Drawing*,[11] by Imitation of Prints, and some of the first Principles of Perspective.

Arithmetick,[12] *Accounts*, and some of the first Principles of *Geometry* and *Astronomy*.

[9] *Milton* proposes, that an Hour and Half before Dinner should be allow'd for Exercise, and recommends among other Exercises, the handling of Arms, but perhaps this may not be thought necessary here . . . *Turnbull*, p. 318. says, "Corporal Exercise invigorates the Soul as well as the Body; let one be kept closely to Reading, without allowing him any Respite from Thinking, or any Exercise to his Body, and were it possible to preserve long, by such a Method, his Liking to Study and Knowledge, yet we should soon find such an one become no less soft in his Mind than in his outward Man. Both Mind and Body would thus become gradually too relaxed, too much unbraced for the Fatigues and Duties of active Life. . . ." See p. 318 to 323.

[10] *'Tis* suppos'd that every Parent would be glad to have their Children skill'd in *Swimming*, if it might be learnt in a Place chosen for its Safety, and under the Eye of a careful Person. Mr. *Locke* says, p. 9. in his *Treatise of Education*; "'Tis that saves many a Man's Life . . . But besides the gaining a Skill which may serve him at Need, the Advantages to Health by often Bathing in cold Water during the Heat of the Summer, are so many, that I think nothing need be said to encourage it." 'Tis some Advantage besides, to be free from the slavish Terrors many of those feel who cannot swim, when they are oblig'd to be on the Water even in crossing a Ferry . . .

[11] *Drawing* is a kind of Universal Language, understood by all Nations. A Man may often express his Ideas, even to his own Countrymen, more clearly with a Lead Pencil, or Bit of Chalk, than with his Tongue. And many can understand a Figure, that do not comprehend a Description in Words, tho' ever so properly chosen. All Boys have an early Inclination to this Improvement, and begin to make Figures of Animals, Ships, Machines, &c. as soon as they can use a Pen: But for want of a little Instruction at that Time, generally are discouraged, and quit the Pursuit . . .

[12] . . . Not only the *Skill*, but the *Habit* of keeping Accounts, should be acquir'd by all, as being necessary to all.

The[13] *English* Language might be taught by Grammar; in which some of our best Writers, as *Tillotson*, *Addison*, *Pope*, *Algernon Sidney*, *Cato*'s Letters, *&c.* should be Classicks: The *Stiles* principally to be cultivated, being the *clear* and the *concise*. Reading should also be taught, and pronouncing, properly, distinctly, emphatically; not with an even Tone, which *under-does*, nor a theatrical, which *over-does* Nature.

To form their Stile, they should be put on Writing[14] Letters to each other, making Abstracts of what they read; or writing the same Things

[13] Mr. *Locke*, speaking of *Grammar*, p. 252. says, "That to those the greatest Part of whose Business in this World is to be done with their Tongues, and with their Pens, it is convenient, if not necessary, that they should speak properly and correctly, whereby they may let their Thoughts into other Mens Minds the more easily, and with the greater Impression. Upon this Account . . . he ought to study *Grammar*, among the other Helps of Speaking well, but it *must be* THE GRAMMAR of His OWN TONGUE, of the Language he uses, that he may understand his own Country Speech nicely, and speak it properly, without shocking the Ears of those it is addressed to with Solecisms and offensive Irregularities . . ."

Dr. *Turnbull*, in his Observations on a liberal Education, says, p. 262. "The *Greeks*, perhaps, made more early Advances in the most useful Sciences than any Youth have done since, chiefly on this Account, that they studied no other Language but their own. This no Doubt saved them very much Time; but they *applied themselves carefully* to the Study of *their own* Language, and were *early* able to speak and write it in *the greatest Perfection* . . ."

Mons. *Simon*, in an elegant Discourse of his among the Memoirs of the Academy of *Belles Lettres* at *Paris*, speaking of the Stress the *Romans* laid on Purity of Language and graceful Pronunciation, adds . . . "Masters of Rhetoric taught them early the Principles, the Difficulties, the Beauties, the Subtleties, the Depths, the Riches of their own Language. When they went from these Schools, they were perfect Masters of it, they were never at a Loss for proper Expressions; and I am much deceived if it was not owing to this, that they produced such excellent Works with *so marvellous Facility.*"

[14] This Mr. *Locke* recommends, *Educ.* p. 284. and says, "The Writing of Letters has so much to do in all the Occurrences of human Life, that no Gentleman can avoid shewing himself in this Kind of Writing. Occasions will daily force him to make this Use of his Pen, which, besides the Consequences that, in his Affairs, the well or ill managing it often draws after it, always lays him open to a severer Examination of his Breeding, Sense and Abilities, than oral Discourses, whose transient Faults dying for the most Part with the Sound that gives them Life, and so not subject to a strict Review, more easily escape Observation and Censure." He adds,

"Had the Methods of Education been directed to their right End, one would have thought this so necessary a Part could not have been neglected, whilst Themes and Verses in Latin, of no Use at all, were so constantly every where pressed, to the Racking of Children's Inventions beyond their Strength, and hindring their chearful Progress by unnatural Difficulties. But Custom has so ordained it, and who dares disobey? . . .

"To speak and write correctly, gives a Grace, and gains a favourable Attention to what one has to say: And since 'tis *English* that an *Englishman* will have constant Use of, that is the Language he should chiefly cultivate, and wherein most Care should be taken to polish and perfect his Stile. To speak or write better *Latin* than *English*, may make a Man be talk'd of, but he will find it more to his Purpose to express himself well in his own Tongue, that he uses every Moment, than to have the vain Commendation of others for a very insignificant Quality . . .

in their own Words; telling or writing Stories lately read, in their own Expressions. All to be revis'd and corrected by the Tutor, who should give his Reasons, explain the Force and Import of Words, *&c.*

To form their[15] Pronunciation, they may be put on making Declamations, repeating Speeches, delivering Orations, *&c.* The Tutor assisting at the Rehearsals, teaching, advising, correcting their Accent, *&c.*

But if[16] HISTORY be made a constant Part of their Reading, such as the Translations of the *Greek* and *Roman* Historians, and the modern Histories of antient *Greece* and *Rome*, &c. may not almost all Kinds of useful Knowledge be that Way introduc'd to Advantage, and with Pleasure to the Student? As

GEOGRAPHY, by reading with Maps, and being required to point out the Places *where* the greatest Actions were done, to give their old and new Names, with the Bounds, Situation, Extent of the Countries concern'd, *&c.*

CHRONOLOGY, by the Help of *Helvicus* or some other Writer of the Kind, who will enable them to tell *when* those Events happened; what Princes were Cotemporaries, what States or famous Men flourish'd about that Time, *&c.* The several principal Epochas to be first well fix'd in their Memories.

I am not here speaking against *Greek* and *Latin*. I think *Latin* at least ought to be well understood by every Gentleman. But whatever foreign Languages a young Man meddles with, that which he should critically study, and labour to get a Facility, Clearness and Elegancy to express himself in, should be *his own*; and to this purpose *he should daily be* EXERCISED in it." . . .

To the same Purpose writes a Person of eminent Learning in a Letter to Dr. *Turnbull*: ". . . But where is English taught at present? Who thinks it of Use to study correctly *that Language* which he is to use *every Day* in his Life, be his Station ever so high, or ever so insignificant. It is in *this* the Nobility and Gentry defend their Country, and serve their Prince in Parliament; in *this* the Lawyers plead, the Divines instruct, and all Ranks of People write their Letters, and transact all their Affairs; and yet who thinks it worth his learning to write *this* even accurately, not to say politely? . . . Few think their Children qualified for a Trade till they have been whipt at a Latin School for five or six Years, to learn a little of that which they are oblig'd to forget; when in those Years right Education would have improv'd their minds, and taught them to acquire Habits of Writing *their own Language* easily under right Direction; and this would have been useful to them as long as they lived." *Introd.* p. 3, 4, 5 . . .

[15] By Pronunciation is here meant, the proper Modulation of the Voice, to suit the Subject with due Emphasis, Action, *&c.* In delivering a Discourse in Publick, design'd to persuade, the *Manner*, perhaps, contributes more to Success, than either the *Matter* or *Method* . . .

[16] As nothing *teaches* (saith Mr. *Locke*) so nothing *delights* more than HISTORY. The first of these recommends it to the Study of grown Men, the latter makes me think it the *fittest* for a young Lad, who as soon as he is instructed in Chronology, and acquainted with the several Epochas in Use in this Part of the World, and can reduce them to the Julian Period, should then have some History put into his Hand. *Educ. p.* 276. . . .

Antient Customs, religious and civil, being frequently mentioned in History, will give Occasion for explaining them; in which the Prints[17] of Medals, Basso Relievo's, and antient Monuments will greatly assist.

Morality,[18] by descanting and making continual Observations on the Causes of the Rise or Fall of any Man's Character, Fortune, Power, *&c.* mention'd in History; the Advantages of Temperance, Order, Frugality, Industry, Perseverance, *&c. &c.*[19] Indeed the general natural Tendency of Reading good History, must be, to fix in the Minds of Youth deep Impressions of the Beauty and Usefulness of Virtue of all Kinds, Publick Spirit, Fortitude, *&c.*

History will show the wonderful Effects of Oratory, in governing, turning and leading great Bodies of Mankind, Armies, Cities, Nations. When the Minds of Youth are struck with Admiration at this,[20] then is the Time to give them the Principles of that Art, which they will study with Taste and Application. Then they may be made acquainted with the best Models among the Antients, their Beauties being particularly pointed out to them. Modern Political Oratory being chiefly performed by the Pen and Press, its Advantages over the Antient in some Respects are to be shown; as that its Effects are more extensive, more lasting, *&c.*

History will also afford frequent Opportunities of showing the Necessity of a *Publick Religion*, from its Usefulness to the Publick; the Advantage of a Religious Character among private Persons; the Mischiefs of Superstition, *&c.* and the Excellency of the Christian Religion above all others antient or modern.[21]

History will also give Occasion to expatiate on the Advantage of Civil Orders and Constitutions, how Men and their Properties are protected by joining in Societies and establishing Government; their Industry encouraged and rewarded, Arts invented, and Life made more

[17] [. . .]

[18] For the Importance and Necessity of moral instructions to Youth, see the latter Notes.

[19] Dr. *Turnbull*, Liberal Education, p. 371, says, "That the useful Lessons which ought to be inculcated upon Youth, are much better taught and enforced from *Characters*, *Actions*, and *Events*, developing the inward Springs of human Conduct, and the different Consequences of Actions, whether with Respect to private or publick Good, than by abstract Philosophical Lectures . . ."

[20] "Rules are best understood, when Examples that confirm them, and point out their Fitness or Necessity, naturally lead one, as it were by the Hand, to take Notice of them . . . [T]o teach Rules abstractly, or without Examples, and before the agreeable Effects the Observance of them tends to produce (which are in Reality their Reason or Foundation) have been felt, *is exceedingly preposterous.*" *Turnbull*, p. 410.

[21] See *Turnbull* on this Head, from p. 386 to 390. very much to the Purpose, but too long to be transcribed here.

comfortable: The Advantages of *Liberty*, Mischiefs of *Licentiousness*, Benefits arising from good Laws and a due Execution of Justice, *&c.* Thus may the first Principles of sound *Politicks*[22] be fix'd in the Minds of Youth.

On *Historical* Occasions, Questions of Right and Wrong, Justice and Injustice, will naturally arise, and may be put to Youth, which they may debate in Conversation and in Writing.[23] When they ardently desire Victory, for the Sake of the Praise attending it, they will begin to feel the Want, and be sensible of the Use of *Logic*, or the Art of Reasoning to *discover* Truth, and of Arguing to *defend* it, and *convince* Adversaries. This would be the Time to acquaint them with the Principles of that Art. *Grotius*, *Puffendorff*, and some other Writers of the same Kind, may be used on these Occasions to decide their Disputes. Publick Disputes[24] warm the Imagination, whet the Industry, and strengthen the natural Abilities.

When Youth are told, that the Great Men whose Lives and Actions they read in History, spoke two of the best Languages that ever were, the most expressive, copious, beautiful; and that the finest Writings, the most correct Compositions, the most perfect Productions of human Wit and Wisdom, are in those Languages, which have endured Ages, and will endure while there are Men; that no Translation can do them justice, or give the Pleasure found in Reading the Originals; that those Languages

[22] Thus, as Milton says, *Educ.* p. 381. should they be instructed in the Beginning, End and Reasons of political Societies; that they may not, in a dangerous Fit of the Commonwealth, be such poor, shaken, uncertain Reeds, of such a tottering Conscience, as many of our great Councellors have lately shown themselves, but stedfast Pillars of the State.

[23] After this, they are to dive into the Grounds of Law and legal Justice; deliver'd first and with best Warrant by *Moses*; and as far as human Prudence can be trusted, in those celebrated Remains of the antient *Grecian* and *Roman* Lawgivers, *&c.* [Milton,] p. 382.

"When he has pretty well digested *Tully*'s Offices, says Mr. *Locke*, p. 277. and added to it *Puffendorff de Officio Hominis & Civs*, it may be seasonable to set him upon *Grotius*, *de Jure Belli & Pacis*, or which perhaps is the better of the two, *Puffendorff de Jure naturali & Gentium*; wherein he will be instructed in the natural Rights of Men, and the Original and Foundations of Society, and the Duties resulting from thence . . ."

[24] Mr. *Walker*, in his excellent Treatise of the Education of young Gentlemen, speaking of *Publick and open Argumentation pro and con*, says p. 124, 125 "*This is it* which brings a Question to a Point, and discovers the very Center and Knot of the Difficulty. *This* warms and *activates* the Spirit in the Search of Truth, excites Notions, and by replying and frequent Beating upon it, *cleanseth* it from the Ashes, and makes it shine and flame out the clearer. Besides, it puts them upon a continual *Stretch* of their Wits to defend their Cause, it makes them quick in Replies, intentive upon their Subject; where the *Opponent* useth all Means to drive his Adversary from his Hold; and the *Answerer* defends himself *sometimes* with the Force of Truth, *sometimes* with the Subtilty of his Wit; and *sometimes* also he escapes in a Mist of Words, and the Doubles of a Distinction, whilst he seeks all Holes and Recesses to shelter his persecuted Opinion and Reputation . . ."

contain all Science; that one of them is become almost universal, being the Language of Learned Men in all Countries; that to understand them is a distinguishing Ornament, *&c.* they may be thereby made desirous of learning those Languages, and their Industry sharpen'd in the Acquisition of them. All intended for Divinity should be taught the *Latin* and *Greek*; for Physick, the *Latin*, *Greek* and *French*; for Law, the *Latin* and *French*; Merchants, the *French*, *German*, and *Spanish*: And though all should not be compell'd to learn *Latin*, *Greek*, or the modern foreign Languages; yet none that have an ardent Desire to learn them should be refused; their *English*, Arithmetick, and other Studies absolutely necessary, being at the same Time not neglected.

If the new *Universal History* were also read, it would give a *connected* Idea of human Affairs, so far as it goes, which should be follow'd by the best modern Histories, particularly of our Mother Country; then of these Colonies; which should be accompanied with Observations on their Rise, Encrease, Use to *Great-Britain*, Encouragements, Discouragements, *&c.* the Means to make them flourish, secure their Liberties, &c.

With the History of Men, Times and Nations, should be read at proper Hours or Days, some of the best *Histories of Nature*[25] which would not only be delightful to Youth, and furnish them with Matter for their Letters, *&c.* as well as other History; but afterwards of great Use to them, whether they are Merchants, Handicrafts, or Divines; enabling the first the better to understand many Commodities, Drugs, *&c.* the second to improve his Trade or Handicraft by new Mixtures, Materials, *&c.* and the last to adorn his Discourses by beautiful Comparisons, and strengthen them by new Proofs of Divine Providence. The Conversation of all will be improved by it, as Occasions frequently occur of making Natural Observations, which are instructive, agreeable, and entertaining in almost all Companies. *Natural History* will also afford Opportunities of introducing many Observations, relating to the Preservation of Health, which may be afterwards of great Use. *Arbuthnot* on Air and *Aliment*, *Sanctorius* on Perspiration, *Lemery* on Foods, and some others, may now be read, and a very little Explanation will make them sufficiently intelligible to Youth.

[25] Rollin, Vol. 4. p. 211. speaking of *Natural Philosophy*, says, "That . . . even Children are capable of Studying Nature, for they have Eyes, and don't want Curiosity; they ask Questions, and love to be informed; and here we need only awaken and keep up in them the Desire of Learning and Knowing, which is natural to all Mankind . . . A Garden, a Country, a Plantation, are all so many Books which lie open to them; but they must have been taught and accustomed to read in them . . ."

While they are reading Natural History, might not a little *Gardening, Planting, Grafting, Inoculating*, &c. be taught and practised; and now and then Excursions made to the neighbouring Plantations of the best Farmers, their Methods observ'd and reason'd upon for the Information of Youth. The Improvement of Agriculture being useful to all,[26] and Skill in it no Disparagement to any.

The History of *Commerce*, of the Invention of Arts, Rise of Manufactures, Progress of Trade, Change of its Seats, with the Reasons, Causes, *&c.* may also be made entertaining to Youth, and will be useful to all. And this, with the Accounts in other History of the prodigious Force and Effect of Engines and Machines used in War, will naturally introduce a Desire to be instructed in[27] *Mechanicks*, and to be inform'd of the Principles of that Art by which weak Men perform such Wonders, Labour is sav'd, Manufactures expedited, *&c. &c.* This will be the Time to show them Prints of antient and modern Machines, to explain them, to let them be[28] copied, and to give Lectures in Mechanical Philosophy.

With the whole should be constantly inculcated and cultivated, that *Benignity of Mind*[29] which shows itself in *searching for* and *seizing* every Opportunity to *serve* and to *oblige*; and is the Foundation of what is called Good Breeding; highly useful to the Possessor, and most agreeable to all.[30]

The Idea of what is *true Merit*, should also be often presented to Youth, explain'd and impress'd on their Minds, as consisting in an *Inclination* join'd with an *Ability* to serve Mankind, one's Country, Friends and Family; which *Ability* is (with the Blessing of God) to be acquir'd or

[26] *Milton* would have the *Latin* Authors on Agriculture taught at School . . . *Hutcheson (Dialogues on Educ.* 303, 2d Vol.) says, "Nor should I think it below the Dignity or Regard of an University, to descend even to the general Precepts of *Agriculture* and *Gardening* . . ." *Locke* also recommends the Study of Husbandry and Gardening, as well as gaining an Insight in several of the manual Arts . . .

[27] How many Mills are built and Machines constructed, at great and fruitless Expence which a little Knowledge in the Principles of Mechanics would have prevented?

[28] [. . .]

[29] "Upon this excellent Disposition (says *Turnbull*, p. 326.) it will be *easy to build* that amiable Quality commonly called GOOD BREEDING, and upon *no other Foundation* can it be raised. For whence else can it spring, but from a general Good-will and Regard for all People, deeply rooted in the Heart, which makes any one that has it, careful not to shew in his Carriage, any Contempt, Disrespect, or Neglect of them, but to express a Value and Respect for them according to their Rank and Condition, suitable to the Fashion and Way of their Country? . . ."

[30] "It is this lovely Quality which gives true Beauty to all other Accomplishments, or renders them useful to their Possessor, in procuring him the Esteem and Good-will of all that he comes near . . ." *Turnbull*, p. 327.

greatly encreas'd by *true Learning*; and should indeed be the great *Aim* and *End*[31] of all Learning.

[Philadelphia: 1749]

[31] To have in View the *Glory* and *Service of God*, as some express themselves, is only the same Thing in other Words. For *Doing Good to Men* is the *only Service of God* in our Power; and to *imitate his Beneficence* is to *glorify him* . . . Mr. *Hutcheson* says, *Dial.* v. 2. p. 97. "The *principal End* of Education is, to *form us wise and good Creatures, useful to others and happy ourselves* . . ." And Mr. *Locke* (p. 84. *Educ.*) says, "'Tis VIRTUE, then, direct VIRTUE, which is to be *aim'd at* in Education. All other Considerations and Accomplishments are nothing in Comparison to this. This is the solid and *substantial* Good, which Tutors should not only read Lectures and talk of, but the *Labour* and *Art of Education* should furnish the Mind with, and *fasten* there, and never cease till the young Man had a true Relish of it, and plac'd his *Strength*, his *Glory*, and his *Pleasure*, in it." . . .

Dr. *Turnbull* has the same Sentiments, with which we shall conclude this Note. "If," says he, "there be any such Thing as DUTY, or any such Thing as HAPPINESS; if there be any Difference between right and wrong Conduct; any Distinction between Virtue and Vice, or Wisdom and Folly; in fine, if there be any such Thing as Perfection or Imperfection belonging to the rational Powers which constitute moral Agents; or if Enjoyments and Pursuits admit of Comparison; *Good Education* must of Necessity be acknowledged to mean, *proper Care* to instruct early in the Science of Happiness and Duty, or in the Art of Judging and *Acting aright* in Life . . . The Way therefore to judge whether Education be on a right Footing or not, is to compare it with the END; or to consider what it does in order to accomplish Youth for choosing and *behaving well* in the various Conditions, *Relations* and Incidents, of Life . . . *Observations on Liberal Education*, p. 175, 176.

CHAPTER 14

Observations concerning the Increase of Mankind, Peopling of Countries, &c.

(1751)

1. Tables of the Proportion of Marriages to Births, of Deaths to Births, of Marriages to the Numbers of Inhabitants, &c. form'd on Observations made upon the Bills of Mortality, Christnings, &c. of populous Cities, will not suit Countries; nor will Tables form'd on Observations made on full settled old Countries, as *Europe*, suit new Countries, as *America*.

2. For People increase in Proportion to the Number of Marriages, and that is greater in Proportion to the Ease and Convenience of supporting a Family. When Families can be easily supported, more Persons marry, and earlier in Life.

3. In Cities, where all Trades, Occupations and Offices are full, many delay marrying, till they can see how to bear the Charges of a Family; which Charges are greater in Cities, as Luxury is more common: many live single during Life, and continue Servants to Families, Journeymen to Trades, &c. hence Cities do not by natural Generation supply themselves with Inhabitants; the Deaths are more than the Births.

4. In Countries full settled, the Case must be nearly the same; all Lands being occupied and improved to the Heighth; those who cannot get Land, must Labour for others that have it; when Labourers are plenty, their Wages will be low; by low Wages a Family is supported with Difficulty; this Difficulty deters many from Marriage, who therefore long continue Servants and single.——Only as the Cities take Supplies of People from the Country, and thereby make a little more Room in the Country; Marriage is a little more incourag'd there, and the Births exceed the Deaths.

5. *Europe* is generally full settled with Husbandmen, Manufacturers, &c. and therefore cannot now much increase in People: *America* is

chiefly occupied by Indians, who subsist mostly by Hunting.——But as the Hunter, of all Men, requires the greatest Quantity of Land from whence to draw his Subsistence, (the Husbandman subsisting on much less, the Gardner on still less, and the Manufacturer requiring least of all), The *Europeans* found *America* as fully settled as it well could be by Hunters; yet these having large Tracks, were easily prevail'd on to part with Portions of Territory to the new Comers, who did not much interfere with the Natives in Hunting, and furnish'd them with many Things they wanted.

6. Land being thus plenty in *America*, and so cheap as that a labouring Man, that understands Husbandry, can in a short Time save Money enough to purchase a Piece of new Land sufficient for a Plantation, whereon he may subsist a Family; such are not afraid to marry; for if they even look far enough forward to consider how their Children when grown up are to be provided for, they see that more Land is to be had at Rates equally easy, all Circumstances considered.

7. Hence Marriages in *America* are more general, and more generally early, than in *Europe*. And if it is reckoned there, that there is but one Marriage per Annum among 100 Persons, perhaps we may here reckon two; and if in *Europe* they have but 4 Births to a Marriage (many of their Marriages being late) we may here reckon 8, of which if one half grow up, and our Marriages are made, reckoning one with another at 20 Years of Age, our People must at least be doubled every 20 Years.

8. But notwithstanding this Increase, so vast is the Territory of *North-America*, that it will require many Ages to settle it fully; and till it is fully settled, Labour will never be cheap here, where no Man continues long a Labourer for others, but gets a Plantation of his own, no Man continues long a journeyman to a Trade, but goes among those new Settlers, and sets up for himself, &c. Hence Labour is no cheaper now, in *Pennsylvania*, than it was 30 Years ago, tho' so many Thousand labouring People have been imported.

9. The Danger therefore of these Colonies interfering with their Mother Country in Trades that depend on Labour, Manufactures, &c. is too remote to require the Attention of *Great-Britain*.

10. But in Proportion to the Increase of the Colonies, a vast Demand is growing for British Manufactures, a glorious Market wholly in the Power of *Britain*, in which Foreigners cannot interfere, which will increase in a short Time even beyond her Power of supplying, tho' her whole Trade

should be to her Colonies:[1] Therefore *Britain* should not too much restrain Manufactures in her Colonies. A wise and good Mother will not do it. To distress, is to weaken, and weakening the Children, weakens the whole Family.

11. Besides if the Manufactures of *Britain* (by Reason of the *American* Demands) should rise too high in Price, Foreigners who can sell cheaper will drive her Merchants out of Foreign Markets; Foreign Manufactures will thereby be encouraged and increased, and consequently foreign Nations, perhaps her Rivals in Power, grow more populous and more powerful; while her own Colonies, kept too low, are unable to assist her, or add to her Strength.

12. 'Tis an ill-grounded Opinion that by the Labour of Slaves, *America* may possibly vie in Cheapness of Manufactures with *Britain*. The Labour of Slaves can never be so cheap here as the Labour of working Men is in *Britain*. Any one may compute it. Interest of Money is in the Colonies from 6 to 10 per Cent. Slaves one with another cost 30 £. Sterling per Head. Reckon then the Interest of the first Purchase of a Slave, the Insurance or Risque on his Life, his Cloathing and Diet, Expences in his Sickness and Loss of Time, Loss by his Neglect of Business (Neglect is natural to the Man who is not to be benefited by his own Care or Diligence), Expence of a Driver to keep him at Work, and his Pilfering from Time to Time, almost every Slave being *by Nature*[2] a Thief, and compare the whole Amount with the Wages of a Manufacturer of Iron or Wool in *England*, you will see that Labour is much cheaper there than it ever can be by Negroes here. Why then will *Americans* purchase Slaves? Because Slaves may be kept as long as a Man pleases, or has Occasion for their Labour; while hired Men are continually leaving their Master (often in the midst of his Business,) and setting up for themselves. § 8.

13. As the Increase of People depends on the Encouragement of Marriages, the following Things must diminish a Nation, *viz.* 1. The being conquered; for the Conquerors will engross as many Offices, and exact as much Tribute or Profit on the Labour of the conquered, as will maintain them in their new Establishment, and this diminishing the Subsistence of the Natives discourages their Marriages, and so gradually diminishes them, while the Foreigners increase. 2. Loss of Territory. Thus the *Britons*

[1] [Remainder of §10 and all of §11 omitted from 1769 edition of *Experiments and Observations*.]

[2] [In 1769 edition of *Experiments and Observations*, Franklin replaced "by Nature" with "from the nature of slavery."]

being driven into *Wales*, and crowded together in a barren Country insufficient to support such great Numbers, diminished 'till the People bore a Proportion to the Produce, while the *Saxons* increased on their abandoned Lands; 'till the Island became full of *English*. And were the *English* now driven into *Wales* by some foreign Nation, there would in a few Years be no more Englishmen in *Britain*, than there are now People in *Wales*. 3. Loss of Trade. Manufactures exported, draw Subsistence from Foreign Countries for Numbers; who are thereby enabled to marry and raise Families. If the Nation be deprived of any Branch of Trade, and no new Employment is found for the People occupy'd in that Branch, it will also be soon deprived of so many People. 4. Loss of Food. Suppose a Nation has a Fishery, which not only employs great Numbers, but makes the Food and Subsistence of the People cheaper: If another Nation becomes Master of the Seas, and prevents the Fishery, the People will diminish in Proportion as the Loss of Employ, and Dearness of Provision, makes it more difficult to subsist a Family. 5. Bad Government and insecure Property. People not only leave such a Country, and settling Abroad incorporate with other Nations, lose their native Language, and become Foreigners; but the Industry of those that remain being discourag'd, the Quantity of Subsistence in the Country is lessen'd, and the Support of a Family becomes more difficult. So heavy Taxes tend to diminish a People. 6. The Introduction of Slaves. The Negroes brought into the *English* Sugar *Islands*, have greatly diminish'd the Whites there; the Poor are by this Means depriv'd of Employment, while a few Families acquire vast Estates; which they spend on Foreign Luxuries, and educating their Children in the Habit of those Luxuries; the same Income is needed for the Support of one that might have maintain'd 100. The Whites who have Slaves, not labouring, are enfeebled, and therefore not so generally prolific; the Slaves being work'd too hard, and ill fed, their Constitutions are broken, and the Deaths among them are more than the Births; so that a continual Supply is needed from *Africa*. The Northern Colonies having few Slaves increase in Whites. Slaves also pejorate the Families that use them; the white Children become proud, disgusted with Labour, and being educated in Idleness, are rendered unfit to get a Living by Industry.

14. Hence the Prince that acquires new Territory, if he finds it vacant, or removes the Natives to give his own People Room; the Legislator that makes effectual Laws for promoting of Trade, increasing Employment, improving Land by more or better Tillage; providing more Food by Fisheries; securing Property, &c. and the Man that invents new

Trades, Arts or Manufactures, or new Improvements in Husbandry, may be properly called *Fathers* of their Nation, as they are the Cause of the Generation of Multitudes, by the Encouragement they afford to Marriage.

15. As to Privileges granted to the married, (such as the *Jus trium Liberorum* among the *Romans*), they may hasten the filling of a Country that has been thinned by War or Pestilence, or that has otherwise vacant Territory; but cannot increase a People beyond the Means provided for their Subsistence.

16. Foreign Luxuries and needless Manufactures imported and used in a Nation, do, by the same Reasoning, increase the People of the Nation that furnishes them, and diminish the People of the Nation that uses them.——Laws therefore that prevent such Importations, and on the contrary promote the Exportation of Manufactures to be consumed in Foreign Countries, may be called (with Respect to the People that make them) *generative Laws*, as by increasing Subsistence they encourage Marriage. Such Laws likewise strengthen a Country, doubly, by increasing its own People and diminishing its Neighbours.

17. Some *European* Nations prudently refuse to consume the Manufactures of *East-India*:——They should likewise forbid them to their Colonies; for the Gain to the Merchant, is not to be compar'd with the Loss by this Means of People to the Nation.

18. Home Luxury in the Great, increases the Nation's Manufacturers employ'd by it, who are many, and only tends to diminish the Families that indulge in it, who are few. The greater the common fashionable Expence of any Rank of People, the more cautious they are of Marriage. Therefore Luxury should never be suffer'd to become common.

19. The great Increase of Offspring in particular Families, is not always owing to greater Fecundity of Nature, but sometimes to Examples of Industry in the Heads, and industrious Education; by which the Children are enabled to provide better for themselves, and their marrying early, is encouraged from the Prospect of good Subsistence.

20. If there be a Sect therefore, in our Nation, that regard Frugality and Industry as religious Duties, and educate their Children therein, more than others commonly do; such Sect must consequently increase more by natural Generation, than any other Sect in *Britain*.——

21. The Importation of Foreigners into a Country that has as many Inhabitants as the present Employments and Provisions for Subsistence will bear; will be in the End no Increase of People; unless the New Comers

have more Industry and Frugality than the Natives, and then they will provide more Subsistence, and increase in the Country; but they will gradually eat the Natives out.——Nor is it necessary to bring in Foreigners to fill up any occasional Vacancy in a Country; for such Vacancy (if the Laws are good, § 14, 16) will soon be filled by natural Generation. Who can now find the Vacancy made in *Sweden*, *France* or other Warlike Nations, by the Plague of Heroism 40 Years ago; in *France*, by the Expulsion of the Protestants; in *England*, by the Settlement of her Colonies; or in *Guinea*, by 100 Years Exportation of Slaves, that has blacken'd half America?——The thinness of Inhabitants in Spain is owing to National Pride and Idleness, and other Causes, rather than to the Expulsion of the *Moors*, or to the making of new Settlements.

22. There is in short, no Bound to the prolific Nature of Plants or Animals, but what is made by their crowding and interfering with each others Means of Subsistence. Was the Face of the Earth vacant of other Plants, it might be gradually sowed and overspread with one Kind only; as, for Instance, with Fennel; and were it empty of other Inhabitants, it might in a few Ages be replenish'd from one Nation only; as, for Instance, with *Englishmen*. Thus there are suppos'd to be now upwards of One Million *English* Souls in *North-America*, (tho' 'tis thought scarce 80,000 have been brought over Sea) and yet perhaps there is not one the fewer in *Britain*, but rather many more, on Account of the Employment the Colonies afford to Manufacturers at Home. This Million doubling, suppose but once in 25 Years, will in another Century be more than the People of *England*, and the greatest Number of *Englishmen* will be on this Side the Water. What an Accession of Power to the *British* Empire by Sea as well as Land! What Increase of Trade and Navigation! What Numbers of Ships and Seamen! We have been here but little more than 100 Years, and yet the Force of our Privateers in the late War, united, was greater, both in Men and Guns, than that of the whole *British* Navy in Queen *Elizabeth's* Time.——How important an Affair then to *Britain*, is the present Treaty for settling the Bounds between her Colonies and the *French*, and how careful should she be to secure Room enough, since on the Room depends so much the Increase of her People?

23. In fine, A Nation well regulated is like a Polypus; take away a Limb, its Place is soon supply'd; cut it in two, and each deficient Part shall speedily grow out of the Part remaining. Thus if you have Room and Subsistence enough, as you may by dividing, make ten Polypes out of

one, you may of one make ten Nations, equally populous and powerful; or rather, increase a Nation ten fold in Numbers and Strength.[3]

And since Detachments of *English* from *Britain* sent to *America*, will have their Places at Home so soon supply'd and increase so largely here; why should the *Palatine Boors* be suffered to swarm into our Settlements, and by herding together establish their Language and Manners to the Exclusion of ours? Why should *Pennsylvania*, founded by the *English*, become a Colony of *Aliens*, who will shortly be so numerous as to Germanize us instead of our Anglifying them, and will never adopt our Language or Customs, any more than they can acquire our Complexion.

24. Which leads me to add one Remark: That the Number of purely white People in the World is proportionably very small. All *Africa* is black or tawny. *Asia* chiefly tawny. *America* (exclusive of the new Comers) wholly so. And in *Europe*, the *Spaniards*, *Italians*, *French*, *Russians* and *Swedes*, are generally of what we call a swarthy Complexion; as are the *Germans* also, the *Saxons* only excepted, who with the *English*, make the principal Body of White People on the Face of the Earth. I could wish their Numbers were increased. And while we are, as I may call it, *Scouring* our Planet, by clearing *America* of Woods, and so making this Side of our Globe reflect a brighter Light to the Eyes of Inhabitants in *Mars* or *Venus*, why should we in the Sight of Superior Beings, darken its People? why increase the Sons of *Africa*, by Planting them in *America*, where we have so fair an Opportunity, by excluding all Blacks and Tawneys, of increasing the lovely White and Red? But perhaps I am partial to the Complexion of my Country, for such Kind of Partiality is natural to Mankind.

[Printed in [William Clarke], *Observations On the late and present Conduct of the French, with Regard to their Encroachments upon the British Colonies in North America . . . To which is added, wrote by another Hand; Observations concerning the Increase of Mankind, Peopling of Countries, &c.* (Boston, 1755)]

[3] [Remainder of text omitted from 1760 and 1761 reprints, and from 1769 edition.]

CHAPTER 15
To James Parker
(20 March 1751)

Dear Mr. Parker,

I have, as you desire, read the Manuscript you sent me; and am of Opinion, with the publick-spirited Author, that securing the Friendship of the *Indians* is of the greatest Consequence to these Colonies; and that the surest Means of doing it, are, to regulate the *Indian* Trade, so as to convince them, by Experience, that they may have the best and cheapest Goods, and the fairest Dealing from the *English*; and to unite the several Governments, so as to form a Strength that the *Indians* may depend on for Protection, in Case of a Rupture with the *French*; or apprehend great Danger from, if they should break with us.

This Union of the Colonies, however necessary, I apprehend is not to be brought about by the Means that have hitherto been used for that Purpose. A Governor of one Colony, who happens from some Circumstances in his own Government, to see the Necessity of such an Union, writes his Sentiments of the Matter to the other Governors, and desires them to recommend it to their respective Assemblies. They accordingly lay the Letters before those Assemblies, and perhaps recommend the Proposal in general Words. But Governors are often on ill Terms with their Assemblies, and seldom are the Men that have the most Influence among them. And perhaps some Governors, tho' they openly recommend the Scheme, may privately throw cold Water on it, as thinking additional publick Charges will make their People less able, or less willing to give to them. Or perhaps they do not clearly see the Necessity of it, and therefore do not very earnestly press the Consideration of it: And no one being present that has the Affair at Heart, to back it, to answer and remove Objections, *&c.* 'tis easily dropt, and nothing is done.——Such an Union is certainly necessary to us all, but more immediately so to your Government. Now, if you were to pick out half a Dozen Men of good

Understanding and Address, and furnish them with a reasonable Scheme and proper Instructions, and send them in the Nature of Ambassadors to the other Colonies, where they might apply particularly to all the leading Men, and by proper Management get them to engage in promoting the Scheme; where, by being present, they would have the Opportunity of pressing the Affair both in publick and private, obviating Difficulties as they arise, answering Objections as soon as they are made, before they spread and gather Strength in the Minds of the People, *&c. &c.* I imagine such an Union might thereby be made and established: For reasonable sensible Men, can always make a reasonable Scheme appear such to other reasonable Men, if they take Pains, and have Time and Opportunity for it; unless from some Circumstances their Honesty and good Intentions are suspected. A voluntary Union entered into by the Colonies themselves, I think, would be preferable to one impos'd by Parliament; for it would be perhaps not much more difficult to procure, and more easy to alter and improve, as Circumstances should require, and Experience direct. It would be a very strange Thing, if six Nations of ignorant Savages should be capable of forming a Scheme for such an Union, and be able to execute it in such a Manner, as that it has subsisted Ages, and appears indissoluble; and yet that a like Union should be impracticable for ten or a Dozen *English* Colonies, to whom it is more necessary, and must be more advantageous; and who cannot be supposed to want an equal Understanding of their Interests.

Were there a general Council form'd by all the Colonies, and a general Governor appointed by the Crown to preside in that Council, or in some Manner to concur with and confirm their Acts, and take Care of the Execution; every Thing relating to Indian Affairs and the Defence of the Colonies, might be properly put under their Management. Each Colony should be represented by as many Members as it pays Sums of Hundred Pounds into the common Treasury for the common Expence; which Treasury would perhaps be best and most equitably supply'd, by an equal Excise on strong Liquors in all the Colonies, the Produce never to be apply'd to the private Use of any Colony, but to the general Service. Perhaps if the Council were to meet successively at the Capitals of the several Colonies, they might thereby become better acquainted with the Circumstances, Interests, Strength or Weakness, *&c.* of all, and thence be able to judge better of Measures propos'd from time to time. At least it might be more satisfactory to the Colonies, if this were propos'd as a Part of the Scheme; for a Preference might create Jealousy and Dislike.

I believe the Place mention'd is a very suitable one to build a Fort on. In Times of Peace, Parties of the Garrisons of all Frontier Forts might be allowed to go out on Hunting Expeditions, with or without Indians, and have the Profit to themselves of the Skins they get: By this Means a Number of Wood-Runners would be form'd, well acquainted with the Country, and of great Use in War Time, as Guides of Parties and Scouts, *&c.*——Every Indian is a Hunter; and as their Manner of making War, *viz.* by Skulking, Surprizing and Killing particular Persons and Families, is just the same as their Manner of Hunting, only changing the Object, Every Indian is a disciplin'd Soldier. Soldiers of this Kind are always wanted in the Colonies in an Indian War; for the *European* Military Discipline is of little Use in these Woods.

Publick Trading Houses would certainly have a good Effect towards regulating the private Trade; and preventing the Impositions of the private Traders; and therefore such should be established in suitable Places all along the Frontiers; and the Superintendant of the Trade, propos'd by the Author, would, I think, be a useful Officer.

The Observation concerning the Importation of *Germans* in too great Numbers into *Pennsylvania*, is, I believe, a very just one. This will in a few Years become a *German* Colony: Instead of their Learning our Language, we must learn their's, or live as in a foreign Country. Already the *English* begin to quit particular Neighbourhoods surrounded by *Dutch*, being made uneasy by the Disagreeableness of disonant Manners; and in Time, Numbers will probably quit the Province for the same Reason. Besides, the *Dutch* under-live, and are thereby enabled to under-work and under-sell the *English*; who are thereby extreamly incommoded, and consequently disgusted, so that there can be no cordial Affection or Unity between the two Nations. How good Subjects they may make, and how faithful to the *British* Interest, is a Question worth considering. And in my Opinion, equal Numbers might have been spared from the *British* Islands without being miss'd there, and on proper Encouragement would have come over. I say without being miss'd, perhaps I might say without lessening the Number of People at Home. I question indeed, whether there be a Man the less in *Britain* for the Establishment of the Colonies. An Island can support but a certain Number of People: When all Employments are full, Multitudes refrain Marriage, 'till they can see how to maintain a Family. The Number of Englishmen in *England*, cannot by their present common Increase be doubled in a Thousand Years; but if half of them were taken away and planted in *America*, where there is Room for them to encrease, and sufficient Employment and Subsistance; the Number of *Englishmen* would be doubled in 100 *Years*: For those left at home, would multiply in that Time so as to fill up the Vacancy, and those here would at least keep Pace with them.

Everyone must approve the Proposal of encouraging a Number of sober discreet Smiths to reside among the *Indians*. They would doubtless be of great Service. The whole Subsistance of *Indians*, depends on keeping their Guns in order; and if they are obliged to make a Journey of two or three hundred Miles to an English Settlement to get a Lock mended; it may, besides the Trouble, occasion the Loss of their Hunting Season. They are People that think much of their temporal, but little of their spiritual Interests; and therefore, as he would be a most useful and necessary Man to them, a Smith is more likely to influence them than a Jesuit; provided he has a good common Understanding, and is from time to time well instructed.

I wish I could offer any Thing for the Improvement of the Author's Piece, but I have little Knowledge, and less Experience in these Matters. I think it ought to be printed; and should be glad there were a more general Communication of the Sentiments of judicious Men, on Subjects so generally interesting; it would certainly produce good Effects. Please to present my Respects to the Gentleman, and thank him for the Perusal of his Manuscript.

I am, Yours affectionately.

[Printed in (Archibald Kennedy), *The Importance of Gaining and Preserving the Friendship of the Indians to the British Interest, Considered* (New York: James Parker, 1751), 27–31]

CHAPTER 16
Rattle-Snakes for Felons
(9 May 1751)

To the Printers of the Gazette

By a Passage in one of your late Papers, I understand that the Government at home will not suffer our mistaken Assemblies to make any Law for preventing or discouraging the Importation of Convicts from Great Britain, for this kind Reason, "*That such Laws are against the Publick Utility, as they tend to prevent the* IMPROVEMENT *and* WELL PEOPLING of the Colonies."

Such a tender *parental* Concern in our *Mother Country* for the *Welfare* of her Children, calls aloud for the highest *Returns* of Gratitude and Duty. This every one must be sensible of: But 'tis said, that in our present Circumstances it is absolutely impossible for us to make *such* as are adequate to the Favour. I own it; but nevertheless let us do our Endeavour. 'Tis something to show a grateful Disposition.

In some of the uninhabited Parts of these Provinces, there are Numbers of these venomous Reptiles we call RATTLE-SNAKES; Felons-convict from the Beginning of the World: These, whenever we meet with them, we put to Death, by Virtue of an old Law, *Thou shalt bruise his Head.* But as this is a sanguinary Law, and may seem too cruel; and as however mischievous those Creatures are with us, they may possibly change their Natures, if they were to change the Climate; I would humbly propose, that this general Sentence of *Death* be changed for *Transportation.*

In the Spring of the Year, when they first creep out of their Holes, they are feeble, heavy, slow, and easily taken; and if a small Bounty were allow'd *per* Head, some Thousands might be collected annually, and *transported* to Britain. There I would propose to have them carefully distributed in *St. James's Park*, in the *Spring-Gardens* and other Places of Pleasure about *London*; in the Gardens of all the Nobility and Gentry throughout the Nation; but particularly in the Gardens of the *Prime Ministers*, the *Lords of Trade* and *Members of Parliament*; for to them we are *most particularly* obliged.

There is no human Scheme so perfect, but some Inconveniencies may be objected to it: Yet when the Conveniencies far exceed, the Scheme is judg'd rational, and fit to be executed. Thus Inconveniencies have been objected to that *good* and *wise* Act of Parliament, by virtue of which all the *Newgates* and *Dungeons* in *Britain* are emptied into the Colonies. It has been said, that these Thieves and Villains introduc'd among us, spoil the Morals of Youth in the Neighbourhoods that entertain them, and perpetrate many horrid Crimes: But let not *private Interests* obstruct *publick Utility*. Our *Mother* knows what is best for us. What is a little *Housebreaking*, *Shoplifting*, or *Highway Robbing*; what is a *Son* now and then *corrupted* and *hang'd*, a Daughter *debauch'd* and *pox'd*, a Wife *stabb'd*, a Husband's *Throat cut*, or a Child's *Brains beat out* with an Axe, compar'd with this "IMPROVEMENT and WELL PEOPLING of the Colonies!"

Thus it may perhaps be objected to my Scheme, that the *Rattle-Snake* is a mischievous Creature, and that his changing his Nature with the Clime is a mere Supposition, not yet confirm'd by sufficient Facts. What then? Is not Example more prevalent than Precept? And may not the honest rough British Gentry, by a Familiarity with these Reptiles, learn to *creep*, and to *insinuate*, and to *slaver*, and to *wriggle* into Place (and perhaps to *poison* such as stand in their Way) Qualities of no small Advantage to Courtiers! In comparison of which "*Improvement* and *Publick Utility*," what is a *Child* now and then kill'd by their venomous Bite,——or even a favourite *Lap-Dog*?

I would only add, That this Exporting of Felons to the Colonies, may be consider'd as a *Trade*, as well as in the Light of a *Favour*. Now all Commerce implies *Returns*: Justice requires them: There can be no Trade without them. And *Rattle-Snakes* seem the most *suitable Returns* for the *Human Serpents* sent us by our *Mother* Country. In this, however, as in every other Branch of Trade, she will have the Advantage of us. She will reap *equal* Benefits without equal Risque of the Inconveniencies and Dangers. For the *Rattle-Snake* gives Warning before he attempts his Mischief; which the Convict does not. I am

Yours, & c.
Americanus.

[Gazette, 9 May 1751]

CHAPTER 17

To Peter Collinson

(9 May 1753)

Sir

I received your Favour of the 29th. August last and thank you for the kind and judicious remarks you have made on my little Piece. Whatever further occurs to you on the same subject, you will much oblige me in communicating it.

I have often observed with wonder, that Temper of the poor English Manufacturers and day Labourers which you mention, and acknowledge it to be pretty general. When any of them happen to come here, where Labour is much better paid than in England, their Industry seems to diminish in equal proportion. But it is not so with the German Labourers; They retain the habitual Industry and Frugality they bring with them, and now receiving higher Wages an accumulation arises that makes them all rich.

When I consider, that the English are the Offspring of Germans, that the Climate they live in is much of the same Temperature; when I can see nothing in Nature that should create this Difference, I am apt to suspect it must arise from Institution, and I have sometimes doubted, whether the Laws peculiar to England which compel the Rich to maintain the Poor, have not given the latter, a Dependance that very much lessens the care of providing against the wants of old Age.

I have heard it remarked that the Poor in Protestant Countries on the Continent of Europe, are generally more industrious than those of Popish Countries, may not the more numerous foundations in the latter for the relief of the poor have some effect towards rendering them less provident. To relieve the misfortunes of our fellow creatures is concurring with the Deity, 'tis Godlike, but if we provide encouragements for Laziness, and supports for Folly, may it not be found fighting against the order of God and Nature, which perhaps has appointed Want and Misery as the proper

Punishments for, and Cautions against as well as necessary consequences of Idleness and Extravagancy.

Whenever we attempt to mend the scheme of Providence and to interfere in the Government of the World, we had need be very circumspect lest we do more harm than Good. In New England they once thought Black-birds useless and mischievous to their corn, they made [Laws] to destroy them, the consequence was, the Black-birds were diminished but a kind of Worms which devoured their Grass, and which the Black-birds had been used to feed on encreased prodigiously; Then finding their Loss in Grass much greater than their saving to corn they wished again for their Black-birds.

We had here some years since a Transylvanian Tartar, who had travelled much in the East, and came hither merely to see the West, intending to go home thro' the spanish West Indies, China &c. He asked me one day what I thought might be the Reason that so many and such numerous nations, as the Tartars in Europe and Asia, the Indians in America, and the Negroes in Africa, continued a wandring careless Life, and refused to live in Cities, and to cultivate the arts they saw practiced by the civilized part of Mankind. While I was considering what answer to make him; I'll tell you, says he in his broken English, God make man for Paradise, he make him for to live lazy; man make God angry, God turn him out of Paradise, and bid him work; man no love work; he want to go to Paradise again, he want to live lazy; so all mankind love lazy. Howe'er this may be it seems certain, that the hope of becoming at some time of Life free from the necessity of care and Labour, together with fear of penury, are the mainsprings of most peoples industry.

To those indeed who have been educated in elegant plenty, even the provision made for the poor may appear misery, but to those who have scarce ever been better provided for, such provision may seem quite good and sufficient, these latter have then nothing to fear worse than their present Conditions, and scarce hope for any thing better than a Parish maintainance; so that there is only the difficulty of getting that maintainance allowed while they are able to work, or a little shame they suppose attending it, that can induce them to work at all, and what they do will only be from hand to mouth.

The proneness of human Nature to a life of ease, of freedom from care and labour appears strongly in the little success that has hitherto attended every attempt to civilize our American Indians, in their present way of living, almost all their Wants are supplied by the spontaneous Productions of Nature, with the addition of very little labour, if hunting and fishing may indeed be called labour when Game is so plenty, they visit us frequently, and see the advantages that Arts, Sciences, and compact Society procure us, they are not deficient in natural understanding and yet they have never shewn any Inclination to change their manner of life for ours, or to learn any of our Arts; When an Indian Child has been brought up among us, taught our language and habituated to our Customs, yet if he goes to see his relations and make one Indian Ramble with them, there is no perswading him ever to return, and that this is not natural [to them] merely as Indians, but as men, is plain from this, that when white persons of either sex have been taken prisoners young by the Indians, and lived a while among them, tho' ransomed by their Friends, and treated with all imaginable tenderness to prevail with them to stay among the English, yet in a Short time they become disgusted with our manner of life, and the care and pains that are necessary to support it, and take the first good Opportunity of escaping again into the Woods, from whence there is no reclaiming them. One instance I remember to have heard, where the person was brought home to possess a good Estate; but finding some care necessary to keep it together, he relinquished it to a younger Brother, reserving to himself nothing but a gun and a match-Coat, with which he took his way again to the Wilderness.

Though they have few but natural wants and those easily supplied. But with us are infinite Artificial wants, no less craving than those of Nature, and much more difficult to satisfy; so that I am apt to imagine that close Societies subsisting by Labour and Arts, arose first not from choice, but from necessity: When numbers being driven by war from their hunting grounds and prevented by seas or by other nations were crowded together into some narrow Territories, which without labour would not afford them Food. However as matters [now] stand with us, care and industry seem absolutely necessary to our well being; they should therefore have every Encouragement we can invent, and not one Motive to diligence be subtracted, and the support of the Poor should not be by maintaining them in Idleness, But by employing them in some kind of labour suited to their Abilities of body &c. as I am informed of late begins to be the practice in many parts of England, where work houses are erected for that purpose. If these were general I should think the Poor would be more careful and work voluntarily and lay up something for themselves against a rainy day, rather than run the risque of being obliged to work at the pleasure of others for a bare subsistence and that too under confinement.

The little value Indians set on what we prize so highly under the name of Learning appears from a pleasant passage that happened some years since at a Treaty between one of our Colonies and the Six Nations; when every thing had been settled to the Satisfaction of both sides, and nothing remained but a mutual exchange of civilities, the English Commissioners told the Indians, they had in their Country a College for the instruction of Youth who were there taught various languages, Arts, and Sciences; that there was a particular foundation in favour of the Indians to defray the expense of the Education of any of their sons who should desire to take the Benefit of it. And now if the Indians would accept of the Offer, the English would take half a dozen of their brightest lads and bring them up in the Best manner; The Indians after consulting on the proposal replied that it was remembered some of their Youths had formerly been educated in that College, but it had been observed that for a long time after they returned to their Friends, they were absolutely good for nothing being neither acquainted with the true methods of killing deer, catching Beaver or surprizing an enemy. The Proposition however, they looked on as a mark of the kindness and good will of the English to the Indian Nations which merited a grateful return; and therefore if the English Gentlemen would send a dozen or two of their Children to Onondago the great Council would take care of their Education, bring them up in really what was the best manner and make men of them.

I am perfectly of your mind, that measures of great Temper are necessary with the Germans: and am not without Apprehensions, that thro' their indiscretion or Ours, or both, great disorders and inconveniences may one day arise among us; Those who come hither are generally of the most ignorant Stupid Sort of their own Nation, and as Ignorance is often attended with Credulity when Knavery would mislead it, and with Suspicion when Honesty would set it right; and as few of the English understand the German Language, and so cannot address them either from the Press or Pulpit, 'tis almost impossible to remove any prejudices they once entertain. Their own Clergy have very little influence over the people; who seem to take an uncommon pleasure in abusing and discharging the Minister on every trivial occasion. Not being used to Liberty, they know not how to make a modest use of it; and as Kolben says of the young Hottentots, that they are not esteemed men till they have shewn their manhood by beating their mothers, so these seem to think themselves not free, till they can feel their liberty in abusing and insulting their Teachers. Thus they are under no restraint of Ecclesiastical Government; They behave, however, submissively enough, at present to the Civil Government which I wish they may continue to do: For I remember when they modestly declined intermeddling in our Elections, but now they come in droves, and carry all before them, except in one or two Counties; Few of their children in the Country learn English; they import many Books from Germany; and of the six printing houses in the Province, two are entirely German, two half German half English, and but two entirely English; They have one German News-paper, and one half German. Advertisments intended to be general are now printed in Dutch and English; the Signs in our Streets have inscriptions in both languages, and in some places only German: They begin of late to make all their Bonds and other legal Writings in their own Language, which (though I think it ought not to be) are allowed good in our Courts, where the German Business so encreases that there is continual need of Interpreters; and I suppose in a few years they will be also necessary in the Assembly, to tell one half of our Legislators what the other half say; In short unless the stream of their importation could be turned from this to other Colonies, as you very judiciously propose, they will soon so out number us, that all the advantages we have will not [in My Opinion] be able to preserve our language, and even our Government will become precarious. The French who watch all advantages, are now [themselves] making a German settlement back of us in the Ilinoes Country, and by means of those Germans they may in time come to an understanding with ours, and indeed in the last war our Germans shewed a general disposition that seems to bode us no good; for when the English who were not Quakers, alarmed by the danger arising from the defenceless state of our Country entered unanimously into an Association within this Government and the lower Countries [Counties] raised armed and Disciplined [near] 10,000 men, the Germans except a very few in proportion to their numbers refused to engage in it, giving out one among another, and even in print, that if they were quiet the French should they take the Country would not molest them; at the same time abusing the Philadelphians for fitting out Privateers against the Enemy; and representing the trouble hazard and Expence of defending the Province, as a greater inconvenience than any that might be expected from a change of Government. Yet I am not for refusing entirely to admit them into our Colonies: all that seems to be necessary is, to distribute them more equally, mix them with the English, establish English Schools where they are now too thick settled, and take some care to prevent the practice lately fallen into by some of the Ship Owners, of sweeping the German Gaols to make up the number of their Passengers. I say I am not against the Admission of Germans in general, for they have their Virtues, their industry and frugality is exemplary; They are excellent husbandmen and contribute greatly to the improvement of a Country.

I pray God long to preserve to Great Britain the English Laws, Manners, Liberties and Religion notwithstanding the complaints so frequent in Your public papers, of the prevailing corruption and degeneracy of your People; I know you have a great deal of Virtue still subsisting among you, and I hope the Constitution is not so near a dissolution, as some seem to apprehend; I do not think you are generally become such Slaves to your Vices, as to draw down that *Justice* Milton speaks of when he says that

> ——sometimes Nations will descend so low
> From reason, which is virtue, that no Wrong,
> But Justice, and some fatal curse annex'd
> Deprives them of their *outward* liberty,
> Their *inward* lost. Parad: lost.[1]

In history we find that Piety, Public Spirit and military Prowess have their Flows, as well as their ebbs, in every nation, and that the Tide is never so low but it may rise again; But should this dreaded fatal change happen in my time, how should I even in the midst of the Affliction rejoice, if we have been able to preserve those invaluable treasures, and can invite the good among you to come and partake of them! O let not Britain seek to oppress us, but like an affectionate parent endeavour to secure freedom to her children; they may be able one day to assist her in defending her own——Whereas a Mortification begun in the Foot may spread upwards to the destruction of the nobler parts of the Body.

I fear I have [already] extended this rambling letter beyond your patience, and therefore conclude with requesting your acceptance of the inclosed Pamphlet from Sir Your most humble servant.

[Papers 4:479–86]

[1] [*Paradise Lost*, 12:97–101.]

CHAPTER 18
To Peter Collinson
(September 1753–January 1754)

With regard to the Germans, I think Methods of great tenderness should be used, and nothing that looks like a hardship be imposed. Their fondness for their own Language and Manners is natural: It is not a Crime. When People are induced to settle a new Country by a promise of Privileges, that Promise should be bonâ fide performed, and the Privileges never infringed: If they are, how shall we be believed another time, when we want to People another Colony? Your first Proposal of establishing English Schools among them is an excellent one; provided they are free Schools, and can be supported. As your Poet, Young says

> . . . The Dutch
> Wou'd fain save all the Money that they Touch.

If they can have English Schooling gratis, as much as they love their own Language they will not pay for German Schooling.

The second Proposal, of an Act of Parliament, disqualifying them to accept of any Post of Trust, Profit or Honour, unless they can speak English intelligbly, will be justifyed by the reason of the thing, and will not seem an hardship; But it does not seem necessary to include the Children. If the Father takes pains to learn English, the same Sense of its usefulness will induce him to teach it to his Children.

The third Proposal, to invalidate all Deeds, Bonds or other legal Writings written in a foreign Language (Wills made on a Man's Death Bed excepted, as an English Scribe may not always be at hand) is not at all amiss. I think it absolutely necessary, and that it cannot be complain'd of.

The fourth Proposal, to suppress all German Printing houses, &c. will seem too harsh. As will the fifth, to prohibit all Importation of German Books. If the other Methods are taken, the Printing Houses will in time wear out, as they become unnecessary, and the Importation of Books will cease of itself.

The sixth Proposal of Encouraging Intermarriages between the English and Germans, by Donations, &c. I think would either cost too much, or have no Effect. The German Women are generally so disagreable to an English Eye, that it wou'd require great Portions to induce Englishmen to marry them. Nor would the German Ideas of Beauty generally agree with our Women; *dick and starcke*, that is, *thick and strong*, always enters into their Description of a pretty Girl: for the value of a Wife with them consists much in the Work she is able to do. So that it would require a round Sum with an English Wife to make up to a Dutch Man the difference in Labour and Frugality. This Matter therefore I think had better be left to itself.

The seventh Proposal of discouraging the sending more Germans to Pennsylvania, is a good one; those who are already here would approve of it. They complain of the late great Importations, and wish they could be prevented. They say, the Germans that came formerly, were a good sober industrious honest People; but now Germany is swept, scour'd and scumm'd by the Merchants, who, for the gain by the Freight, bring all the Refuse Wretches poor and helpless who are burthensome to the old Settlers, or Knaves and Rascals that live by Sharking and Cheating them. The Stream may therefore be well enough turned to the other Colonies you mention. And our Land Owners will have no Cause to complain, if English, Welsh, and Protestant Irish are encouraged to come hither instead of Germans, which will still continue the rising Value of Lands; and at the same time by mixing with our Germans restore by degrees the Predominancy of our Language &c. Nor would the British Subjects be miss'd at home, if my Opinions in the Paper I formerly sent on the Peopling of Countries, are right, as I still think they really are.

[Papers 5:158–60]

CHAPTER 19
Join or Die
(9 May 1754)

Friday last an Express arrived here from Major Washington, with Advice, that Mr. Ward, Ensign of Capt. Trent's Company, was compelled to surrender his small Fort in the Forks of Monongahela to the French, on the 17th past; who fell down from Venango with a Fleet of 360 Battoes and Canoes, upwards of 1000 Men, and 18 Pieces of Artillery, which they planted against the Fort; and Mr. Ward having but 44 Men, and no Cannon to make a proper Defence, was obliged to surrender on Summons, capitulating to march out with their Arms, &c. and they had accordingly joined Major Washington, who was advanced with three Companies of the Virginia Forces, as far as the New Store near the Allegheny Mountains, where the Men were employed in clearing a Road for the Cannon, which were every Day expected with Col. Fry, and the Remainder of the Regiment.——We hear farther, that some few of the English Traders on the Ohio escaped, but 'tis supposed the greatest Part are taken, with all their Goods, and Skins, to the Amount of near 20,000£. The Indian Chiefs, however, have dispatch'd Messages to Pennsylvania, and Virginia, desiring that the English would not be discouraged, but send out their Warriors to join them, and drive the French out of the Country before they fortify; otherwise the Trade will be lost, and, to their great Grief, an eternal Separation made between the Indians and their Brethren the English. 'Tis farther said, that besides the French that came down from Venango, another Body of near 400 is coming up the Ohio; and that 600 French Indians, of the Chippaways and Ottaways, are coming down Siota River, from the Lake, to join them; and many more French are expected from Canada; the Design being to establish themselves, settle their Indians, and build Forts just on the Back of our Settlements in all our Colonies; from which Forts, as they did from Crown-Point, they may send out their Parties to kill and scalp the Inhabitants, and ruin the Frontier Counties.

Accordingly we hear, that the Back Settlers in Virginia, are so terrify'd by the Murdering and Scalping of the Family last Winter, and the Taking of this Fort, that they begin already to abandon their Plantations, and remove to Places of more Safety.——The Confidence of the French in this Undertaking seems well-grounded on the present disunited State of the British Colonies, and the extreme Difficulty of bringing so many different Governments and Assemblies to agree in any speedy and effectual Measures for our common Defence and Security; while our Enemies have the very great Advantage of being under one Direction, with one Council, and one Purse. Hence, and from the great Distance of Britain, they presume that they may with Impunity violate the most solemn Treaties subsisting between the two Crowns, kill, seize and imprison our Traders, and confiscate their Effects at Pleasure (as they have done for several Years past) murder and scalp our Farmers, with their Wives and Children, and take an easy Possession of such Parts of the British Territory as they find most convenient for them; which if they are permitted to do, must end in the Destruction of the British Interest, Trade and Plantations in America.

[Gazette, 9 May 1754]

CHAPTER 20

Reasons and Motives for the Albany Plan of Union

(July 1754)

1. *Reasons and Motives on which the Plan of Union was formed*

The Commissioners from a number of the northern colonies being met at *Albany*, and considering the difficulties that have always attended the most necessary general measures for the common defence, or for the annoyance of the enemy, when they were to be carried through the several particular assemblies of all the colonies; some assemblies being before at variance with their governors or councils, and the several branches of the government not on terms of doing business with each other; others taking the opportunity, when their concurrence is wanted, to push for favourite laws, powers, or points that they think could not at other times be obtained, and so *creating* disputes and quarrels; one assembly waiting to see what another will do, being afraid of doing more than its share, or desirous of doing less; or refusing to do any thing, because its country is not at present so much exposed as others, or because another will reap more immediate advantage; from one or other of which causes, the assemblies of six (out of seven) colonies applied to, had granted no assistance to *Virginia*, when lately invaded by the *French*, though purposely convened, and the importance of the occasion earnestly urged upon them: Considering moreover, that one principal encouragement to the French, in invading and insulting the British American dominions, was their knowledge of our disunited state, and of our weakness arising from such want of union; and that from hence different colonies were, at different times, extremely harassed, and put to great expence both of blood and treasure, who would have remained in peace, if the enemy had had cause to fear the drawing on themselves the resentment and power of the whole; the said Commissioners, considering also the present incroachments of the French, and the mischievous consequences that may be expected from them, if not opposed with our force, came to an unanimous resolution,——*That an union of the colonies is absolutely necessary for their preservation.*

The *manner* of forming and establishing this union was the next point. When it was considered that the colonies were seldom all in equal danger at the same time, or equally near the danger, or equally sensible of it; that some of them had particular interests to manage, with which an union might interfere; and that they were extremely jealous of each other;——it was thought impracticable to obtain a joint agreement of all the colonies to an union, in which the expence and burthen of defending any of them should be divided among them all; and if ever acts of assembly in all the colonies could be obtained for that purpose, yet as any colony, on the least dissatisfaction, might repeal its own act and thereby withdraw itself from the union, it would not be a stable one, or such as could be depended on: for if only one colony should, on any disgust withdraw itself, others might think it unjust and unequal that they, by continuing in the union, should be at the expence of defending a colony which refused to bear its proportionable part, and would therefore one after another, withdraw, till the whole crumbled into its original parts.——Therefore the commissioners came to another previous resolution, viz. *That it was necessary the union should be established by act* of *parliament.*

They then proceeded to sketch out a *plan of union*, which they did in a plain and concise manner, just sufficient to shew their sentiments of the kind of union that would best suit the circumstances of the colonies, be most agreeable to the people, and more effectually promote his Majesty's service and the general interest of the British empire.——This was respectfully sent to the assemblies of the several colonies for their consideration, and to receive such alterations and improvements as they should think fit and necessary; after which it was proposed to be transmitted to *England* to be perfected, and the establishment of it there humbly solicited.

This was as much as the commissioners could do.

II. Reasons against partial Unions

It was proposed by some of the Commissioners to form the colonies into two or three distinct unions; but for these reasons that proposal was dropped even by those that made it; [viz.]

1. In all cases where the strength of the whole was necessary to be used against the enemy, there would be the same difficulty in degree, to bring the several unions to unite together, as now the several colonies; and consequently the same delays on our part and advantage to the enemy.

2. Each union would separately be weaker than when joined by the whole, obliged to exert more force, be more oppressed by the expence, and the enemy less deterred from attacking it.

3. Where particular colonies have *selfish views*, as New York with regard to Indian trade and lands; or are *less exposed*, being covered by others, as New Jersey, Rhode Island, Connecticut, Maryland; or have *particular whims and prejudices* against warlike measures in general, as Pennsylvania, where the Quakers predominate; such colonies would have more weight in a partial union, and be better able to oppose and obstruct the measures necessary for the general good, than where they are swallowed up in the general union.

4. The *Indian* trade would be better regulated by the union of the whole than by partial unions. And as *Canada* is chiefly supported by that trade, if it could be drawn into the hands of the *English*, (as it might be if the Indians were supplied on moderate terms, and by honest traders appointed by and acting for the public) that alone would contribute greatly to the weakening of our enemies.

5. The establishing of new colonies westward on the *Ohio* and the lakes, (a matter of considerable importance to the increase of *British* trade and power, to the breaking that of the *French*, and to the protection and security of our present colonies,) would best be carried on by a joint union.

6. It was also thought, that by the frequent meetings-together of commissioners or representatives from all the colonies, the circumstances of the whole would be better known, and the good of the whole better provided for; and that the colonies would by this connection learn to consider themselves, not as so many independent states, but as members of the same body; and thence be more ready to afford assistance and support to each other, and to make diversions in favour even of the most distant, and to join cordially in any expedition for the benefit of all against the common enemy.

These were the principal reasons and motives for forming the plan of union as it stands. To which may be added this, that as the union of the [*the remainder of this article is lost*].

III. *Plan of a proposed Union of the several Colonies of* Massachusett's Bay, New Hampshire, Connecticut, Rhode Island, New York, New Jersey, Pensylvania, Maryland, Virginia, North Carolina, and South Carolina *for their mutual Defence and Security, and for extending the* British *Settlements in* North America, *with the Reasons and Motives for each Article of the Plan [as far as could be remembered]*

It is proposed.——That humble application be made for an act of parliament of Great Britain, by virtue of which one general government may be formed in America including all the said colonies, within and under which government each colony may retain its present constitution, except to the particulars wherein a change may be directed by the said act as hereafter follows.

President General, and Grand Council

That the said general government be administered by a President General to be appointed and supported by the crown; and a Grand Council to be chosen by the representatives of the people of the several colonies met in their respective assemblies.

It was thought that it would be best the President General should be supported as well as appointed by the crown; that so all disputes between him and the Grand Council concerning his salary might be prevented; as such disputes have been frequently of mischievous consequence in particular colonies, especially in time of public danger. The quit-rents of crown-lands in America, might in a short time be sufficient for this purpose.——The choice of members for the grand council is placed in the house of representatives of each government, in order to give the people a share in this new general government, as the crown has its share by the appointment of the President General.

But it being proposed by the gentlemen of the council of *New York*, and some other counsellors among the commissioners, to alter the plan in this particular, and to give the governors and council of the several provinces a share in the choice of the grand council, or at least a power of approving and confirming or of disallowing the choice made by the house of representatives, it was said:

"That the government or constitution proposed to be formed by the plan, consists of two branches; a President General appointed by the crown, and a council chosen by the people, or by the people's representatives, which is the same thing.

"That by a subsequent article, the council chosen by the people can effect nothing without the consent of the President General appointed by the crown; the crown possesses therefore full one half of the power of this constitution.

"That in the British constitution, the crown is supposed to possess but one third, the Lords having their share.

"That this constitution seemed rather more favourable for the crown.

"That it is essential to English liberty, [that] the subject should not be taxed but by his own consent or the consent of his elected representatives.

"That taxes to be laid and levied by this proposed constitution will be proposed and agreed to by the representatives of the people, if the plan in this particular be preserved:

"But if the proposed alteration should take place, it seemed as if matters may be so managed as that the crown shall finally have the appointment not only of the President General, but of a majority of the grand council; for, seven out of eleven governors and councils are appointed by the crown:

"And so the people in all the colonies would in effect be taxed by their governors.

"It was therefore apprehended that such alterations of the plan would give great dissatisfaction, and that the colonies could not be easy under such a power in governors, and such an infringement of what they take to be *English* liberty.

"Besides, the giving a share in the choice of the grand council would not be equal with respect to all the colonies, as their constitutions differ. In some, both governor and council are appointed by the crown. In others, they are both appointed by the proprietors. In some, the people have a share in the choice of the council; in others, both government and council are wholly chosen by the people. But the house of representatives is every where chosen by the people; and therefore placing the right of choosing the grand council in the representatives, is equal with respect to all.

"That the grand council is intended to represent all the several houses of representatives of the colonies, as a house of representatives doth the several towns or counties of a colony. Could all the people of a colony be consulted and unite in public measures, a house of representatives would be needless: and could all the assemblies conveniently consult and unite in general measures, the grand council would be unnecessary.

"That a house of commons or the house of representatives, and the grand council, are thus alike in their nature and intention. And as it would seem improper that the King or house of Lords should have a power of disallowing or appointing members of the house of commons;——so likewise that a governor and council appointed by the crown should have a power of disallowing or appointing members of the grand council, (who, in this constitution, are to be the representatives of the people.)

"If the governors and councils therefore were to have a share in the choice of any that are to conduct this general government, it should seem more proper that they chose the President General. But this being an office of great trust and importance to the nation, it was thought better to be filled by the immediate appointment of the crown.

"The power proposed to be given by the plan to the grand council is only a concentration of the powers of the several assemblies in certain points for the general welfare; as the power of the President General is of the powers of the several governors in the same points.

"And as the choice therefore of the grand council by the representatives of the people, neither gives the people any new powers, nor diminishes the power of the crown, it was thought and hoped the crown would not disapprove of it."

Upon the whole, the commissioners were of opinion, that the choice was most properly placed in the representatives of the people.

Election of Members

That within months after the passing such act, the house of representatives that happen to be sitting within that time, or that shall be especially for that purpose convened, may and shall choose members for the grand council, in the following proportion, that is to say,

Massachussett's Bay 7
New Hampshire 2
Connecticut 5
Rhode Island 2
New York 4
New Jerseys 3

Pensylvania	6
Maryland	4
Virginia	7
North Carolina	4
South Carolina	4
	48

It was thought that if the least colony was allowed two, and the others in proportion, the number would be very great and the expence heavy; and that less than two would not be convenient, as a single person, being by any accident prevented appearing at the meeting, the colony he ought to appear for would not be represented. That as the choice was not immediately popular, they would be generally men of good abilities for business, and men of reputation for integrity; and that forty-eight such men might be a number sufficient. But, though it was thought reasonable that each colony should have a share in the representative body in some degree, according to the proportion it contributed to the general treasury; yet the proportion of wealth or power of the colonies is not to be judged by the proportion here fixed; because it was at first agreed that the greatest colony should not have more than seven members, nor the least less than two: and the settling these proportions between these two extremes was not nicely attended to, as it would find itself, after the first election from the sums brought into the treasury, as by a subsequent article.

Place of first Meeting

——who shall meet for the first time at the city of *Philadelphia* in Pennsylvania, being called by the President General as soon as conveniently may be after his appointment.

Philadelphia was named as being the nearer the center of the colonies where the Commissioners would be well and cheaply accommodated. The high-roads through the whole extent, are for the most part very good, in which forty or fifty miles a day may very well be and frequently are travelled. Great part of the way may likewise be gone by water.——In summer-time the passages are frequently performed in a week from *Charles Town* to Philadelphia and New York; and from *Rhode Island* to New York through the Sound in two or three days; and from *New York* to Philadelphia by water and land in two days, by stage-boats and wheel-carriages that set out every other day. The journey from *Charles*

Town to Philadelphia may likewise be facilitated by boats running up Chesapeak Bay three hundred miles.——But if the whole journey be performed on horseback, the most distant members, *(viz.* the two from *New Hampshire* and from *South Caro*lina) may probably render themselves at Philadelphia in fifteen or twenty-days;——the majority may be there in much less time.

New Election

That there shall be a new election of the members of the Grand Council every three years; and on the death or resignation of any member, his place shall be supplied by a new choice at the next sitting of the assembly of the colony he represented.

Some colonies have annual assemblies, some continue during a governor's pleasure; three years was thought a reasonable medium, as affording a new member time to improve himself in the business, and to act after such improvement; and yet giving opportunities, frequent enough, to change him if he has misbehaved.

Proportion of Members after the first three Years

That after the first three years, when the proportion of money arising out of each colony to the general treasury can be known, the number of members to be chosen for each colony shall from time to time, in all ensuing elections, be regulated by that proportion (yet so as that the number to be chosen by any one province be not more than seven, nor less than two.)

By a subsequent article it is proposed, that the general council shall lay and levy such general duties as to them may appear most equal and least burthensome, &c. Suppose, for instance, they lay a small duty or excise on some commodity imported into or made in the colonies, and pretty generally and equally used in all of them; as rum perhaps, or wine: the yearly produce of this duty or excise, if fairly collected, would be in some colonies greater, in others less, as the colonies are greater or smaller. When the collectors accounts are brought in, the proportions will appear; and from them it is proposed to regulate the proportion of representatives to be chosen at the next general election, within the limits however of seven and two. These numbers may therefore vary in course of years, as the colonies may in the growth and increase of people. And thus the quota of tax from each colony would naturally vary with its circumstances; thereby preventing all disputes and dissatisfactions about the just proportions due from each; which might otherwise produce pernicious consequences, and destroy the harmony and good agreement that ought to subsist between the several parts of the union.

Meetings of the Grand Council, and Call

That the Grand Council shall meet once in every year and oftener if occasion require, at such time and place as they shall adjourn to at the last preceding meeting, or as they shall be called to meet at by the President General on any emergency; he having first obtained in writing the consent of seven of the members to such call, and sent due and timely notice to the whole.

It was thought, in establishing and governing new colonies or settlements, regulating *Indian* trade, *Indian* treaties, &c. there would be every year sufficient business arise to require at least one meeting, and at such meeting many things might be suggested for the benefit of all the colonies. This annual meeting may either be at a time or place certain, to be fixed by the President General and grand council at their first meeting; or left at liberty, to be at such time and place as they shall adjourn to, or be called to meet at by the President General.

In *time of war* it seems convenient, that the meeting should be in that colony, which is nearest the seat of action.

The power of calling them on any emergency seemed necessary to be vested in the President General; but that such power might not be wantonly used to harass the members, and oblige them to make frequent long journies to little purpose, the consent of seven at least to such call was supposed a convenient guard.

Continuance

That the Grand Council have power to choose their speaker; and shall neither be dissolved, prorogued, nor continued sitting longer than six weeks at one time; without their own consent or the special command of the crown.

The speaker should be presented for approbation; it being convenient, to prevent misunderstandings and disgusts, that the mouth of the council should be a person agreeable, if possible, both to the council and the President General.

Governors have sometimes wantonly exercised the power of proroguing or continuing the sessions of assemblies, merely to harass the members and compel a compliance; and sometimes dissolve them on slight disgusts. This it was feared might be done by the President General, if not provided against: and the inconvenience and hardship would be greater in the general government than in particular colonies, in proportion to the distance the members must be from home, during sittings, and the long journies some of them must necessarily take.

Members' Allowance

That the members of the Grand Council shall be allowed for their service ten shillings sterling *per diem*, during their session and journey to and from the place of meeting; twenty miles to be reckoned a day's journey.

It was thought proper to allow *some* wages, lest the expence might deter some suitable persons from the service;——and not to allow *too great* wages, lest unsuitable persons should be tempted to cabal for the employment for the sake of gain.——Twenty miles was set down as a day's journey to allow for accidental hinderances on the road, and the greater expences of travelling than residing at the place of meeting.

Assent of President General and his Duty

That the assent of the President General be requisite to all acts of the Grand Council; and that it be his office and duty to cause them to be carried into execution.

The assent of the President General to all acts of the grand council was made necessary, in order to give the crown its due share of influence in this government, and connect it with that of *Great Britain*. The President General, besides one half of the legislative power, hath in his hands the whole executive power.

Power of President General and Grand Council Treaties of Peace and War

That the President General, with the advice of the Grand Council, hold or direct all Indian treaties in which the general interest of the colonies may be concerned; and make peace or declare war with Indian nations.

The power of making peace or war with *Indian* nations is at present supposed to be in every colony, and is expressly granted to some by charter, so that no new power is hereby intended to be granted to the colonies.—— But as, in consequence of this power, one colony might make peace with a nation that another was justly engaged in war with; or make war on slight occasions without the concurrence or approbation of neighbouring colonies, greatly endangered by it; or make particular treaties of neutrality in case of a general war, to their own private advantage in trade, by supplying the common enemy; of all which there have been instances——it was thought better to have all treaties of a general nature under a general direction; that so the good of the whole may be consulted and provided for.

Indian Trade

That they make such laws as they judge necessary for regulating all Indian trade.

Many quarrels and wars have arisen between the colonies and Indian nations, through the bad conduct of traders; who cheat the Indians after making them drunk, &c. to the great expence of the colonies both in blood and treasure. Particular colonies are so interested in the trade as not to be willing to admit such a regulation as might be best for the whole; and therefore it was thought best under a general direction.

Indian Purchases

That they make all purchases from Indians for the crown, of lands not now within the bounds of particular colonies or that shall not be within their bounds when some of them are reduced to more convenient dimensions.

Purchases from the Indians made by private persons, have been attended with many inconveniences. They have frequently interfered, and occasioned uncertainty of titles, many disputes and expensive law-suits, and hindered the settlement of the land so disputed. Then the Indians have been cheated by such private purchases, and discontent and wars have been the consequence. These would be prevented by public fair purchases.

Several of the colony charters in America extend their bounds to the *South Sea*, which may be perhaps three or four thousand miles in length to one or two hundred miles in breadth. It is supposed they must in time be reduced to dimensions more convenient for the common purposes of government.

Very little of the land in those grants is yet purchased of the Indians.

It is much cheaper to purchase of them, than to take and maintain the possession by force: for they are generally very reasonable in their demands for land; and the expence of guarding a large frontier against their incursions is vastly great; because all must be guarded and always guarded, as we know not where or when *to expect them.*

New Settlements

That they make new settlements on such purchases by granting lands in the King's name, reserving a quit-rent to the crown for the use of the general treasury.

It is supposed better that there should be one purchaser than many; and that the crown should be that purchaser, or the union in the name of the crown. By this means the bargains may be more easily made, the price not inhanced by numerous bidders, future disputes about private Indian purchases, and monopolies of vast tracts to particular persons (which are prejudicial to the settlement and peopling of a country) prevented; and the land being again granted in small tracts to the settlers, the quit-rents reserved may in time become a fund for support of government, for defence of the country, ease of taxes, &c.

Strong forts on the lakes, the Ohio, &c. may at the same time they secure our present frontiers, serve to defend new colonies settled under their protection; and such colonies would also mutually defend and support such forts, and better secure the friendship of the far Indians.

A particular colony has scarce strength enough to extend itself by new settlements, at so great a distance from the old: but the joint force of the union might suddenly establish a new colony or two in those parts, or extend an old colony to particular passes, greatly to the security of our present frontiers, increase of trade and people, breaking off the French communication between *Canada* and *Louisiana*, and speedy settlement of the intermediate lands.

The power of settling new colonies is therefore thought a valuable part of the plan; and what cannot so well be executed by two unions as by one.

Laws to govern them

That they make laws for regulating and governing such new settlements, till the crown shall think fit to form them into particular governments.

The making of laws suitable for the new colonies, it was thought would be properly vested in the President General and grand council; under whose protection they will at first necessarily be, and who would be well acquainted with their circumstances, as having settled them. When they are become sufficiently populous, they may by the crown, be formed into compleat and distinct governments.

The appointment of a Sub-president by the crown, to take place in case of the death or absence of the President General, would perhaps be an improvement of the plan; and if all the governors of particular provinces were to be formed into a standing council of state, for the advice and assistance of the President General, it might be another considerable improvement.

Raise Soldiers and equip Vessels, &c.

That they raise and pay soldiers and build forts for the defence of any of the colonies, and equip vessels of force to guard the coasts and protect the trade on the ocean, lakes, or great rivers; but they shall not impress men in any colony without the consent of the legislature.

It was thought, that quotas of men to be raised and paid by the several colonies, and joined for any public service, could not always be got together with the necessary expedition. For instance, suppose one thousand men should be wanted in *New Hampshire* on any emergency; to fetch them by fifties and hundreds out of every colony as far as *South Carolina*, would be inconvenient, the transportation chargeable, and the occasion perhaps passed before they could be assembled; and therefore that it would be best to raise them (by offering bounty-money and pay) near the place where they would be wanted, to be discharged again when the service should be over.

Particular colonies are at present backward to build forts at their own expence, which they say will be equally useful to their neighbouring colonies; who refuse to join, on a presumption that such forts *will* be built and kept up, though they contribute nothing. This unjust conduct weakens the whole; but the forts being for the good of the whole, it was thought best they should be built and maintained by the whole, out of the common treasury.

In the time of war, small vessels of force are sometimes necessary in the colonies to scour the coast of small privateers. These being provided by the Union, will be an advantage in turn to the colonies which are situated on the sea, and whose frontiers on the land-side, being covered by other colonies, reap but little immediate benefit from the advanced forts.

Power to make Laws, lay Duties, &c.

That for these purposes they have power to make laws, and lay and levy such general duties, imports, or taxes, as to them shall appear most equal and just, (considering the ability and other circumstances of the inhabitants in the several colonies,) and such as may be collected with the least inconvenience to the people; rather discouraging luxury, than loading industry with unnecessary burthens.

The laws which the President General and grand council are impowered to make, *are such only* as shall be necessary for the government of the settlements; the raising, regulating and paying soldiers for the general service; the regulating of Indian trade; and laying and collecting the general duties and taxes. (They should also have a power to restrain the exportation of provisions to the enemy from any of the colonies, on particular occasions, in time of war.) But it is not intended that they may interfere with the constitution and government of the particular colonies; who are to be left to their own laws, and to lay, levy, and apply their own taxes as before.

General Treasurer and Particular Treasurer

That they may appoint a General Treasurer and Particular Treasurer in each government when necessary; and from time to time may order the sums in the treasuries of each government into the general treasury; or draw on them for special payments, as they find most convenient.

The treasurers here meant are only for the general funds; and not for the particular funds of each colony, which remain in the hands of their own treasurers at their own disposal.

Money how to issue

Yet no money to issue but by joint orders of the President General and Grand Council; except where sums have been appropriated to particular purposes, and the President General is previously impowered by an act to draw for such sums.

To prevent misapplication of the money, or even application that might be dissatisfactory to the crown or the people, it was thought necessary to join the President General and grand council in all issues of money.

Accounts

That the general Accounts shall be yearly settled and reported to the several assemblies.

By communicating the accounts yearly to each assembly, they will be satisfied of the prudent and honest conduct of their representatives in the grand council.

Quorum

That a quorum of the Grand Council impowered to act with the President General, do consist of twenty-five members; among whom there shall be one or more from a majority of the colonies.

The quorum seems large, but it was thought it would not be satisfactory to the colonies in general, to have matters of importance to the whole transacted by a smaller number, or even by this number of twenty-five, unless there were among them one at least from a majority of the colonies; because otherwise the whole quorum being made up of members from three or four colonies at one end of the union, something might be done that would not be equal with respect to the rest, and thence dissatisfactions and discords might rise to the prejudice of the whole.

Laws to be transmitted

That the laws made by them for the purposes aforesaid shall not be repugnant, but, as near as may be, agreeable to the laws of England, and shall be transmitted to the King in council for approbation as soon as may be after their passing; and if not disapproved within three years after presentation, to remain in force.

This was thought necessary for the satisfaction of the crown, to preserve the connection of the parts of the *British* empire with the whole, of the members with the head, and to induce greater care and circumspection in making of the laws, that they be good in themselves and for the general benefit.

Death of the President General

That in case of the death of the President General, the speaker of the Grand Council for the time being shall succeed, and be vested with the same powers and authorities, to continue till the King's pleasure be known.

It might be better, perhaps, as was said before, if the crown appointed a Vice President, to take place on the death or absence of the President General; for so we should be more sure of a suitable person at the head of the colonies. On the death or absence of both, the speaker to take place (or rather the eldest King's-governor) till his Majesty's pleasure be known.

Officers how appointed

That all military commission officers, whether for land or sea service, to act under this general constitution, shall be nominated by the President General; but the approbation of the Grand Council is to be obtained, before they receive their commissions. And all civil officers are to be nominated by the Grand Council, and to receive the President General's approbation before they officiate.

It was thought it might be very prejudicial to the service, to have officers appointed unknown to the people, or unacceptable; the generality of Americans serving willingly under officers they know; and not caring to engage in the service under strangers, or such as are often appointed by governors through favour or interest. The service here meant, is not the stated settled service in standing troops; but any sudden and short service, either for defence of our own colonies, or invading the enemies country; (such as, the expedition to *Cape Breton* in the last war; in which many substantial farmers and tradesmen engaged as common soldiers under officers of their own country, for whom they had an esteem and affection; who would not have engaged in a standing army, or under officers from England.)——It was therefore thought best to give the council the power of approving the officers, which the people will look upon as a great security of their being good men. And without some such provision as this, it was thought the expence of engaging men in the service on any emergency would be much greater, and the number who could be induced to engage much less; and that therefore it would be most for the King's service and general benefit of the nation, that the prerogative should relax a little in this particular throughout all the colonies in America; as it had already done much more in the charters of some particular colonies, viz. *Connecticut* and *Rhode Island.*

The civil officers will be chiefly treasurers and collectors of taxes; and the suitable persons are most likely to be known by the council.

Vacancies how supplied

But in case of vacancy by death, or removal of any officer civil or military under this constitution, the governor of the province in which such vacancy happens, may appoint till the pleasure of the President General and Grand Council can be known.

The vacancies were thought best supplied by the governors in each province, till a new appointment can be regularly made; otherwise the service might suffer before the meeting of the President General and grand council.

Each Colony may defend itself on Emergency, &c.

That the particular military as well as civil establishments in each colony remain in their present state, the general constitution notwithstanding; and that on sudden emergencies any colony may defend itself and lay the accounts of expence thence arising before the President General and general council, who may allow and order payment of the same as far as they judge such accounts just and reasonable.

Otherwise the Union of the whole would weaken the parts, contrary to the design of the union. The accounts are to be judged of by the President General and grand council, and allowed if found reasonable: this was thought necessary to encourage colonies to defend themselves, as the expence would be light when borne by the whole; and also to check imprudent and lavish expence in such defences.

Remark, Feb. 9. 1789.

On Reflection it now seems probable, that if the foregoing Plan or some thing like it, had been adopted and carried into Execution, the subsequent Separation of the Colonies from the Mother Country might not so soon have happened, nor the Mischiefs suffered on both sides have occurred, perhaps during another Century. For the Colonies, if so united, would have really been, as they then thought themselves, sufficient to their own Defence, and being trusted with it, as by the Plan, an Army from Britain, for that purpose would have been unnecessary: The Pretences for framing the Stamp-Act would then not have existed, nor the other Projects for drawing a Revenue from America to Britain by Acts of Parliament, which were the Cause of the Breach, and attended with such terrible Expence of Blood and Treasure: so that the different Parts of the Empire might still have remained in Peace and Union. But the Fate of this Plan was singular. For tho' after many Days thorough Discussion of all its Parts in Congress it was unanimously agreed to, and Copies ordered to be sent to the Assembly of each Province for Concurrence, and one to the Ministry in England for the Approbation of the Crown. The Crown disapprov'd it, as having plac'd too much Weight in the democratic Part of the Constitution; and every Assembly as having allowed too much to Prerogative. So it was totally rejected.

[Vaughan 85–119; Papers 5:417]

CHAPTER 21
To Governor Shirley
(December 1754),
with a Preface
(8 February 1766)

To the PRINTER *of the* LONDON CHRONICLE.

Sir,

In July 1754, when from the encroachments of the French in America on the lands of the crown, and the interruption they gave to the commerce of this country among the Indians, a war was apprehended, commissioners from a number of the colonies met at Albany, to form a PLAN of UNION for their common defence. The plan they agreed to was in short this; "That a grand council should be formed, of members to be chosen by the assemblies and sent from all the colonies; which council, together with a governor general to be appointed by the crown, should be empowered to make general laws to raise money in all the colonies for the defence of the whole." This plan was sent to the government here for approbation: had it been approved and established by authority from hence, English America thought itself sufficiently able to cope with the French, without other assistance; several of the colonies having alone in former wars withstood the whole power of the enemy, unassisted not only by the mother country, but by any of the neighbouring provinces. The plan however was not approved here: but a new one was formed instead of it, by which it was proposed, that "the Governors of all the colonies, attended by one or two members of their respective councils, should assemble, concert measures for the defence of the whole, erect forts where they judged proper, and raise what troops they thought necessary, with power to draw on the treasury here for the sums that should be wanted; and the treasury to be reimbursed by a tax laid on the colonies by act of parliament." This new plan being communicated by Governor *Shirley* to a gentleman of Philadelphia, then in Boston, (who hath very eminently distinguished himself, before and since that time, in the literary world, and whose judgment, penetration and candor, as well as his readiness and ability to suggest, forward, or carry into execution every scheme of public utility, hath most deservedly endeared him not only to our fellow subjects throughout the whole continent of North-America, but to his numberless friends on this side the Atlantic) occasioned the following remarks from him, which perhaps may contribute in some degree to its being laid aside. As they very particularly show the then sentiments of the Americans on the subject of a parliamentary tax, *before* the French power in that country was subdued, and *before* the late restraints on their commerce, they satisfy me, and I hope they will convince your readers, contrary to what has been advanced by some of your correspondents, that those particulars have had no share in producing the present opposition to such a tax, nor in the disturbances occasioned by it; which these papers indeed do almost prophetically foretell. For this purpose, having accidentally fallen into my hands, they are communicated to you by one who is, not *partially*, but in the *most enlarged sense*,

A LOVER OF BRITAIN.

SIR, *Tuesday Morning* [December 3, 1754].

I return the loose sheets of the plan, with thanks to your Excellency for communicating them.

I apprehend, that excluding the *People* of the Colonies from all share in the choice of the Grand Council, will give extreme dissatisfaction, as well as the taxing them by Act of Parliament, where they have no Representative. It is very possible, that this general Government might be as well and faithfully administer'd without the people, as with them; but where heavy burthens are to be laid on them, it has been found useful to make it, as much as possible, their own act; for they bear better when they have, or think they have some share in the direction; and when any public measures are generally grievous or even distasteful to the people, the wheels of Government must move more heavily.

SIR, Boston. December 4.1754

I mention'd it Yesterday to your Excellency as my Opinion, that Excluding the People of the Colonies from all Share in the Choice of the Grand Council would probably give extreme Dissatisfaction, as well as the Taxing them by Act of Parliament where they have no Representative. In Matters of General Concern to the People, and especially where Burthens are to be laid upon them, it is of Use to consider as well what they will *be apt* to think and say, as what they *ought* to think: I shall, therefore, as your Excellency requires it of me, briefly mention what of either Kind occurs at present, on this Occasion.

First, they will say, and perhaps with Justice, that the Body of the People in the Colonies are as loyal, and as firmly attach'd to the present Constitution and reigning Family, as any Subjects in the King's Dominions; that there is no Reason to doubt the Readiness and Willingness of their Representatives to grant, from Time to Time, such Supplies, for the Defence of the Country, as shall be judg'd necessary, so far as their Abilities will allow: That the People in the Colonies, who are to feel the immediate Mischiefs of Invasion and Conquest by an Enemy, in the Loss of their Estates, Lives and Liberties, are likely to be better Judges of the Quantity of Forces necessary to be raised and maintain'd, Forts to be built and supported, and of their own Abilities to bear the Expence, than the Parliament of England at so great a Distance. That Governors often come to the Colonies meerly to make Fortunes, with which they intend to return to Britain, are not always Men of the best Abilities and Integrity, have no Estates here, nor any natural Connections with us, that should make them heartily concern'd for our Welfare; and might possibly be sometimes fond of raising and keeping up more Forces than necessary, from the Profits accruing to themselves, and to make Provision for their Friends and Dependents. That the Councellors in most of the Colonies, being appointed by the Crown, on the Recommendation of Governors, are often of small Estates, frequently dependant on the Governors for Offices, and therefore too much under Influence. That there is therefore great Reason to be jealous of a Power in such Governors and Councils, to raise such Sums as they shall judge necessary, by Draft on the Lords of the Treasury, to be afterwards laid on the Colonies by Act of Parliament, and paid by the People here; since they might abuse it, by projecting useless Expeditions, harrassing the People, and taking them from their Labour to execute such Projects, and meerly to create Offices and Employments, gratify their Dependants and divide Profits. That the Parliament of England is at a great Distance, subject to be misinform'd by such Governors and Councils, whose united Interests might probably secure them against the Effect of any Complaints from hence. That it is suppos'd an undoubted Right of Englishmen not to be taxed but by their own Consent given thro' their Representatives. That the Colonies have no Representatives in Parliament. That to propose taxing them by Parliament, and refusing them the Liberty of chusing a Representative Council, to meet in the Colonies, and consider and judge of the Necessity of any General Tax and the Quantum, shews a Suspicion of their Loyalty to the Crown, or Regard for their Country, or of their Common Sense and Understanding, which they have not deserv'd. That compelling the Colonies to pay Money without their Consent would be rather like raising Contributions in an Enemy's Country, than taxing of Englishmen for their own publick Benefit. That it would be treating them as a conquer'd People, and not as true British Subjects. That a Tax laid by the Representatives of the Colonies might easily be lessened as the Occasions should lessen, but being once laid by Parliament, under the Influence of the Representations made by Governors, would probably be kept up and continued, for the Benefit of Governors, to the grievous Burthen and Discouragement of the Colonies, and preventing their Growth and Increase. That a Power in Governors to march the Inhabitants from one End of the British and French Colonies to the other, being a Country of at least 1500 Miles square, without the Approbation or Consent of their Representatives first obtain'd to such Expeditions, might be grievous and ruinous to the People, and would put them on a Footing with the Subjects of France in Canada, that now groan under such Oppression from their Governor, who for two Years past has harrass'd them with long and destructive Marches to the Ohio. That if the Colonies in a Body may be well governed by Governors and Councils appointed by the Crown, without Representatives, particular Colonies may as well or better be so governed; a Tax may be laid on them all by Act of Parliament, for Support of Government, and their Assemblies be dismiss'd as a useless Part of their Constitution. That the Powers propos'd, by the Albany Plan of Union to be vested in a Grand Council representative of the People, even with Regard to Military Matters, are not so great as those the Colonies of Rhode Island and Connecticut are intrusted with, and have never abused; for by this Plan the President-General is appointed by the Crown, and controlls all by his Negative; but in those Governments the People chuse the Governor, and yet allow him no Negative. That the British Colonies, bordering on the French, are properly Frontiers of the British Empire; and that the Frontiers of an Empire are properly defended at the joint Expence of the Body of People in such Empire. It would now be thought hard, by Act of Parliament, to oblige the Cinque Ports or Sea Coasts of Britain to maintain the whole Navy, because they are more immediately defended by it, not allowing them, at the same Time, a Vote in chusing Members of Parliament: And if the Frontiers in America must bear the Expence of their own Defence, it seems hard to allow them no Share in Voting the Money, judging of the Necessity and Sum, or advising the Measures. That besides the Taxes necessary for the Defence of the Frontiers, the Colonies pay yearly great Sums to the Mother Country unnotic'd: For Taxes, paid in Britain by the Land holder or Artificer, must enter into and increase the Price of the Produce of Land, and of Manufactures made of it; and great Part of this is paid by Consumers in the Colonies, who thereby pay a considerable Part of the British Taxes. We are restrain'd in our Trade with Foreign Nations, and where we could be supplied with any Manufactures cheaper from them, but must buy the same dearer from Britain, the Difference of Price is a clear Tax to Britain. We are oblig'd to carry great Part of our Produce directly to Britain, and where the Duties there laid upon it lessens its Price to the Planter, or it sells for less than it would in Foreign Markets, the Difference is a Tax paid to Britain. Some Manufactures we could make, but are forbid, and must take them of British Merchants; the whole Price of these is a Tax paid to Britain. By our greatly increasing the *Consumption* and *Demand* of British Manufactures, their Price is considerably rais'd of late Years; the Advance is clear Profit to Britain, and enables its People better to pay great Taxes; and much of it being paid by us is clear Tax to Britain. In short, as we are not suffer'd to regulate our Trade, and restrain the Importation and Consumption of British Superfluities, (as Britain can the Consumption of Foreign Superfluities) our whole Wealth centers finally among the Merchants and Inhabitants of Britain, and if we make them richer, and enable them better to pay their Taxes, it is nearly the same as being taxed ourselves, and equally beneficial to the Crown. These Kind of Secondary Taxes, however, we do not complain of, tho' we have no Share in the Laying or Disposing of them; but to pay immediate heavy Taxes, in the Laying Appropriation or Disposition of which, we have no Part, and which perhaps we may know to be as unnecessary as grievous, must seem hard Measure to Englishmen, who cannot conceive, that by hazarding their Lives and Fortunes in subduing and settling new Countries, extending the Dominion and encreasing the Commerce of their Mother Nation, they have forfeited the native Rights of Britons, which they think ought rather to have been given them, as due to such Merit, if they had been before in a State of Slavery.

These, and such Kind of Things as these, I apprehend will be thought and said by the People, if the propos'd Alteration of the Albany Plan should take Place. Then, the Administration of the Board of Governors and Council so appointed, not having any Representative Body of the People to approve and unite in its Measures, and conciliate the Minds of the People to them, will probably become suspected and odious. Animosities and dangerous Feuds will arise between the Governors and Governed, and every Thing go into confusion. Perhaps I am too apprehensive in this Matter, but having freely given my Opinion and Reasons, your Excellency can better judge whether there be any Weight in them. And the Shortness of the Time allow'd me will I hope, in some Degree, excuse the Imperfections of this Scrawl.

With the greatest Respect and Fidelity, I am, Your Excellency's most obedient and most humble Servant.

SIR, *Boston, Dec. 22*, 1754

Since the conversation your Excellency was pleased to honour me with, on the subject of uniting the Colonies more intimately with Great Britain, by allowing them Representatives in Parliament, I have something further considered that matter, and am of opinion, that such an Union would be very acceptable to the Colonies, provided they had a reasonable number of Representatives allowed them; and that all the old Acts of Parliament restraining the trade or cramping the manufactures of the Colonies, be at the same time repealed, and the British Subjects on this side the water put, in those respects, on the same footing with those in Great Britain, 'till the new Parliament, representing the whole, shall think it for the interest of the whole to re-enact some or all of them: It is not that I imagine so many Representatives will be allowed the Colonies, as to have any great weight by their numbers; but I think there might be sufficient to occasion those laws to be better and more impartially considered, and perhaps to overcome the private interest of a petty corporation, or of any particular set of artificers or traders in England, who heretofore seem, in some instances, to have been more regarded than all the Colonies, or than was consistent with the general interest, or best national good. I think too, that the government of the Colonies by a Parliament, in which they are fairly represented, would be vastly more agreeable to the people, than the method lately attempted to be introduced by Royal Instructions, as well as more agreeable to the nature of an English Constitution, and to English Liberty; and that such laws as now seem to bear hard on the Colonies, would (when judged by such a Parliament for the best interest of the whole) be more chearfully submitted to, and more easily executed.

I should hope too, that by such an union, the people of Great Britain and the people of the Colonies would learn to consider themselves, not as belonging to different Communities with different Interests, but to one Community with one Interest, which I imagine would contribute to strengthen the whole, and greatly lessen the danger of future separations.

It is, I suppose, agreed to be the general interest of any state, that it's people be numerous and rich; men enow to fight in its defence, and enow to pay sufficient taxes to defray the charge; for these circumstances tend to the security of the state, and its protection from foreign power: But it seems not of so much importance whether the fighting be done by John or Thomas, or the tax paid by William or Charles: The iron manufacture employs and enriches British Subjects, but is it of any importance to the state, whether the manufacturers live at Birmingham or Sheffield, or both, since they are still within its bounds, and their wealth and persons at its command? Could the Goodwin Sands be laid dry by banks, and land equal to a large country thereby gain'd to England, and presently filled with English Inhabitants, would it be right to deprive such Inhabitants of the common privileges enjoyed by other Englishmen, the right of vending their produce in the same ports, or of making their own shoes, because a merchant, or a shoemaker, living on the old land, might fancy it more for his advantage to trade or make shoes for them? Would this be right, even if the land were gained at the expence of the state? And would it not seem less right, if the charge and labour of gaining the additional territory to Britain had been borne by the settlers themselves? And would not the hardship appear yet greater, if the people of the new country should be allowed no Representatives in the Parliament enacting such impositions? Now I look on the Colonies as so many Counties gained to Great Britain, and more advantageous to it than if they had been gained out of the sea around its coasts, and joined to its land: For being in different climates, they afford greater variety of produce, and materials for more manufactures; and being separated by the ocean, they increase much more its shipping and seamen; and since they are all included in the British Empire, which has only extended itself by their means; and the strength and wealth of the parts is the strength and wealth of the whole; what imports it to the general state, whether a merchant, a smith, or a hatter, grow rich in *Old* or *New* England? And if, through increase of people, two smiths are wanted for one employed before, why may not the *new* smith be allowed to live and thrive in the *new Country*, as well as the *old* one in the *Old*? In fine, why should the countenance of a state be *partially* afforded to its people, unless it be most in favour of those, who have most merit? and if there be any difference, those, who have most contributed to enlarge Britain's empire and commerce, encrease her strength, her wealth, and the numbers of her people, at the risque of their own lives and private fortunes in new and strange countries, methinks ought rather to expect some preference.

With the greatest respect and esteem I have the honour to be

Your Excellency's most obedient
and most humble servant.

[*The London Chronicle*, 8 February 1766; Papers 5:443–7]

CHAPTER 22

Preface to *Poor Richard Improved*: Father Abraham's Speech[1] (7 July 1757)

Courteous Reader,

I have heard that nothing gives an Author so great Pleasure, as to find his Works respectfully quoted by other learned Authors. This Pleasure I have seldom enjoyed; for tho' I have been, if I may say it without Vanity, an *eminent Author* of Almanacks annually now a full Quarter of a Century, my Brother Authors in the same Way, for what Reason I know not, have ever been very sparing in their Applauses; and no other Author has taken the least Notice of me, so that did not my Writings produce me some solid *Pudding*, the great Deficiency of *Praise* would have quite discouraged me.

I concluded at length, that the People were the best judges of my Merit; for they buy my Works; and besides, in my Rambles, where I am not personally known, I have frequently heard one or other of my Adages repeated, with, *as Poor Richard says*, at the End on't; this gave me some Satisfaction, as it showed not only that my Instructions were regarded, but discovered likewise some Respect for my Authority; and I own, that to encourage the Practice of remembering and repeating those wise Sentences, I have sometimes *quoted myself* with great Gravity.

Judge then how much I must have been gratified by an Incident I am going to relate to you. I stopt my Horse lately where a great Number of People were collected at a Vendue of Merchant Goods. The Hour of Sale not being come, they were conversing on the Badness of the Times, and one of the Company call'd to a plain clean old Man, with white Locks, *Pray, Father* Abraham, *what think you of the Times? Won't these heavy Taxes quite ruin the Country? How shall we be ever able to pay them? What*

[1] [Father Abraham's speech has also been printed under the title *The Way to Wealth*.]

would you advise us to?——Father *Abraham* stood up, and reply'd, If you'd have my Advice, I'll give it you in short, for a *Word to the Wise is enough*, and *many Words won't fill a Bushel*, as *Poor Richard says.* They join'd in desiring him to speak his Mind, and gathering round him, he proceeded as follows;

"Friends, says he, and Neighbours, the Taxes are indeed very heavy, and if those laid on by the Government were the only Ones we had to pay, we might more easily discharge them; but we have many others, and much more grievous to some of us. We are taxed twice as much by our *Idleness*, three times as much by our *Pride*, and four times as much by our *Folly*, and from these Taxes the Commissioners cannot ease or deliver us by allowing an Abatement. However let us hearken to good Advice, and something may be done for us; *God helps them that help themselves*, as *Poor Richard* says, in his Almanack of 1733.

It would be thought a hard Government that should tax its People one tenth Part of their *Time*, to be employed in its Service. But *Idleness* taxes many of us much more, if we reckon all that is spent in absolute *Sloth*, or doing of nothing, with that which is spent in idle Employments or Amusements, that amount to nothing. *Sloth*, by bringing on Diseases, absolutely shortens Life. *Sloth, like Rust, consumes faster than Labour wears, while the used Key is always bright*, as *Poor Richard* says. But *dost thou love Life, then do not squander Time, for that's the Stuff Life is made of*, as *Poor Richard* says.——How much more than is necessary do we spend in Sleep! forgetting that *The sleeping Fox catches no Poultry*, and that *there will be sleeping enough in the Grave*, as *Poor Richard* says. If Time be of all Things the most precious, *wasting Time* must be, as *Poor Richard* says, *the greatest Prodigality*, since, as he elsewhere tells us, *Lost Time is never found again*; and what we call *Time-enough, always proves little enough*: Let us then be up and be doing, and doing to the Purpose; so by Diligence shall we do more with less Perplexity. *Sloth makes all Things difficult, but Industry all easy*, as *Poor Richard* says; and *He that riseth late, must trot all Day, and shall scarce overtake his Business at Night.* While *Laziness travels so slowly, that Poverty soon overtakes him*, as we read in *Poor Richard*, who adds, *Drive thy Business, let not that drive thee;* and *Early to Bed, and early to rise, makes a Man healthy, wealthy and wise.*

So what signifies *wishing* and *hoping* for better Times. We may make these Times better if we bestir ourselves. *Industry need not wish*, as *Poor Richard* says, and *He that lives upon Hope will die fasting. There are no Gains, without Pains*; then *Help Hands, for I have no Lands*, or if I have, they are smartly taxed. And, as *Poor Richard* likewise observes, *He that hath a Trade hath an Estate*, and *He that hath a Calling hath an Office of Profit and Honour*; but then the *Trade* must be worked at, and the *Calling* well followed, or neither the *Estate*, nor the *Office*, will enable us to pay our Taxes.——If we are industrious we shall never starve; for, as *Poor Richard* says, *At the working Man's House* Hunger *looks in, but dares not enter.* Nor will the Bailiff nor the Constable enter, for *Industry pays Debts, while Despair encreaseth them*, says *Poor Richard.*——What though you have found no Treasure, nor has any rich Relation left you a Legacy, *Diligence is the Mother of Good lucks* as *Poor Richard* says, and *God gives all Things to Industry.* Then *plough deep, while Sluggards sleep, and you shall have Corn to sell and to keep*, says *Poor Dick.* Work while it is called To-day, for you know not how much you may be hindered To-morrow, which makes *Poor Richard* say, *One To-day is worth two Tomorrows*; and farther, *Have you somewhat to do To-morrow, do it To-day.* If you were a Servant, would you not be ashamed that a good Master should catch you idle? Are you then your own Master, *be ashamed to catch yourself idle*, as *Poor Dick* says. When there is so much to be done for yourself, your Family, your Country, and your gracious King, be up by Peep of Day; *Let not the Sun look down and say, Inglorious here he lies.* Handle your Tools without Mittens; remember that *the Cat in Gloves catches no Mice*, as *Poor Richard* says. 'Tis true there is much to be done, and perhaps you are weak handed, but stick to it steadily, and you will see great Effects, for *constant Dropping wears away Stones*, and by *Diligence and Patience the Mouse ate in two the Cable*; and *little Strokes fell great Oaks*, as *Poor Richard* says in his Almanack, the Year I cannot just now remember.

Methinks I hear some of you say, *Must a Man afford himself no Leisure?*——I will tell thee, my Friend, what *Poor Richard* says, *Employ thy Time well if thou meanest to gain Leisure*; and, *since thou art not sure of a Minute, throw not away an Hour.* Leisure, is Time for doing something useful; this Leisure the diligent Man will obtain, but the lazy Man never; so that, as *Poor Richard* says, a *Life of Leisure and a Life of Laziness are two Things.* Do you imagine that Sloth will afford you more Comfort than Labour? No, for as *Poor Richard* says, *Trouble springs from Idleness, and grievous Toil from needless Ease. Many without Labour, would live by their* WITS *only, but they break for want of Stock.* Whereas Industry gives Comfort, and Plenty, and Respect: *Fly Pleasures, and they'll follow you. The diligent Spinner has a large Shift*; and *now I have a Sheep and a Cow, every Body bids me Good morrow*; all which is well said by *Poor Richard.*

But with our Industry, we must likewise be *steady, settled* and *careful*, and oversee our own Affairs *with our own Eyes*, and not trust too much to others; for, as *Poor Richard* says,

I never saw an oft removed Tree,
Nor yet an oft removed Family,
That throve so well as those that settled be.

And again, *Three Removes is as bad as a Fire*; and again, *Keep thy Shop, and thy Shop will keep thee*; and again, *If you would have your Business done, go; If not, send.* And again,

He that by the Plough would thrive,
Himself must either hold or drive.

And again, *The Eye of a Master will do more Work than both his Hands*; and again, *Want of Care does us more Damage than Want of Knowledge*; and again, *Not to oversee Workmen, is to leave them your Purse open.* Trusting too much to others Care is the Ruin of many; for, as the *Almanack* says, *In the Affairs of this World, Men are saved, not by Faith, but by the Want of it*; but a Man's own Care is profitable; for, saith *Poor Dick*, *Learning is to the Studious*, and *Riches to the Careful*, as well as *Power to the Bold*, and *Heaven to the Virtuous.* And farther, *If you would have a faithful Servant, and one that you like, serve yourself.* And again, he adviseth to Circumspection and Care, even in the smallest Matters, because sometimes *a little Neglect may breed great Mischief*; adding, *For want of a Nail the Shoe was lost; for want of a Shoe the Horse was lost; and for want of a Horse the Rider was lost*, being overtaken and slain by the Enemy, all for want of Care about a Horse-shoe Nail.

So much for Industry, my Friends, and Attention to one's own Business; but to these we must add *Frugality*, if we would make our *Industry* more certainly successful. A Man may, if he knows not how to save as he gets, *keep his Nose all his Life to the Grindstone*, and die not worth a *Groat* at last. *A fat Kitchen makes a lean Will*, as *Poor Richard* says; and,

Many Estates are spent in the Getting,
Since Women for Tea forsook Spinning and Knitting,
And Men for Punch forsook Hewing and Splitting.

If you would be wealthy, says he, in another Almanack, *think of Saving as well as of Getting: The* Indies *have not made Spain rich, because her* Outgoes *are greater than her* Incomes. Away then with your expensive Follies, and you will not have so much Cause to complain of hard Times, heavy Taxes, and chargeable Families; for, as *Poor Dick* says,

Women and Wine, Game and Deceit,
Make the Wealth small, and the Wants great.

And farther, *What maintains one Vice, would bring up two Children.* You may think perhaps, That a *little* Tea, or a *little* Punch now and then, Diet a *little* more costly, Clothes a *little* finer, and a *little* Entertainment now and then, can be no *great* Matter; but remember what *Poor Richard* says, *Many* a Little *makes a Mickle*; and farther, *Beware of* little *Expences; a small Leak will sink a great Ship*; and again, *Who Dainties love, shall Beggars prove*; and moreover, *Fools make Feasts, and wise Men eat them.*

Here you are all got together at this Vendue of *Fineries* and *Knicknacks.* You call them *Goods*, but if you do not take Care, they will prove *Evils* to some of you. You expect they will be sold *cheap*, and perhaps they may for less than they cost; but if you have no Occasion for them, they must be *dear* to you. Remember what *Poor Richard* says, *Buy what thou hast no Need of, and ere long thou shalt sell thy Necessaries.* And again, *At a great Pennyworth pause a while*: He means, that perhaps the Cheapness is *apparent* only, and not *real*; or the Bargain, by straitning thee in thy Business, may do thee more Harm than Good. For in another Place he says, *Many have been ruined by buying good Pennyworths.* Again, *Poor Richard* says, *'Tis foolish to lay out Money in a Purchase of Repentance*; and yet this Folly is practised every Day at Vendues, for want of minding the Almanack. *Wise Men*, as *Poor Dick* says, *learn by others Harms, Fools scarcely by their own*; but, *Felix quem faciunt aliena Pericula cautum.* Many a one, for the Sake of Finery on the Back, have gone with a hungry Belly, and half starved their Families; *Silks and Sattins, Scarlet and Velvets*, as *Poor Richard* says, *put out the Kitchen Fire.* These are not the *Necessaries* of Life; they can scarcely be called the *Conveniencies*, and yet only because they look pretty, how many *want* to *have* them. The *artificial* Wants of Mankind thus become more numerous than the *natural*; and, as *Poor Dick* says, *For one* poor *Person, there are an hundred* indigent. By these, and other Extravagancies, the Genteel are reduced to Poverty, and forced to borrow of those whom they formerly despised, but who through *Industry* and *Frugality* have maintained their Standing; in which Case it appears plainly, that a *Ploughman on his Legs is higher than a Gentleman on his Knees*, as *Poor Richard* says. Perhaps they have had a small Estate left them, which they knew not the Getting of; they think *'tis Day, and will never be Night*; that a little to be spent out of *so much*, is not worth minding; (*a Child and a Fool*, as *Poor Richard* says, *imagine* Twenty Shillings *and Twenty Years can never be spent*) but, *always taking out of the Meal-tub, and never putting in, soon comes to the Bottom*; then, as *Poor Dick* says, *When the Well's dry, they know the Worth of Water*. But this they might have known before, if they had taken his Advice; *If you would know the Value of Money, go and try to borrow some*; for, *he that goes a borrowing goes a sorrowing*; and indeed so does he that lends to such People, when he goes *to get it in again*.——*Poor Dick* farther advises, and says,

> *Fond* Pride of Dress, *is sure a very Curse;*
> *E'er* Fancy *you consult, consult your Purse.*

And again, *Pride is as loud a Beggar as Want, and a great deal more saucy*. When you have bought one fine Thing you must buy ten more, that your Appearance may be all of a Piece; but *Poor Dick* says, *'Tis easier to* suppress *the first Desire than to* satisfy *all that follow it*. And 'tis as truly Folly for the Poor to ape the Rich, as for the Frog to swell, in order to equal the Ox.

> *Great Estates may venture more,*
> *But little Boats should keep near Shore.*

'Tis however a Folly soon punished; *for Pride that dines on Vanity sups on Contempt*, as *Poor Richard* says. And in another Place, *Pride breakfasted with Plenty, dined with Poverty, and supped with Infamy*. And after all, of what Use is this *Pride of Appearance*, for which so much is risked, so much is suffered? It cannot promote Health, or ease Pain; it makes no Increase of Merit in the Person, it creates Envy, it hastens Misfortune.

> *What is a Butterfly? At best*
> *He's but a Caterpillar drest.*
> *The gaudy Fop's his Picture just,*

as *Poor Richard* says.

But what Madness must it be to *run in Debt* for these Superfluities! We are offered, by the Terms of this Vendue, *Six Months Credit*; and that perhaps has induced some of us to attend it, because we cannot spare the ready Money, and hope now to be fine without it. But, ah, think what you do when you run in Debt; *You give to another Power over your Liberty*. If you cannot pay at the Time, you will be ashamed to see your Creditor; you will be in Fear when you speak to him; you will make poor pitiful sneaking

Excuses, and by Degrees come to lose your Veracity, and sink into base downright lying; for, as *Poor Richard* says, *The second Vice is Lying, the first is running in Debt.* And again, to the same Purpose, *Lying rides upon Debt's Back.* Whereas a freeborn *Englishman* ought not to be ashamed or afraid to see or speak to any Man living. But Poverty often deprives a Man of all Spirit and Virtue: *'Tis hard for an empty Bag to stand upright*, as *Poor Richard* truly says. What would you think of that Prince, or that Government, who should issue an Edict forbidding you to dress like a Gentleman or a Gentlewoman, on Pain of Imprisonment or Servitude? Would you not say, that you are free, have a Right to dress as you please, and that such an Edict would be a Breach of your Privileges, and such a Government tyrannical? And yet you are about to put yourself under that Tyranny when you run in Debt for such Dress! Your Creditor has Authority at his Pleasure to deprive you of your Liberty, by confining you in Gaol for Life, or to sell you for a Servant, if you should not be able to pay him! When you have got your Bargain, you may, perhaps, think little of Payment; but *Creditors, Poor Richard* tells us, *have better Memories than Debtors*; and in another Place says, *Creditors are a superstitious Sect, great Observers of set Days and Times.* The Day comes round before you are aware, and the Demand is made before you are prepared to satisfy it. Or if you bear your Debt in Mind, the Term which at first seemed so long, will, as it lessens, appear extreamly short. *Time* will seem to have added Wings to his Heels as well as Shoulders. *Those have a short Lent*, saith *Poor Richard, who owe Money to be paid at Easter.* Then since, as he says, *The Borrower is a Slave to the Lender, and the Debtor to the Creditor*, disdain the Chain, preserve your Freedom; and maintain your Independency: Be *industrious* and *free*; be *frugal* and *free.* At present, perhaps, you may think yourself in thriving Circumstances, and that you can bear a little Extravagance without Injury; but,

For Age and Want, save while you may;
No Morning Sun lasts a whole Day,

as *Poor Richard* says.——Gain may be temporary and uncertain, but ever while you live, Expence is constant and certain; and *'tis easier to build two Chimnies than to keep one in Fuel*, as *Poor Richard* says. So *rather go to Bed supperless than rise in Debt.*

Get what you can, and what you get hold;
'Tis the Stone that will turn all your Lead into Gold,

as *Poor Richard* says. And when you have got the Philosopher's Stone, sure you will no longer complain of bad Times, or the Difficulty of paying Taxes.

This Doctrine, my Friends, is *Reason* and *Wisdom*; but after all, do not depend too much upon your own *Industry*, and *Frugality*, and *Prudence*, though excellent Things, for they may all be blasted without the Blessing of Heaven; and therefore ask that Blessing humbly, and be not uncharitable to those that at present seem to want it, but comfort and help them. Remember *Job* suffered, and was afterwards prosperous.

And now to conclude, *Experience keeps a dear School, but Fools will learn in no other, and scarce in that*; for it is true, *we may give Advice, but we cannot give Conduct*, as *Poor Richard* says: However, remember this, *They that won't be counselled, can't be helped* as *Poor Richard* says: And farther, That *if you will not hear Reason, she'll surely rap your Knuckles.*

Thus the old Gentleman ended his Harangue. The People heard it, and approved the Doctrine, and immediately practised the contrary, just as if it had been a common Sermon; for the Vendue opened, and they began to buy extravagantly, notwithstanding all his Cautions, and their own Fear of Taxes.——I found the good Man had thoroughly studied my Almanacks, and digested all I had dropt on those Topicks during the Course of Five-and-twenty Years. The frequent Mention he made of me must have tired any one else, but my Vanity was wonderfully delighted with it, though I was conscious that not a tenth Part of the Wisdom was my own which he ascribed to me, but rather the *Gleanings* I had made of the Sense of all Ages and Nations. However, I resolved to be the better for the Echo of it; and though I had at first determined to buy Stuff for a new Coat, I went away resolved to wear my old One a little longer. *Reader*, if thou wilt do the same, thy Profit will be as great as mine.

I am, as ever,
Thine to serve thee,
RICHARD SAUNDERS.

July 7, 1757.

[*Poor Richard improved: Being an Almanack and Ephemeris . . . for the Year of our Lord 1758* (Philadelphia: B. Franklin and D. Hall, 1758)]

CHAPTER 23
To ____
(13 December 1757)[1]

Dear Sir

I have read your Manuscript with some Attention. By the Arguments it contains against the Doctrine of a particular Providence, tho' you allow a general Providence, you strike at the Foundation of all Religion: For without the Belief of a Providence that takes Cognizance of, guards and guides and may favour particular Persons, there is no Motive to Worship a Deity, to fear its Displeasure, or to pray for its Protection. I will not enter into any Discussion of your Principles, tho' you seem to desire it; At present I shall only give you my Opinion that tho' your Reasonings are subtle, and may prevail with some Readers, you will not succeed so as to change the general Sentiments of Mankind on that Subject, and the Consequence of printing this Piece will be a great deal of Odium drawn upon your self, Mischief to you and no Benefit to others. He that spits against the Wind, spits in his own Face. But were you to succeed, do you imagine any Good would be done by it? You yourself may find it easy to live a virtuous Life without the Assistance afforded by Religion; you having a clear Perception of the Advantages of Virtue and the Disadvantages of Vice, and possessing a Strength of Resolution sufficient to enable you to resist common Temptations. But think how great a Proportion of Mankind consists of weak and ignorant Men and Women, and of inexperienc'd and inconsiderate Youth of both Sexes, who have need of the Motives of Religion to restrain them from Vice, to support their Virtue, and retain them in the Practice of it till it becomes *habitual*, which is the great Point for its Security; And perhaps you are indebted to her originally that is to your Religious Education, for the Habits of Virtue upon which you now justly value yourself. You might easily display your excellent Talents of reasoning on a less hazardous Subject, and thereby obtain Rank

[1] [Both the date and the addressee of this letter are subjects of debate. Here I follow the Papers.]

with our most distinguish'd Authors. For among us, it is not necessary, as among the Hottentots that a Youth to be receiv'd into the Company of Men, should prove his Manhood by beating his Mother. I would advise you therefore not to attempt unchaining the Tyger, but to burn this Piece before it is seen by any other Person, whereby you will save yourself a great deal of Mortification from the Enemies it may raise against you, and perhaps a good deal of Regret and Repentance. If Men are so wicked as we now see them *with Religion* what would they be if *without it*? I intend this Letter itself as a *Proof* of my Friendship and therefore add no *Professions* of it, but subscribe simply Yours.

[Papers 7:294–5]

CHAPTER 24
To Lord Kames
(3 May 1760)

My dear Lord,

Your obliging Favour of January 24th. found me greatly indispos'd with an obstinate Cold and Cough accompany'd with Feverish Complaints and Headachs, that lasted long and harass'd me greatly, not being subdu'd at length but by the whole Round of Cupping, Bleeding, Blistering, &c. When I had any Intervals of Ease and Clearness, I endeavour'd to comply with your Request, in writing something on the present Situation of our Affairs in America, in order to give more correct Notions of the British Interest with regard to the Colonies, than those I found many sensible Men possess'd of. Inclos'd you have the Production, such as it is.[1] I wish it may in any Degree be of Service to the Publick. I shall at least hope this from it for my own Part, that you will consider it as a Letter from me to you, and accept its Length as some Excuse for its being so long acoming.

I am now reading, with great Pleasure and Improvement, your excellent Work, the Principles of Equity. It will be of the greatest Advantage to the judges in our Colonies, not only in those which have Courts of Chancery, but also in those which having no such Courts are obliged to mix Equity with the Common Law. It will be of the more Service to the Colony Judges, as few of them have been bred to the Law. I have sent a Book to a particular Friend, one of the Judges of the Supreme Court in Pennsylvania.

I will shortly send you a Copy of the Chapter you are pleas'd to mention in so obliging a Manner; and shall be extreamly oblig'd in receiving a Copy of the Collection of Maxims for the Conduct of Life, which you are preparing for the Use of your Children. I purpose, likewise, a little Work for the Benefit of Youth, to be call'd *The Art of Virtue.* From the Title I think you will hardly conjecture what the Nature of such a Book

[1] [*The Interest of Great Britain Considered, with Regard to her Colonies, And the Acquisitions of Canada and Guadaloupe* (London, 1760).]

may be. I must therefore explain it a little. Many People lead bad Lives that would gladly lead good ones, but know not *how* to make the Change. They have frequently *resolv'd* and *endeavour'd* it; but in vain, because their Endeavours have not been properly conducted. To exhort People to be good, to be just, to be temperate, &c. without *shewing* them *how* they shall *become* so, seems like the ineffectual Charity mention'd by the Apostle, which consisted in saying to the Hungry, the Cold, and the Naked, *be ye fed, be ye warmed, be ye clothed*, without shewing them how they should get Food, Fire or Clothing. Most People have naturally *some* Virtues, but none have naturally *all* the Virtues. To *acquire* those that are wanting, and *secure* what we acquire as well as those we have naturally, is the Subject of *an Art*. It is as properly an Art, as Painting, Navigation, or Architecture. If a Man would become a Painter, Navigator, or Architect, it is not enough that he is *advised* to be one, that he is *convinc'd* by the Arguments of his Adviser that it would be for his Advantage to be one, and that he *resolves* to be one, but he must also be taught the Principles of the Art, be shewn all the Methods of Working, and how to acquire the *Habits* of using properly all the Instruments; and thus regularly and gradually he arrives by Practice at some Perfection in the Art. If he does not proceed thus, he is apt to meet with Difficulties that discourage him, and make him drop the Pursuit. My *Art of Virtue* has also its Instruments, and teaches the Manner of Using them. Christians are directed to have *Faith in Christ*, as the effectual Means of obtaining the Change they desire. It may, when sufficiently strong, be effectual with many. A full Opinion that a Teacher is infinitely wise, good, and powerful, and that he will certainly reward and punish the Obedient and Disobedient, must give great Weight to his Precepts, and make them much more attended to by his Disciples. But all Men cannot have Faith in Christ; and many have it in so weak a Degree, that it does not produce the Effect. Our *Art of Virtue* may therefore be of great Service to those who have not Faith, and come in Aid of the weak Faith of others. Such as are naturally well-disposed, and have been carefully educated, so that good Habits have been early established, and bad ones prevented, have less Need of this Art; but all may be more or less benefited by it. It is, in short, to be adapted for universal Use. I imagine what I have now been writing will seem to savour of great Presumption; I must therefore speedily finish my little Piece, and communicate the Manuscript to you, that you may judge whether it is possible to make good such Pretensions. I shall at the same time hope for the Benefit of your Corrections.

My respectful Compliments to Lady Kames and your amiable Children, in which my Son joins. With the sincerest Esteem and Attachment, I am, My Lord, Your Lordship's most obedient and most humble Servant.

[Papers 9:103–6]

CHAPTER 25

On the Price of Corn, and Management of the Poor

(29 November 1766)

To Messieurs the PUBLIC *and* Co.

I Am one of that class of people that feeds you all, and at present is abus'd by you all;——in short I am a *Farmer.*

By your News-papers we are told, that God had sent a very short harvest to some other countries of Europe. I thought this might be in favour to Old England; and that now we should get a good price for our grain, which would bring in millions among us, and make us flow in money, that to be sure is scarce enough.

But the wisdom of Government forbad the exportations.

Well, says I, then we must be content with the market price at home.

No, says my Lords the mob, you sha'n't have that. Bring your corn to market if you dare;——we'll sell it for you, for less money, or take it for nothing.

Being thus attack'd by both ends *of the Constitution*, the head and the tail *of Government*, what am I to do?

Must I keep my corn in barn to feed and increase the breed of rats?——be it so;——they cannot be less thankful than those I have been used to feed.

Are we Farmers the only people to be grudged the profits of honest labour?——And why?——One of the late scribblers against us gives a bill of fare of the provisions at my daughter's wedding, and proclaims to all the world that we had the insolence to eat beef and pudding!——Has he never read that precept in the good book, *Thou shat not muzzle the mouth of the ox that treadeth out the corn*; or does he think us less worthy of good living than our oxen?

O, but the Manufacturers! the Manufacturers! they are to be favour'd, and they must have bread at a cheap rate!

Hark-ye, Mr. Oaf;——The Farmers live splendidly, you say. And pray, would you have them hoard the money they get?——Their fine cloaths and furniture, do they make them themselves, or for one another, and so keep the money among them? Or do they employ these your darling Manufacturers, and so scatter it again all over the nation?

My wool would produce me a better price if it were suffer'd to go to foreign markets. But that, Messieurs the Public, your laws will not permit. It must be kept all at home, that our *dear* Manufacturers may have it the cheaper. And then, having yourselves thus lessened our encouragement for raising sheep, you curse us for the scarcity of mutton!

I have heard my grandfather say, that the Farmers submitted to the prohibition on the exportation of wool, being made to expect and believe, that when the Manufacturer bought his wool cheaper, they should have their cloth cheaper. But the deuce a bit. It has been growing dearer and dearer from that day to this. How so? why truly the cloth is exported; and that keeps up the price.

Now if it be a good principle, that the exportation of a commodity is to be restrain'd, that so our own people at home may have it the cheaper, stick to that principle, and go thorough stitch with it. Prohibit the exportation of your cloth, your leather and shoes, your iron ware, and your manufactures of all sorts, to make them all cheaper at home. And cheap enough they will be, I'll warrant you——till people leave off making them.

Some folks seem to think they ought never to be easy, till *England* becomes another *Lubberland*, where 'tis fancied the streets are paved with penny rolls, the houses tiled with pancakes, and chickens ready roasted cry, come eat me.

I say, when you are sure you have got a good principle, stick to it, and carry it thorough.——I hear 'tis said, that though it was *necessary and right* for the M——y to advise a prohibition of the exportation of corn, yet it was *contrary to law*; and also, that though it was *contrary to law* for the mob to obstruct the waggons, yet it was *necessary and right.*——Just the same thing, to a tittle. Now they tell me, an act of indemnity ought to pass in favour of the M——y, to secure them from the consequences of having acted illegally.——If so, pass another in favour of the mob. Others say, some of the mob ought to be hanged, by way of example.——If so,——but I say no more than I have said before, *when you are sure that you have got a good principle, go thorough with it.*

You say, poor labourers cannot afford to buy bread at a high price, unless they had higher wages.——Possibly.——But how shall we Farmers be able to afford our labourers higher wages, if you will not allow us to get, when we might have it, a higher price for our corn?

By all I can learn, we should at least have had a guinea a quarter more if the exportation had been allowed. And this money England would have got from foreigners.

But, it seems, we Farmers must take So much less, that the poor may have it so much cheaper.

This operates then as a tax for the maintenance of the poor.——A very good thing, you will say. But I ask, Why a partial tax? Why laid on us Farmers only?——If it be a good thing, pray, Messrs. the Public, take your share of it, by indemnifying us a little out of your public treasury. In doing a good thing there is both honour and pleasure;——you are welcome to your part of both.

For my own part, I am not so well satisfied of the goodness of this thing. I am for doing good to the poor, but I differ in opinion of the means.——I think the best way of doing good to the poor, is not making them easy *in* poverty, but leading or driving them *out* of it. In my youth I travelled much, and I observed in different countries, that the more public provisions were made for the poor, the less they provided for themselves, and of course became poorer. And, on the contrary, the less was done for them, the more they did for themselves, and became richer. There is no country in the world where so many provisions are established for them; so many hospitals to receive them when they are sick or lame, founded and maintained by voluntary charities; so many alms-houses for the aged of both sexes, together with a solemn general law made by the rich to subject their estates to a heavy tax for the support of the poor. Under all these obligations, are our poor modest, humble, and thankful; and do they use their best endeavours to maintain themselves, and lighten our shoulders of this burthen?——On the contrary, I affirm that there is no country in the world in which the poor are more idle, dissolute, drunken, and insolent. The day you passed that act, you took away from before their eyes the greatest of all inducements to industry, frugality, and sobriety, by giving them a dependance on somewhat else than a careful accumulation during youth and health, for support in age or sickness. In short, you offered a premium for the encouragement of idleness, and you should not now wonder that it has had its effect in the increase of poverty. Repeal that law, and you will soon see a change in their manners. St. *Monday*, and St. *Tuesday*, will cease to be holidays. SIX *days shalt thou labour*, though one of the old commandments long treated as out of date, will again be looked upon as a respectable precept; industry will increase, and with it plenty among the lower people; their circumstances will mend, and more will be done for their happiness by inuring them to provide for themselves, than could be done by dividing all your estates among them.

Excuse me, Messrs. the Public, if upon this *interesting* subject, I put you to the trouble of reading a little of *my* nonsense. I am sure I have lately read a great deal of *yours*; and therefore from you (at least from those of you who are writers) I deserve a little indulgence.

I am, your's, &c.
ARATOR.

[*The London Chronicle*, 29 November 1766]

CHAPTER 26
To Lord Kames
(25 February 1767)

My dear Friend,

I Received your Favour of Jan. 19. You have kindly reliev'd me from the Pain I had long been under. You are Goodness itself.

I ought long since to have answered yours of Dec. 25.1765. I never receiv'd a Letter that contain'd Sentiments more suitable to my own. It found me under much Agitation of Mind on the very important Subject it treated. It fortified me greatly in the Judgment I was inclined to form (tho' contrary to the general Vogue) on the then delicate and critical Situation of Affairs between Britain and her Colonies; and on that weighty Point their Union: You guess'd aright in supposing I could not be a Mute in that Play. I was extreamly busy, attending Members of both Houses, informing, explaining, consulting, disputing, in a continual Hurry from Morning to Night till the Affair was happily ended. During the Course of it, being called before the House of Commons, I spoke my Mind pretty plainly. Inclos'd I send you the imperfect Account that was taken of that Examination; you will there see how intirely we agree, except in a Point of Fact of which you could not but be mis-inform'd, the Papers at that time being full of mistaken Assertions, that the Colonies had been the Cause of the War, and had ungratefully refus'd to bear any part of the Expence of it. I send it you now, because I apprehend some late Incidents are likely to revive the Contest between the two Countries. I fear it will be a mischievous one. It becomes a Matter of great Importance that clear Ideas should be formed on solid Principles, both in Britain and America, of the true political Relation between them, and the mutual Duties belonging to that Relation. Till this is done, they will be often jarring. I know none whose Knowledge, Sagacity and Impartiality, qualify them so thoroughly for such a Service, as yours do you. I wish therefore you would consider it. You may thereby be the happy Instrument of great Good to the Nation, and of preventing much Mischief and Bloodshed. I am fully persuaded with you, that a consolidating Union, by a fair and equal Representation of all the Parts of this Empire in Parliament, is the only firm Basis on which its political Grandeur and Stability can be founded. Ireland once wish'd it, but now rejects it. The Time has been when the Colonies might have been pleas'd with it; they are now indifferent about it; and, if 'tis much longer delay'd, they too will refuse it. But the *Pride* of *this People* cannot bear the Thoughts of it. Every Man in England seems to consider himself as a Piece of a Sovereign over America; seems to jostle himself into the Throne with the King, and talks of OUR *Subjects in the Colonies*. The Parliament cannot well and wisely make Laws suited to the Colonies, without being properly and truly informed of their Circumstances, Abilities, Temper, &c. This it cannot be without Representatives from thence. And yet it is fond of this Power, and averse to the only Means of duly acquiring the necessary Knowledge for exercising it, which is desiring to be *omnipotent* without being *omniscient*.

I have mentioned that the Contest is like to be revived. It is on this Occasion. In the same Session with the Stamp Act, an Act was pass'd to regulate the Quartering of Soldiers in America. When the Bill was first brought in, it contain'd a Clause empowering the Officers to quarter their Soldiers in private Houses; this we warmly oppos'd, and got it omitted. The Bill pass'd however, with a Clause that empty Houses, Barns, &c. should be hired for them; and that the respective Provinces where they were, should pay the Expence, and furnish Firing, Bedding, Drink, and some other Articles, to the Soldiers, gratis. There is no way for any Province to do this, but by the Assembly's making a Law to raise the Money. Pennsylvania Assembly has made such a Law. New York Assembly has refus'd to do it. And now all the Talk here is to send a Force to compel them.

The Reasons given by the Assembly to the Governor for their Refusal, are, That they understand the Act to mean the furnishing such things to Soldiers only while on their March thro' the Country, and not to great Bodies of Soldiers, to be fixt as at present in the Province, the Burthen in the latter Case being greater than the Inhabitants can bear: That it would put it in the Power of the Captain General to oppress the Province at pleasure, &c. But there is suppos'd to be another Reason at bottom, which they intimate, tho' they do not plainly express it; to wit, that it is of the nature of an *internal Tax* laid on them by Parliament, which has no Right so to do. Their Refusal is here called Rebellion, and Punishment is thought of.

Now waiving that Point of Right, and supposing the Legislatures in America subordinate to the Legislature of Great Britain, one might conceive, I think, a Power in the superior Legislature to *forbid* the inferior Legislature's making particular Laws; but to *enjoin* it to make a particular Law, contrary to its own Judgment, seems improper, an Assembly or Parliament not being an *executive* Officer of Government, whose Duty it is, in Law-making, to obey Orders; but a *deliberative* Body, who are to consider what comes before them, its Propriety, Practicability, or Possibility, and to determine accordingly. The very Nature of a Parliament seems to be destroy'd, by supposing it may be bound and compell'd by a Law of a superior Parliament to make a Law contrary to its own Judgment.

Indeed the Act of Parliament in question has not, as in other Acts, when a Duty is injoined, directed a Penalty on Neglect or Refusal, and a Mode of Recovering that Penalty. It seems therefore to the People in America as a mere Requisition, which they are at Liberty to comply with or not as it may suit or not suit the different Circumstances of different Colonies. Pennsylvania has therefore voluntarily comply'd. New York, as I said before, has refus'd. The Ministry that made the Act, and all their Adherents, call out for Vengeance. The present Ministry are perplext, and the Measures they will finally take on the Occasion are unknown. But sure I am, that, if Force is us'd, great Mischief will ensue, the Affections of the People of America to this Country will be alienated, your Commerce will be diminished, and a total Separation of Interests be the final Consequence.

It is a common but mistaken Notion here, that the Colonies were planted at the Expence of Parliament, and that therefore the Parliament has a Right to tax them, &c. The Truth is, they were planted at the Expence of private Adventurers, who went over there to settle with Leave of the King given by Charter. On receiving this Leave and these Charters, the Adventurers voluntarily engag'd to remain the King's Subjects, though in a foreign Country, a Country which had not been conquer'd by either King or Parliament, but was possess'd by a free People. When our Planters arriv'd, they purchas'd the Lands of the Natives without putting King or Parliament to any Expence. Parliament had no hand in their Settlement, was never so much as consulted about their Constitution, and took no kind of Notice of them till many Years after they were established; never attempted to meddle with the Government of them, till that Period when it destroy'd the Constitution of all Parts of the Empire, and usurp'd a Power over Scotland, Ireland, Lords and King. I except only the two modern

Colonies, or rather Attempts to make Colonies, (for they succeed but poorly, and as yet hardly deserve the Name of Colonies) I mean Georgia and Nova Scotia, which have been hitherto little better than Parliamentary Jobbs. Thus all the Colonies acknowledge the King as their Sovereign: His Governors there represent his Person. Laws are made by their Assemblies or little Parliaments, with the governor's Assent, subject still to the King's Pleasure to confirm or annul them. Suits arising in the Colonies, and Differences between Colony and Colony, are not brought before your Lords of Parliament, as those within the Realm, but determined by the King in Council. In this View they seem so many separate little States, subject to the same Prince. The Sovereignty of the King is therefore easily understood. But nothing is more common here than to talk of the *Sovereignty of Parliament*, and the *Sovereignty of this Nation* over the Colonies; a kind of Sovereignty the Idea of which is not so clear, nor does it clearly appear on what Foundations it is established. On the other hand it seems necessary for the common Good of the Empire, that a Power be lodg'd somewhere to regulate its general Commerce; this, as Things are at present circumstanc'd, can be plac'd no where so properly as in the Parliament of Great Britain; and therefore tho' that Power has in some Instances been executed with great Partiality to Britain and Prejudice to the Colonies, they have nevertheless always submitted to it. Customhouses are established in all of them by Virtue of Laws made here, and the Duties constantly paid, except by a few Smugglers, such as are here and in all Countries; but internal Taxes laid on them by Parliament are and ever will be objected to, for the Reasons that you will see in the mentioned Examination.

Upon the whole, I have lived so great a Part of my Life in Britain, and have formed so many Friendships in it, that I love it and wish its Prosperity, and therefore wish to see that Union on which alone I think it can be secur'd and establish'd. As to America, the Advantages of such an Union to her are not so apparent. She may suffer at present under the arbitrary Power of this Country; she may suffer for a while in a Separation from it; but these are temporary Evils that she will outgrow. Scotland and Ireland are differently circumstanc'd. Confin'd by the Sea, they can scarcely increase in Numbers, Wealth and Strength so as to overbalance England. But America, an immense Territory, favour'd by Nature with all Advantages of Climate, Soil, great navigable Rivers and Lakes, &c. must become a great Country, populous and mighty; and will in a less time than is generally conceiv'd be able to shake off any Shackles that maybe impos'd on her, and perhaps place them on the Imposers. In the mean time, every Act of Oppression will sour their Tempers, lessen greatly if not annihilate the Profits of your Commerce with them, and hasten their final Revolt: For the Seeds of Liberty are universally sown there, and nothing can eradicate them. And yet there remains among that People so much Respect, Veneration and Affection for Britain, that, if cultivated prudently, with kind Usage and Tenderness for their Privileges, they might be easily govern'd still for Ages, without Force or any considerable Expence. But I do not see here a sufficient Quantity of the Wisdom that is necessary to produce such a Conduct, and I lament the Want of it.

. . . This is unexpectedly grown a long Letter. The Visit to Scotland, and the Art of Virtue, we will talk of hereafter. It is now time to say, that I am, with increasing Esteem and Affection, My dear Friend, Yours ever

[Papers 14:62–71]

CHAPTER 27

Causes of the American Discontents Before 1768

(7 January 1768)

To the PRINTER

The Waves never rise but when the Winds blow.

Prov.

SIR,

As the cause of the present ill-humour in America, and of the Resolutions taken there to purchase less of our manufactures, does not seem to be generally understood, it may afford some satisfaction to your Readers, if you give them the following short historical state of facts.

From the time that the Colonies were first considered as capable of granting aids to the Crown, down to the end of the last war, it is said, that the constant mode of obtaining those aids was by Requisition made from the Crown through its Governors to the several Assemblies, in circular letters from the Secretary of State in his Majesty's name, setting forth the occasion, requiring them to take the matter into consideration; and expressing a reliance on their prudence, duty and affection to his Majesty's Government, that they would grant such sums, or raise such numbers of men, as were suitable to their respective circumstances.

The Colonies being accustomed to this method, have from time to time granted money to the Crown, or raised troops for its service, in proportion to their abilities, and, during all the last war beyond their abilities, so that considerable sums were return'd them yearly by Parliament, as they had exceeded their proportion.

Had this happy method been continued (a method that left the King's subjects in those remote countries the pleasure of showing their zeal and loyalty, and of imagining that they recommended themselves to their Sovereign by the liberality of their voluntary grants) there is no doubt but all the money that could reasonably be expected to be rais'd from them in any manner, might have been obtained, without the least heart-burning, offence, or breach of the harmony, of affections and interests, that so long subsisted between the two countries.

It has been thought wisdom in a Government exercising sovereignty over different kinds of people, to have some regard to prevailing and established opinions among the people to be governed, wherever such opinions might in their effects obstruct or promote publick measures.——If they tend to obstruct publick service, they are to be changed before we act against them, and they can only be changed by reason and persuasion.——But if public service can be carried on without thwarting those opinions, if they can be, on the contrary, made subservient to it, they are not unnecessarily to be thwarted, how absurd soever such popular opinions may be in their natures.——This had been the wisdom of our Government with respect to raising money in the Colonies. It was well known that the Colonists universally were of opinion, that no money could be levied from English subjects, but by their own consent, given by themselves or their chosen Representatives. That therefore whatever money was to be raised from the people in the Colonies, must first be granted by their Assemblies, as the money raised in Britain is first to be granted by the House of Commons. That this right of granting their own money was essential to English liberty; and that if any man, or body of men, in which they had no Representative of their chusing, could tax them at pleasure, they could not be said to have any property, any thing they could call their own. But as these opinions did not hinder their granting money voluntarily and amply, whenever the Crown, by its servants, came into their Assemblies (as it does into its Parliaments of Britain and Ireland) and demanded aids therefore that method was chosen rather than the baneful one of arbitrary taxes.

I do not undertake here to support those opinions; they have been refuted by a late Act of Parliament, declaring its own power; which very Parliament, however, shew'd wisely so much tender regard to those inveterate prejudices, as to repeal a tax that had odiously militated against them.——And those prejudices are still so fixed and rooted in the Americans, that it has been supposed not a single man among them has been convinced of his error by that Act of Parliament.

The Minister, therefore, who first projected to lay aside the accustomed method of requisition, and to raise money on America by Stamps, seems not to have acted wisely in deviating from that method (which the Colonists looked upon as constitutional) and thwarting unnecessarily, the general fixed prejudices of so great a number of the King's subjects. It was not, however, for want of knowledge that what he was about to do would give them great offence; he appears to have been very sensible of this, and apprehensive that it might occasion some disorders, to prevent or suppress which he projected another Bill, that was brought in the same Session with the Stamp Act, whereby it was to be made lawful for Military Officers in the Colonies to quarter their Soldiers in private houses. This seemed intended to awe the people into a compliance with the other Act. Great opposition, however, being raised here against the Bill, by the Agents from the Colonies, and the Merchants trading thither, the Colonists declaring that under such a power in the Army, no one could look on his house as his own, or think he had a home, when Soldiers might be thrust into it and mix'd with his family, at the pleasure of an Officer, that part of the Bill was dropt; but there still remained a clause, when it passed into a Law, to oblige the several Assemblies to provide quarters for the soldiers, furnishing them with fire, bedding, candles, small beer or rum, and sundry other articles, at the expence of the several Provinces.——And this Act continued in force when the Stamp Act was repealed, though if obligatory on the Assemblies, it equally militated against the American principle abovementioned, that money is not to be raised on English subjects without their consent.

The Colonies nevertheless, being put into high good humour by the repeal of the Stamp Act, chose to avoid fresh dispute upon the other, it being temporary, and soon to expire, never (as they hoped) to revive again; and in the mean time they, by various ways, provided for the quartering of the troops, either by Acts of their own Assemblies, without taking notice of the Acts of Parliament, or by some variety or small diminution (as of salt and vinegar) in the supplies required by the Act, that what they did might appear a voluntary act of their own, and not done in obedience to an Act of Parliament, which they thought contrary to right, and therefore void of itself.

It might have been well if the matter had thus passed without notice; but an officious Governor having written home an angry and aggravating letter upon this conduct in the Assembly of his province, the outed projector of the Stamp Act and his adherents, then in the opposition, raised such a clamour against America, as in rebellion, &c. and against those who had been for the repeal of the Stamp Act, as having thereby been encouragers of this supposed rebellion, that it was thought necessary to enforce the Quartering Act by another Act of Parliament, taking away from the

Province of New-York, which had been the most explicit in its refusal, all the powers of legislation, till it should have complied with that act: The news of which greatly alarmed the people every where in America, as the language of such an act seemed to them to be——Obey implicitly laws made by the Parliament of Great Britain, to force money from you without your consent, or you shall enjoy no rights or privileges at all.

At the same time the late Chancellor of the Exchequer, desirous of ingratiating himself with the opposition, or driven to it by their clamours, projected the levying more money from America, by new duties on various articles of our own manufacture, as glass, paper, painters colours, &c. appointing a new Board of Customs, and sending over a set of Commissioners (with large salaries) to be established at Boston, who were to have the care of collecting those duties; which were, by the act, expressly mentioned to be intended for the payment of the salaries of Governors, Judges, and other Officers of the Crown in America, it being a pretty general opinion here, that those Officers ought not to depend on the people there for any part of their support.

It is not my intention to combat this opinion. But perhaps it may be some satisfaction to the Public to know what ideas the Americans have on the subject. They say then, as to Governors, that they are not like Princes whose posterity have an inheritance in the government of a nation, and therefore an interest in its prosperity; they are generally strangers to the Provinces they are sent to govern; have no estate, natural connection, or relation there, to give them an affection for the country; that they come only to make money as fast as they can, are frequently men of vicious characters and broken fortunes, sent merely to get them off the hands of a Minister somewhere; that as they intend staying in the country no longer than their government continues, and purpose to leave no family behind them, they are apt to be regardless of the good will of the people, and care not what is said or thought of them after they are gone. Their situation gives them many opportunities of being vexatious, and they are often so, notwithstanding their dependance on the Assemblies for all that part of their support that does not arise from fees established by law, but would probably be much more so if they were to be supported by money drawn from the people, without the consent or good will of the people, which is the professed design of this act. That if by means of these forced duties, government is to be supported in America, without the intervention of the Assemblies, their Assemblies will soon be looked upon as useless, and a Governor will not call them, as having nothing to hope from their meeting, and perhaps something to fear from their enquiries into and remonstrances against his mal-administration; that thus the people will be deprived of their most essential rights; that its being, as at present, a Governor's interest to cultivate the good will, by promoting the welfare of the people he governs, can be attended with no prejudice to the Mother Country, since all the laws he may be prevailed on to give his assent to, are subject to revision here, and if reported against by the Board of Trade, as hurtful to the interest of this Country, may and are immediately repealed by the Crown; nor dare he pass any law contrary to his instructions, as he holds his office during the pleasure of the Crown, and his securities are liable for the penalties of their bonds if he contravenes those instructions.

This is what they say as to Governors.

As to Judges they alledge, that being appointed from hence, by the Crown and holding their commissions, not during good behaviour, as in Britain, but during pleasure, all the weight of interest would be thrown into one of the scales, (which ought to be held even) if the salaries are also to be paid out of duties forced upon the people without their consent, and independent of their Assemblies' approbation or disapprobation of the Judges behavior; that whenever the Crown will grant commissions to able and honest Judges during good behaviour, the Assemblies will settle permanent and ample salaries on them during their commissions; but at present they have no other means of getting rid of an ignorant, unjust Judge (and some of scandalous characters have, they say, been sometimes sent them) but by starving him out.

I do not suppose these reasonings of the Americans will appear here to have much weight. I do not produce them with an expectation of convincing your readers. I relate them merely in pursuance of the task I have imposed on myself, to be an impartial Historian of American facts and opinions.

F. B.

To the Printer

The Colonists being greatly alarmed, as I observed in my last, by the news of the act for abolishing the legislature of New-York, and the imposition of these new duties professedly for such disagreeable and to them appearing dangerous purposes; accompanied by a new set of Revenue Officers, with large appointments, which gave strong suspicions that more business of the same kind was soon to be provided for them, that they might earn these salaries, began seriously to consider their situation, and to revolve afresh in their minds grievances which from their respect and love for this country, they had long borne, and seemed almost willing to forget. They reflected how lightly the interest of all America had been esteemed here, when the interest of a few inhabitants of Great Britain happened to have the smallest competition with it. That thus the whole American people were forbidden the advantage of a direct importation of wine, oil, and fruit, from Portugal, but must take them loaded with all the expences of a voyage of one thousand leagues round about, being to be landed first in England to be re-shipped for America; expences amounting, in war time, at least to thirty per cent. more than otherwise they would have been charged with, and all this, merely that a few Portugal Merchants in London might gain a commission on those goods passing through their hands.——Portugal Merchants, by the bye, who can complain loudly of the smallest hardships laid on their trade by foreigners, and yet even the last year could oppose with all their influence the giving ease to their fellow-subjects under so heavy an oppression——That on a frivolous complaint of a few Virginia Merchants, nine Colonies were restrained from making paper money, though become absolutely necessary to their internal commerce, from the constant remittance of their gold and silver to Britain.——But not only the interest of a particular body of Merchants, the interest of any small body of British Tradesmen or Artificers, has been found, they say, to outweigh that of all the King's subjects in the Colonies.

There cannot be a stronger natural right than that of a man's making the best profit he can of the natural produce of his lands, provided he does not thereby hurt the State in general. Iron is to be found every where in America, and beaver furs are the natural produce of that country. Hats, and nails, and steel, are wanted there as well as here. It is of no importance to the common welfare of the Empire, whether a subject gets his living by making hats on this or that side of the water; yet the Hatters of England have prevailed so far as to obtain an Act in their own favour, restraining that manufacture in America, in order to oblige the Americans to send their beaver to England to be manufactured, and purchase back the hats loaded with the charges of a double transportation. In the same manner have a few Nail-makers, and still a smaller body of Steel-makers (perhaps there are not half a dozen of these in England) prevailed totally to forbid, by an act of Parliament, the erecting of slitting-mills and steel-furnaces in America, that the Americans may be obliged to take nails for their buildings, and steel for their tools from these artificers under the same disadvantages. Added to these, the Americans remembered the act authorizing the most cruel insult that perhaps was ever offered by one people to another, that of emptying our gaols into their settlements (Scotland too has within these two years obtained the privilege it had not before, of sending its rogues and villains also to the Plantations) an insult aggravated by that barbarous ill-placed sarcasm in a report of the Board of Trade, when one of the Provinces complained of the act. "It is necessary that it should be continued for the Better Peopling of your Majesty's Colonies." I say, reflecting on these things, the Americans said to one another (their news papers are full of such discourses) these people are not content with making a monopoly of us, forbiding us to trade with any other country of Europe, and compelling us to buy every thing of them, though in many articles we could furnish ourselves 10, 20, and even 50 per cent. cheaper elsewhere; but now they have as good as declared they have a right to tax us, *ad libitum*, internally and externally; and that our constitution and liberties shall all be taken away if we do not submit to that claim. They are not content with the high prices at which they sell us their goods, but have now begun to enhance those prices by new duties; and by the expensive apparatus of a new set of Officers, they appear to intend an augmentation and multiplication of those burthens that shall still be more grievous to us. Our people have been foolishly fond of their superfluous modes and manufactures, to the impoverishing our country, carrying off all our cash, and loading us with debt; they will not suffer us to restrain the luxury of our inhabitants as they do that of their own, by laws; they can make laws to discourage or prohibit the importation of French superfluities; but though those of England are as ruinous to us as the French ones are to them; if we make a law of that kind, they immediately repeal it. Thus they get all our money from us by trade, and every profit we can any where make by our fishery, our produce, and our commerce, centers finally with them! but this does not satisfy. It is time then to take care of ourselves by the best means in our power. Let us unite in solemn resolutions and engagements with and to each other, that we will give these new Officers as little trouble as possible by not consuming the British manufactures on which they are to levy the duties. Let us agree to consume no more of their expensive gew-gaws; let us live frugally; and let us industriously manufacture what we can for ourselves; thus we shall be able honourably to discharge the debts we already owe them, and after that we may be able to keep some money in our country, not only for the uses of our internal commerce, but for the service of our gracious Sovereign, whenever he shall have occasion for it, and think proper to require it of us in the old constitutional manner. For notwithstanding the reproaches thrown out against us in their public papers and pamphlets; notwithstanding we have been reviled in their Senate as rebels and traitors, we are truly a loyal people. Scotland has had its rebellions, and England its plots, against the present royal family; but America is untainted with those crimes; there is in it scarce a man, there is not a single native of our country who is not firmly attached to his King by principle and by affection. But a new kind of loyalty seems to be required of us, a loyalty to Parliament; a loyalty that is to extend, it seems, to a surrender of all our properties, whenever a House of Commons, in which there is not a single Member of our chusing, shall think fit to grant them away without our consent, and to a patient suffering the loss of our privileges, as Englishmen, if we cannot submit to make such surrender. We were separated too far from Britain by the ocean, but we were united strongly to it by respect and love, so that we could at any time freely have spent our lives and little fortunes in its cause; but this unhappy new system of politics tends to dissolve those bands of union, and to sever us for ever. Woe to the man that first adopted it! Both countries will long have cause to execrate his memory.

These are the wild ravings of the at present half distracted Americans. To be sure no reasonable man in England can approve of such sentiments, and, as I said before, I do not pretend to support or justify them; but I sincerely wish, for the sake of the manufactures and commerce of Great Britain, and for the sake of the strength a firm union with our growing colonies would give us, that these people had never been thus needlessly driven out of their senses.

F. B.

[First printed in *The London Chronicle*, 7 January 1768 and reprinted, with Franklin's corrections, an 30 August and 1 September 1774. The latter is reproduced here.]

CHAPTER 28

The Somersett Case and the Slave Trade

(20 June 1772)

It is said that some generous humane persons subscribed to the expence of obtaining liberty by law for Somerset the Negro.——It is to be wished that the same humanity may extend itself among numbers; if not to the procuring liberty for those that remain in our Colonies, at least to obtain a law for abolishing the African commerce in Slaves, and declaring the children of present Slaves free after they become of age.

By a late computation made in America, it appears that there are now eight hundred and fifty thousand Negroes in the English Islands and Colonies; and that the yearly importation is about one hundred thousand, of which number about one third perish by the gaol distemper on the passage, and in the sickness called the *seasoning* before they are set to labour. The remnant makes up the deficiencies continually occurring among the main body of those unhappy people, through the distempers occasioned by excessive labour, bad nourishment, uncomfortable accommodation, and broken spirits. Can sweetening our tea, &c. with sugar, be a circumstance of such absolute necessity? Can the petty pleasure thence arising to the taste, compensate for so much misery produced among our fellow creatures, and such a constant butchery of the human species by this pestilential detestable traffic in the bodies and souls of men?——*Pharisaical Britain!* to pride thyself in setting free *a single Slave* that happens to land on thy coasts, while thy Merchants in all thy ports are encouraged by thy laws to continue a commerce whereby so many *hundreds of thousands* are dragged into a slavery that can scarce be said to end with their lives, since it is entailed on their posterity!

[*The London Chronicle*, 20 June 1772]

CHAPTER 29

Rules by Which a Great Empire May Be Reduced to a Small One

(11 September 1773)

For the Public Advertiser.

[Presented privately to a *late Minister*, when he entered upon his Administration; and now first published.]

An ancient Sage valued himself upon this, that tho' he could not fiddle, he knew how to make a *great City* of a *little one*. The Science that I, a modern Simpleton, am about to communicate is the very reverse.

I address myself to all Ministers who have the Management of extensive Dominions, which from their very Greatness are become troublesome to govern, because the Multiplicity of their Affairs leaves no Time for *fiddling*.

I. In the first Place, Gentlemen, you are to consider, that a great Empire, like a great Cake, is most easily diminished at the Edges. Turn your Attention therefore first to your remotest Provinces; that as you get rid of them, the next may follow in Order.

II. That the Possibility of this Separation may always exist, take special Care the Provinces are never incorporated with the Mother Country, that they do not enjoy the same common Rights, the same Privileges in Commerce, and that they are governed by *severer* Laws, all of *your enacting*, without allowing them any Share in the Choice of the Legislators. By carefully making and preserving such Distinctions, you will (to keep to my Simile of the Cake) act like a wise Gingerbread Baker, who, to facilitate a Division, cuts his Dough half through in those Places, where, when bak'd, he would have it *broken to Pieces*.

III. These remote Provinces have perhaps been acquired, purchas'd, or conquer'd, at the *sole Expence* of the Settlers or their Ancestors, without the Aid of the Mother Country. If this should happen to increase her *Strength* by their growing Numbers ready to join in her Wars, her *Commerce* by their growing Demand for her Manufactures, or her *Naval Power* by greater Employment for her Ships and Seamen, they may probably suppose some Merit in this, and that it entitles them to some Favour; you are therefore to *forget it all*, or resent it as if they had done you Injury. If they happen to be zealous Whigs, Friends of Liberty, nurtur'd in Revolution Principles, *remember all that* to their Prejudice, and contrive to punish it: For such Principles, after a Revolution is thoroughly established, are of *no more Use*, they are even *odious* and *abominable*.

IV. However peaceably your Colonies have submitted to your Government, shewn their Affection to your Interest, and patiently borne their Grievances, you are to *suppose* them always inclined to revolt, and treat them accordingly. Quarter Troops among them, who by their Insolence may *provoke* the rising of Mobs, and by their Bullets and Bayonets *suppress* them. By this Means, like the Husband who uses his Wife ill *from Suspicion*, you may in Time convert your *Suspicions* into *Realities*.

V. Remote Provinces must have *Governors*, and *Judges*, to represent the Royal Person, and execute every where the delegated Parts of his Office and Authority. You Ministers know, that much of the Strength of Government depends on the *Opinion* of the People; and much of that Opinion on the Choice of Rulers placed immediately over them. If you send them wise and good Men for Governors, who study the Interest of the Colonists, and advance their Prosperity, they will think their King wise and good, and that he wishes the Welfare of his Subjects. If you send them learned and upright Men for judges, they will think him a Lover of Justice. This may attach your Provinces more to his Government. You are therefore to be careful who you recommend for those Offices.——If you can find Prodigals who have ruined their Fortunes, broken Gamesters or Stock-Jobbers, these may do well as *Governors*; for they will probably be rapacious, and provoke the People by their Extortions. Wrangling Proctors and petty-fogging Lawyers too are not amiss, for they will be for ever disputing and quarrelling with their little Parliaments. If withal they should be ignorant, wrong-headed and insolent, so much the better. Attorneys Clerks and Newgate Solicitors will do for *Chief-Justices*, especially if they hold their Places *during your Pleasure*:—— And all will contribute to impress those ideas of your Government that are proper for a People *you would wish to renounce it*.

VI. To confirm these impressions, and strike them deeper, whenever the Injured come to the Capital with Complaints of Mal-administration,

Oppression, or Injustice, punish such Suitors with long Delay, enormous Expence, and a final judgment in Favour of the Oppressor. This will have an admirable Effect every Way. The Trouble of future Complaints will be prevented, and Governors and Judges will be encouraged to farther Acts of Oppression and Injustice; and thence the People may become more disaffected, *and at length desperate.*

VII. When such Governors have crammed their Coffers, and made themselves so odious to the People that they can no longer remain among them with Safety to their Persons, recall and *reward* them with Pensions. You may make them *Baronets* too, if that respectable Order should not think fit to resent it. All will contribute to encourage new Governors in the same Practices, and make the supreme Government *detestable.*

VIII. If when you are engaged in War, your Colonies should vie in liberal Aids of Men and Money against the common Enemy, upon your simple Requisition, and give far beyond their Abilities, reflect, that a Penny taken from them by your Power is more honourable to you than a Pound presented by their Benevolence. Despise therefore their voluntary Grants, and resolve to harrass them with novel Taxes. They will probably complain to your Parliaments that they are taxed by a Body in which they have no Representative, and that this is contrary to common Right. They will petition for Redress. Let the Parliaments flout their Claims, reject their Petitions, refuse even to suffer the reading of them, and treat the Petitioners with the utmost Contempt. Nothing can have a better Effect, in producing the Alienation proposed; for though many can forgive injuries, *none ever forgave Contempt.*

IX. In laying these Taxes, never regard the heavy Burthens those remote People already undergo, in defending their own Frontiers, supporting their own provincial Governments, making new Roads, building Bridges, Churches and other public Edifices, which in old Countries have been done to your Hands by your Ancestors, but which occasion constant Calls and Demands on the Purses of a new People. Forget the *Restraints* you lay on their Trade for *your own* Benefit, and the Advantage a *Monopoly* of this Trade gives your exacting Merchants. Think nothing of the Wealth those Merchants and your Manufacturers acquire by the Colony Commerce; their encreased Ability thereby to pay Taxes at home; their accumulating, in the Price of their Commodities, most of those Taxes, and so levying them from their consuming Customers: All this, and the Employment and Support of thousands of your Poor by the Colonists, you are *intirely to forget.* But remember to make your arbitrary Tax more grievous to your

Provinces, by public Declarations importing that your Power of taxing them has *no limits*, so that when you take from them without their Consent a Shilling in the Pound, you have a clear Right to the other nineteen. This will probably weaken every Idea of *Security in their Property*, and convince them that under such a Government *they have nothing they can call their own*; which can scarce fail of producing *the happiest Consequences!*

X. Possibly indeed Some of them might still comfort themselves, and say, "Though we have no Property, we have yet *something* left that is valuable; we have constitutional *Liberty* both of Person and of Conscience. This King, these Lords, and these Commons, who it seems are too remote from us to know us and feel for us, cannot take from us our *Habeas Corpus* Right, or our Right of Trial *by a Jury of our Neighbours*: They cannot deprive us of the Exercise of our Religion, alter our ecclesiastical Constitutions, and compel us to be Papists if they please, or Mahometans." To annihilate this Comfort, begin by Laws to perplex their Commerce with infinite Regulations impossible to be remembered and observed; ordain Seizures of their Property for every Failure; take away the Trial of such Property by Jury, and give it to arbitrary Judges of your own appointing, and of the lowest Characters in the Country, whose Salaries and Emoluments are to arise out of the Duties or Condemnations, and whose Appointments are *during Pleasure*. Then let there be a formal Declaration of both Houses, that Opposition to your Edicts is *Treason*, and that Persons suspected of Treason in the Provinces may, according to some obsolete Law, be seized and sent to the Metropolis of the Empire for Trial; and pass an Act that those there charged with certain other Offences shall be sent away in Chains from their Friends and Country to be tried in the same Manner for Felony. Then erect a new Court of Inquisition among them, accompanied by an armed Force, with Instructions to transport all such suspected Persons, to be ruined by the Expence if they bring over Evidences to prove their Innocence, or be found guilty and hanged if they can't afford it. And lest the People should think you cannot possibly go any farther, pass another solemn declaratory Act, that "King, Lords, and Commons had, hath, and of Right ought to have, full Power and Authority to make Statutes of sufficient Force and Validity to bind the unrepresented Provinces IN ALL CASES WHATSOEVER." This will include *spiritual* with temporal; and taken together, must operate wonderfully to your Purpose, by convincing them, that they are at present under a Power something like that spoken of in the Scriptures, which can not only *kill their Bodies*, but *damn their Souls* to all Eternity, by compelling them, if it pleases, *to worship the Devil*.

XI. To make your Taxes more odious, and more likely to procure Resistance, send from the Capital a Board of Officers to superintend the Collection, composed of the most *indiscreet, ill-bred* and *insolent* you can find. Let these have large Salaries out of the extorted Revenue, and live in open grating Luxury upon the Sweat and Blood of the Industrious, whom they are to worry continually with groundless and expensive Prosecutions before the above-mentioned arbitrary Revenue-Judges, all *at the Cost of the Party prosecuted* tho' acquitted, because *the King is to pay no Costs.*——Let these Men *by your Order* be exempted from all the common Taxes and Burthens of the Province, though they and their Property are protected by its Laws. If any Revenue Officers are *suspected* of the least Tenderness for the People, discard them. If others are justly complained of, protect and reward them. If any of the Under-officers behave so as to provoke the People to drub them, promote those to better Offices: This will encourage others to procure for themselves such profitable Drubbings, by multiplying and enlarging such Provocations, and *all with work towards the End you aim at.*

XII. Another Way to make your Tax odious, is to misapply the Produce of it. If it was originally appropriated for the *Defence* of the Provinces and the better Support of Government, and the Administration of justice where it may be *necessary*, then apply none of it to that *Defence*, but bestow it where it is *not necessary*, in augmented Salaries or Pensions to every Governor who has distinguished himself by his Enmity to the People, and by calumniating them to their Sovereign. This will make them pay it more unwillingly, and be more apt to quarrel with those that collect it, and those that imposed it, who will quarrel again with them, and all shall contribute to your *main Purpose* of making them *weary* of *your Government.*

XIII. If the People of any Province have been accustomed to support their own Governors and Judges to Satisfaction, you are to apprehend that such Governors and Judges may be thereby influenced to treat the People kindly, and to do them Justice. This is another Reason for applying Part of that Revenue in larger Salaries to such Governors and Judges, given, as their Commissions are, *during your Pleasure* only, forbidding them to take any Salaries from their Provinces; that thus the People may no longer hope any Kindness from their Governors, or (in Crown Cases) any Justice from their Judges. And as the Money thus mis-applied in one Province is extorted from all, probably *all will resent the Misapplication.*

XIV. If the Parliaments of your Provinces should dare to claim Rights or complain of your Administration, order them to be harass'd with repeated

Dissolutions. If the same Men are continually return'd by new Elections, adjourn their Meetings to some Country Village where they cannot be accommodated, and there keep them *during Pleasure*; for this, you know, is your PREROGATIVE; and an excellent one it is, as you may manage it, to promote Discontents among the People, diminish their Respect, and *increase their Disaffection*.

XV. Convert the brave honest Officers of your Navy into pimping Tide-waiters and Colony Officers of the Customs. Let those who in Time of War fought gallantly in Defence of the Commerce of their Countrymen, in Peace be taught to prey upon it. Let them learn to be corrupted by great and real Smugglers; but (to shew their Diligence) scour with armed Boats every Bay, Harbour, River, Creek, Cove or Nook throughout the Coast of your Colonies, stop and detain every Coaster, every Wood-boat, every Fisherman, tumble their Cargoes, and even their Ballast, inside out and upside down; and if a Penn'orth of Pins is found un-entered, let the Whole be seized and confiscated. Thus shall the Trade of your Colonists suffer more from their Friends in Time of Peace, than it did from their Enemies in War. Then let these Boats Crews land upon every Farm in their Way, rob the Orchards, steal the Pigs and Poultry, and insult the Inhabitants. If the injured and exasperated Farmers, unable to procure other Justice, should attack the Agressors, drub them and burn their Boats, you are to call this *High Treason* and *Rebellion*, order Fleets and Armies into their Country, and threaten to carry all the offenders three thousand Miles to be hang'd, drawn and quartered. *O! this will work admirably*.

XVI. If you are told of Discontents in your Colonies, never believe that they are general, or that you have given Occasion for them; therefore do not think of applying any Remedy, or of changing any offensive Measure. Redress no Grievance, lest they should be encouraged to demand the Redress of some other Grievance. Grant no Request that is just and reasonable, lest they should make another that is unreasonable. Take all your Informations of the State of the Colonies from your Governors and Officers in Enmity with them. Encourage and reward these *Leasing-makers*; secrete their lying Accusations lest they should be confuted; but act upon them as the clearest Evidence, and believe nothing you hear from the Friends of the People. Suppose all *their* Complaints to be invented and promoted by a few factious Demagogues, whom if you could catch and hang, all would be quiet. Catch and hang a few of them accordingly; and the *Blood of the Martyrs* shall *work Miracles* in favour of your Purpose.

XVII. If you see *rival Nations* rejoicing at the Prospect of your Disunion with your Provinces, and endeavouring to promote it: If they translate, publish and applaud all the Complaints of your discontented Colonists, at the same Time privately stimulating you to severer Measures; let not that *alarm* or offend you. Why should it? since you all mean *the same Thing*.

XVIII. If any Colony should at their own Charge erect a Fortress to secure their Port against the Fleets of a foreign Enemy, get your Governor to betray that Fortress into your Hands. Never think of paying what it cost the Country, for that would *look*, at least, like some Regard for Justice; but turn it into a Citadel to awe the Inhabitants and curb their Commerce. If they should have lodged in such Fortress the very Arms they bought and used to aid you in your Conquests, seize them all, 'twill provoke like *Ingratitude* added to *Robbery*. One admirable Effect of these Operations will be, to discourage every other Colony from erecting such Defences, and so their and your Enemies may more easily invade them, to the great Disgrace of your Government, and of course *the Furtherance of your Project*.

XIX. Send Armies into their Country under Pretence of protecting the Inhabitants; but instead of garrisoning the Forts on their Frontiers with those Troops, to prevent Incursions, demolish those Forts, and order the Troops into the Heart of the Country, that the Savages may be encouraged to attack the Frontiers, and that the Troops may be protected by the Inhabitants: This will seem to proceed from your Ill will or your Ignorance, and contribute farther to produce and strengthen an Opinion among them, *that you are no longer fit to govern them*.

XX. Lastly, Invest the General of your Army in the Provinces with great and unconstitutional Powers, and free him from the Controul of even your own Civil Governors. Let him have Troops enow under his Command, with all the Fortresses in his Possession; and who knows but (like some provincial Generals in the Roman Empire, and encouraged by the universal Discontent you have produced) he may take it into his Head to set up for himself. If he should, and you have carefully practised these few *excellent Rules* of mine, take my Word for it, all the Provinces will immediately join him, and you will that Day (if you have not done it sooner) get rid of the Trouble of governing them, and all the *Plagues* attending their *Commerce* and Connection from thenceforth and for ever.

Q.E.D.

[*The Public Advertiser*, 11 September 1773]

CHAPTER 30

An Edict by the King of Prussia

(22 September 1773)

For the Public Advertiser.

The SUBJECT of the following Article of FOREIGN INTELLIGENCE being exceeding EXTRAORDINARY, is the Reason of its being separated from the usual Articles of *Foreign News*.

Dantzick, September 5.

We have long wondered here at the Supineness of the English Nation, under the Prussian Impositions upon its Trade entering our Port. We did not till lately know the *Claims*, antient and modern, that hang over that Nation, and therefore could not suspect that it might submit to those Impositions from a Sense of *Duty*, or from Principles of *Equity*. The following *Edict*, just made public, may, if serious, throw some Light upon this Matter.

"FREDERICK, by the Grace of God, King of *Prussia*, &c. &c. &c. to all present and to come,[1] HEALTH. The Peace now enjoyed throughout our Dominions, having afforded us Leisure to apply ourselves to the Regulation of Commerce, the Improvement of our Finances, and at the same Time the easing our *Domestic Subjects* in their Taxes: For these Causes, and other good Considerations us thereunto moving, We hereby make known, that after having deliberated these Affairs in our Council, present our dear Brothers, and other great Officers of the State, Members of the same, WE, of our certain Knowledge, full Power and Authority Royal, have made and issued this present Edict, viz.

"WHEREAS it is well known to all the World, that the first German Settlements made in the Island of Britain, were by Colonies of People, Subjects to our renowned Ducal Ancestors, and drawn from *their* Dominions,

[1] *A tous presens et à venir*. Orig.

under the Conduct of *Hengist*, *Horsa*, *Hella*, *Uffa*, *Cerdicus*, *Ida*, and others; and that the said Colonies have flourished under the Protection of our august House, for Ages past, have never been *emancipated* therefrom, and yet have hitherto yielded little Profit to the same. And whereas We Ourself have in the last War fought for and defended the said Colonies against the Power of *France*, and thereby enabled them to make Conquests from the said Power in *America*, for which we have not yet received adequate Compensation. And whereas it is just and expedient that a Revenue should be raised from the said Colonies in *Britain* towards our Indemnification; and that those who are Descendants of our antient Subjects, and thence still owe us due Obedience, should contribute to the replenishing of our Royal Coffers, as they must have done had their Ancestors remained in the Territories now to us appertaining: WE do therefore hereby ordain and command, That from and after the Date of these Presents, there shall be levied and paid to our Officers of the Customs, on all Goods, Wares and Merchandizes, and on all Grain and other Produce of the Earth exported from the said Island of *Britain*, and on all Goods of whatever Kind imported into the same, a *Duty of Four and an Half* per Cent. *ad Valorem*, for the Use of us and our Successors.——And that the said Duty may more effectually be collected, We do hereby ordain, that all Ships or Vessels bound from *Great Britain* to any other Part of the World, or from any other Part of the World to *Great Britain*, shall in their respective Voyages touch at our Port of KONINGSBERG, there to be unladen, searched, and charged with the said Duties.

"AND whereas there have been from Time to Time discovered in the said Island of *Great Britain* by our Colonists there, many Mines or Beds of Iron Stone; and sundry Subjects of our antient Dominion, skilful in converting the said Stone into Metal, have in Times past transported themselves thither, carrying with them and communicating that Art; and the Inhabitants of the said Island, *presuming* that they had a natural Right to make the best Use they could of the natural Productions of their Country for their own Benefit, have not only built Furnaces for smelting the said Stone into Iron, but have erected Plating Forges, Slitting Mills, and Steel Furnaces, for the more convenient manufacturing of the same, thereby endangering a Diminution of the said Manufacture in our antient Dominion. WE *do therefore* hereby farther ordain, that from and after the Date hereof, no Mill or other Engine for Slitting or Rolling of Iron, or any Plating Forge to work with a Tilt-Hammer, or any Furnace for making Steel, shall be erected or continued in the said Island of *Great Britain*:

And the Lord Lieutenant of every County in the said Island is hereby commanded, on Information of any such Erection within his County, to order and by Force to cause the same to be abated and destroyed, as he shall answer the Neglect thereof to Us at his Peril.——But We are nevertheless graciously pleased to permit the Inhabitants of the said Island to transport their Iron into *Prussia*, there to be manufactured, and to them returned, they paying our Prussian Subjects for the Workmanship, with all the Costs of Commission, Freight and Risque coming and returning, any Thing herein contained to the contrary notwithstanding.

"WE do not however think fit to extend this our Indulgence to the Article of *Wool*, but meaning to encourage not only the manufacturing of woollen Cloth, but also the raising of Wool in our antient Dominions, and to prevent *both*, as much as may be, in our said Island, We do hereby absolutely forbid the Transportation of Wool from thence even to the Mother Country *Prussia*; and that those Islanders may be farther and more effectually restrained in making any Advantage of their own Wool in the Way of Manufacture, We command that none shall be carried *out of one County into another*, nor shall any Worsted-Bay, or Woollen-Yarn, Cloth, Says, Bays, Kerseys, Serges, Frizes, Druggets, Cloth-Serges, Shalloons, or any other Drapery Stuffs, or Woollen Manufactures whatsoever, made up or mixt with Wool in any of the said Counties, be carried into any other County, or be Water-borne even across the smallest River or Creek, on Penalty of Forfeiture of the same, together with the Boats, Carriages, Horses, &c. that shall be employed in removing them. *Nevertheless* Our loving Subjects there are hereby permitted, (if they think proper) to use all their Wool as *Manure for the Improvement of their Lands*.

"AND whereas the Art and Mystery of making *Hats* hath arrived at great Perfection in *Prussia*, and the making of Hats by our remote Subjects ought to be as much as possible restrained. And forasmuch as the Islanders before-mentioned, being in Possession of Wool, Beaver, and other Furs, have *presumptuously* conceived they had a Right to make some Advantage thereof, by manufacturing the same into Hats, to the Prejudice of our domestic Manufacture, WE do therefore hereby strictly command and ordain, that no Hats or Felts whatsoever, dyed or undyed, finished or unfinished, shall be loaden or put into or upon any Vessel, Cart, Carriage or Horse, to be transported or conveyed *out of one County* in the said Island *into another County*, or to *any other Place whatsoever*, by any Person or Persons whatsoever, on Pain of forfeiting the same, with a Penalty of *Five Hundred Pounds* Sterling for every Offence. Nor shall any

Hat-maker in any of the said Counties employ more than two Apprentices, on Penalty of *Five Pounds* Sterling per Month: We intending hereby that such Hat-makers, being so restrained both in the Production and Sale of their Commodity, may find no Advantage in continuing their Business.——But lest the said Islanders should suffer Inconveniency by the Want of Hats, We are farther graciously pleased to permit them to send their Beaver Furs to *Prussia*; and We also permit Hats made thereof to be exported from *Prussia* to *Britain*, the People thus favoured to pay all Costs and Charges of Manufacturing, Interest, Commission to Our Merchants, Insurance and Freight going and returning, as in the Case of Iron.

"And lastly, Being willing farther to favour Our said Colonies in *Britain*, We do hereby also ordain and command, that all the Thieves, Highway and Street-Robbers, House-breakers, Forgerers, Murderers, So[domi]tes, and Villains of every Denomination, who have forfeited their Lives to the Law in *Prussia*, but whom We, in Our great Clemency, do not think fit here to hang, shall be emptied out of our Gaols into the said Island of *Great Britain for the* BETTER PEOPLING *of that Country*.

"We flatter Ourselves that these Our Royal Regulations and Commands will be thought *just* and *reasonable* by Our much-favoured Colonists in *England*, the said Regulations being copied from their own Statutes of 10 and 11 Will. III. C. 10.——5 Geo. II. C. 22.——23 Geo. II. C. 29.——4 Geo. I. C. II. and from other equitable Laws made by their Parliaments, or from Instructions given by their Princes, or from Resolutions of both Houses entered into for the GOOD *Government* of their own Colonies in *Ireland* and *America*.

"And all Persons in the said Island are hereby cautioned not to oppose in any wise the Execution of this Our Edict, or any Part thereof, such opposition being HIGH TREASON, of which all who are suspected shall be transported in Fetters from *Britain* to *Prussia*, there to be tried and executed according to the *Prussian Law*.

"Such is our Pleasure.

"Given at *Potsdam* this twenty-fifth Day of the Month of August, One Thousand Seven Hundred and Seventy-three, and in the Thirty-third Year of our Reign.

"By the KING in his Council RECHTMÆSSIG, *Secr.*"

Some take this Edict to be merely one of the King's *Jeux d'Esprit*: Others suppose it serious, and that he means a Quarrel with England: But all here think the Assertion it concludes with, "that these Regulations are copied from Acts of the English Parliament respecting their Colonies," a very *injurious* one: it being impossible to believe, that a People distinguish'd for their *Love of Liberty*, a Nation so *wise*, so *liberal in its Sentiments*, so *just and equitable* towards its *Neighbours*, should, from mean and *injudicious* Views of *petty immediate Profit*, treat *its own Children* in a Manner so *arbitrary* and TYRANNICAL!

[*The Public Advertiser*, 22 September 1773]

CHAPTER 31

On a Proposed Act to Prevent Emigration

([December?] 1773)

To the Printer of the Publick Advertiser

Sir,

You give us in your Paper of Tuesday, the 16th of November, what is called "the Plan of an Act to be proposed at the next Meeting of Parliament to prevent the Emigration of our People." I know not from what Authority it comes, but as it is very circumstantial, I must suppose some such Plan may be really under Consideration, and that this is thrown out to feel the Pulse of the Publick. I shall therefore, with your leave, give my Sentiments of it in your Paper.

During a Century and half that Englishmen have been at Liberty to remove if they pleased to America, we have heard of no Law to restrain that Liberty, and confine them as Prisoners in this Island. Nor do we perceive any ill Effects produced by their Emigration. Our Estates far from diminishing in Value thro' a Want of Tenants, have been in that Period more than doubled; the Lands in general are better cultivated; their increased Produce finds ready Sale at an advanced Price, and the Complaint has for some time been, not that we want Mouths to consume our Meat, but that we want Meat for our Number of Mouths.

Why then is such a restraining Law *now* thought necessary? A Paragraph in the same Paper from the *Edinburgh Courant* may perhaps throw some Light upon this Question. We are there told "that 1500 People have emigrated to America from the Shire of Sutherland within these two Years, and carried with them £7500 Sterling; which exceeds a Years Rent of the whole County; and that the single Consideration of the *Misery* which most of these People *must suffer* in America, independent of the Loss of Men and Money to the Mother Country, should engage the Attention not only of the *landed Interest, but of Administration*." The humane Writer of this Paragraph, may, I fancy, console himself, with the Reflection, that perhaps the apprehended future Sufferings of those Emigrants will never exist: for that it was probably the authentic Accounts they had received from Friends already settled there, of the Felicity to be enjoyed in that Country, with a thorough Knowledge of their own Misery at home, which induced their Removal. And, as a Politician, he may be comforted by assuring himself, that if they really meet with greater Misery in America, their future Letters lamenting it, will be more credited than the *Edinburgh Courant*, and effectually without a Law put a Stop to the Emigration. It seems some of the Scottish Chiefs, who delight no longer to live upon their Estates in the honourable Independence they were born to, among their respecting Tenants, but chuse rather a Life of Luxury, tho' among the Dependants of a Court, have lately raised their Rents most grievously to support the Expence. The Consuming of those Rents in London, tho' equally prejudicial to the poor County of *Sutherland*, no Edinburgh Newspaper complains of; but now that the oppressed Tenants take Flight and carry with them what might have supported the Landlords London Magnificence, he begins to *feel* for the MOTHER-COUNTRY, and its enormous *Loss* of £7500 carried to her Colonies! *Administration* is called upon to remedy the Evil, by another Abridgement of ENGLISH LIBERTY. And surely Administration should do something for these Gentry, as they do any thing for Administration.

But is there not an easier Remedy? Let them return to their Family Seats, live among their People, and instead of fleecing and skinning, patronize and cherish them; promote their Interest, encourage their Industry, and make their Situation comfortable. If the poor Folks are happier at home than they can be abroad, they will not lightly be prevailed with to cross the Ocean. But can their Lord blame them for leaving home in search of better Living, when he first sets them the Example?

I would consider the proposed Law,

1st. As to the NECESSITY of it.

2dly. The PRACTICABILITY.

3dly. The POLICY, if practicable.

and 4thly. The JUSTICE of it.

Pray spare me room for a few Words on each of these Heads.

1st. As to the *Necessity* of it.

If any Country has more People than can be comfortably subsisted in it, some of those who are incommoded, may be induced to emigrate. As long as the new Situation shall be *far* preferable to the old, the Emigration may possibly continue. But when many of those who at home interfered with others of the same Rank, (in the Competition for Farms, Shops, Business, Offices, and other Means of Subsistence) are gradually withdrawn, the Inconvenience of that Competition ceases; the Number remaining no longer half starve each other, they find they can now subsist comfortably, and tho' perhaps not quite so well as those who have left them, yet the inbred Attachment to a native Country is sufficient to overbalance a moderate Difference, and thus the Emigration ceases naturally. The Waters of the Ocean may move in Currents from one Quarter of the Globe to another, as they happen in some places to be accumulated and in others diminished; but no Law beyond the Law of Gravity, is necessary to prevent their Abandoning any Coast entirely. Thus the different Degrees of Happiness of different Countries and Situations find or rather make their Level by the flowing of People from one to another, and where that Level is once found, the Removals cease. Add to this, that even a real Deficiency of People in any Country occasioned by a wasting War or Pestilence, is speedily supply'd by earlier and of course more prolific Marriages, encouraged by the greater Facility of obtaining the Means of Subsistence. So that a Country half depopulated would soon be repeopled, till the Means of Subsistence were equalled by the Population. All Encrease beyond that Point must perish, or flow off into more favourable Situations. Such Overflowings there have been of Mankind in all Ages, or we should not now have had so many Nations. But to apprehend absolute Depopulation from that Cause, and call for a Law to prevent it, is calling for a Law to stop the Thames, lest its Waters, by what leave it daily at Gravesend, should be quite exhausted. Such a Law therefore I do not conceive to be *Necessary*.

2dly. As to the *Practicability*.

When I consider the Attempts of this kind that have been made, first in the time of Archbishop Laud, by Orders of Council, to stop the Puritans who were flying from his Persecutions, into New-England, and next by

Louis XIV, to retain in his Kingdom the persecuted Huguenots; and how ineffectual all the Power of our Crown, with which the Archbishop armed himself, and all the more absolute Power of that great French Monarch, were, to obtain the End for which they were exerted. When I consider too, the extent of Coast to be guarded, and the Multitude of Cruizers necessary effectually to make a Prison of the island for this confinement of free Englishmen, who naturally love Liberty, and would probably by the very Restraint be more stimulated to break thro' it, I cannot but think such a Law IMPRACTICABLE. The Offices would not be applied to for Licences, the Ports would not be used for Embarcation. And yet the People disposed to leave us would, as the Puritans did, get away by Shipfuls.

3dly. As to the *Policy* of the Law.

Since, as I have shewn, there is no Danger of depopulating Britain, but that the Places of those who depart will soon be filled up equal to the Means of obtaining a Livelihood, let us see whether there are not some general *Advantages* to be expected from the present Emigration. The new Settlers in America, finding plenty of Subsistence, and Land easily acquired whereon to seat their Children, seldom postpone Marriage thro' fear of Poverty. Their natural Increase is therefore in a proportion far beyond what it would have been if they had remained here. New Farms are daily every where forming in those immense Forests, new Towns and Villages rising; hence a growing Demand for our Merchandise, to the greater Employment of our Manufacturers and the enriching of our Merchants. By this natural Increase of People, the Strength of the Empire is increased; Men are multiplied out of whom new Armies may be formed on Occasion, or the old recruited. The long extended Sea Coast too, of that vast Country, the great maritime Commerce of its Parts with each other, its many navigable Rivers and Lakes, and its plentiful Fisheries, breed multitudes of Seamen, besides those created and supported by its Voyages to Europe; a thriving Nursery this, for the manning of our Fleets in time of War, and maintaining our Importance among foreign Nations, by that Navy which is also our best Security against invasions from our Enemies. An Extension of Empire by Conquest of inhabited Countries is not so easily obtained, it is not so easily secured, it alarms more the neighbouring States, it is more subject to Revolts, and more apt to occasion new Wars. The Increase of Dominion by Colonies proceeding from yourselves, and by the natural Growth of your own People, cannot be complained of by your Neighbours as an Injury, none have a right to be offended with it. Your new Possessions are therefore more secure, they are more cheaply gained, they are attached to your Nation by natural Alliance and Affection, and thus they afford an additional Strength more certainly to be depended on, than any that can be acquired by a Conquering Power, tho' at an immense Expence of Blood and Treasure. These methinks are national Advantages that more than equiponderate with the Inconveniencies suffered by a few Scotch or Irish Landlords, who perhaps may only find it necessary to abate a little of their present Luxury, or of those advanced Rents they now so unfeelingly demand. From these Considerations, I think I may conclude that the restraining Law proposed, would if practicable be IMPOLITIC.

4thly. As to the *Justice* of it.

I apprehend that every Briton who is made unhappy at home, has a Right to remove from any Part of his King's Dominions into those of any other Prince where he can be happier. If this should be denied me, at least it will be allowed that he has a Right to remove into any other Part of the same Dominions. For by this Right so many Scotchmen remove into England, easing their own Country of its supernumeraries, and benefitting ours by their Industry. And this is the Case with those who go to America. Will not these Scottish Lairds be satisfied unless a Law passes to pin down all Tenants to the Estate they are born on, *(adscriptitii glebae)* to be bought and sold with it? God has given to the Beasts of the Forest and to the Birds of the Air a Right when their Subsistence fails in one Country, to migrate into another, where they can get a more comfortable Living; and shall Man be denyed a Privilege enjoyed by Brutes, merely to gratify a few avaricious Landlords? Must Misery be made *permanent*, and suffered by *many* for the Emolument of One? While the Increase of Human Beings is prevented, and thousands of their Offspring stifled as it were in the Birth, that this petty Pharaoh may enjoy an *Excess* of Opulence? God commands to increase and replenish the Earth: The proposed Law would forbid increasing, and confine Britons to their present Number, keeping half that Number too, in wretchedness. The Common People of Britain and of Ireland, contributed by the Taxes they paid, and by the Blood they lost, to the Success of that War, which brought into our Hands the vast unpeopled Territories of North America; a Country favoured by Heaven with all the Advantages of Soil and Climate; Germans are now pouring into it, to take Possession of it, and fill it with their Posterity; and shall

Britons, and Irelanders, who have a much better Right to it, be forbidden a Share of it, and instead of enjoying there the Plenty and Happiness that might reward their Industry, be compelled to remain here in Poverty and Misery? Considerations such as these persuade me, that the proposed Law would be both UNJUST and INHUMAN.

If then it is *unnecessary, impracticable, impolitic*, and *unjust*, I hope our Parliament will never receive the Bill, but leave Landlords to their own Remedy, an Abatement of Rents and Frugality of Living; and leave the Liberties of Britons and Irishmen at least as extensive as it found them. I am, Sir, Yours &c.

A Friend to the Poor.

[Papers 20:522–8]

CHAPTER 32
Proposed Articles of Confederation
(21 July 1775)

Articles of Confederation and perpetual Union, entred into by the Delegates of the several Colonies of New Hampshire &c. in general Congress met at Philadelphia, May 10. 1775.

Art. I. The Name of the Confederacy shall henceforth be *The United Colonies of North America.*

Art. II. The said United Colonies hereby severally enter into a firm League of Friendship with each other, binding on themselves and their Posterity, for their common Defence against their Enemies, for the Security of their Liberties and Propertys, the Safety of their Persons and Families, and their mutual and general welfare.

Art. III. That each Colony shall enjoy and retain as much as it may think fit of its own present Laws, Customs, Rights, Privileges, and peculiar Jurisdictions within its own Limits; and may amend its own Constitution as shall seem best to its own Assembly or Convention.

Art. IV. That for the more convenient Management of general Interests, Delegates shall be annually elected in each Colony to meet in General Congress at such Time and Place as shall be agreed on in the next preceding Congress. Only where particular Circumstances do not make a Deviation necessary, it is understood to be a Rule, that each succeeding Congress be held in a different Colony till the whole Number be gone through, and so in perpetual Rotation; and that accordingly the next Congress after the present shall be held at Annapolis in Maryland.

Art. V. That the Power and Duty of the Congress shall extend to the Determining on War and Peace, to sending and receiving Ambassadors, and entring into Alliances, the Reconciliation with Great Britain; the Settling all Disputes and Differences between Colony and Colony about Limits or any other cause if such should arise; and the Planting of new Colonies when proper. The Congress shall also make such general Ordinances as tho' necessary to the General Welfare, particular Assemblies cannot be competent to; viz. those that may relate to our general Commerce or general Currency; to the Establishment of Posts; and the Regulation of our common Forces. The Congress shall also have the Appointment of all Officers civil and military, appertaining to the general Confederacy, such as General Treasurer Secretary, &c.

Art. VI. All Charges of Wars, and all other general Expences to be incurr'd for the common Welfare, shall be defray'd out of a common Treasury, which is to be supply'd by each Colony in proportion to its Number of Male Polls between 16 and 60 Years of Age; the Taxes for paying that proportion are to be laid and levied by the Laws of each Colony.

Art. VII. The Number of Delegates to be elected and sent to the Congress by each Colony, shall be regulated from time to time by the Number of such Polls return'd, so as that one Delegate be allowed for every 5000 Polls. And the Delegates are to bring with them to every Congress an authenticated Return of the number of Polls in their respective Provinces, which is to be annually taken, for the Purposes abovementioned.

Art. VIII. At every Meeting of the Congress One half of the Members return'd exclusive of Proxies be necessary to make a Quorum, and Each Delegate at the Congress, shall have a Vote in all Cases; and if necessarily absent, shall be allowed to appoint any other Delegate from the same Colony to be his Proxy, who may vote for him.

Art. IX. An executive Council shall be appointed by the Congress out of their own Body, consisting of 12 Persons; of whom in the first Appointment one Third, viz. 4, shall be for one Year, 4 for two Years, and 4 for three Years, and as the said Terms expire, the vacancies shall be filled by Appointments for three Years, whereby One Third of the Members will be changed annually. And each Person who has served the said Term of three Years as Counsellor, shall have a Respite of three Years, before he can be elected again. This Council (of whom two thirds shall be a Quorum) in the Recess of the Congress is to execute what shall have been enjoin'd thereby; to manage the general continental Business and Interests to receive Applications from foreign Countries; to prepare Matters for the Consideration of the Congress; to fill up *(pro tempore)* continental Offices that fall vacant; and to draw on the General Treasurer for such Monies as may be necessary for general Services, and appropriated by the Congress to such Services.

Art. X. No Colony shall engage in an offensive War with any Nation of Indians without the Consent of the Congress, or great Council abovementioned, who are first to consider the Justice and Necessity of such War.

Art. XI. A perpetual Alliance offensive and defensive, is to be entered into as soon as may be with the Six Nations; their Limits to be ascertain'd and secur'd to them; their Land not to be encroach'd on, nor any private or Colony Purchases made of them hereafter to be held good; nor any Contract for Lands to be made but between the Great Council of the Indians at Onondaga and the General Congress. The Boundaries and Lands of all the other Indians shall also be ascertain'd and secur'd to them in the same manner; and Persons appointed to reside among them in proper Districts, who shall take care to prevent Injustice in the Trade with them, and be enabled at our General Expence by occasional small Supplies, to relieve their personal Wants and Distresses. And all Purchases from them shall be by the Congress for the General Advantage and Benefit of the United Colonies.

Art. XII. As all new Institutions may have Imperfections which only Time and Experience can discover, it is agreed, that the General Congress from time to time shall propose such Amendment of this Constitution as may be found necessary; which being approv'd by a Majority of the Colony Assemblies, shall be equally binding with the rest of the Articles of this Confederation.

Art. XIII. Any and every Colony from Great Britain upon the Continent of North America not at present engag'd in our Association, may upon Application and joining the said Association, be receiv'd into this Confederation, viz. Ireland the West India Islands, Quebec, St. Johns, Nova Scotia, Bermudas, and the East and West Floridas: and shall thereupon be entitled to all the Advantages of our Union, mutual Assistance and Commerce.

These Articles shall be propos'd to the several Provincial Conventions or Assemblies, to be by them consider'd, and if approv'd they are advis'd to impower their Delegates to agree to and ratify the same in the ensuing Congress. After which the *Union* thereby establish'd is to continue firm till the Terms of Reconciliation proposed in the Petition of the last Congress to the King are agreed to; till the Acts since made restraining the American Commerce and Fisheries are repeal'd; till Reparation is made for the Injury done to Boston by shutting up its Port; for the Burning of Charlestown;

and for the Expence of this unjust War; and till all the British Troops are withdrawn from America. On the Arrival of these Events the Colonies are to return to their former Connection and Friendship with Britain: But on Failure thereof this Confederation is to be perpetual.

[Papers 22:120–5]

CHAPTER 33

The Morals of Chess

(before 28 June 1779)

[Playing at Chess is the most ancient and the most universal game known among men; for its original is beyond the memory of history, and it has, for numberless ages, been the amusement of all the civilised nations of Asia, the Persians, the Indians, and the Chinese. Europe has had it above a thousand years; the Spaniards have spread it over their part of America; and it has lately to make its appearance in the United States. It is so interesting in itself, as not to need the view of gain to induce engaging in it; and thence it is seldom played for money. Those therefore who have leisure for such diversions, cannot find one that is more innocent: and the following piece, written with a view to correct (among a few young friends) some little improprieties in the practice of it, shows at the same time, that it may, in its effects on the mind, be not merely innocent, but advantageous, to the vanquished as well as to the victor.]

The game of Chess is not merely an idle Amusement. Several very valuable qualities of the mind, useful in the course of human Life, are to be acquired or strengthened by it, so as to become habits, ready on all occasions. For Life is a kind of Chess, in which we have often points to gain, and Competitors or Adversaries to contend with; and in which there is a vast variety of good and ill Events, that are in some degree the Effects of Prudence or the want of it. By playing at Chess, then, we may learn,

I. *Foresight*, which looks a little into futurity, and considers the consequences that may attend an action: for it is continually occurring to the Player, "If I move this piece, what will be the advantages or disadvantages of my new situation? What Use can my Adversary make of it to annoy me? What other moves can I make to support it, and to defend myself from his attacks?"

II. *Circumspection*, which surveys the whole Chessboard, or scene of action; the relations of the several pieces and situations, the Dangers they are respectively exposed to, the several possibilities of their aiding each other; the probabilities that the Adversary may make this or that move, and attack this or the other Piece, and what different Means can be used to avoid his stroke, or turn its consequences against him.

III. *Caution*, not to make our moves too hastily. This habit is best acquired by observing strictly the laws of the Game; such as, *If you touch a piece, you must move it somewhere; if you set it down, you must let it stand.* And it is therefore best that these rules should be observed, as the Game becomes thereby more the image of human Life, and particularly of War; in which, if you have incautiously put yourself into a bad and dangerous position, you cannot obtain your Enemy's Leave to withdraw your Troops, and place them more securely, but you must abide all the consequences of your rashness.

And *lastly*, we learn by chess the habit of not being discouraged by *present* bad appearances in the state of our affairs, the habit of hoping for a favourable change, and that of persevering in the search of resources. The Game is so full of Events, there is such a variety of turns in it, the Fortune of it is so subject to sudden Vicissitudes, and one so frequently, after long contemplation, discovers the means of extricating one's self from a supposed insurmountable Difficulty, that one is encouraged to continue the Contest to the last, in hopes of Victory by our own skill, or at least of giving a stale mate, by the Negligence of our Adversary. And whoever considers, what in Chess he often sees instances of, that particular pieces of success are apt to produce Presumption, and its consequent Inattention, by which more is afterwards lost than was gained by the preceding Advantage, while misfortunes produce more care and attention, by which the loss may be recovered, will learn not to be too much discouraged by the present success of his Adversary, nor to despair of final good fortune, upon every little Check he receives in the pursuit of it.

That we may therefore be induced more frequently to chuse this beneficial amusement, in preference to others which are not attended with the same advantages, every Circumstance that may increase the pleasure of it should be regarded; and every action or word that is unfair, disrespectful, or that in any way may give uneasiness, should be avoided, as contrary to the immediate intention of both the Players, which is to pass the Time agreeably.

Therefore, first, it is agreed to play according to the strict rules, then those rules are to be exactly observed by both parties, and should not be insisted on for one side, while deviated from by the other——for this is not equitable.

Secondly, if it is agreed not to observe the rules exactly, but one party demands indulgencies, he should then be as willing to allow them to the other.

Thirdly, no false move should ever be made to extricate yourself out of a difficulty, or to gain an advantage. There can be no pleasure in playing with a person once detected in such unfair practice.

Fourthly, if your adversary is long in playing, you ought not to hurry him, or express any uneasiness at his delay. You should not sing, nor whistle, nor look at your watch, nor take up a book to read, nor make a tapping with your feet on the floor, or with your fingers on the table, nor do anything that may disturb his attention. For all these things displease; and they do not show your skill in playing, but your craftiness or your rudeness.

Fifthly, you ought not to endeavour to amuse and deceive your adversary, by pretending to have made bad moves, and saying you have now lost the game, in order to make him secure and careless, and inattentive to your schemes: for this is fraud, and deceit, not skill in the game.

Sixthly, you must not, when you have gained a victory, use any triumphing or insulting expression, nor show too much pleasure; but endeavour to console your adversary, and make him less dissatisfied with himself by every kind and civil expression, that may be used with truth, such as, "you understand the game better than I, but you are a little inattentive;" or, "you play too fast;" or, "you had the best of the game but something happened to divert your thoughts, and that turned it in my favour."

Seventhly, if you are a spectator, while others play, observe the most perfect silence. For if you give advice, you offend both parties, him against whom you give it, because it may cause the loss of his game; him in whose favour you give it, because, though it be good, and he follows it, he loses the pleasure he might have had, if you had permitted him to think until it occurred to himself. Even after a move or moves, you must not, by replacing the pieces, shew how it might have been played better; for that displeases, and may occasion disputes or doubts about their true situation. All talking to the players lessens or diverts their attention, and is therefore unpleasing. Nor should you give the least hint to either party, by any kind of noise or motion. If you do, you are unworthy to be a spectator. If you have a mind to exercise or show your judgments, do it in playing your own game, when you have an opportunity, not in criticising or meddling with, or counselling, the play of others.

Lastly, if the game is not to be played rigorously, according to the rules above mentioned, then moderate your desire of victory over your adversary, and be pleased with one over yourself. Snatch not eagerly at every advantage offered by his unskilfulness or inattention; but point out to him kindly that by such a move he places or leaves a piece in danger and unsupported; that by another he will put his king in a dangerous situation, &c. By this generous civility (so opposite to the unfairness above forbidden) you may, indeed, happen to lose the game to your opponent; but you will win what is better, his esteem, his respect, and his affection, together with the silent approbation and good will of impartial spectators.

[Writings 7:357–62]

CHAPTER 34

To Madame Brillon: The Whistle

(10 November 1779)

I received my dear Friend's two Letters, one for Wednesday & one for Saturday. This is again Wednesday. I do not deserve one for to day, because I have not answered the former. But indolent as I am, and averse to Writing, the Fear of having no more of your pleasing Epistles, if I do not contribute to the Correspondance, obliges me to take up my Pen: And as M. B. has kindly sent me Word, as he sets out to-morrow to see you; instead of spending this Wednesday Evening as I have long done its Name-sakes, in your delightful Company, I sit down to spend it in thinking of you, in writing to you, and in reading over and over again our Letters.

I am charm'd with your Description of Paradise, and with your Plan of living there. And I approve much of your Conclusion, that in the mean time we should draw all the Good we can from this World. In my Opinion we might all draw more Good, from it than we do, and suffer less Evil, if we would but take care *not to give too much for our Whistles*. For to me it seems that most of the unhappy People we meet with, are become so by Neglect of that Caution.

You ask what I mean?——You love Stories, and will excuse my telling you one of my self. When I was a Child of seven Years old, my Friends on a Holiday fill'd my little Pocket with Halfpence. I went directly to a Shop where they sold Toys for Children; and being charm'd with the Sound of a Whistle that I met by the way, in the hands of another Boy, I voluntarily offer'd and gave all my Money for it. When I came home, whistling all over the House, much pleas'd with my Whistle, but disturbing all the Family, my Brothers, Sisters and Cousins, understanding the Bargain I had made, told me I had given four times as much for it as it was worth, put me in mind what good Things I might have bought with the rest of the Money, and laught at me so much for my Folly that I cry'd with Vexation; and the Reflection gave me more Chagrin than the Whistle gave me Pleasure.

This however was afterwards of use to me, the Impression continuing on my Mind; so that often when I was tempted to buy some unnecessary thing, I said to my self, *Do not give too much for the Whistle*; and I sav'd my Money.

As I grew up, came into the World, and observed the Actions of Men, I thought I met many *who gave too much for the Whistle.*——When I saw one ambitious of Court Favour, sacrificing his Time in Attendance at Levees, his Repose, his Liberty, his Virtue and perhaps his Friend, to obtain it; I have said to my self, *This Man gives too much for his Whistle.*——When I saw another fond of popularity, constantly employing himself in political Bustles, neglecting his own Affairs, and ruining them by that Neglect, *He pays*, says I, *too much for his Whistle.*——If I knew a Miser, who gave up every kind of comfortable Living, all the Pleasure of doing Good to others, all the Esteem of his Fellow Citizens, and the Joys of benevolent Friendship, for the sake of Accumulating Wealth, *Poor Man*, says I, *you pay too much for your Whistle.*——When I met with a Man of Pleasure, sacrificing every laudable Improvement of his Mind or of his Fortune, to mere corporeal Satisfactions, and ruining his Health in their Pursuit, *Mistaken Man*, says I, *you are providing Pain for your self instead of Pleasure, you pay too much for your Whistle.*——If I see one fond of Appearance, of fine Cloaths, fine Houses, fine Furniture, fine Equipages, all above his Fortune, for which he contracts Debts, and ends his Career in a Prison; *Alas*, says I, *he has paid too much for his Whistle.*——When I saw a beautiful sweet-temper'd Girl, marry'd to an ill-natured Brute of a Husband; *What a Pity*, says I, that *she should pay so much for a Whistle!* —— In short, I conceiv'd that great Part of the Miseries of Mankind, were brought upon them by the false Estimates they had made of the Value of Things, and by their *giving too much for the Whistle.*

Yet I ought to have Charity for these unhappy People, when I consider that with all this Wisdom of which I am boasting, there are certain things in the World so tempting; for Example the Apples of King John, which happily are not to be bought, for if they were put to sale by Auction, I might very easily be led to ruin my self in the Purchase, and find that I had once more *given too much for the Whistle.*

Adieu, my dearest Friend, and believe me ever yours very sincerely and with unalterable Affection.

[Papers 31:69–77]

CHAPTER 35
To Joseph Priestley
(8 February 1780)

Dear Sir,

Your kind Letter of Sept. 27. came to hand but very lately, the Bearer having staid long in Holland.

I always rejoice to hear of your being still employ'd in Experimental Researches into Nature, and of the Success you meet with. The rapid Progress *true* Science now makes, occasions my Regretting sometimes that I was born so soon. It is impossible to imagine the Height to which may be carried in a 1000 Years the Power of Man over Matter. We may perhaps learn to deprive large Masses of their Gravity and give them absolute Levity, for the sake of easy Transport. Agriculture may diminish its Labour and double its Produce. All Diseases may by sure means be prevented or cured, not excepting even that of Old Age, and our Lives lengthened at pleasure even beyond the antediluvian Standard. O that moral Science were in as fair a Way of Improvement, that Men would cease to be Wolves to one another, and that human Beings would at length learn what they now improperly call Humanity.——

I am glad my little Paper on the Aurora Borealis pleas'd. If it should occasion farther Enquiry, and so produce a better Hypothesis, it will not be wholly useless——

I am ever, with the greatest & most sincere Esteem, Dear Sir, Yours very affectionately

Separate Paper

I have considered the Situation of that Person very attentively; I think that with a little help from the *Moral Algebra*, he might form a better Judgment than any other Person can form for him. But since my Opinion seems to desired, I give it for continuing to the End of the Term under all the present Disagreeable Circumstances. The Connection will then die a natural Death. No Reason will be expected to be given for the Separation, and of course no Offence taken at Reasons given. The Friendship may still subsist, and in some other way be useful.——The Time diminishes daily, and is usefully employ'd. All human Situations have their Inconveniencies. We *feel* those that we find in the present, and we neither *feel* nor *see* those that exist in another. Hence we make frequent and troublesome Changes without Amendment, and often for the Worse. In my Youth I was Passenger in a little Sloop, descending the River Delaware. There being no Wind, we were obliged, when the Ebb was spent, to cast anchor, and wait for the next. The Heat of the Sun on the Vessel was excessive, the Company Strangers to me and not very agreeable. Near the River Side I saw what I took to be a pleasent green Meadow, in the Middle of which was a large shady Tree, where it strook my Fancy, I could sit and read, having a Book in my Pocket, and pass the Time agreably till the Tide turned. I therefore prevail'd with the Captain to put me ashore. Being landed I found the greatest Part of my Meadow was really a Marsh, in crossing which to come at my Tree, I was up to the Knees in Mire: And I had not plac'd my self under its Shade five Minutes before the Muskitoes in Swarms found me out, attack'd my Legs, Hands and Face, and made my Reading and my Rest impossible: So that I return'd to the Beach, and call'd for the Boat to come and take me aboard again, where I was obliged to bear the Heat I had strove to quit, and also the Laugh of the Company.——Similar Cases in the Affairs of Life have since frequently fallen under my Observation.——

[Papers 31:455–7]

CHAPTER 36
To Joseph Priestley
(7 June 1782)

Dear Sir,

I received your kind Letter of the 7th of April, also one of the 3d of May. I have always great Pleasure in hearing from you, in learning that you are well, and that you continue your Experiments. I should rejoice much if I could once more recover the Leisure to search with you into the Works of Nature, I mean the inanimate, not the animate or moral Part of them. The more I discover'd of the former, the more I admir'd them; the more I know of the latter, the more I am disgusted with them. Men I find to be a Sort of Beings very badly constructed, as they are generally more easily provok'd than reconcil'd, more disposed to do Mischief to each other than to make Reparation, much more easily deceiv'd than undeceiv'd, and having more Pride and even Pleasure in killing than in begetting one another, for without a Blush they assemble in great armies at Noon Day to destroy, and when they have kill'd as many as they can, they exaggerate the Number to augment the fancied Glory; but they creep into Corners or cover themselves with the Darkness of Night, when they mean to beget, as being asham'd of a virtuous Action. A virtuous Action it would be, and a vicious one the killing of them, if the Species were really worth producing or preserving; but of this I begin to doubt. I know you have no such Doubts, because, in your zeal for their Welfare, you are taking a great deal of Pains to save their Souls. Perhaps as you grow older you may look upon this as a hopeless Project, or an idle Amusement, repent of having murdered in mephitic Air so many honest harmless Mice, and wish that to prevent Mischief you had used Boys and Girls instead of them. In what Light we are view'd by superior Beings, may be gathered from a Piece of late West India News, which possibly has not yet reach'd you. A young Angel of Distinction being sent down to this World on some Business for the first time, had an old Courier-Spirit assigned him as a Guide.

They arriv'd over the Seas of Martinico in the middle of the long Day of obstinate Fights between the Fleets of Rodney and De Grasse. When thro' the Clouds of Smoke he saw the Fire of the Guns, the Decks cover'd with mangled Limbs, and Bodies dead or dying, the Ships sinking, burning, or blown into the Air, and the Quantity of Pain, Misery, and Destruction, the Crews yet alive were thus with so much Eagerness dealing round to one another; he turn'd angrily to his Guide, and said, You blundering Blockhead, you are ignorant of your Business; you undertook to conduct me to the Earth, and you have brought me into Hell!——No, Sir, says the Guide; I have made no mistake; this is really the Earth, and these are Men. Devils never treat one another in this cruel manner; they have more Sense, and more of what Men (vainly) call *Humanity!*

But to be serious, my dear old Friend, I love you as much as ever, and I love all the honest Souls that meet at the London Coffeehouse. I only wonder how it happen'd that they and my other Friends in England, came to be such good Creatures in the midst of so perverse a Generation. I long to see them and you once more, and I labour for Peace with more earnestness, that I may again be happy in your sweet society . . .

Adieu, and believe me ever, yours most affectionately,

[Papers 37:444–46]

CHAPTER 37
To Richard Price
(13 June 1782)

Dear Sir,

I received a few Days since your kind Letter of the 27th past, by Messrs. Milford and Brown. It gave me great Pleasure to hear of your Welfare. All that come with a line from you are welcome.

I congratulate you on the late Revolution in your Public Affairs. Much good may arise from it, though possibly not all that good men, and even the new ministers themselves may have wished or expected. The Change however in the Sentiments of the Nation, in which I see evident effects of your Writing, with those of our deceas'd friend Mr. Burgh, and others of our valuable Club, should encourage you to proceed. The ancient Roman and Greek Orators could only speak to the Number of Citizens capable of being assembled within the Reach of their Voice: Their Writings had little Effect because the Bulk of the People could not read. Now by the Press we can speak to Nations; and good Books and well written Pamphlets have great and general Influence. The Facility, with which the same Truths may be repeatedly enforc'd by placing them daily in different lights, in Newspapers which are everywhere read, gives a great Chance of establishing them. And we now find that it is not only right to strike while the Iron is hot, but that it is very practicable to heat it by continual Striking.——I suppose all may now correspond with more Freedom, and I shall be glad to hear from you as often as may be convenient to you. Please to present my best Respects to our good old Friends of the London Coffee house. I often figure to myself the Pleasure I should have in being once more seated among them. With the greatest and most sincere Esteem and affection, I am, my dear Friend, Your ever,

[Papers 37:472–73]

CHAPTER 38
To Robert Morris
(25 December 1783)

Sir,

I have received your Favour of the 30th of September, for which I thank you. My Apprehension that the Union between France and our States might be diminished by Accounts from hence, was occasioned by the extravagant and violent Language held here by a Public Person[1] in public Company, which had that Tendency; and it was natural for me to think his Letters might hold the same Language; in which I was right; for I have since had Letters from Boston informing me of it. Luckily here, and I hope there, it is imputed to the true Cause; a Disorder in the Brain; which tho' not constant has its Fits too frequent. I will not fill my Letter with an Account of those Discourses; Mr. Laurens when you see him, can give it to you; I mean such as he heard in Company with other Persons; for I would not desire him to relate private Conversations. They distress'd me much at the Time, being then at your earnest Instances soliciting for more Aids of Money, the Success of which Solicitation such ungrateful and provoking Language might I feared have had a Tendency to prevent. Enough of this at present.——

I have been exceedingly hurt and afflicted by the Difficulty some of your late Bills met with in Holland. As soon as I receiv'd the Letter from Messrs. Willinck & Co. which I inclose, I sent for Mr. Grand, who brought me a Sketch of his Account with you, by which it appear'd that the Demands upon us, existing and expected, would more than absorb the Funds in his Hands. We could not indulge the smallest Hope of obtaining further Assistance here, the Public Finances being in a State of Embarrassment, private Persons full of Distrust occasioned by the late Stoppage of Payment at the Caisse d'Escompte, and Money in general extreamly scarce . . .

[1] [John Adams.]

The Remissness of our People in Paying Taxes is highly blameable, the Unwillingness to pay them is still more so. I see in some Resolutions of Town-Meetings, a Remonstrance against giving Congress a Power to take as they call it, *the People's Money* out of their Pockets tho' only to pay the Interest and Principal of Debts duly contracted. They seem to mistake the Point. Money justly due from the People is their Creditors' Money, and no longer the Money of the People, who, if they withold it, should be compell'd to pay by some Law. All Property indeed, except the Savage's temporary Cabin, his Bow, his Matchcoat, and other little Acquisitions absolutely necessary for his Subsistence, seems to me to be the Creature of public Convention. Hence the Public has the Right of Regulating Descents and all other Conveyances of Property, and even of limiting the Quantity and the Uses of it. All the Property that is necessary to a Man for the Conservation of the Individual and the Propagation of the Species, is his natural Right which none can justly deprive him of: But all Property superfluous to such purposes is the Property of the Publick, who by their Laws have created it, and who may therefore by other Laws dispose of it, whenever the Welfare of the Publick shall demand such Disposition. He that does not like civil Society on these Terms, let him retire and live among Savages.——He can have no right to the Benefits of Society who will not pay his Club towards the Support of it.

. . . With sincere Regard and Attachment, I am ever, Dear Sir, Your most &c.

[LC Box 21]

CHAPTER 39

Remarks Concerning the Savages of North-America

(1783)

SAVAGES we call them, because their Manners differ from ours, which we think the Perfection of Civility. They think the same of theirs.

Perhaps if we could examine the Manners of different Nations with Impartiality, we should find no People so rude as to be without any Rules of Politeness; nor any so polite as not to have some Remains of Rudeness.

The Indian Men when young are Hunters and Warriors; when old, Counsellors; for all their Government is by Counsel of the Sages; there is no Force, there are no Prisons, no Officers to compel Obedience, or inflict Punishment.——Hence they generally study Oratory; the best Speaker having the most Influence. The Indian Women till the Ground, dress the Food, nurse and bring up the Children, and preserve and hand down to Posterity the Memory of public Transactions. These Employments of Men and Women are accounted natural and honourable. Having few artificial Wants, they have abundance of Leisure for Improvement by Conversation. Our laborious Manner of Life compared with theirs, they esteem slavish and base; and the Learning on which we value ourselves, they regard as frivolous and useless. An Instance of this occurr'd at the Treaty of Lancaster in Pennsylvania, anno 1744, between the Government of Virginia and the Six Nations. After the principal Business was settled, the Commissioners from Virginia acquainted the Indians by a Speech, that there was at Williamsburg a College, with a Fund for Educating Indian Youth; and that if the Six Nations would send down half a dozen of their young Lads to that College, the Government would take Care that they should be well provided for, and instructed in all the Learning of the White People. It is one of the Indian Rules of Politeness not to answer a public Proposition the same day that it is made; they think it would be treating it as a light matter, and that they show it Respect by taking time to consider it, as of a Matter important. They therefore deferr'd their Answer till the Day following; when their Speaker began by expressing their deep Sense of the kindness of the Virginia Government in making them that Offer, for we know, says he, that you highly esteem the kind of Learning taught in those Colleges, and that the Maintenance of our young Men while with you, would be very expensive to you. We are convinc'd therefore that you mean to do us Good by your Proposal, and we thank you heartily. But you who are wise must know, that different Nations have different Conceptions of Things, and you will therefore not take it amiss if our Ideas of this kind of Education happen not to be the same with yours. We have had some Experience of it: Several of our young People were formerly brought up at the Colleges of the Northern Provinces; they were instructed in all your Sciences; but, when they came back to us they were bad Runners, ignorant of every means of living in the Woods, unable to bear either Cold or Hunger, knew neither how to build a Cabin, take a Deer or kill an Enemy, spoke our Language imperfectly, were therefore neither fit for Hunters Warriors, or Counsellors, they were totally good for nothing.——We are however not the less oblig'd by your kind Offer, tho' we decline accepting it; and to show our grateful Sense of it, if the Gentlemen of Virginia will send us a Dozen of their Sons, we will take great Care of their Education, instruct them in all we know, and *make MEN* of them.——

Having frequent Occasions to hold public Councils, they have acquired great Order and Decency in conducting them. The old Men sit in the foremost Ranks, the Warriors in the next, and the Women and Children in the hindmost. The Business of the Women is to take exact Notice of what passes, imprint it in their Memories, for they have no Writing, and communicate it to their Children. They are the Records of the Councils, and they preserve Traditions of the Stipulations in Treaties 100 Years back, which when we compare with our Writings we always find exact. He that would speak rises. The rest observe a profound Silence. When he has finish'd and sits down; they leave him 5 or 6 Minutes to recollect, that if he has omitted any thing he intended to say, or has any thing to add, he may rise again and deliver it. To interrupt another, even in common Conversation, is reckon'd highly indecent. How different this is, from the conduct of a polite British House of Commons, where scarce a day passes without some Confusion, that makes the Speaker hoarse in calling to Order and how different from the Mode of Conversation in many polite Companies of Europe, where if you do not deliver your

Sentence with great Rapidity, you are cut off in the middle of it by the Impatient Loquacity of those you converse with, and never suffer'd to finish it.——

The Politeness of these Savages in Conversation is indeed carried to Excess, since it does not permit them to contradict or deny the Truth of what is asserted in their Presence. By this means they indeed avoid Disputes, but then it becomes difficult to know their Minds, or what Impression you make upon them. The Missionaries who have attempted to convert them to Christianity, all complain of this as one of the great Difficulties of their Mission. The Indians hear with Patience the Truths of the Gospel explain'd to them, and give their usual Tokens of Assent and Approbation: you would think they were convinc'd. No such Matter. It is mere Civility. A Swedish Minister, having assembled the Chiefs of the Susquehanah Indians, made a Sermon to them, acquainting them with the principal historical Facts on which our Religion is founded, such as the Fall of our first Parents by eating an Apple; the coming of Christ, to repair the Mischief; his Miracles and Suffering, &c. When he had finished, an Indian Orator stood up to thank him. "What you have told us, says he, is all very good. It is indeed bad to eat Apples. It is better to make them all into Cyder. We are much oblig'd by your kindness in coming so far to tell us these Things which you have heard from your Mothers; in return I will tell you some of those we have heard from ours. In the Beginning our Fathers had only the Flesh of Animals to subsist on, and if their Hunting was unsuccessful, they were starving. Two of our young Hunters having kill'd a Deer, made a Fire in the Woods to broil some Part of it. When they were about to satisfy their Hunger, they beheld a beautiful young Woman descend from the Clouds, and seat herself on that Hill which you see yonder among the blue Mountains. They said to each other, It is a Spirit that perhaps has smelt our broiling Venison and wishes to eat of it: Let us offer some to her. They presented her with the Tongue, She was pleas'd with the Taste of it, and said, Your kindness shall be rewarded: Come to this Place after thirteen Moons, and you shall find something that will be of great Benefit in nourishing you and your Children to the latest Generations. They did so, and, to their Surprise found Plants they had never seen before, but which from that ancient time have been constantly cultivated among us to our great Advantage. Where her right Hand had touch'd the Ground they found Maize; Where her left hand had touch'd it, they found Kidney Beans, and where her Backside had rested on it, they found Tobacco.——The good Missionary disgusted with this idle Tale, said, What I delivered to you were sacred Truths, but what you tell me is mere Fable, Fiction and Falshood. The Indian offended, reply'd, My Brother, it seems your Friends have not done you Justice in your Education, they have not well instructed you in the Rules of common Civility. You saw that we who understand and practise those Rules, believ'd all your Stories: Why do you refuse to believe ours?——

When any of them come into our Towns, our People are apt to croud round them, gaze upon them, and incommode them where they desire to be private; this they esteem great Rudeness, and the Effect of Want of Instruction in the Rules of Civility and good Manners. We have, say they, as much Curiosity as you, and when you come into our Towns, we wish for Opportunities of looking at you; but for this purpose we hide ourselves behind Bushes where you are to pass, and never intrude ourselves into your Company.——

Their Manner of entring one anothers villages has likewise its Rules. It is reckon'd uncivil in travelling Strangers to enter a Village abruptly, without giving Notice of their Approach. Therefore as soon as they arrive within Hearing, they stop and hollow, remaining there till invited to enter. Two old Men usually come out to them, and lead them in. There is in every Village a vacant Dwelling called the Strangers House. Here they are plac'd, while the old Men go round from Hut to Hut, acquainting the Inhabitants that Strangers are arriv'd who are probably hungry and weary; and every one sends them what he can spare of Victuals and Skins to repose on. When the Strangers are refresh'd, Pipes and Tobacco are brought; and then, but not before, Conversation begins, with Enquiries who they are, whither bound, what News, &c. and it usually ends with Offers of Service if the Strangers have occasion of Guides or any Necessaries for continuing their Journey, and nothing is exacted for the Entertainment.

The same Hospitality esteem'd among them as a principal Virtue, is practis'd by private Persons, of which Conrad Weiser, our Interpreter gave me the following Instance. He had been naturaliz'd among the Six Nations, and spoke well the Mohock Language. In going thro' the Indian Country to carry a Message from our Governor to the Council at Onondaga, he call'd at the Habitation of Canassetego an old Acquaintance, who embrac'd him, spread Furs for him to sit on, plac'd before him some boil'd Beans and Venison, and mix'd some Rum and Water for his Drink. When he was well refresh'd, and had lit his Pipe, Canassetego began to converse with him, ask'd how he had far'd the many Years since they had seen each other, whence he then came, what occasion'd the Journey, &c. &c. Conrad answered all his Questions, and when the Discourse began to flag, the Indian to continue it, said, Conrad, you have lived long among the white People and know something of their Customs. I have been sometimes at Albany, and have observed that once in Seven Days they shut up their Shops, and assemble all in the great House; tell me what it is for? What do they do there?——They meet there, says Conrad, to hear and learn good Things. I do not doubt says the Indian, that they tell you so: They have told me the same; But I doubt the Truth of what they say, and I will tell you my Reasons. I went lately to Albany to sell my Skins, and buy Blankets, Knives, Powder, Rum, &c. You know I us'd generally to deal with Hans Hanson, but I was a little inclin'd this time to try some other Merchant; however, I call'd first upon Hans, and ask'd him what he would give for Beaver. He said he could not give more than four Shillings a Pound; but says he, I cannot talk on Business now; this is the Day when we meet together to learn good Things, and I am going to the Meeting. So I thought to myself, since we cannot do any Business to day, I may as well go to the Meeting too; and I went with him. There stood up a Man in Black, and began to talk to the People very angrily. I did not understand what he said; but perceiving that he look'd much at me and at Hanson, I imagin'd he was angry at seeing me there; so I went out, sat down near the House, struck Fire and lit my Pipe, waiting till the Meeting should break up. I thought too that the Man had mention'd something of Beaver, and I suspected it might be the Subject of their Meeting. So when they came out, I accosted my Merchant, Well, Hans, says I, I hope you have agreed to give more than four Shillings a Pound. No, says he, I cannot give so much; I cannot give more than three Shillings and sixpence. I then spoke to several other Dealers, but they all sung the same song. Three and sixpence, Three and sixpence. This made it clear to me that my Suspicion was right; and that whatever they pretended of meeting to learn Good Things, the real purpose was to consult how to cheat Indians in the Price of Beaver. Consider but a little, Conrad, and you must be of my Opinion. If they met so often to learn Good Things, they would certainly have learnt some before this time. But they are still ignorant. You know our Practice. If a white Man in travelling thro' our Country, enters one of our Cabins, we all treat him as I treat you; we dry him if he is wet, we warm him if he is cold, we give him Meat and Drink that he may allay his Thirst and Hunger, and spread soft Furs for him to rest and sleep on: We demand nothing in return.[1] But if I go into a white Man's House at Albany, and ask for Victuals and Drink, they say, where is your Money? and if I have none; they say, Get out you Indian Dog. You see they have not yet learnt those little Good Things, that we need no Meetings to be instructed in, because our Mothers taught them to us when we were Children: And therefore, it is impossible their Meeting Should be as they say, for any such purpose, or have any such Effect. They are only to contrive *the Cheating of Indians in the Price of Beaver.*——

[LC Box 26]

[1] It is remarkable that in all Ages and Countries Hospitality has been allow'd as the Virtue of those whom the civilized were pleas'd to call Barbarians. The Greeks celebrated the Scythians for it. The Saracens possess'd it eminently, and it is to this day the reigning Virtue of the wild Arabs. St. Paul, too, in the Relation of his Voyage and Shipwreck on the Island of Melita says *the Barbarous People shewed us no little Kindness; for they kindled a Fire, and received us every one, because of the present Rain, and because of the Cold.* [Acts 28:2]

CHAPTER 40
To Sarah Franklin Bache
(26 January 1784)

My dear Child,

Your Care in sending me the Newspapers is very agreable to me. I received by Capt. Barney those relating to the Cincinnati. My Opinion of the Institution cannot be of much Importance. I only wonder that when the united Wisdom of our Nation had, in the Articles of Confederation, manifested their Dislike of establishing Ranks of Nobility by Authority either of the Congress or of any particular State, a Number of private Persons should think proper to distinguish themselves and their Posterity from their fellow Citizens, and form an Order of hereditary Knights, in direct Opposition to the solemnly declared Sense of their Country. I imagine it must be likewise contrary to the Good Sense of most of those drawn into it, by the Persuasion of its Projectors, who have been too much struck with the Ribbands and Crosses they have seen among them, hanging to the Buttonholes of Foreign Officers. And I suppose those who disapprove of it have not hitherto given it much Opposition, from a Principle a little like that of your Mother, relating to punctilious Persons, who are always exacting little Observances of Respect, that *if People can be pleased with small Matters, it is a pity but they should have them.* In this View, perhaps I should not myself, if my Advice had been ask'd, have objected to their wearing their Ribband and Badge according to their Fancy, tho' I certainly should to the entailing it as an Honour on their Posterity. For Honour worthily obtain'd as that for Example of our Officers, is in its Nature a personal Thing, and incommunicable to any but those who had some Share in obtaining it. Thus among the Chinese, the most ancient, and from long Experience the wisest of Nations, Honour does not *descend* but *ascends*. If a man from his Learning, his Wisdom or his Valour, is promoted by the Emperor to the Rank of Mandarin, his Parents are immediately intitled to all the same Ceremonies of Respect from the People, that are establish'd as due to the Mandarin himself; on this Supposition, that it must have been owing to the Education, Instruction, and good Example afforded him by his Parents that he was rendered capable of serving the Publick. This *ascending Honour* is therefore useful to the State as it encourages Parents to give their Children a good and virtuous Education. But the *descending Honour*, to Posterity who could have no Share in obtaining it, is not only groundless and absurd, but often hurtful to that Posterity, since it is apt to make them proud, disdaining to be employed in useful Arts, and thence falling into Poverty and all the Meannesses, Servility and Wretchedness attending it; which is the present case with much of what is called the *Noblesse* in Europe. Or if, to keep up the Dignity of the Family, Estates are entailed entire on the Eldest Male Heir, another Pest to Industry and Improvement of the Country is introduced, which will be follow'd by all the odious Mixture of Pride and Beggary, and Idleness, that have half depopulated Spain, occasioning continual Extinction of Families by the Discouragements of Marriage. I wish therefore that the Cincinnati, if they must go on with their Project, would direct the Badges of their Order to be worn by their Parents instead of handing them down to their Children. It would be a good Precedent, and might have good Effects. It would also be a kind of Obedience to the fourth Commandment, in which God enjoins us to *honour* our Father and Mother, but has nowhere directed us to *honour* our Children. And certainly no mode of honouring those immediate Authors of our Being can be more effectual, than that of doing praiseworthy Actions, which reflect honour on those who gave us our Education; or more becoming, than that of manifesting by some public Expression or Token that it is to their Instruction and Example we ascribe the Merit of those Actions.

But the Absurdity of *descending* Honours is not a mere Matter of philosophical Opinion, it is capable of mathematical Demonstration. A Man's Son, for instance, is but half of his Family, the other half belonging to the Family of his Wife. His Son too, marrying into another Family, his Share in the Grandson is but a fourth; In the Great Grandson, by the same Process, it is but an Eighth. In the next Generation a Sixteenth: The next a Thirty-second. The next a Sixty-fourth. The next an Hundred and twenty-eighth. The next a Two hundred and Fifty-sixth: and the next a Five hundred and twelfth. Thus in Nine Generations, which will not require more than 300 years, (no very great Antiquity for a Family) our present Chevalier of the Order of Cincinnatus's Share in the then existing Knight will be but a 512th part; which, allowing the present certain Fidelity of American Wives to be insur'd down through all those Nine Generations, is so small a Consideration, that methinks no reasonable Man would hazard for the sake of it the disagreable Consequences of the Jealousy, Envy and Ill-will of his Countrymen.——

Let us go back with our Calculation from this young Noble, the 512th part of the present Knight, thro' his nine Generations till we return to the Year of the Institution. He must have had a Father and Mother, they are two. Each of them had a Father and Mother, they are four. Those of the next preceding Generation will be eight; the next Sixteen; the next thirty-two; the next Sixty-four; the next One hundred and Twenty-eight; the next Two hundred and fifty-six; and the ninth in this Retrocession Five hundred and twelve, who must be now existing, and all contribute their Proportion of this future Chevalier de Cincinnatus. These with the rest, make together as follows

	2
	4
	8
	16
	32
	64
	128
	256
	512
Total	1022

One Thousand and Twenty-two Men and Women Contributors to the Formation of one Knight. And if we are to have a Thousand of these future Knights, there must be now and hereafter existing One Million and Twenty two Thousand Fathers and Mothers who are to contribute to their Production, unless a Part of the Number are employ'd in making more Knights than One. Let us strike off then the 22,000 on the Supposition of this double Employ, and then consider whether after a reasonable Estimation of the Number of Rogues, and Fools, and Royalists and Scoundrels and Prostitutes that are mix'd with and help to make up necessarily their Million of Predecessors, Posterity will have much reason to boast of the noble Blood of the then existing Set of Chevaliers de Cincinnatus. I hope therefore that the Order will drop this part of their Project, and content themselves as the Knights of the Garter, Bath, Thistle, St. Louis and other Orders of Europe do, with a Life Enjoyment of their little Badge and Ribband, and let the Distinction die with those who have merited it. This I imagine will give no Offence. For my own Part, I shall think it a Convenience when I go into a Company where there may be Faces unknown to me, if I discover by this Badge the Persons who merit some particular Expression of my Respect; and it will save modest Virtue the Trouble of calling for our Regard, by awkward roundabout Intimations of having been heretofore employ'd in the Continental Service.

The Gentleman who made the Voyage to France to provide the Ribbands and Medals has executed his Commission. To me they seem tolerably done, but all such Things are criticis'd. Some find fault with the Latin, as wanting classic Elegance and Correctness; and, since our Nine Universities were not able to furnish better Latin, it was Pity, they say, that the Mottos had not been in English. Others object to the Title, as not properly assumable by any but Gen. Washington, who serv'd without Pay. Others object to the Bald Eagle, as looking too much like a *Dindon*, or Turkey. For my own part I wish the Bald Eagle had not been chosen as the Representative of our Country. He is a Bird of bad moral Character. He does not get his living honestly. You may have seen him perch'd on some dead Tree near the River, where, too lazy to fish for himself, he watches the Labour of the Fishing Hawk; and, when that diligent Bird has at length taken a Fish, and is bearing it to his Nest for the support of his Mate and young Ones, the Bald Eagle pursues him and takes it from him. With all this Injustice, he is never in good Case but like those among Men who live by Sharping and Robbing, he is generally poor and often very lousy. Besides he is a rank Coward: the little *King Bird* not bigger than a Sparrow attacks him boldly and drives him out of the District. He is therefore by no means a proper Emblem for the brave and honest Cincinnati of America who have driven all the *King birds* from our Country; tho' exactly fit for that Order of Knights which the French call *Chevaliers d'Industrie*. I am on this account not displeas'd that the Figure is not known as a Bald Eagle, but looks more like a Turkey. For in Truth the Turkey is in Comparison a much more respectable Bird, and withal a true original Native of America. Eagles have been found in all Countries, but the Turkey was peculiar to ours, the first of the Species seen in Europe being brought to France by the Jesuits from Canada, and serv'd up at the Wedding Table of Charles the ninth. He is besides, tho' a little vain and silly, a Bird of Courage, and would not hesitate to attack a Grenadier of the British Guards, who should presume to invade his FarmYard with a red Coat on.

I shall not enter into the Criticisms made upon their Latin. The gallant Officers of America may not have the Merit of being great Scholars, but they undoubtedly merit much as brave Soldiers from their Country, which should therefore not leave them merely to *Fame* for their *Virtutis Premium*; which is one of their Latin Mottos. Their *Esto perpetua* another is an excellent Wish, if they meant it for their Country, bad, if intended for their Order. The States should not only restore to them the *Omnia* of their first Motto[1] which many of them have left and lost, but pay them justly, and reward them generously. They should not be suffered to remain with their new-created Chivalry *entirely* in the Situation of the Gentleman in the Story, which their *Omnia reliquit* reminds me of. You know every thing makes me recollect some Story. He had built a very fine House, and thereby much impair'd his Fortune. He had a Pride however in showing it to his Acquaintance. One of them after viewing it all remark'd a Motto over the Door, ŌIA VANITAS. What, says he, is the Meaning of this ŌIA? tis a Word I don't understand. I will tell you, says the Gentleman; I had a mind to have the Motto cut on a Piece of smooth Marble, but there was not room for it between the Ornaments to be put in Characters large enough to be read. I therefore made use of a Contraction antiently very common in Latin Manuscripts, by which the m's and n'*s* in Words are omitted, and the Omission noted by a little Dash above, which you may see there; so that the Word is *Omnia*, *omnia vanitas*. O, says his Friend, I now comprehend the Meaning of your Motto, it relates to your Edifice; and signifies, that if you have abridged your *Omnia*, you have, nevertheless, left your VANITAS legible at full length.

I am ever, Your affectionate Father,

[LC Box 22]

[1] Omnia reliquit servare Rempublicam.

CHAPTER 41

Information to Those Who Would Remove to America

(February 1784)

Many Persons in Europe having directly or by Letters, express'd to the Writer of this, who is well acquainted with North-America, their Desire of transporting and establishing themselves in that Country; but who appear to him to have formed thro' Ignorance, mistaken Ideas and Expectations of what is to be obtained there; he thinks it may be useful, and prevent inconvenient, expensive and fruitless Removals and Voyages of improper Persons, if he gives some clearer and truer Notions of that Part of the World than appear to have hitherto prevailed.

He finds it is imagined by Numbers that the Inhabitants of North-America are rich, capable of rewarding, and dispos'd to reward all sorts of Ingenuity; that they are at the same time ignorant of all the Sciences; and consequently that Strangers possessing Talents in the Belles-Letters, fine Arts, &c. must be highly esteemed, and so well paid as to become easily rich themselves; that there are also abundance of profitable Offices to be disposed of, which the Natives are not qualified to fill; and that having few Persons of Family among them, Strangers of Birth must be greatly respected, and of course easily obtain the best of those Offices, which will make all their Fortunes: that the Governments too, to encourage Emigrations from Europe, not only pay the Expence of personal Transportation, but give Lands gratis to Strangers, with Negroes to work for them, Utensils of Husbandry, and Stocks of Cattle. These are all wild Imaginations; and those who go to America with Expectations founded upon them, will surely find themselves disappointed.

The Truth is, that tho' there are in that Country few People so miserable as the Poor of Europe, there are also very few that in Europe would be called rich: it is rather a general happy Mediocrity that prevails. There are few great Proprietors of the Soil, and few Tenants; most People cultivate their own Lands, or follow some Handicraft or Merchandise; very few rich enough to live idly upon their Rents or Incomes; or to pay the high Prices given in Europe, for Paintings, Statues, Architecture and the other Works of Art that are more curious than useful. Hence the natural Geniuses, that have arisen in America, with such Talents, have uniformly quitted that Country for Europe, where they can be more suitably rewarded. It is true that Letters and mathematical Knowledge are in Esteem there, but they are at the same time more common than is apprehended; there being already existing nine Colleges or Universities, viz. four in New England, and one in each of the Provinces of New York, New Jersey, Pennsylvania, Maryland and Virginia, all furnish'd with learned Professors; besides a number of smaller Academies: These educate many of their Youth in the Languages and those Sciences that qualify men for the Professions of Divinity, Law or Physick. Strangers indeed are by no means excluded from exercising those Professions, and the quick Increase of Inhabitants everywhere gives them a Chance of Employ, which they have in common with the Natives. Of civil Offices or Employments, there are few; no superfluous Ones as in Europe; and it is a Rule establish'd in some of the States, that no Office should be so profitable as to make it desirable. The 36th Article of the Constitution of Pennsilvania, runs expressly in these Words: *As every Freeman, to preserve his Independence, (if he has not a sufficient Estate) ought to have some Profession, Calling, Trade or Farm, whereby he may honestly subsist, there can be no Necessity for, nor Use in, establishing Offices of Profit; the usual Effects of which are Dependance and Servility, unbecoming Freemen, in the Possessors and Expectants; Faction, Contention, Corruption, and Disorder among the People. Wherefore, whenever an Office, thro' Increase of Fees or otherwise, becomes so profitable as to occasion many to apply for it, the Profits ought to be lessened by the Legislature.*

These Ideas prevailing more or less in all the United States, it cannot be worth any Man's while, who has a means of Living at home, to expatriate himself in hopes of obtaining a profitable civil Office in America; and as to military Offices, they are at an End with the War; the Armies being disbanded. Much less is it adviseable for a Person to go thither who has no other Quality to recommend him but his Birth. In Europe it has indeed its Value, but it is a Commodity that cannot be carried to a worse Market than that of America, where people do not enquire concerning a Stranger, *What IS he?* but, *What can he DO?* If he has any useful Art, he is welcome; and if he exercises it and behaves well, he will be respected by all that know him; but a mere Man of Quality, who on that Account wants to live upon the Public, by some Office or Salary, will be despis'd and disregarded. The Husbandman is in honor there, and even the Mechanic, because their Employments are useful. The People have a saying, that God Almighty is himself a Mechanic, the greatest in the Universe; and he is respected and admired more for the Variety, Ingenuity and Utility of his Handiworks, than for the Antiquity of his Family. They are pleas'd with the Observation of a Negro, and frequently mention it, that *Boccarorra* (meaning the White man) make de Blackman workee, make de Horse workee, make de Ox workee, make ebery ting workee; only de Hog. He de hog, no workee; he eat, he drink, he walk about, he go to sleep when he please, *he libb like a Gentleman.* According to these Opinions of the Americans, one of them would think himself more oblig'd to a Genealogist, who could prove for him that his Ancestors and Relations for ten Generations had been Ploughmen, Smiths, Carpenters, Turners, Weavers, Tanners, or even Shoemakers, and consequently that they were useful Members of Society; than if he could only prove that they were Gentlemen, doing nothing of Value, but living idly on the Labour of others, mere *fruges consumere nati*,[1] and otherwise *good* for *nothing*, till by their Death their Estates, like the Carcass of the Negro's Gentleman-Hog, come to be *cut up*.

With regard to Encouragements for Strangers from Government, they are really only what are derived from good Laws and Liberty. Strangers are welcome because there is room enough for them all, and therefore the old Inhabitants are not jealous of them; the Laws protect them sufficiently, so that they have no need of the Patronage of great Men; and every one will enjoy securely the Profits of his Industry. But if he does not bring a Fortune with him, he must work and be industrious to live. One or two Years Residence gives him all the Rights of a Citizen; but the Government does not at present, whatever it may have done in former times, hire People to become Settlers, by Paying their Passages, giving Land, Negroes, Utensils, Stock, or any other kind of Emolument whatsoever. In short America is the Land of Labour, and by no means what the English call *Lubberland*, and the French *Pays de Cocagne*, where the streets are said to be pav'd with half-peck Loaves, the Houses til'd with Pancakes, and where the Fowls fly about ready roasted, crying, *Come eat me!*

[1] *There are a Number of us born*
Merely to eat up the corn. – Watts

Who then are the kind of Persons to whom an Emigration to America may be advantageous? And what are the Advantages they may reasonably expect?

Land being cheap in that Country, from the vast Forests still void of Inhabitants, and not likely to be occupied in an Age to come, insomuch that the Propriety of an hundred Acres of fertile Soil full of Wood may be obtained near the Frontiers in many Places for Eight or Ten Guineas, hearty young Labouring Men, who understand the Husbandry of Corn and Cattle, which is nearly the same in that Country as in Europe, may easily establish themselves there. A little Money sav'd of the good Wages they receive there while they work for others, enables them to buy the Land and begin their Plantation, in which they are assisted by the Good Will of their Neighbours and some Credit. Multitudes of poor People from England, Ireland, Scotland and Germany, have by this means in a few Years become wealthy Farmers, who in their own Countries, where all the Lands are fully occupied, and the Wages of Labour low, could never have emerged from the poor Condition wherein they were born.

From the Salubrity of the Air, the healthiness of the Climate, the plenty of good Provisions, and the Encouragement to early Marriages, by the certainty of Subsistence in cultivating the Earth, the Increase of Inhabitants by natural Generation is very rapid in America, and becomes still more so by the Accession of Strangers; hence there is a continual Demand for more Artisans of all the necessary and useful kinds, to supply those Cultivators of the Earth with Houses, and with Furniture and Utensils of the grosser Sorts which cannot so well be brought from Europe. Tolerably good Workmen in any of those mechanic Arts, are sure to find Employ, and to be well paid for their Work, there being no Restraints preventing Strangers from exercising any Art they understand, nor any Permission necessary. If they are poor, they begin first as Servants or Journeymen; and if they are sober, industrious and frugal, they soon become Masters, establish themselves in Business, marry, raise Families, and become respectable Citizens.

Also, Persons of moderate Fortunes and Capitals, who having a Number of Children to provide for, are desirous of bringing them up to Industry, and to secure Estates for their Posterity, have Opportunities of doing it in America, which Europe does not afford. There they may be taught and practise profitable mechanic Arts, without incurring Disgrace on that Account; but on the contrary acquiring Respect by such Abilities. There small Capitals laid out in Lands, which daily become more valuable by the

Increase of People, afford a solid Prospect of ample Fortunes thereafter for those Children. The Writer of this has known several Instances of large Tracts of Land, bought on what was then the Frontier of Pennsylvania, for Ten Pounds per hundred Acres, which, after twenty Years, when the Settlements had been extended far beyond them, sold readily, without any Improvement made upon them, for three Pounds per Acre. The Acre in America is the same with the English Acre or the Acre of Normandy.

Those who desire to understand the State of Government in America, would do well to read the Constitutions of the several States, and the Articles of Confederation that bind the whole together for general Purposes under the Direction of one Assembly called the Congress. These Constitutions have been printed, by Order of Congress in America; two Editions of them have also been printed in London, and a good Translation of them into French has lately been published at Paris.

Several of the Princes of Europe having of late Years, from an Opinion of Advantage to arise by producing all Commodities and Manufactures within their own Dominions, so as to diminish or render useless their Importations, have endeavoured to entice Workmen from other Countries, by high Salaries, Privileges, &c. Many Persons pretending to be skilled in various great Manufactures, imagining that America must be in Want of them, and that the Congress would probably be dispos'd to imitate the Princes above mentioned, have proposed to go over, on Condition of having their Passages paid, Lands given, Salaries appointed, exclusive Privileges for Terms of Years, &c. Such Persons on reading the Articles of Confederation will find that the Congress have no Power committed to them, or Money put into their Hands, for such purposes; and that if any such Encouragement is given, it must be by the Government of some separate State. This however has rarely been done in America; and when it has been done it has rarely succeeded, so as to establish a Manufacture which the Country was not yet so ripe for as to encourage private Persons to set it up; Labour being generally too dear there, and Hands difficult to be kept together, every one desiring to be a Master, and the Cheapness of Land enclining many to leave Trades for Agriculture. Some indeed have met with Success, and are carried on to Advantage; but they are generally such as require only a few Hands, or wherein great Part of the Work is perform'd by Machines. Goods that are bulky, and of so small Value as not well to bear the Expence of Freight, may often be made cheaper in the Country than they can be imported; and the Manufacture of such Goods will be profitable wherever there is a sufficient Demand. The Farmers in America produce indeed a good deal of Wool and Flax; and none is exported, it is all work'd up; but it is in the Way of Domestic Manufacture for the Use of the Family. The buying up Quantities of Wool and Flax with the Design to employ Spinners, Weavers, &c. and form great Establishments, producing Quantities of Linen and Woollen Goods for Sale, has been several times attempted in different Provinces; but those Projects have generally failed, Goods of equal Value being imported cheaper. And when the Governments have been solicited to support such Schemes by Encouragements, in Money, or by imposing Duties on Importation of such Goods, it has been generally refused, on this Principle, that if the Country is ripe for the Manufacture, it may be carried on by private Persons to Advantage; and if not, it is a Folly to think of forcing Nature. Great Establishments of Manufacture, require great Numbers of Poor to do the Work for small Wages; these Poor are to be found in Europe, but will not be found in America, till the Lands are all taken up and cultivated, and the excess of People who cannot get Land, want Employment. The Manufacture of Silk, they say, is natural in France, as that of Cloth in England, because each Country produces in Plenty the first Material: But if England will have a Manufacture of Silk as well as that of Cloth, and France one of Cloth as well as that of Silk, these unnatural Operations must be supported by mutual Prohibitions or high Duties on the Importation of each others Goods, by which means the Workmen are enabled to tax the home Consumer by greater Prices, while the higher Wages they receive makes them neither happier nor richer, since they only drink more and work less. Therefore the Governments in America do nothing to encourage such Projects. The People by this Means are not impos'd on, either by the Merchant or Mechanic; if the Merchant demands too much Profit on imported Shoes, they buy of the Shoemaker: and if he asks too high a Price, they take them of the Merchant: thus the two Professions are Checks on each other. The Shoemaker however has on the whole a considerable Profit upon his Labour in America, beyond what he had in Europe, as he can add to his Price a Sum nearly equal to all the Expences of Freight and Commission, Risque or Insurance, &c. necessarily charged by the Merchant. And the Case is the same with the Workmen in every other Mechanic Art. Hence it is that Artisans generally live better and more easily in America than in Europe, and such as are good Œconomists make a comfortable Provision for Age, and for their Children. Such may therefore remove with Advantage to America.

In the old longsettled Countries of Europe, all Arts, Trades, Professions, Farms, &c. are so full that it is difficult for a poor Man who has Children, to place them where they may gain, or learn to gain a decent Livelihood. The Artisans, who fear creating future Rivals in Business, refuse to take Apprentices, but upon Conditions of Money, Maintenance or the like, which the Parents are unable to comply with. Hence the Youth are dragg'd up in Ignorance of every gainful Art, and oblig'd to become Soldiers or Servants or Thieves, for a Subsistence. In America the rapid Increase of Inhabitants takes away that Fear of Rivalship, and Artisans willingly receive Apprentices from the hope of Profit by their Labour during the Remainder of the Time stipulated after they shall be instructed. Hence it is easy for poor Families to get their Children instructed; for the Artisans are so desirous of Apprentices, that many of them will even give Money to the Parents to have Boys from ten to fifteen Years of Age bound Apprentices to them till the Age of twenty one; and many poor Parents have by that means, on their Arrival in the Country, raised Money enough to buy Land sufficient to establish themselves, and to subsist the rest of their Family by Agriculture. These Contracts for Apprentices are made before a Magistrate, who regulates the Agreement according to Reason and Justice; and having in view the Formation of a future useful Citizen, obliges the Master to engage by a written Indenture, not only that during the time of Service stipulated, the Apprentice shall be duly provided with Meat, Drink, Apparel, washing and Lodging, and at its Expiration with a compleat new Suit of Cloths, but also that he shall be taught to read, write and cast Accompts, and that he shall be well instructed in the Art or Profession of his Master, or some other, by which he may afterwards gain a Livelihood, and be able in his turn to raise a Family. A Copy of this Indenture is given to the Apprentice or his Friends, and the Magistrate keeps a Record of it, to which Recourse may be had, in case of Failure by the Master in any Point of Performance. This desire among the Masters to have more Hands employ'd in working for them, induces them to pay the Passages of young Persons, of both Sexes, who, on their Arrival agree to serve them one, two, three or four Years; those who have already learnt a Trade agreeing for a shorter Term in proportion to their Skill and the consequent immediate Value of their Service; and those who have none, agreeing for a longer Term, in Consideration of being taught an Art their Poverty would not permit them to acquire in their own Country.

The almost general Mediocrity of Fortune that prevails in America, obliging its People to follow some Business for Subsistence, those Vices that arise usually from Idleness are in a great Measure prevented. Industry and constant Employment are great Preservatives of the Morals and Virtue of a Nation. Hence bad Examples to Youth are more rare in America, which must be a comfortable Consideration to Parents. To this may be truly added, that serious Religion under its various Denominations, is not only tolerated but respected and practised. Atheism is unknown there, Infidelity rare and secret, so that persons may live to a great Age in that Country without having their Piety shock'd by meeting with either an Atheist or an Infidel. And the Divine Being seems to have manifested his Approbation of the mutual Forbearance and Kindness with which the different Sects treat each other, by the remarkable Prosperity with which he has been pleased to favour the whole Country.

[Passy: 1784]

CHAPTER 42
To Benjamin Vaughan
(26 July 1784)

Dear Friend,

. . . You ask, "what Remedy I have for the growing Luxury of my Country, which gives so much *Offence* to all *English Travellers*——without Exception." I answer that I think it exaggerated, and that Travellers are no good Judges whether our Luxury is growing or diminishing. Our People are hospitable, and have indeed too much Pride in displaying upon their Tables before Strangers the Plenty and Variety that our Country affords. They have the Vanity too of sometimes borrowing one another's Plate to entertain more splendidly.——Strangers being invited from House to House, and meeting every Day with a Feast, imagine what they see is the ordinary Way of living of all the Families where they dine; when perhaps each Family lives a Week after upon the Remains of the Dinner given. It is, I own, a Folly in our People to give *such Offence* to *English* Travellers. The first part of the Proverb is thereby verified, that *Fools make Feasts*. I wish in this Case the other were as true, *and wise Men eat them*. These Travellers might one would think find some Fault they could more decently reproach us with, than that of our excessive Civility to them as Strangers.

I have not indeed yet thought of a Remedy for Luxury. I am not sure that in a great State it is capable of a Remedy. Nor that the Evil is in itself always so great as it is represented. Suppose we include in the Definition of Luxury all unnecessary Expence, and then let us consider whether Laws to prevent such Expence are possible to be executed in a great Country; and whether if they could be executed, our People generally would be happier or even richer. Is not the Hope of one day being able to purchase and enjoy Luxuries a great Spur to Labour and Industry? May not Luxury therefore produce more than it consumes, if without such a Spur People would be as they are naturally enough inclined to be, lazy and indolent? To this purpose I remember a Circumstance. The Skipper of a Shallop employed between Cape May and Philadelphia, had done us some small Service for which he refused Pay. My Wife understanding that he had a Daughter, sent her as a Present a new-fashioned Cap. Three Years After, this Skipper being at my House with an old Farmer of Cape May his Passenger, he mentioned the Cap and how much his Daughter had been pleased with it; but says he it proved a dear Cap to our Congregation.——How so? When my Daughter appeared in it at Meeting, it was so much admired, that all the Girls resolved to get such Caps from Philadelphia; and my Wife and I computed that the whole could not have cost less than a hundred Pound. True says the Farmer, but you do not tell all the Story; I think the Cap was nevertheless an Advantage to us; for it was the first thing that put our Girls upon Knitting worsted Mittens for Sale at Philadelphia, that they might have wherewithal to buy Caps and Ribbands there; and you know that that Industry has continued and is likely to continue and increase to a much greater Value, and answer better Purposes. Upon the whole I was more reconciled to this little Piece of Luxury; since not only the Girls were made happier by having fine Caps, but the Philadelphians by the Supply of warm Mittens.

In our Commercial Towns upon the Seacoast, Fortunes will occasionally be made. Some of those who grow rich, will be prudent, live within Bounds, and preserve what they have gained for their Posterity. Others fond of showing their Wealth, will be extravagant and ruin themselves. Laws cannot prevent this; and perhaps it is not always an Evil to the Publick. A Shilling spent idly by a Fool, may be picked up by a Wiser Person who knows better what to do with it. It is therefore not lost. A vain silly Fellow builds a fine House, furnishes it richly, lives in it expensively, and in few Years ruins himself, but the Masons, Carpenters, Smiths and other honest Tradesmen have been by his Employ assisted in maintaining and raising their Families, the Farmer has been paid for his Labour and encouraged, and the Estate is now in better Hands. In some Cases indeed certain Modes of Luxury may be a publick Evil in the same Manner as it is a Private one. If there be a Nation for Instance, that exports its Beef and Linnen to pay for its Importation of Claret and Porter, while a great Part of its People live upon Potatoes and wear no Shirts, wherein does it differ from the Sot who lets his Family starve and sells his Clothes to buy Drink? Our American Commerce is I confess a little in this way. We sell our Victuals to your Islands for Rum and Sugar; the Substantial

Necessaries of Life for Superfluities. But we have Plenty and live well nevertheless; tho' by being soberer, we might be richer. By the by, here is just issued an Arret of Council, taking off all the Duties upon the Exportation of Brandies, which it is said will render them cheaper in America than your Rum, in which case there is no doubt but they will be preferr'd, and we shall be better able to bear your Restrictions on our Commerce. There are Views here by augmenting their Settlements of being able to supply the growing People of North America with the Sugar that may be wanted there. On the whole I guess England will get as little by the Commercial War she has begun with us as she did by the Military. But to return to *Luxury*.

The vast Quantity of Forest Lands we yet have to clear and put in order for Cultivation, will for a long time keep the Body of our Nation laborious and frugal. Forming an Opinion of our People and their Manners by what is seen among the Inhabitants of the Seaports, is judging from an improper Sample. The People of the Trading Towns may be rich and luxurious, while the Country possesses all the Virtues that tend to private Happiness and publick Prosperity. Those Towns are not much regarded by the Country. They are hardly considered as an essential Part of the States. And the Experience of the last War has shown, that their being in the Possession of the Enemy, did not necessarily draw on the Subjection of the Country, which bravely continued to maintain its Freedom and Independence notwithstanding.——

It has been computed by some Political Arithmetician, that if every Man and Woman would work four Hours each Day on something useful, that Labour would produce sufficient to procure all the Necessaries and Comforts of Life, Want and Misery would be banished out of the World, and the rest of the 24 Hours might be Leisure and Pleasure.

What occasions then so much Want and Misery? It is the Employment of Men and Women in Works, that produce neither the Necessaries nor Conveniences of Life, who, with those who do nothing, consume the Necessaries raised by the Laborious——To explain this——

The first Elements of Wealth are obtained by Labour from the Earth and Waters. I have Land and raise Corn. With this if I feed a Family that does nothing, my Corn will be consum'd and at the end of the Year I shall be no richer than I was at the Beginning. But if while I feed them I employ them, some in Spinning others in hewing Timber and sawing Boards, others in making Bricks &c. for Building; the Value of my Corn will be arrested, and remain with me, and at the end of the Year we may all be better clothed and better lodged. And if instead of employing a Man I feed, in making Bricks, I employ him in fiddling for me, the Corn he eats is gone, and no Part of his Manufacture remains to augment the Wealth and Conveniencies of the Family. I shall therefore be the poorer for this fiddling Man, unless the rest of My Family work more or eat less to make up the Deficiency he occasions.——

Look round the World and see the Millions employ'd in doing nothing, or in something that amounts to nothing when the Necessaries and Conveniencies of Life are in Question. What is the Bulk of Commerce, for which we fight and destroy each other but the Toil of Millions for Superfluities to the great Hazard and Loss of many Lives by the constant Dangers of the Sea. How much Labour Spent in Building and Fitting great Ships to go to China and Arabia for Tea and for Coffee, to the West Indies for Sugar, to America for Tobacco! These Things cannot be called the Necessaries of Life, for our Ancestors lived very comfortably without them.

A Question may be asked, Could all these People now employed in raising, making or carrying Superfluities, be subsisted by raising Necessaries? I think they might. The World is large, and a great Part of it still uncultivated. Many hundred Millions of Acres in Asia, Africa and America, are still Forest, and a great Deal even in Europe. On 100 Acres of this Forest a Man might become a substantial Farmer, and 100,000 Men employed in clearing each his 100 Acres, (instead of being as they are French Hairdressers) would hardly brighten a Spot big enough to be Visible from the Moon, unless with Herschell's Telescope, so vast are the Regions still in [the] World unimproved.

'Tis however some Comfort to reflect that upon the whole the Quantity of Industry and Prudence among Mankind exceeds the Quantity of Idleness and Folly. Hence the Increase of good Buildings, Farms cultivated, and populous Cities filled with Wealth all over Europe, which a few Ages since were only to be found on the Coasts of the Mediterranean. And this notwithstanding the mad Wars continually raging, by which are often destroyed in one Year the Works of many Years Peace. So that we may hope the Luxury of a few Merchants on the Sea Coast, will not be the Ruin of America.

One Reflection more, and I will end this long rambling Letter. Almost all the Parts of our Bodies require some Expence. The Feet demand Shoes, the Legs Stockings, the rest of the Body Clothing, and the Belly a good deal of Victuals. *Our* Eyes, tho' exceedingly useful, ask when reasonable, only the cheap Assistance of *Spectacles*, which could not much impair our Finances. But THE EYES OF OTHER PEOPLE are the Eyes that ruin us. If all but myself were blind, I should want neither fine Clothes, fine Houses nor Fine Furniture.

Adieu, my dear Friend. I am Yours ever

[LC Box 22]

CHAPTER 43
At the Constitutional Convention
(June–September 1787)

Speech on the Subject of Salaries (2 June)

Sir,

It is with Reluctance that I rise to express a Disapprobation of any one Article of the Plan for which we are so much obliged to the honourable Gentleman who laid it before us. From its first Reading I have borne a good Will to it, and in general wish'd it Success. In this Particular of Salaries to the Executive Branch, I happen to differ; and as my Opinion may appear new and chimerical, it is only from a Persuasion that it is right, and from a Sense of Duty that I hazard it. The Committee will judge [of my] Reasons when they have heard them, and their Judgment may possibly change mine.——I think I see Inconveniences in the Appointment of Salaries, I see none in refusing them, but on the contrary great Advantages.

Sir, there are two Passions which have a powerful Influence in the Affairs of Men. These are *Ambition* and *Avarice*; the Love of Power and the Love of Money. Separately each of these has great Force in prompting Men to Action; but when united in View of the same Object, they have in many Minds the most violent Effects. Place before the Eyes of such Men a [Post] of *Honour* that shall at the same time be a Place of *Profit*, and they will move Heaven and Earth to obtain it. The vast Number of such Places it is that renders the British Government so tempestuous. The Struggles for them are the true Source of all those Factions which are perpetually dividing the Nation, distracting its Councils, hurrying it sometimes into fruitless, and mischievous Wars, and often compelling a Submission to dishonourable Terms of Peace.

And of what kind are the men that will strive for this profitable Pre-eminence, thro' all the Bustle of Cabal, the Heat of Contention, the infinite mutual Abuse of Parties, tearing to Pieces the best of Characters? It will not be the wise and moderate, the Lovers of Peace and good Order, the men fittest for the Trust. It will be the Bold and the Violent, the Men of strong Passions and [in]defatigable Activity in their selfish Pursuits. These will thrust themselves into your Government, and be your Rulers.——And these too will be mistaken in the expected Happiness of their Situation: For their vanquish'd Competitors of the same Spirit and from the same Motives will perpetually be endeavouring to distress their Administration, thwart their Measures, and render them odious to the People.

Besides these Evils, Sir, tho' we may set out in the Beginning with moderate Salaries, we shall find that such will not be of long Continuance. Reasons will never be wanting for propos'd Augmentations. And there will always be a Party for giving more to the Rulers, that the Rulers may be able in Return to give more to them. Hence as all History informs us, there has been in every State and Kingdom a constant kind of Warfare between the Governing and the Governed: the one striving to obtain more for its Support, and the other to pay less. And this has alone occasion'd great Convulsions, actual civil Wars, ending either in dethroning of the Princes or enslaving of the People. Generally indeed the Ruling Power carries its Point, and we see the Revenues of Princes constantly increasing, and we see that they are never satisfied, but always in want of more. The more the People are discontented with the Oppression of Taxes; the greater Need the Prince has of Money to distribute among his Partisans and pay the Troops that are to suppress all Resistance, and enable him to plunder at Pleasure. There is scarce a King in a hundred who would not, if he could, follow the Example of Pharaoh, get first all the Peoples Money, then all their Lands, and then make them and their Children Servants for ever. It will be said, that we don't propose to establish Kings.——I know it.—— But there is a natural Inclination in Mankind to Kingly Government. It sometimes relieves them from Aristocratic Domination. They had rather have one Tyrant than 500. It gives more of the Appearance of Equality among Citizens; and that they like. I am apprehensive, therefore,—— perhaps too apprehensive, that the Government of these States, may in future times, end in a Monarchy. But this Catastrophe I think may be long delay'd, if in our propos'd System we do not sow the Seeds of Contention Faction and Tumult by making our Posts of Honour Places of Profit. If we do, I fear that tho' we employ at first a Number and not a single Person, the Number will in time be set aside, it will only nourish the Fœtus of a King, (as the honourable Gentleman from Virginia very aptly express'd it) and a King will the sooner be set over us.

It may be imagined by some that this is an Utopian Idea, and that we can never find Men to serve us in the Executive Department, without paying them well for their Services. I conceive this to be a Mistake. Some existing Facts present themselves to me, which incline me to a contrary Opinion. The High Sheriff of a County in England is an honourable Office, but it is not a profitable one. It is rather expensive, and therefore not sought for. But yet it is executed, and well executed, and usually by some of the principal Gentlemen of the County. In France, the Office of Counsellor or Member of their judiciary Parliaments, is more honourable. It is therefore purchas'd at a high Price: There are indeed Fees on the Law Proceedings, which are divided among them, but these Fees do not amount to more than three per Cent on the Sum paid for the Plan. Therefore as legal Interest is there at five per Cent they in fact pay two per Cent for being allow'd to do the Judiciary Business of the Nation, which is at the same time entirely exempt from the Burthen of paying them any Salaries for their Services. I do not however, mean to recommend this as an eligible Mode for our judiciary Department. I only bring the Instance to show that the Pleasure of doing Good and serving their Country, and the Respect such Conduct entitles them to, are sufficient Motives with some Minds to give up a great Portion of their Time to the Public, without the mean Inducement of pecuniary Satisfaction.——

Another Instance is that of a respectable Society, who have made the Experiment, and practis'd it with Success, now more than a hundred years.——I mean the Quakers. It is an establish'd Rule with them that they are not to go to Law, but in their Controversies they must apply to their Monthly, Quarterly and Yearly Meetings. Committees of these sit with Patience to hear the Parties, and spend much time in composing their Differences. In doing this, they are supported by a Sense of Duty; and the Respect paid to Usefulness. It is honourable to be so employ'd, but it was never made profitable by Salaries, Fees, or Perquisites. And indeed in all Cases of public Service, the less the Profit the greater the Honour.

To bring the Matter nearer home, have we not seen the great and most important of our Offices, that of General of our Armies, executed for Eight Years together, without the smallest Salary, by a patriot whom I will not now offend by any other Praise; and this thro' Fatigues and Distresses in common with the other brave Men his military Friends and Companions, and the constant Anxieties peculiar to his Station? and shall we doubt finding three or four Men in all the United States, with public Spirit enough to bear Sitting in peaceful Council, for perhaps an equal Term, merely to preside over our civil Concerns, and see that our Laws are duly executed. Sir, I have a better Opinion of our Country. I think we shall never be without a sufficient Number of wise and good Men to undertake and execute well and faithfully the Office in question.

Sir, the Saving of the Salaries, that may at first be propos'd, is not an Object with me. The subsequent Mischief of proposing them are what I apprehend. And therefore it is that I move the Amendment. If it is not seconded or accepted, I must be contented with the Satisfaction of having deliver'd my Opinion frankly, and done my Duty.

Speech in a Committee of the Convention on the Proportion of Representation and Votes (11 June)

Mr. Chairman,

It has given me great Pleasure to observe that till this Point, *the Proportion of Representation*, came before us, our Debates were carry'd on with great Coolness and Temper. If any thing of a contrary kind has on this Occasion appeared, I hope it will not be repeated; for we are sent hither to *consult*, not to *contend*, with each other; and Declaration of a fix'd Opinion and of determined Resolutions never to change it, neither enlighten nor convince us. Positiveness and Warmth on one side naturally beget their like on the other; and tend to create and augment Discord and Division, in a great Concern, wherein Harmony and Union are extremely necessary, to give Weight to our Counsels, and render them effectual in promoting and securing the common Good.

I must own that I was originally of Opinion it would be better if every Member of Congress, or our national Council, were to consider himself rather as a Representative of the Whole, than as an Agent for the Interests of a particular State, in which Case the Proportion of Members for each State would be of less Consequence, and it would not be very material whether they voted by States or individually. But as I find this is not [to] be expected, I now think the Number of Representatives should bear some Proportion to the Number of the Represented, and that the Decisions should be by the Majority of Members, not by the Majority of States. This is objected to, from an Apprehension that the greater States would then swallow up the Smaller. I do not at present clearly see what Advantage the greater States could propose to themselves by swallowing the smaller and therefore do not apprehended they would attempt it. I recollect that in the Beginning of this Century, when the Union was propos'd of the two Kingdoms, England and Scotland, the Scotch Patriots were full of Fears, that unless they had an equal Number of Representatives in Parliament they should be ruined by the Superiority of the English. They finally agreed however that the different Proportions of Importance in the Union of the two Nations should be attended to, whereby they were to have only Forty Members in the House of Commons, and only Sixteen of their Peers were to sit in the House of Lords, A very great Inferiority of Numbers! And yet to this Day I do not recollect that any thing has been done in the Parliament of Great Britain to the Prejudice of Scotland; and whoever looks over the Lists of Publick Officers Civil and Military of that Nation will find, I believe that the North Britons enjoy at least their full proportion of Emolument.

But, Sir, in the present Mode of Voting by States, it is equally in the Power of the lesser States to swallow up the greater; and this is mathematically demonstrable. Suppose, for example, that 7 smaller States had each 3 Members in the House, and the Six larger to have one with another 6 Members. And that upon a Question, two Members of each smaller State should be in the Affirmative, and one in the Negative; they will make

Affirmatives,	14	Negatives	7
And that all the larger States should be unanimously in the negative, they would make		Negatives	36
		In all	43

It is then apparent that the 14 carry the Question against the 43, and the Minority overpowers the Majority, contrary to the common Practice of Assemblies in all Countries and Ages.

The greater States, Sir, are naturally as unwilling to have their Property left in the Disposition of the smaller, as the smaller are to leave theirs in the Disposition of the greater. An honourable Gentleman has to avoid this difficulty, hinted a Proposition of equalizing the States. It appears to me an equitable one and I should for my own Part, not be against such a Measure, if it might be found practicable. Formerly, indeed, when almost every Province had a different Constitution some with greater others with fewer Privileges, it was of Importance to the Borderers, when their Boundaries were contested, whether, by running the Division Lines they were placed on one Side or the other. At present when such Differences are done away, it is less material. The Interest of a State is made up of the Interests of its individual Members. If they are not injured, the State is not injured. Small States are more easily well and happily governed than large ones. If therefore in such an equal Division, it should be found necessary to diminish Pennsylvania, I should not be averse to the giving a Part of it to New Jersey, and another to Delaware: But as there would probably be considerable Difficulties in adjusting such a Division; and however equally made at first, it would be continually varying by the Augmentation of Inhabitants in some States and their more fixed proportion in others; and thence frequent Occasion for new Divisions; I beg leave to propose for the Consideration of the Committee another Mode, which appears to me, to be as equitable, more easily carry'd into Practice, and more permanent in its Nature.

Let the weakest State say what Proportion of Money or Force it is able and willing to furnish for the general Purposes of the Union.

Let all the others oblige themselves to furnish each an equal Proportion.

The whole of these joint Supplies to be absolutely in the Disposition of Congress.

The Congress in this Case to be compos'd of an equal Number of Delegates from each State:

And their Decisions to be by the Majority of individual Members voting.

If these joint and equal Supplies should on particular Occasions not be sufficient, Let Congress make Requisitions on the richer and more powerful States for further Aids, to be voluntarily afforded; so leaving each State the Right of considering the Necessity and Utility of the Aid desired, and of giving more or less as it should be found proper.

This Mode is not new; it was formerly practic'd with Success by the British Government, with respect to Ireland and the Colonies. We sometimes gave even more than they expected or thought just to accept; and in the last War, carried on while we were united, they gave us back in 5 Years a Million Sterling. We should probably have continu'd such voluntary Contributions, whenever the Occasions appear'd to require them for the common Good of the Empire: It was not till they chose to force us, and to deprive us of the Merit and Pleasure of voluntary Contributions, that we refus'd and resisted. Those Contributions however were to be dispos'd of at the Pleasure of a Government in which we had no Representative. I am therefore persuaded that they will not be refus'd to one in which the Representation shall be equal.

My learned Colleague has already mentioned that the present method of voting by States, was submitted to originally by Congress, under a Conviction of its Impropriety, Inequality and Injustice. This appears in the Words of their Resolution. It is of Sept. 6, 1774. The words are,

"Resolved, That in determining Questions in this Congress, each Colony or Province shall have one Vote: The Congress not being possessed of or at present able to procure Materials for ascertaining the Importance of each Colony."

Motion for Prayers in the Convention (28 June)

Mr. President,

The small Progress we have made after 4 or 5 Weeks close Attendance and continual Reasonings with each other, our different Sentiments on almost every Question, several of the last producing as many *Noes* as *Ayes,* is methinks a melancholy Proof of the Imperfection of the Human Understanding. We indeed seem to feel our own want of political Wisdom, since we have been running all about in search of it. We have gone back to ancient History for Models of Government, and examin'd the different Forms of those Republics, which, having been originally form'd with the Seeds of their own Dissolution, now no longer exist. And we have view'd modern States all round Europe, but find none of their Constitutions suitable to our Circumstances.

In this Situation of this Assembly, groping, as it were, in the dark, to find Political Truth, and scarce able to distinguish it when presented to us, how has it happened, Sir, that we have not, hitherto once thought of humbly applying to the Father of Lights to illuminate our Understandings? In the Beginning of the Contest with Britain, when we were sensible of Danger, we had daily Prayers in this Room for the Divine Protection. Our Prayers, Sir, were heard;——and they were graciously answered. All of us, who were engag'd in the Struggle, must have observ'd frequent Instances of a Superintending Providence in our Favour. To that kind Providence we owe this happy Opportunity of Consulting in Peace on the Means of establishing our future national Felicity. And have we now forgotten that powerful Friend? or do we imagine we no longer need its Assistance? I have lived, Sir, a long time; and the longer I live, the more convincing proofs I see of this Truth, *That* GOD *governs in the Affairs of Men!*——And if a Sparrow cannot fall to the Ground without his Notice, is it probable that an Empire can rise without his Aid?——We have been assured, Sir, in the Sacred Writings, that "except the Lord build the House, they labour in vain that build it." I firmly believe this;——and I also believe that without his concurring Aid, we shall succeed in this political Building no better than the Builders of Babel: We shall be divided by our little partial local Interests, our Projects will be confounded and we ourselves shall become a Reproach and a Byeword down to future Ages. And what is worse, Mankind may hereafter, from this unfortunate Instance, despair of establishing Government by human Wisdom, and leave it to Chance, War and Conquest.

I therefore beg leave to move,

That henceforth Prayers, imploring the Assistance of Heaven, and its Blessing on our Deliberations, be held in this Assembly every Morning before we proceed to Business; and that one or more of the Clergy of this City be requested to officiate in that Service.[1]

Speech in the Convention at the Conclusion of its Deliberations (17 September)

Mr. President,

I confess that I do not entirely approve of this Constitution at present, but Sir, I am not sure I shall never approve it: For, having lived long, I have experienced many Instances of being obliged by better Information or fuller Consideration, to change Opinions even on important Subjects, which I once thought right, but found to be otherwise. It is therefore that the older I grow the more apt I am to doubt my own Judgment, and to pay more Respect to the Judgment of others. Most Men indeed as well as most Sects in Religion, think themselves in Possession of all Truth, and that wherever others differ from them it is so far Error. Steele, a Protestant in a Dedication tells the Pope, that the only Difference between our two Churches in their opinions of the Certainty of their Doctrine, is, the Romish Church is infallible, and the Church of England is never in the wrong. But tho' many private Persons think almost as highly of their own Infallibility, as of that of their Sect, few express it so naturally as a certain French Lady, who in a little Dispute with her Sister, said, I don't know

[1] The Convention, except three or four Persons, thought Prayers unnecessary!

how it happens, Sister, but I meet with no body but myself that's *always* in the right. *Il n'y a que moi qui a toujours raison.*

In these Sentiments, Sir, I agree to this Constitution, with all its Faults, if they are such; because I think a General Government necessary for us, and there is no *Form* of Government but what may be a Blessing to the People if well administered; and I believe farther that this is likely to be well administered for a Course of Years, and can only End in Despotism as other Forms have done before it, when the People shall become so corrupted as to need Despotic Government, being incapable of any other. I doubt too whether any other Convention we can obtain, may be able to make a better Constitution: For when you assemble a Number of Men, to have the Advantage of their joint Wisdom, you inevitably assemble with those Men all their Prejudices, their Passions, their Errors of Opinion, their local Interests, and their selfish Views. From such an Assembly can a perfect Production be expected? It therefore astonishes me, Sir, to find this System approaching so near to Perfection as it does and I think it will astonish our Enemies, who are waiting with Confidence to hear that our Councils are confounded, like those of the Builders of Babel, and that our States are on the Point of Separation, only to meet hereafter for the Purpose of cutting one anothers Throats. Thus I consent, Sir, to this Constitution because I expect no better, and because I am not sure that it is not the best. The Opinions I have had of its Errors I sacrifice to the Public Good. I have never whisper'd a Syllable of them abroad. Within these Walls they were born, and here they shall die. If every one of us in returning to our Constituents were to report the Objections he has had to it, and endeavour to gain Partizans in support of them, we might prevent its being generally received, and thereby lose all the salutary Effects and great Advantages resulting naturally in our favour among foreign Nations, as well as among ourselves, from our real or apparent Unanimity. Much of the Strength and Efficiency of any Government in procuring and securing Happiness to the People depends on Opinion, on the general Opinion of the Goodness of that Government as well as of the Wisdom and Integrity of its Governors. I hope therefore for our own Sakes, as a Part of the People, and for the sake of our Posterity we shall act heartily and unanimously in recommending this Constitution, wherever our Influence may extend, and turn our future Thoughts and Endeavours to the Means of having it well administered.——

On the whole Sir, I cannot help expressing a Wish, that every Member of the Convention who may still have Objections to it, would with me on this Occasion doubt a little of his own Infallibility, and to make *manifest* our *Unanimity*, put his Name to this Instrument.——

Then the Motion was made for adding the last Formula, viz. Done in Convention by the Unanimous Consent &c. ——which was agreed to and added accordingly.

[LC Box 24; Cornell University Bound MS 4600 548++]

CHAPTER 44

Queries and Remarks Respecting Alterations in the Constitution of Pennsylvania

(November 1789)

I. Of the Executive Branch

"Your executive should consist of a single Person."

On this I would ask, Is he to have no Council? How is he to be informed of the State and Circumstances of the different Counties, their Wants, their Abilities, their Dispositions, and the Characters of the principal People, respecting their Integrity, Capacities and Qualifications for Offices? Does not the present Construction of our Executive provide well for these particulars? And during the Number of Years it has existed, has its Errors or Failures in answering the End of its Appointment been more or greater than might have been expected from a single Person?

"But an Individual is more easily watched and controlled than any greater Number."

On this I would ask, Who is to watch and controul him? And by what Means is he to be controuled? Will not those Means, whatever they are, and in whatever Body vested, be subject to the same Inconveniencies of Expence, Delay, Obstruction of good Intentions, &c., which are objected to the present Executive?

II. The Duration of the Appointment

"This should be governed by the following Principles——the Independency of the Magistrate, and the Stability of his Administration; neither of which can be secured but by putting both beyond the Reach of every annual Gust of Folly and of Faction."

On this it may be asked, Ought it not also to be put beyond the Reach of every *triennial*, *quinquennial*, or *septennial* Gust of Folly and of Faction; and in short beyond the Reach of Folly and of Faction at any Period whatever? Does not this Reasoning aim at establishing a Monarchy at least for Life, like that of Poland? or to prevent the Inconveniencies, such as that Kingdom is subject to in a new Election on every Decease, does it not point to an hereditary succession? Are the Freemen of Pennsylvania convinced, from a View of the History of such Governments, that it will be for their Advantage to submit themselves to a Government of such Construction?

III. On the Legislative Branch

"A plural Legislature is as necessary to good Government, as a single Executive. It is not enough that your Legislature should be numerous, it should also be divided. Numbers alone are not a sufficient Barrier against the Impulses of Passion, the Combinations of Interest, the Intrigues of Faction, the Haste of Folly or the Spirit of Encroachment. One Division should watch over and controul the other, supply its Wants, correct its Blunders, and cross its Designs, should they be criminal or erroneous. Wisdom is the specific Quality of the Legislature, grows out of the Number of the Body, and is made up of the Portions of Sense and Knowledge which each Member brings to it."

On this it may be asked, May not the Wisdom brought to the Legislature by each Member be as effectual a Barrier against the Impulses of Passion, &c. when the Members are united in one Body as when they are divided? If one Part of the Legislature may controul the Operations of the other, may not the Impulses of Passion, the Combinations of Interest, the Intrigues of Faction, the Haste of Folly, or the Spirit of Encroachment in one of those Bodies obstruct the Good proposed by the other and frustrate its Advantages to the Public? Have we not experienced in this Colony, when a Province under the Government of the Proprietors, the Mischiefs of a second Branch existing in the Proprietary-Family, countenanced and aided by an Aristocratic Council? How many Delays and what great Expences were occasioned in carrying on the public Business; and what a Train of Mischiefs, even to the preventing of the Defence of the Province during several Years, when distressed by an Indian War, by the iniquitous Demand, that the Proprietary Property should be exempt from Taxation? The Wisdom of a few Members in one single Legislative Body may it not frequently stifle bad Motions in their Infancy, and so prevent their being adopted; whereas if those wise Men, in Case of a double Legislature, should happen to be in that Branch wherein the Motion did not arise, may it not, after being adopted by the other occasion lengthy Disputes and Contentions between the two Bodies, expensive to the Public, obstructing the public Business and promoting Factions among the People, many Tempers naturally adhering obstinately to Measures they have once publicly adopted? Have we not seen in one of our neighbouring States a bad Measure adopted by one Branch of the Legislature for Want of the Assistance of some more intelligent Members, who had been packed into the other, occasion many Debates, conducted with much Asperity, which could not be settled but by an expensive, general Appeal to the People? And have we not seen, in another neighbouring State, a similar Difference between the two Branches, occasioning long Debates and Contentions, whereby the State was prevented, for many Months, enjoying the Advantage of having Senators in the Congress of the United States? And has our present Legislative in one Assembly committed any Errors of Importance, which they have not remedied, or may not easily remedy; more easily probably than if divided into two Branches? And if the Wisdom brought by the Members to the Assembly is divided into two Branches may it not be too weak in each to support a good Measure, or obstruct a bad one? The Division of the Legislature into two or three Branches in England, was it the Product of Wisdom, or the Effect of Necessity, arising from the preexisting Prevalence of an odious Feudal System? which Government notwithstanding this Division is now become in Fact an absolute Monarchy, since the King, by bribing the Representatives with the People's Money, carries, by his Ministers, all the Measures that please him, which is equivalent to governing without a Parliament, and renders the Machine of Government much more complex and expensive, and from its being more complex, more easily put out of Order? Has not the famous political Fable of the Snake with two Heads and one Body some useful Instruction contained in it? She was going to a Brook to drink, and in her Way was to pass thro' a Hedge, a Twig of which opposed her direct Course; one Head chose to go on the right side of the Twig, the other on the left; so that Time was spent in the Contest, and before the Decision was completed, the poor Snake died with Thirst.

"Hence it is that the two Branches should be elected by Persons differently qualified; and in short, that, as far as possible, they should be made to represent different Interests.

Under this Reasoning I would establish a Legislature of two Houses. The Upper should represent the Property; the Lower the Population of the State. The upper should be chosen by Freemen possessing in Lands and Houses one thousand Pounds, the Lower by all such as had resided four Years in the Country and paid Taxes. The first should be chosen for four, the last for two Years; They should in Authority be coequal."

Several Questions may arise upon this Proposition. 1st. What is the Proportion of Freemen possessing Lands and Houses of one thousand Pounds value compared to that of Freemen whose Possessions are inferior? Are they as one to ten? Are they even as one to twenty? I should doubt whether they are as one to fifty. If this Minority is to chose a Body expressly to controul that which is to be chosen by the great Majority of the Freemen, what have this great Majority done to forfeit so great a Portion of their Right in Elections? Why is this Power of Controul, contrary to the spirit of all Democracies, to be vested in a Minority, instead of a Majority? Then is it intended or is it not that the Rich should have a Vote in the Choice of Members for the lower House, while those of inferior Property are deprived of the Right of voting for Members of the upper House? And why should the upper House, chosen by a Minority, have equal Power with the lower, chosen by a Majority? Is it supposed that Wisdom is the necessary Concomitant of Riches, and that one Man worth a thousand Pound must have as much Wisdom as twenty, who have each only 999? And why is Property to be represented at all?——Suppose one of our Indian Nations should now agree to form a civil Society, each Individual would bring into the Stock of the Society little more Property than his Gun and his Blanket; for at present he has no other; we know that when one of them has attempted to keep a few Swine, he has not been able to maintain a Property in them, his Neighbours thinking they have a Right to kill and eat them whenever they want Provision; it being one of their Maxims, that Hunting is free for all: the Accumulation therefore of Property in such a Society, and its Security to Individuals in every Society must be an Effect of the Protection afforded to it by the joint Strength of the Society, in the Execution of its Laws; private Property therefore is a Creature of Society and is subject to the Calls of that Society, whenever its Necessities shall require it, even to its last Farthing; its Contributions therefore to the public Exigencies are not to be considered as conferring a Benefit on the Public, entitling the Contributors to the Distinctions of Honour and Power; but as the Return of an Obligation previously received or the Payment of a just Debt. The Combinations of Civil Society are not like those of a Set of Merchants who club their Property in different Proportions for Building and Freighting a Ship, and may therefore have some Right to vote in the Disposition of the Voyage in a greater or less Degree according to their respective Contributions; but the important Ends of Civil Society are the personal Securities of Life and Liberty; these remain the same in every Member of the Society; and the poorest continues to have an equal Claim to them with the most opulent, whatever Difference Time, Chance or Industry may occasion in their Circumstances. On these Considerations I am sorry to see the Signs this Paper I have been considering affords of a Disposition among some of our People to commence an Aristocracy, by giving the Rich a predominancy in Government, a Choice peculiar to themselves in one half the Legislature, to be proudly called the UPPER House, and the other Branch, chosen by the Majority of the People, degraded by the Denomination of the LOWER; and giving to this *upper House* a Permanency of four Years, and but two to the *lower*. I hope therefore that our Representatives in the Convention will not hastily go into these Innovations, but take the Advice of the Prophet, "Stand in the old Ways, view the ancient Paths, consider them well, and be not among those that are given to Change."

[LC Box 25]

CHAPTER 45
On the Slave Trade
(25 March 1790)

To The Editor Of The Federal Gazette

Sir,

Reading last night in your excellent paper the speech of Mr. Jackson in Congress, against their meddling with the affair of slavery, or attempting to mend the condition of the slaves, it put me in mind of a similar one made about one hundred years since, by Sidi Mehemet Ibrahim, a member of the Divan of Algiers, which may be seen in Martin's account of his consulship, anno 1687. It was against granting the petition of the Sect called *Erika*, or Purists, who prayed for the abolition of piracy and slavery as being unjust.——Mr. Jackson does not quote it; perhaps he has not seen it.——If therefore some of its reasonings are to be found in his eloquent speech, it may only show that men's interests and intellects operate and are operated on with surprising similarity in all countries and climates, when under similar circumstances.——The African's speech, as translated, is as follows:

"*Allah Bismillah, &c. God is great, and Mahomet is his Prophet.*

"Have these *Erika* considered the consequences of granting their petition? If we cease our cruises against the christians, how shall we be furnished with the commodities their countries produce, and which are so necessary for us? If we forbear to make slaves of their people, who, in this hot climate, are to cultivate our lands? Who are to perform the common labours of our city, and in our families? Must we not then be our own slaves? And is there not more compassion and more favour due to us as Mussulmen, than to these christian dogs? We have now above 50,000 slaves in and near Algiers.——This number, if not kept up by fresh supplies, will soon diminish, and be gradually annihilated. If we then cease taking and plundering the Infidel ships, and making slaves of the seamen and passengers, our lands will become of no value for want of cultivation; the rents of houses in the city will sink one half; and the revenues of government arising from its share of prizes be totally destroyed. And for what? to gratify the whims of a whimsical sect! who would have us not only forbear making more slaves, but even to manumit those we have.——But who is to indemnify their masters for the loss? Will the state do it? Is our treasury sufficient? Will the *Erika* do it? Can they do it? Or would they, to do what they think justice to the slaves, do a greater injustice to the owners? And if we set our slaves free, what is to be done with them? Few of them return to their countries, they know too well the greater hardships they must there be subject to: they will not embrace our holy religion: they will not adopt our manners: our people will not pollute themselves by intermarrying with them: must we maintain them as beggars in our streets, or suffer our properties to be the prey of their pillage; for men accustom'd to slavery will not work for a livelihood when not compelled.——And what is there so pitiable in their present condition? Were they not slaves in their own countries? Are not Spain, Portugal, France and the Italian states, governed by despots, who hold all their subjects in slavery, without exception? Even England treats its sailors as slaves, for they are, whenever the government pleases, seized and confined in ships of war, condemned not only to work but to fight for small wages or a mere subsistence, not better than our slaves are allowed by us. Is their condition then made worse by their falling into our hands? No, they have only exchanged one slavery for another: and I may say a better: for here they are brought into a land where the sun of Islamism gives forth its light, and shines in full splendor, and they have an opportunity of making themselves acquainted with the true doctrine, and thereby saving their immortal souls. Those who remain at home have not that happiness. Sending the slaves home then, would be sending them out of light into darkness.——I repeat the question, what is to be done with them? I have heard it suggested, that they may be planted in the wilderness, where there is plenty of land for them to subsist on, and where they may flourish as a free state;——but they are, I doubt, too little disposed to labour without compulsion, as well as too ignorant to establish a good government, and the wild Arabs would soon molest and destroy or again enslave them. While serving us, we take care to provide them with every thing, and they are treated with humanity. The labourers in their own countries, are, as I am well informed, worse fed, lodged and cloathed. The condition of most of them is therefore already mended, and requires no further improvement. Here their lives are in safety.——They are not liable to be impressed for soldiers, and forced to cut one another's christian throats, as in the wars of their own countries.——If some of the religious mad bigots who now teaze us with their silly petitions, have in a fit of blind zeal freed their slaves, it was not generosity, it was not humanity that moved them to the action; it was from the conscious burthen of a load of sins, and hope from the supposed merits of so good a work to be excused from damnation.——How grossly are they mistaken in imagining slavery to be disallowed by the Alcoran! Are not the two precepts, to quote no more, *Masters treat your slaves with kindness: Slaves serve your masters with cheerfulness and fidelity*, clear proofs to the contrary? Nor can the plundering of infidels be in that sacred book forbidden, since it is well known from it, that God has given the World and all that it contains to his faithful Mussulmen, who are to enjoy it of right as fast as they can conquer it. Let us then hear no more of this detestable proposition, the manumission of christian slaves, the adoption of which would, by depreciating our lands and houses, and thereby depriving so many good citizens of their properties, create universal discontent, and provoke insurrections, to the endangering of government, and producing general confusion. I have therefore no doubt, but this wise Council will prefer the comfort and happiness of a whole nation of true believers, to the whim of a few *Erika*, and dismiss their petition."

The Result was, as *Martin* tells us, that the Divan came to this resolution, "The Doctrine that plundering and enslaving the Christians is unjust, is at best *problematical*; but that it is the interest of this state to continue the practice, is clear; therefore let the petition be rejected."

And it was rejected accordingly.

And since like motives are apt to produce in the minds of men like opinions and resolutions, may we not, Mr. Brown, venture to predict, from this account, that the petitions to the parliament of England for abolishing the slave trade, to say nothing of other legislatures, and the debates upon them, will have a similar conclusion.

I am, Sir,
Your constant Reader and humble Servant,
Historicus.

[*The Federal Gazette and Philadelphia Evening Post*, 25 March 1790]

Index

Index

Index

CAMBRIDGE TEXTS IN THE HISTORY OF POLITICAL THOUGHT

Titles published in the series thus far

Aquinas *Political Writings* (edited by R.W. Dyson)
0 521 375959 paperback

Aristotle *The Politics* and *The Constitution of Athens* (edited by Stephen Everson)
0 521 48400 6 paperback

Arnold *Culture and Anarchy and other writings* (edited by Stefan Collini)
0 521 37796 X paperback

Astell *Political Writings* (edited by Patricia Springborg)
0 521 42845 9 paperback

Augustine *The City of God against the Pagans* (edited by R. W. Dyson)
0 521 46843 4 paperback

Augustine *Political Writings* (edited by E. M. Atkins and R. J. Dodaro)
0 521 44697 X paperback

Austin *The Province of Jurisprudence Determined* (edited by Wilfrid E. Rumble)
0 521 44756 9 paperback

Bacon *The History of the Reign of King Henry VII* (edited by Brian Vickers)
0 521 58663 1 paperback

Bagehot *The English Constitution* (edited by Paul Smith)
0 521 46942 2 paperback

Bakunin *Statism and Anarchy* (edited by Marshall Shatz)
0 521 36973 8 paperback

Baxter *Holy Commonwealth* (edited by William Lamont)
0 521 40580 7 paperback

Bayle *Political Writings* (edited by Sally L. Jenkinson)
0 521 47677 1 paperback

Beccaria *On Crimes and Punishments and other writings* (edited by Richard Bellamy)
0 521 47982 7 paperback

Bentham *Fragment on Government* (introduction by Ross Harrison)
0 521 35929 5 paperback

Bernstein *The Preconditions of Socialism* (edited by Henry Tudor)
0 521 39808 8 paperback

Bodin *On Sovereignty* (edited by Julian H. Franklin)
0 521 34992 3 paperback

Bolingbroke *Political Writings* (edited by David Armitage)
0 521 58697 6 paperback

Bossuet *Politics Drawn from the Very Words of Holy Scripture* (edited by Patrick Riley)
0 521 36807 3 paperback

The British Idealists (edited by David Boucher)
0 521 45951 6 paperback

Burke *Pre-Revolutionary Writings* (edited by Ian Harris)
0 521 36800 6 paperback

Cavendish *Political Writings* (edited by Susan James)
0 521 63350 8 paperback

Christine De Pizan *The Book of the Body Politic* (edited by Kate Langdon Forhan)
0 521 42259 0 paperback

Cicero *On Duties* (edited by M. T. Griffin and E. M. Atkins)
0 521 34835 8 paperback

Cicero *On the Commonwealth* and *On the Laws* (edited by James E. G. Zetzel)
0 521 45959 1 paperback

Comte *Early Political Writings* (edited by H. S. Jones)
0 521 46923 6 paperback

Conciliarism and Papalism (edited by J. H. Burns and Thomas M. Izbicki)
0 521 47674 7 paperback

Constant *Political Writings* (edited by Biancamaria Fontana)
0 521 31632 4 paperback

Dante *Monarchy* (edited by Prue Shaw)
0 521 56781 5 paperback

Diderot *Political Writings* (edited by John Hope Mason and Robert Wokler)
0 521 36911 8 paperback

The Dutch Revolt (edited by Martin van Gelderen)
0 521 39809 6 paperback

Early Greek Political Thought from Homer to the Sophists (edited by Michael Gagarin and Paul Woodruff)
0 521 43768 7 paperback

The Early Political Writings of the German Romantics (edited by Frederick C. Beiser)
0 521 44951 0 paperback

The English Levellers (edited by Andrew Sharp)
0 521 62511 4 paperback

Erasmus *The Education of a Christian Prince* (edited by Lisa Jardine)
0 521 58811 1 paperback

Fenelon *Telemachus* (edited by Patrick Riley)
0 521 45662 2 paperback

Ferguson *An Essay on the History of Civil Society* (edited by Fania Oz-Salzberger) paperback
0 521 44736 4

Filmer *Patriarcha* and Other Writings (edited by Johann P. Sommerville)
0 521 39903 3 paperback

Fletcher *Political Works* (edited by John Robertson)
0 521 43994 9 paperback

Sir John Fortescue *On the Laws and Governance of England* (edited by Shelley Lockwood)
0 521 58996 7 paperback

Fourier *The Theory of the Four Movements* (edited by Gareth Stedman Jones and Ian Patterson)
0 521 35693 8 paperback

Franklin *The Autobiography* and Other Writings on Politics, Economics, and Virtue (edited by Alan Houston)
0 521 54265 0 paperback

Gramsci *Pre-Prison Writings* (edited by Richard Bellamy)
0 521 42307 4 paperback

Guicciardini *Dialogue on the Government of Florence* (edited by Alison Brown)
0 521 45623 1 paperback

Hamilton, Madison, and Jay (writing as 'Publius') *The Federalist* with *The Letters* of 'Brutus' (edited by Terence Ball)
0 521 00121 8 paperback

Harrington *A Commonwealth of Oceana* and *A System of Politics* (edited by J. G. A. Pocock)
0 521 42329 5 paperback

Hegel *Elements of the Philosophy of Right* (edited by Allen W. Wood and H. B. Nisbet)
0 521 34888 9 paperback

Hegel *Political Writings* (edited by Laurence Dickey and H. B. Nisbet)
0 521 45979 3 paperback

Hobbes *On the Citizen* (edited by Michael Silverthorne and Richard Tuck)
0 521 43780 6 paperback

Hobbes *Leviathan* (edited by Richard Tuck)
0 521 56797 1 paperback

Hobhouse *Liberalism and Other Writings* (edited by James Meadowcroft)
0 521 43726 1 paperback

Hooker *Of the Laws of Ecclesiastical Polity* (edited by A. S. McGrade)
0 521 37908 3 paperback

Hume *Political Essays* (edited by Knud Haakonssen)
0 521 46639 3 paperback

King James VI and I *Political Writings* (edited by Johann P. Sommerville)
0 521 44729 1 paperback

Jefferson *Political Writings* (edited by Joyce Appleby and Terence Ball)
0 521 64841 6 paperback

John of Salisbury *Policraticus* (edited by Cary Nederman)
0 521 36701 8 paperback

Kant *Political Writings* (edited by H. S. Reiss and H. B. Nisbet)
0 521 39837 1 paperback

Knox *On Rebellion* (edited by Roger A. Mason)
0 521 39988 2 paperback

Kropotkin *The Conquest of Bread and other writings* (edited by Marshall Shatz)
0 521 45990 7 paperback

Lawson *Politica sacra et civilis* (edited by Conal Condren)
0 521 39248 9 paperback

Leibniz *Political Writings* (edited by Patrick Riley)
0 521 35899X paperback

The Levellers (edited by Andrew Sharp)
0 521 62511 4 paperback

Locke *Political Essays* (edited by Mark Goldie)
0 521 47861 8 paperback

Locke *Two Treatises of Government* (edited by Peter Laslett)
0 521 35730 6 paperback

Loyseau *A Treatise of Orders and Plain Dignities* (edited by Howell A. Lloyd)
0 521 45624 X paperback

Luther and Calvin on Secular Authority (edited by Harro Höpfl)
0 521 34986 9 paperback

Machiavelli *The Prince* (edited by Quentin Skinner and Russell Price)
0 521 34993 1 paperback

de Maistre *Considerations on France* (edited by Isaiah Berlin and Richard Lebrun)
0 521 46628 8 paperback

Maitland *State, Trust and Corporation* (edited by David Runciman and Magnus Ryan)
0 521 526302 paperback

Malthus *An Essay on the Principle of Population* (edited by Donald Winch)
0 521 42972 2 paperback

Marsiglio of Padua *Defensor minor* and *De translatione Imperii* (edited by Cary Nederman)
0 521 40846 6 paperback

Marx *Early Political Writings* (edited by Joseph O'Malley)
0 521 34994 X paperback

Marx *Later Political Writings* (edited by Terrell Carver)
0 521 36739 5 paperback

James Mill *Political Writings* (edited by Terence Ball)
0 521 38748 5 paperback

J. S. Mill *On Liberty*, with *The Subjection of Women* and *Chapters on Socialism*
(edited by Stefan Collini)
0 521 37917 2 paperback

Milton *Political Writings* (edited by Martin Dzelzainis)
0 521 34866 8 paperback

Montesquieu *The Spirit of the Laws* (edited by Anne M. Cohler, Basia Carolyn Miller and Harold Samuel Stone)
0 521 36974 6 paperback

More *Utopia* (edited by George M. Logan and Robert M. Adams)
0 521 52540 3 paperback

Morris *News from Nowhere* (edited by Krishan Kumar)
0 521 42233 7 paperback

Nicholas of Cusa *The Catholic Concordance* (edited by Paul E. Sigmund)
0 521 56773 4 paperback

Nietzsche *On the Genealogy of Morality* (edited by Keith Ansell-Pearson)
0 521 40610 2 paperback

Paine *Political Writings* (edited by Bruce Kuklick)
0 521 66799 2 paperback

Plato *The Republic* (edited by G. R. F. Ferrari and Tom Griffith)
0 521 48443 X

Plato *Statesman* (edited by Julia Annas and Robin Waterfield)
0 521 44778 X paperback

Price *Political Writings* (edited by D. O. Thomas)
0 521 40969 1 paperback

Priestley *Political Writings* (edited by Peter Miller)
0 521 42561 1 paperback

Proudhon *What is Property?* (edited by Donald R. Kelley and Bonnie G. Smith)
0 521 40556 4 paperback

Pufendorf *On the Duty of Man and Citizen according to Natural Law* (edited by James Tully)
0 521 35980 5 paperback

The Radical Reformation (edited by Michael G. Baylor)
0 521 37948 2 paperback

Rousseau *The Discourses and other early political writings* (edited by Victor Gourevitch)
0 521 42445 3 paperback

Rousseau *The Social Contract and other later political writings* (edited by Victor Gourevitch)
0 521 42446 1 paperback

Seneca *Moral and Political Essays* (edited by John Cooper and John Procope)
0 521 34818 8 paperback

Sidney *Court Maxims* (edited by Hans W. Blom, Eco Haitsma Mulier and Ronald Janse)
0 521 46736 5 paperback

Sorel *Reflections on Violence* (edited by Jeremy Jennings)
0 521 55910 3 paperback

Spencer *The Man versus the State* and *The Proper Sphere of Government* (edited by John Offer)
0 521 43740 7 paperback

Stirner *The Ego and Its Own* (edited by David Leopold)
0 521 45647 9 paperback

Thoreau *Political Writings* (edited by Nancy Rosenblum)
0 521 47675 5 paperback

Tonnies *Community and Civil Society* (edited by Jose Harris and Margaret Hollis)
0 521 561191 paperback

Utopias of the British Enlightenment (edited by Gregory Claeys)
0 521 45590 1 paperback

Vico *The First New Science* (edited by Leon Pompa)
0 521 38726 4 paperback

Vitoria *Political Writings* (edited by Anthony Pagden and Jeremy Lawrance)
0 521 36714 X paperback

Voltaire *Political Writings* (edited by David Williams)
0 521 43727 X paperback

Weber *Political Writings* (edited by Peter Lassman and Ronald Speirs)
0 521 39719 7 paperback

William of Ockham *A Short Discourse on Tyrannical Government* (edited by A. S. McGrade and John Kilcullen)
0 521 35803 5 paperback

William of Ockham *A Letter to the Friars Minor and other writings* (edited by A. S. McGrade and John Kilcullen)
0 521 35804 3 paperback

Wollstonecraft *A Vindication of the Rights of Men* and *A Vindication of the Rights of Woman* (edited by Sylvana Tomaselli)
0 521 43633 8 paperback